Ethics and the
Autonomy of Philosophy

Ethics and the Autonomy of Philosophy

Breaking Ties with Traditional Christian Praxis and Theory

Bernard James Walker

☙PICKWICK *Publications* · Eugene, Oregon

ETHICS AND THE AUTONOMY OF PHILOSOPHY
Breaking Ties with Traditional Christian Praxis and Theory

Copyright © 2014 Bernard James Walker. All rights reserved. Except for brief quotations in critical publications or reviews, no part of this book may be reproduced in any manner without prior written permission from the publisher. Write: Permissions, Wipf and Stock Publishers, 199 W. 8th Ave., Suite 3, Eugene, OR 97401.

Scripture quotations taken from the *New American Standard Bible*, Copyright © 1960, 1962, 1963, 1968, 1971, 1972, 1973, 1975, 1977, 1995 by The Lockman Foundation. Used by permission. (www.Lockman.org)

Pickwick Publications
An Imprint of Wipf and Stock Publishers
199 W. 8th Ave., Suite 3
Eugene, OR 97401

www.wipfandstock.com

ISBN 13: 978-1-62564-364-3

Cataloging-in-Publication data:

Walker, Bernard James

Ethics and the autonomy of philosophy : breaking ties with traditional Christian praxis and theory / Bernard James Walker.

xiv + 308 p. ; 23 cm. —Includes bibliographical references and index(es).

ISBN 13: 978-1-62564-364-3

1. Ethics. 2. Christian ethics. I. Title.

BJ1012 .W33 2014

Manufactured in the U.S.A.

I would like to dedicate this book to my wife Denise and two daughters, Gabriella and Jordan. I hope they will follow in my shoes as a scholar on the subject matter of their choice. I would also like to dedicate this book to a good friend of mine from Jackson, Mississippi. His name is Lem Smith III and was a gentle, sensitive, and kind person. Lem passed away February 16, 2014.

Contents

Acknowledgments | ix

Introduction | xi

1. A Deconstruction of Pop Ethics: A Discussion of the Ethical Views of the Man on the Streets (MOTS) | 1

2. Ethics and Epistemic Myopia: Its Nature, Its Sources, and Its Cures | 23

3. A Construction of Formal Ethics: Reflections on the Phrases Moral Facts, Good, Right, Bad, Wrong, Inappropriate, Rude, and Offensive; and Reflection on the Implications of the Word Ought | 55

4. Reflections on the Varieties of Normative Ethics: Discerning What We Ought to Do and How We Ought to Be | 74

5. Swimming through the Murky Waters of Ethics Mixed with Religion: A Discussion of the Ways Religion Does and Does Not Import an Influence on Ethics | 134

6. Taking Sides on Some Polemic Social Issues in Applied Ethics: Affirmative Action, the Death Penalty, and Abortion | 180

Appendix | 269

Bibliography | 293

Scripture Index | 301

Subject Index | 303

Acknowledgments

I WOULD LIKE TO express thanks to the following young and fine philosophers and biblical scholars who helped make this book possible by providing assistance in the manuscript formation: Ashish Varma, Chad McIntosh, Dima Kotik, Dr. Jason Li, and Dr. David Rim. I would also like to thank Dr. David Nah and Dr. Paul K. Moser for their helpful commentary input.

Introduction

THIS TEXT IS INTENDED to be a companion to an introduction to ethics text that essentially consists of primary texts from various philosophers. As a companion, it consists of chapters reflecting on the major categories of ethics such as moral epistemology, metaethics, axiology, normative ethics, and applied ethics. There is even an appendix on critical thinking for ethical decision-making. I am passionate about the content of this text because all too often texts written with a Christian audience in mind force Scripture to address ethical issues that Scripture does not necessarily address. The adage that you can't make a turnip bleed comes to mind. Moreover, Christian authors of similar ethical textbooks sometimes have an axe to grind, such as recapturing ethics for Christ or doing apologetics under the disguise of ethics. Texts written this way often use philosophy as a means to ground the author's theological end or the status quo of the author's particular brand of Christianity, e.g., evangelicalism or liberalism. My text does not do this. I begin and end with ethics within a philosophical context rather than a theological context, come what may. As a philosophical text, it maintains a broad Christian theological worldview; however, it is not concerned with defending certain theological traditions where reality and reason speak otherwise. It also addresses issues many Christian authors find too polemical to discuss.

The following are unique features of my text. In chapter 1 I introduce metaethics in a negative way by discussing what ethics is not about. Here in chapter 1 I engage the perspectives of the man on the streets (MOTS) or technically what society and culture say ethics is about. With no interest in defending the MOTS, I detail the pitfalls of the various MOTS views in circulation. All too often ethics texts fail to present and engage the perspective of the untrained and unreflective thinker who is best described by the views currently flowing in contemporary society, viz., cultural relativism, skepticism, etc. It is important to address the MOTS views of ethics because many readers of this text will identify with these views, but prior to reading the critical analysis of these views, will fail to see what is so problematic with these views. It is my opinion that since the MOTS is so interwoven in the psyche of so many people, a critique and dismissal of the MOTS is categorical. In would be natural to move from this negative discussion of what ethics is not about to a formal introduction to metaethics; however, other "clean up" matters are in order. In chapter 2, I shift to moral epistemology with a focus on ethical bias, or what I call epistemic myopia. We cannot do and understand what ethics is without first admitting and being aware that we as moral discerners and judges can be clouded in our ethical thinking. Our noetic structure is often shaped by baggage that leads us away from what would be rational and objective ethical thinking. This is no condemnation on anyone in particular as it is an indictment on all humans as conceivers. We all fall short of objectivity for various reasons and knowing this unfortunate fact allows us to prepare and fight against bias. After this "clean up" conversation with application is done, I move on to chapter 3 to positively discuss metaethics. Here I explain the various ethics terms we use as members of the moral community, e.g., what the terms good, bad, right, wrong, inappropriate, rude, and offensive mean. I also provide a detailed discussion of the meaning and implications of the word "ought" because it entails a restriction on what our ethical behavior and judgments are. In short, if a person S ought to do some act X, then S is limited or constrained in such a way that what she does is not unlimited like a choice for a dish in a restaurant is unlimited, given the items available. In chapter 4 I move on to discuss the various historical normative ethical theories that quantify what are right and wrong actions. I critically discuss some of the pros and cons of natural law theory, deontology, utilitarianism, theories of rights, virtue ethics, and end with an accumulative approach to making ethical decisions that appeals to several of the normative ethical theories discussed. In chapter 5 I address the obvious question Christians have about the relationship between ethics and God. To the surprise of many Christians there are several possible relationships God could have to ethics, and the distinction among these relationships is clarified. However, contrary to much Christian tradition and scholarship, I argue that God is not related to ethics in the manner that God grounds or makes actions right or wrong. With that said, I map out ways God and the revelation of God in Jesus Christ have strongly influenced what humans globally believe and what many moral agents have done and do despite the perennial struggle humans have with self-centeredness. Finally in chapter 6 I move on to applied ethics. Here I first address racism and advances a liberal view on racism and social ethics that is absent in most evangelical social ethics texts. Contrary to many, if not most, evangelical philosophers, I talk of the existence of structural/institutional racism and defend affirmative action as a partial way to remedy the social and economic disparities of minorities and African Americans in particular. Next I discuss capital punishment. This is particularly a topic that has both ethical and biblical concerns since the Bible actually condones the death penalty. If God commands the death penalty for ethical reasons, then God's prescriptions would be universally applicable for all times and places. This leads to troubling consequences when we consider the crimes for which the Bible says a person can be sentenced to death. As a result I argue that the references and prescriptions for the death penalty in the Old Testament are either elliptical and hyperbolic or commanded for theological reasons instead of ethical reasons. Finally I move from death to life and discuss reproductive issues, particularly abortion. On the topic of abortion, I show how the traditional view that personhood begins at conception or is constituted biologically is problematic on some fronts. Although I defend a pro-life position throughout the discussion on abortion, I add that the notion (1) personhood begins at conception and (2) the embryo is you (a person) cannot be definitively argued from a philosophical perspective or even affirmed biblically. There are too many metaphysical uncertainties that prevent a ruling in favor of (1) and (2) with certainty. My book ends with an appendix explaining several informal fallacies. The appendix on fallacies is helpful. It is important to recognize fallacies for two reasons: (1) so that you can critically deconstruct an ethical position you may not agree with if it contains fallacies; and (2) so that you do not fall prey to fallacies in the construction of the defense of your own view.

1

A Deconstruction of Pop Ethics: A Discussion of the Ethical Views of the Man on the Streets (MOTS)

IN THIS CHAPTER WE will not per se do ethics or solve ethical issues and dilemmas. Rather we will look into the very nature of what ethics is. After all, how can we do ethics if we don't know exactly what it is we are doing? This chapter is a demolition chapter. Before we talk about what ethics is about, we will look at what it is not about. This requires a deconstruction of popular conceptions of what ethics is about in terms of what these views say we can and cannot know about ethics and what they claim is the basis of what makes actions right or wrong. So let us dive in.

The Three Levels of Ethics

When the question is raised as to what ethics is about, there are at least three major answers that philosophers give. In a broad sense, if we want to know the nature of ethics in terms of how ethics differs from other disciplines or if we want to know the meaning of the concepts used in ethics, then we are looking at and concerned with the foundation of ethics. In essence we are stepping outside of ethics and looking into it. Doing so places us at a level where we are not doing ethics but coming to terms with what ethics is about. Talk of "aboutness" in philosophy is a *meta*-issue (*meta-* is the Greek preposition for about). In short, before we can do ethics, we need to know what it is we are involved in or what ethics is about and philosophers call this *metaethics*. Metaethics will be the focus of this current chapter. If, on the other hand, we want to do ethics, we need some algorithm or methodology for discovering what is ethical (e.g., ethically right or wrong actions). This takes us a step above the foundation of ethics to the level or *normative ethics*. Normative ethics is named such because our focus here is on what moral agents ought to do and ought not to do. In either case, talk of "ought" is equivalent to what is normative. In its strongest sense, ought requires or entails we have a duty to do or refrain from some action. Finally, once we have a methodology to work from, we are now in a position to discover what we ought to do or ought not to do and, given our understanding of the nature of ethics from metaethics, we know the sense of ought that applies to ethics and not to chemistry or sports. We can, thus, decide what is ethically right or wrong to do on any given topics that we apply ethics to. When we apply ethics to a given subject matter, we are doing what philosophers call *applied ethics*. For example, when we apply ethics to medicine, we are doing bioethics or health care ethics; when we apply ethics to the business world and to business practices, we are doing business ethics. The number of topics is indefinite.

The MOTS on Ethics

As already mentioned, the focus of this chapter is a look at metaethics by negation. It is not difficult to find views on ethical and social issues that have little or no logical backing and support. These same views are often incoherent as well. Watch any talk show and copious examples of faulty, fallacious reasoning will greet you. Why? Because such shows discuss very emotional topics. The average person is often clear in their thinking when their subject matter is mathematics, physics or science in general; however, when there is room for a person's emotions, values, and preferences to enter the discussion, faulty thinking runs rampant. If emotions, values, and preferences are not the culprit, then faulty thinking has its origin in a passive commitment to societal consensus, i.e., everybody believes X so X must be true. In either case, I refer to these approaches to ethics as the views on the streets or the views of the "man on the streets" (or as an acronym, MOTS). Often a person committed to the "MOTS" talks about ethics in one of four ways. All four views share the common view that justification is not essential to the correctness of an ethical judgment. Thus they are opposed to the correctness of ethical judgments being evidence based or a matter of logical coherence and consistency.

For most of the ethical MOTS views, ethics is a matter of what some specified group or person says and nothing more. Finally they are opposed to judging the actions of others or other societies or cultures. Let us take a look at each view and determine what is problematic with each one. Some of the terms used to describe the four views are not formally stipulated by anyone other than myself (the author of this book), but the concepts behind the words are embraced by society at large.

Deificationism

A person who is a deificationist says, "We all make mistakes. Who am I or you to judge anyone; only God and saints can judge and decide morality." According to this MOTS view, only saintly people like the Pope, Martin Luther King Jr., the Dali Lama, Mother Teresa or some other saintly person can discern what is morally right or wrong. Supposedly, the logic seems to be, only saintly people have a clear and distinct insight into moral issues. Ultimately, or course, deificationists hold that only God should be in the business of judging but these saints have a privileged, secondary role in judging also. Thus the rest of humanity should avoid making ethical judgments and leave this task to the saintly experts or God. This MOTS view of ethics *deifies* ethics. It makes ethics a divine discipline and places it in the hands of idealized persons who have a divine, saintly character.

Sometimes when a deificationist is asked whether her actions are right or wrong, she responds by saying, "That is between me and God." Some years ago, a previously unknown nurse named Darva Conger became famous on a reality show when she was selected as the bride of millionaire Rick Rockwell. After her popularity from the show she was asked to pose for *Playboy*. Despite an earlier claim she made that she is against pornography and that she considers herself a Christian, she agreed to pose nude for a large sum of money. In a network interview she was asked how she managed to reconcile her "Christianity" with her *Playboy* photographs. She played the role of a deificationist quite well. She responded by saying that there is a big difference between posing nude and posing pornographically and that the only person that should judge her is God. Obviously this is a red herring fallacy.[1] Darva did not actually answer the question presented to her, for the question was not whether God would condone or condemn her choice, but whether her choice was wrong. A similar response was given by a young woman who is identified as the greatest woman in porn. In an interview with the cable

---

1. See appendix for a discussion of red herring.

channel, VH1, she stated that despite her copious pornographic films, she is quite religious. Those who judge her know that they are wrong, she says, for only God can judge. Again, God has and will judge every action a person commits. But this is an issue about the punishment or reward for actions we do, not with whether God deems our actions as right or wrong. In other words, the issue of an action being wrong or right is a separate issue from an action being punished or rewarded.

What are further problems with deificationism? First, deificationism entails skepticism for all but the saintly and thus requires the average person to abandon her attempt to be moral or to hold others ethically accountable. To assert that an imperfect character disqualifies a person from discerning an ethical wrong or right action is absurd. Imagine a person stumbling upon a man raping a person. Would it make sense for that person to say about the rapist's action, "Who am I to judge him? I am not perfect so who am I to judge this man's sexual action"? Surely not. To suggest otherwise is puzzling to common sensibilities. Are humans so imperfect as to be unable to also judge child abuse as ethically wrong? If the deificationist had her way, without the guidance of the "saints" no human behavior could be discerned as ethically right or wrong.

If there is any value to drawing attention to the imperfect nature of a person's character it is in the context of the person's character being inconsistent with what the person deems ethically right or wrong. What the deification should say is that a person is hypocritical in her judgments when guilty of the same action that her judgments condemn. This point is wonderfully illustrated in the New Testament by Jesus Christ. In the book of Matthew, Jesus says:

> Do not judge so that you will not be judged. For in the way you judge, you will be judged; and by your standard of measure, it will be measured to you. Why do you look at the speck that is in your brother's eye, but do not notice the log that is in your own eye? (Matt 7: 1-3, 4, NASB)

Here Jesus does not forbid judging simpliciter nor does he deny that a person's judgment is correct; rather he admonishes the person judging to be free of the same error depicted in the judgment. Otherwise the person is guilty of hypocrisy.

A second problem with deificationism is its claim that a virtuous character is required to discern whether an action is morally right or wrong. This claim could not be farther from the truth. When the deificationist notes that most people in the world make mistakes and are not perfect, they make a correct but tangential claim. We should take note here that the deificationist's move to point out the depravity of human nature is a red herring. Sure no one is perfect. We all make mistakes and have our shortcomings; however, our fallible nature does not stop us from knowing what is right and wrong. When the deificationist points out that she is imperfect like most people in the world, she has already discerned a standard of moral perfection that she does not meet. Thus her claim is self-defeating. To put the point another way, a person like Hitler, a drug dealer and a pimp can discern what actions are right and wrong even when they are guilty of the very action they may condemn. They may not be ideal members of society, but their incorrigible nature does not make them incapable of *knowing* right from wrong.

Autonomism

A person who is an autonomist says, "I decide for myself what is right and wrong. Who are you to judge me? This is a free country…I am entitled to liberty and freedom of choice…be tolerant. Morality is personal. Everyone should mind her own business. I do what I feel like doing. I am a grown woman. You can't tell me what to do." Like the deificationist, the autonomist denies that people should be in the business of judging another person's actions. The difference between the two is that autonomists do believe that they can judge their own actions to be right or wrong. They simply deny that anyone else can judge their actions.

Ultimately, for the autonomist, whatever a person says is right is right *for* them. This is the most self-serving of any ethical view. Imagine waking up one morning as an autonomist. You are hungry so you venture via someone else's car, without their permission, to a very expensive restaurant. According to how autonomists think, for you to take someone else's car without their permission is not wrong if "you say so." After eating the food at the fine restaurant, you decide not to pay for the food, because you say it is not wrong to eat and not pay. Next, you decide to go somewhere for entertainment. You steal a person's wallet and pay for clothes from *Sax Fifth Avenue* with that person's credit card. Stealing the wallet is not wrong because you say it is not wrong. You are still within your rights to hold this view even after viewing photos of the person's family in the wallet. In the end, all of what you do is justified simply because you say you are right. After all, for autonomism, ethics is a personal issue. What *is* right or wrong is up to each individual to decide in light of the individual's personal feelings or beliefs. Now waking up in the morning and committing your day to such a schedule sounds ridiculous, but this state of affairs is logically consistent and an extension of autonomism. The following are comments from a paper written by an autonomist on abortion. She argued:

> I believe a woman has a right to have an abortion anytime she wants to because it is her choice. Who gives the government, society or God the right to tell a woman what to do with her body. Only the woman can make that call. I do not care what the circumstances are for the abortion. Even if what she aborts is a fully developed baby, a woman need not justify her action to anyone, even God.

Autonomism is a version of what we will later call ethical relativism. So relative to each person, a judgment is correct regardless of the circumstances and consequences that result from it. Accordingly, ethics is relative to each individual's personal moral beliefs.

There are several problems that can be pointed out with autonomism. They all stem from the autonomist's claim that ethics is a personal issue. First, it leads to conflicting conclusions about what is morally right. If two autonomists met and one of them acted in a morally relevant way toward the other one, who would be morally right? For example, suppose one autonomist took the credit card of the other autonomist and stated that his action was morally right. Suppose the other autonomist, whose credit card was taken, thought that the act of taking his credit card was wrong. Both men could not be correct and surely neither is correct merely because each said he was correct. Their judgments are contradictory to each other.

Secondly, autonomism is in direct conflict with the nature of the normative nature of ethical judgments. Ethical judgments like all normative judgments, by definition, tell us what we ought to do. If someone wants to live a healthy life, she ought to limit the fat in her diet. If someone wants to live a self-serving life, she ought to be concerned about no one else unless others further her well-being. If someone wants to be a great basketball player, she ought to practice basketball. In all cases, normative judgments presuppose a standard. The standard tells us what we ought to do. By definition, autonomism does not presuppose a standard. For the autonomist, she does whatever she believes is right to do independent of any standard. Thus autonomism can never be an ethical position to hold since it does not require that a person ought to act a certain way.

Autonomism fails to make a subjective/objective distinction about judgments. When a person says, "The pepperoni pizza was great," her statement expresses a taste, not a proposition. Tastes are neither true nor false. In this case, the statement is about the taste of pizza for the person who makes the statement. The fact is pizza is neither great nor bad. The terms "great" and "bad" refer to the taste of a particular person. Tastes vary from person to person and they are neither true nor false. Ask yourself the question, what is a true taste or what is a false taste? Moreover, a person's taste can change over time. Consider another example: "Leisure suits are ugly." A person may have loved the look of leisure suits in the past, but presently deplore their look as out of vogue. Like food, a taste for clothes is relative to persons, times and locations. Statements about tastes are *subjective* or *collectively subjective*. Subjective matters are about internal states in our bodies. Thus tastes cannot be shared by more than one person. (Two people cannot have the same taste although their experiences may be similar about the same object, e.g., a slice of apple pie.) Ethical matters, on the other hand, are objective in that what is constituted as ethical is determined by a standard independent of our tastes and desires. The standard in turn is determined by states of affairs in the world. Moreover, because ethical matters are normative, they place a demand on all persons related to them in that people are expected to behave a certain way. By the same token, subjective matters cannot be normative because the taste a person has is generally beyond her choosing. Even when a person can "acquire" a taste, the taste in question is not something obligated to have since it does not impact the well-being of an individual human being, e.g., the taste for olives.

When you critically think about ethical issues, the arguments you eventually construct should be no different from the arguments you construct for non-ethical issues. The evidence you use to support your conclusion can never be "personal reasons." If your reasons were personal, they would hold or be true only for yourself. In other words, to speak of reasons being personal is to claim that reasons are *for* a particular person and not *for* anyone else. When a person says that murder is wrong, surely the reason why murder is wrong is not because of some reason that is morally relevant or true just *for* that person. If this were so, then the reason why murder is wrong would be justification only for the person who has the reason. In other words, the truth that murder is wrong would hold only for the person who has the "personal reason." No ethical judgment is morally right or wrong simply because you say so.

Subjectivism

A MOTS view similar to autonomism is what ethicists call ethical subjectivism. Ethical subjectivism is the view that a person's ethical judgments are true only in the sense that the judgments accurately express that person's *perception* of the ethical nature of a situation rather than accurately expressing the ethical nature of a situation. To say that rape is wrong, for the subjectivist, is merely to express an individual person's view of the ethical status of rape such that saying rape is not wrong expresses some other individual person's view of the ethical status of rape. To be sure, people do have different ethical views, but ethical subjectivism holds that no one person's view is correct in the sense that the view maps onto some ethical facts in the world. Here, ethical judgments state truths about their speaker rather than truths about ethical actions. The difference between autonomism and ethical subjectivism is that the former view aims to give an account of how matters are concerning some ethical situation while the latter view aims to give an account of what a person's view is of the ethical situation.

Like autonomism, ethical subjectivism is problematic. Ethical subjectivism does not allow for ethical disagreement. How can two persons who express different ethical judgments ever have ethical disagreement since their judgments are true or false in virtue of reporting their own perspectives and not true or false in virtue of reporting what is the case about an ethical matter? Different ethical judgments would be on par with judgments about the taste of a pizza for two persons having different judgments about the pizza's taste. To assert the judgment that a pizza tastes good or bad is merely to state what is true about how each person making the judgments experiences the pizza. Obviously, the pizza is not both good and bad. This shows that if ethical judgments are merely true in virtue of them accurately reporting a person's perspective on an ethical issue, then ethical judgments are never about ethical situations.

Skepticism

A mark of a moral skeptic is the frequency of asked questions. Common questions asked are: "Who is to say what is wrong or right?" "Who knows what's right?" or "Who are you to tell me I'm wrong?" The moral skeptic is unsure about matters of good or bad and right or wrong.[2] Moral skeptics deny truth claims about ethical matters often because of the perennial debates people have about what actions are right or wrong. The mere fact that people do not agree as to what "is the case" concerning some matter does not entail that no truth can be had about the matter. It may be the case that in a particular dispute about whether an action is right or wrong, one of the people disputing the matter may be wrong but refuses to admit it.

Let us consider the abortion issue. It is a polemic issue that continues to leave people either on the pro-choice side or the pro-life side of the fence. People are also split on the death penalty issue. In general, people are split on the moral rightness or wrongness of many actions. But this fact does not entail that no one has the moral truth on the disputed issues. The presence of disagreement does not entail the absence of moral truth. Imagine the debate about slavery in the United States. Nowadays, there are few, if any, who would claim that slavery is not a moral injustice except for hard core racists. However, if the skeptic is correct about the implications of disagreement, then abolitionists could not claim to know that slavery is an injustice since slave owners disagreed with them!

Perhaps an effective way a person can refute the moral skeptic is to appeal to the skeptic's self-interest. For example, ask the skeptic to share with you all the important things in his life. Perhaps he will mention family members and material possessions. Now ask the skeptic would it be morally wrong, for example, to take his credit cards, home and car without requesting them. Or ask the skeptic would it be wrong to violently attack a person dear to himself. To be a real skeptic he would have to say he does not want you to take his possessions and that he does not want you to attack his significant other, but he could not say your actions are wrong. In other words, he can express negative feelings about your actions but he cannot say you *should not* act in the manner you do. Why?

---

2. While skepticism is normally classified under metaethics, I place it under MOTS because the sense of skepticism here refers to an unreflected rejection of the human knower to know which things have value and which ethical judgments are true or false.

Because the skeptic claims that he does not know what is right or wrong. To adhere to skepticism prevents any reflection on issues like abortion, euthanasia, affirmative action, genocide and famine. What position one takes on these issues, according to skepticism, may generate negative or positive feelings but it could not be discerned as correct.

Ethical Relativism

This MOTS ethical view allows for moral judgments; however, the rightness or wrongness of a judgment depends on (a) the beliefs of a society/culture,[3] (b) the beliefs at a given place or (c) the beliefs at a given time. An ethical relativist would hold that "Everyone has their own beliefs...x is wrong for us but may not be wrong for someone else in another country."

Ethical relativism (aka as cultural relativism) *about a society holds that the beliefs of society determine what is morally right and wrong.* Here to find out what is wrong or right, the ethical relativist says we should check with the beliefs of our society. Consequently, the basis for rape being wrong is only because a given society or most societies condemn it, given the time or location of the societies. So there is a metaphysical[4] and epistemological[5] claim being made here: first society functions as an epistemological basis for discerning the correctness of our ethical beliefs and society also serves as a metaphysical basis for what makes our belief correct. Essentially ethical relativism collapses and grounds the ethical content of states of affairs in the world into any given society's beliefs. There are several problems with this form of ethical relativism.

First, we need to know what is meant by "society." Who are the members of society? For starters, each of us is a member of society and this is where the problems begin. If each of us is a member of society, then according to ethical relativism, each of us determines what is ethically right and wrong. But if this is true, why do we need to check with society if we are the ones determining ethics? Moreover, if we are members of society, then we also possess the power to make our judgments be true. Perhaps

---

3. A distinction can be made between society and culture. A society may contain several cultures or just one. In any case a given society is the summation of the cultures or is identical to the one culture if there is only one culture in the society.

4. Metaphysics concerns the nature of what something actually is; it is the study of a thing's essence or what makes the "thing" be what it is.

5. As we will see later in chapter 2, epistemology is the study of knowledge and concerns our beliefs and opinions among other things.

the ethical relativist means that ethics is determined by the views of the majority. This approach sounds a bit more plausible. To determine if our ethical judgments are correct we simply check to see what the majority of people in society say is ethically right and wrong. If there is a match between our judgments and society's judgments, then we know our judgments are correct. Yet plausibility does not mean correct. Never did nor ever will any majority make what is right or wrong. Suppose the majority of a society suddenly decided that killing people over the age of 65 should be permitted? According to relativism, this would be ethically justified for the simple reason that the majority of society is the basis of what we know is true and the basis of some action being true.

Secondly what if there is no dominant ethical view in society concerning some issue? Rather suppose that there are several cultures or subgroups in society (relative to age, gender, sex or ethnicity). Which subgroup would be correct? According to ethical relativism, all the subgroups would equally be correct about their judgments. For example, suppose the judgment to kill people over the age of 65 was determined by everyone under the age of 65 and those who are against this judgment were over the age of 65. Suppose also that these two groups are equally divided in terms of numbers. Ethical relativism could not tell us how to decide what to do in this case since 50 percent of society agrees with the judgment and 50 percent of society does not agree with the judgment. To be sure if ethical relativism is correct, then both subgroups would be correct. Thus terminating the life of members in society who are over the age of 65 would be both right and wrong.

Ethical relativism according to place holds that different places (viz., countries, cultures, etc.) have their own ethical beliefs and each place's ethical beliefs are equally true. So what may be ethically wrong in the United States may not be ethically wrong in China or what may be ethically wrong in the American culture may not be ethically wrong in the Chinese culture. Sometimes defenders of ethical relativism of this sort charge anyone who condemns a practice in another country as arrogant. In this case, the ethical relativist asserts, "Who do you think you are condemning a country half way around the world for their ethical practices? If that is what they do over there, let them do it. They have their ethics, we have ours. Do you think you are better than they are?" Let us consider an ethical practice that most Americans would consider abhorrent. A practice common in the Middle East allows men to beat and then kill a female member of their family when the female member does something to shame the family. It is known as "honor killing." What the female does could be as simple as marrying someone other than the man her parents arranged for her to marry. It is not a rare occurrence for a brother to stab his sister to death multiple times because she married outside her parent's arrangements. Amazingly, the ethical relativist would not condemn this practice, even upon reflection! Or consider an example that Ruth Benedict appeals to in her justification of ethical relativism:

> Among the Kwakiutl it did matter whether a relative had died in bed of disease, or by the hand of an enemy, in either case death was an affront to be wiped out by the death of another person. The fact that one had been caused to mourn was proof that one had been put upon. A chief's sister and her daughter had gone up to Victoria, and either because they drank bad whiskey or because their boat capsized they never came back. The chief called together his warriors, "Now I ask you, tribes, who shall wail? Shall I do it or shall another?" The spokesman answered, of course, "Not you, Chief. Let some other of the tribes." Immediately they set up the war pole to announce their intention of wiping out the injury, and gathered a war party. They set out, and found seven men and children asleep and killed them. "Then they felt good when they arrived at Sebaa in the evening."[6]

The ethical relativist would have us believe that every culture and country has its own set of ethical practices, and who is anyone to question the Middle Eastern and Kwakiutl practices? After all, the people in various cultural settings accept their ethical mores, so why shouldn't we tolerant them?

There are several problems with this approach to ethical relativism. First, if this type of ethical relativist had his way, then Hitler should have never been stopped; Apartheid should never have been ruled illegal; and the "ethnic cleansing" in Kosovo should have been allowed. In general, the problem with this form of ethical relativism is no different from that of ethical relativism based on society.

Secondly, this form of ethical relativism allows any action to have ethical acceptability so long as some country believes the action is ethically acceptable. Thus social and ethical reform and social and ethical reformers are concepts that would be anchored in the air, lacking any meaning. Any change within a society, if it occurs, should be by chance and not intentional unless the given society agreed to change. Nevertheless, the

---

6. Benedict, "Defense of Ethical Relativism," 61–62.

change could not be classified as progress since ethical values do not exist beyond prescriptions of what a society calls ethical values.

Ethical relativism about time holds that ethics judgments are correct in virtue of the time period they are made. Thus for some action that was considered wrong 50 years ago would not be wrong today if no one believes it is wrong. Accordingly, ethics changes with the times. For ethical relativists, anyone who denies this relativistic dictum is branded "old fashioned." A relativist of this sort would say, "My grandmother and mother believed that X was immoral, but times have changed." The relativist is correct that ethical *views* change over time, but this fact does not entail that *ethics* varies over time. At best, if ethical views change over time this simply shows that our discernment of what is ethically right or wrong is greater or worse. But the rightness or wrongness of an action remains the same.

Consider the case of Jim Crowism in the United States. Over 50 years ago, many people in the United States believed that races should be kept separate and valued according to a racial hierarchy. At public washrooms and water fountains were signs reading, "Colored Only" and "Whites Only." Today many Americans are more ethically mature to see that such thinking is flawed. Jim Crowism was wrong 50 years ago and is wrong today. What changed was the view of many Americans *about* Jim Crowism, not the wrongness of Jim Crowism.

For all forms of ethical relativism, the main error committed is the conflation of objective judgments with subjective and conventional judgments. Judgments that are conventional and subjective correspond *merely to our own desires and beliefs*; they do not correspond to the world independently of our conception of the world. Subjective judgments are true reports just of and for the person asserting the judgments. The following would be examples of subjective judgments: Pepperoni pizza tastes good; blue is a pretty color; Reggae sounds great; and Leisure suits are ugly. While others may assert the truth of these judgments, they are reports of the internal states of the speaker asserting the judgments. As explained earlier in this chapter, they are true in virtue of reporting what is factually the case of the speaker asserting the judgment. They are not literally reports of the objects they predicate. That is to say, the speaker who asserts that pepperoni pizza tastes good is not literally reporting facts about pepperoni pizza as she is about the reaction her tastes buds have to pepperoni pizza. Clearly someone else could assert the judgment that pepperoni pizza is terrible and surely both speakers could not be speaking the truth if their judgments were literally reporting facts about pepperoni pizza itself. Tastes are not in pizza, they are in us. Tastes and internal states often change over time and are neither true nor false.

Let us take a few examples. Leisure suits were popular in the early 1970s. Since then their presence on the earth has all but disappeared. A case could be made that no one would find leisure suits pleasurable to wear. They are simply not in style. Leisure suits are still leisure suits and will continue to be what they are. They can no more change what they are than the color red can stop being the color red. What has changed, however, is their being in style. This, however, is a reflection of us, people in culture and society. What may be fashionable today may not be fashionable tomorrow. Indeed, fashion is relative. But this should come as no surprise since fashion is a matter of taste. Similarly, conventional judgments stemming from culture and society are true not for any empirical, logical or justifiable reasons of any sort; they are true merely because a given society, culture or even organization says so or for some historical reason. For example, it is true that a touchdown plus a field goal equals seven points in football. But there is no empirical, logical or justifiable reason why this judgment is true. The judgment is true simply because the NFL organization, and inventors of American football, like Walter Camp, declared that a touchdown and field goal would amount to this score. They could have equally declared that a touchdown equals two points like a score does in basketball; there are no facts in the world or logical constraints that prevent this from ever happening. The same basis for truth would hold true for other conventional judgments grounded in culture and society. Consider the following: Boy babies ought to wear blue and girl babies ought to wear pink; a king in chess can move only one square; An American motorist should drive a vehicle on the right side of the road; and wedding engagements require a ring for the potential bride. In all these examples, the truth of the judgments obtain merely because some culture/society declared these judgments to be true. There is nothing about the world *per se* that requires these cultural/societal judgments to be true. Consider the above example about the side of the road the United States has stipulated for a car to drive on and, say, England. In the United States, cars drive on the right side of the road. In England, cars drive on the left side of the road. Neither way is correct. There are no reasons to prefer one way correct and the other way incorrect. Nevertheless, from the perspective of the law, drivers *ought* to drive on either side of the road in light of what the traffic laws stipulate in the United States and England respectively.

Now imagine if ethical judgments were merely instances of subjective judgments or instances of conventional judgments of culture or society, then the truth of ethical judgments would be stipulated in the same manner as that of subjective or conventional judgments. Thus ethical judgments would be true merely because they report some speaker's internal states or because they report the collective attitude or consensus of a culture or society. Beyond these types of contingent verbal and psychological groundings, there would be nothing about ethical judgments that make them correct. Rape and child abuse, for instance, would be wrong merely because a person, culture, or society simply declared that they are wrong.

Against ethical relativism, ethical judgments are true because they point out normative states of affairs about the actual world or some possible world. They are not made true because they are merely stipulated by a person, culture, or society. Specifically, these actual or potential states of affairs in the world (or what we call "truth bearers" in epistemology) are about some person's autonomy or well-being, at least theoretically.[7] From an epistemological perspective, our justification for believing an ethical judgment to be true is based on these same truth bearers rather than on mere individual or collective beliefs or sentiments.

It goes without saying that even within a given culture, there are practices, and beliefs about those practices, that are prescribed as ethical. Even here these ethical beliefs and practices are not correct "just because" the culture says so. To be sure, if a given culture condemned child abuse simply because child abuse was traditionally condemned in that society, this would be an instance of ethical relativism(tradition could have easily condoned child abuse). However the same culture could condemn child abuse because child abuse by definition and in fact traumatizes children. So the fact that a given culture has ethical beliefs does not entail that those beliefs are unfounded or not based on the actual well-being of some person. Nevertheless, whether the culture has cogent reasons for its ethical practices and beliefs, or merely grounds its ethical practices and beliefs in tradition, matters. A culture that abides by the belief that child prostitution is permissible is an ethical belief that is per se unethical, regardless if the belief is based on reasons or tradition. Such a belief should be disregarded. Now this strong stand against tradition goes against a commonly held claim that traditions should be respected. To the contrary, this claim is confusing

---

7. As with legal issues, a jury's verdict (judgment) is based on evidence or facts in the world that pertains to the alleged crime regardless if the jury's verdict is correct or incorrect. The same would be true of ethical judgments.

"respect for ethical beliefs and practices" within a culture with "respect for customs" within a culture. So given this bifurcation between traditions qua ethical judgments and traditions qua customs, it would be important to say a thing or two about how to decide what beliefs within a given culture fall under ethics and what beliefs within a culture fall under customs.

Customs are meaningful, existential ways people behave within a society or culture. Specifically, customs involve the way people eat food, dress, marry and even greet each other in public. For example, in some Asian countries, people bow to each other as a means to greet each other. In Scotland, men for traditional purposes sometimes wear a skirt-like garment called a kilt. In some countries, men greet each other with a kiss. In India, the duration of a wedding is over several days. None of these practices are right or wrong. In some cases, it is just a brute fact that practices are done the way they are done. Surely there may be some causal, historical explanation to account for the origin of these practices, but there are no normative reasons why the practices ought to be carried out in the fashion that they are carried out. What customs are practiced in country X may not be the customs practiced in country Y. Customs are *relative* to what is valued and *believed* by those in a particular country or culture. Moreover, customs can change relative to time differences.

Well, how are customs and ethics different? Obviously, to answer this question we need to know what ethics entails. We will look at this issue in more detail later, but some features of ethics may include the following: a condemnation of behavior that violates the respect or autonomy of someone or causes harm without the person's consent, particularly when no greater good is achieved by the harm. Thus any customs that sanction such behavior cannot *be* customs even when they are considered customs by members of the culture that adopt them. Instead they become immoral acts. Let us consider, for example, female castration or what is also known as female mutilation that is a customary practice in some countries. Young girls in these countries are restrained by older women and then their clitoris is cut (often by using a dull razor blade). The intended result is for these young girls not to develop sexual desires. This is a benefit for their future husbands since their husbands will not have to worry about them having sexual desires for another man. Female castration curtails adultery on the part of the wives. But surely it can be seen that this practice violates the respect of the young girls and, in fact, it causes them unnecessary harm and pain. So while female castration may be considered a custom in some countries, it is, in fact, an immoral act done to victimized girls. A rejoinder to this objection is that the cultural practice is ethically permissible in cases where the girls voluntarily choose to undergo the procedure. In such cases, it is said, the young ladies are exercising their autonomy. If autonomy is the issue here, it is a modified autonomy. In countries that condone female castration, females are also regulated to a second class status. Their ability to function as autonomous citizens is difficult in light of discriminatory practices that prevent them from obtaining employment. The male in such counties is the source of economic security. Being a wife unfortunately has great benefits. It is not difficult to see how females could convince themselves to undergo castration if this is a cultural precondition for economic security.

Applying the Principle of Charity to Those Who Embrace the MOTS

It should be obvious, upon reflection on the objections just presented to the ethical forms of MOTS, what is rationally problematic with such views. Nevertheless, the MOTS are ubiquitous and quite popular in society; after all, MOTS is an acronym for "man on the streets." So what is the pull the MOTS have on people? Why are they so popular? Are people really not sophisticated enough to discern the incoherence of the MOTS? Perhaps there is no one answer but a series of answers that could be given.

Four come to mind. The first two reasons are sociological. People tend to practice and preach in disjointed ways. It is doubtful that many people practice the MOTS. When someone has been treated unjustly that person can stipulate why they were treated unjustly and their reasons have nothing to do with the reasons being warranted simply because society endorses them. However, there is an assumption in society and among humanity at large that what ought to be preached or what normative stance to take as far as what makes an action right or wrong is some form of MOTS. This assumption is derived from yet another assumption that ethics should be approached this way because the issue has been settled in the past (in the same manner that the earth has been proven to be round and needs no further discussion) that ethics is a matter of personal or cultural belief. So everyone has a duty to carrying on the tradition.

The second sociological reason turns on the issue of respect and rights. According to many people unless there is a consensus in society that some action is wrong, then no particular person has a right to tell another person what she should or should not do. This unwritten rule about "rights" says members of society have a right to tell another person not to beat their 5 year old son till he is hospitalized but members do not have a right to tell another member what is right or wrong on issues concerning their own personhood, e.g., issues where there is no consensus like abortion, euthanasia, or sexual practices.

A third reason has to do with dehumanizing others' character. A consistent theme in the MOTS is an emphasis on not judging others. As a result some may find a departure from the MOTS's dictum "do not judge" problematic or difficult to do. This dictum "You ought not to judge" is ambiguous or incoherent. Let us begin with the matter of ambiguity. Does the dictum assert that a person's belief should not be judged as true or false, or does the dictum assert that the person's character or being should not be judged? From what has been said about judging, there are three types of judgments: judgment of a person's action, character or being. Surely judging a person's character is often wrong and more importantly judging a person qua human being as less valuable than ourselves is categorically wrong. A person may do something despicable or unethical, but surely this should not call for a condemnation of a person's character as despicable or unethical. While no person's character is good in an absolute sense, many people have characters that in many ways seek to do good or what is right. This understanding of human nature is consistent with the teaching of the Bible that "for all have sinned and fall short of the glory of God," and "nothing good dwells in me, that is, in my flesh" (Rom 3:23; 7:18). To be sure Paul does not say that human nature is incorrigible; rather, he says that the principle of sin or "flesh" is sinfully incorrigible. This distinction Paul makes implies that human nature is not simple but is an integrated whole. Common everyday experience reveals that humanity is capable of seeking what is good, e.g., it is natural for mothers to seek the good of their child. But because humans are fallen, it can also be said that humans can be driven or compelled to act from the sin principle, which among other things is self-focused and opposes God's authority. Since human character has both altruistic and self-interest elements, it follows that humans can seek either good or bad. For any given individual, the good elements of her character may or may not outweigh the bad elements of her character. This complexity in human character shows that actions do not entail a specified character that is wholly good or wholly bad. It is a complex issue of how choices a person makes, environment and natural tendencies within the person contribute to the person's character in terms of whether it is dominated by goodness or badness. In light of these considerations, in as much as two people may disagree about what to do in a given ethical situation, what should not *per se* be center stage is either person's character in terms of traits as integrity and sense of decency. It would be a hasty generalization to assume from one ethical situation that a person has a bad character. At most what could be determined is that the person made a right or wrong decision. Judgments of character are appropriate only after significant episodes of consistent decisions to do the wrong thing.

Even when a person's action is an extension of her character, say as with Hitler, the person's worth as a person should[8] remain intake. Even Hitler is a valuable being, because he is a rational being made in the image of God. If we judge Hitler as worthless, we disregard the image of God that he is made in. It is worth noting that Dietrich Bonheoffer, aware of Hitler's value, attempted to assassinate Hitler near the end of the WWII. However, in his failed attempt to do so, Bonheoffer did not devalue the worth of Hitler's personhood. Nevertheless Bonheoffer's action was guided by his assessment of Hitler's actions; not Hitler's character. Bonheoffer knew that Hitler was the main cause behind the carnage in Europe. He also knew that Hitler's diabolical character was incorrigible, so an attempt to negotiate with Hitler would be fruitless. With Hitler dead, the carnage in Europe would very likely stop. The ascription of a person's character as good or bad does not entail that their actions will be right or wrong respectfully. Good people are capable of wrong actions and bad people are capable of right actions. Failure to make this action verses character distinction leads to the unfortunate consequence of judging a person's character because of their actions.

Also, when the sense of the dictum pertains not to a person's character but to the person's belief about a prescribed action, it becomes incoherent. For person A to tell person B that she ought not to tell person C what to do (i.e., judge person C), person A is in turn judging person B's belief and telling person B what to do, viz., not tell C what to do. But this is incoherent.

Finally, there is an epistemic reason. All too often the expression about not being in another person's shoes is mentioned in ethical conversations to imply the need for sympathy. It also implies the inability to know all the significant circumstances that lead a person to do what she did or did not

---

8. The "should" here will be defended in chapters 4, 5, and 6, where the value of persons is discussed.

do or implies the inability to critique another cultural practice. To be sure, our cognitive limitations, due to our own ignorance of other cultures or another person's circumstances, are grounds for forgoing a judgment on the rightness or wrongness of some action or practice. Admitting as much, however, does not entail or imply judging others or knowing that some action is right or wrong is simpliciter impossible.

That All Important Question: What Makes an Action Right or Wrong?

Looking back on the various MOTS views of ethics, a core problem with all of them is that they are not evidence based and the fact of the matter is that ethics is evidence based. To be sure, as we will see in chapter 3, some metaethicists deny that there are any normative or moral features in the world; however, with the exception of a nihilist, even they admit that ethics is about facts in the world even if the facts are not normative. Unfortunately, some people make ethics to be about mere beliefs (opinions in particular) and by default adopt some version of the MOTS. Accordingly, it escapes their notice that the fact rape, for example, causes mental and physical trauma to its victim has everything to do with the wrongness of rape. Instead, they immediately assert that rape is wrong because society, religion, or their individual opinion condemns it. The problems with opinion qua "mere belief" have already been stated. However, it is important to extend that discussion to point out the proper role of "mere belief" in ethics or to any cognitive discipline for that matter.

First, one would be intellectually irresponsible to hold an opinion without some degree of evidence to support the opinion. To be sure, opinions are not indubitable, proven fact, or irrefutable, but some opinions are better than others and to hold an opinion without any supporting evidence or pragmatic reason for doing so is again intellectually irresponsible and irrational.

Secondly, even with evidence, opinions do not make any state of affairs obtain. Proven beliefs are called truths, but even here proven beliefs do not determine or ground reality; instead they inform us what states of affairs obtain or do not obtain. For example, asserting that the earth is 92,955,807 miles from the sun is a truth. Now what makes the earth be this distance from the sun is not the truth we assert, that is discerned from mathematics, physics, etc. What makes the earth be 92, 955,807 miles from sun is the fact of the distance between the two bodies. This causal inertness of beliefs, even true beliefs, applies to ethics as well. People who make ethics to be about mere beliefs or even people who say proven beliefs make an action right or wrong, fail to make a distinction between (a) what makes an action right or wrong and (b) how a person knows an action is right or wrong.

Consider the following example about pathology and doctors' views about a pathology. Suppose you were experiencing pain in your abdominal area and you were discharging blood in your stool. You decide to go to a GI doctor and she rules out colon cancer and hemorrhoids after a few tests, e.g., a colonoscopy. However, she says her personal opinion is that you have a rare disease X. You are not convinced that you have disease X and so you go to another GI doctor. He says his personal opinion is that you have disease Y. At this point you do not know which doctor, if either of them, is correct, but for sure they both have personal opinions that could be true and both opinions are evidence based. Suppose the second doctor is correct and you are asked what makes you have disease Y; hopefully you don't say "I know I have disease Y because the second doctor said so based on his interpretation of test results" or "I had a gut feeling I had the disease." If you said this, you would not be answering the question given to you; you would be answering how you knew you had disease Y. The beliefs or test results of the second doctor does not make you have disease Y. What makes you have the disease Y (or even X) are the interaction of things like DNA, foreign bodies, radiation, etc. . . . items in the world as opposed to the doctor's beliefs or test results. If you were asked how you knew you had disease Y, then the expected answer would be either the opinion of the second doctor or her test results. The same is true of ethical beliefs. Our ethical beliefs should be evidence based, but even here, our beliefs do not make actions right or wrong. The rejoinder that medicine and ethics are radically different subject matters by the fact that the former always has consensus among those in the medical field and the claims of medicine are never proven false ignores the example just given about disease X and Y or fails to appreciate how medicine works.

Conclusion

It could be argued that talk of ethics being evidence based begs the question of who knows what actually is wrong or right. Even if it is true that some action cannot be right for one person and wrong for another, the objection goes, who determines who is correct if person A says X is wrong and person B says X is right? This objection to ethics being evidence based misses the point about what "evidence based" means. There may not be a non-question begging way to know who is right and who is wrong about some ethical issue, but this epistemic problem does not prevent ethics from being about affairs out there in the world. A car, for example, has a color, even if two people disagree about what that color is. Uncertainty and lack of consensus about what ethical judgments are true does not entail the absence of ethical truth.

2

Ethics and Epistemic Myopia: Its Nature, Its Sources, and Its Cures

. . . and you will know the truth, and the truth will make you free.

—JOHN 8:32 (NASB)

If those who are called philosophers, particularly the Platonists, have said anything which is true and consistent with our faith, we must not reject it, but claim it for our own use, in the knowledge that they must possess it unlawfully. . . . [P]agan learning is not entirely made up of false teaching and superstitions. . . . It contains also some excellent teachings, well suited to be used by truth, and excellent moral values. Indeed, some truths are even found among them which relate to the worship of the one God.

—ST. AUGUSTINE, AD 397, *DE DOCTRINA CHRISTIANA*[1]

IN THIS CHAPTER WE will take a look at epistemology in the context of ethics. We will first explore what epistemology is simpliciter and then consider the trappings of a poorly processed epistemology that leads to a plethora of ethically wrong decisions or ethically wrong actions, both historically speaking and as a matter of a general rule. Specifically we will look at a belief, attitude, perceptual, and evaluating disease I call epistemic myopia. Myopia prevents us from seeing and evaluating the world objectively. By its very nature, sufferers of myopia are unaware they suffer from it. From their perspective, however, they see and value affairs in the world objectively. People in general understand the concept of epistemic myopia but often are not aware they suffer from it. We will end this

---

1. St. Augustine, *De doctrina Christiana* 2.40.60, 64.

chapter with a discussion on how to check for and avoid myopia so as to pursue ethically sound decision making as a general rule. So let us start with a brief description of what epistemology is all about.

Epistemology and Ethics

Epistemology is "the study of knowledge." The etiology of the word is from two Greek words *episteme* (meaning knowledge) and *logos* (meaning an account). Here we ask questions like: What is the difference between a true belief and a justified true belief? What is knowledge? Are some beliefs justified by non-beliefs, like sensory states? Can I know that an external world exists? Is truth objective or merely a creation of my culture? Can I know anything? What kinds of things can I have knowledge about? The first conflict in the Bible centered around issues in epistemology. Satan told Eve that eating from the tree of knowledge would make her wise (knowing good and evil), and that God did not speak the truth when he told Eve she would die if she ate from the tree.

The goal of this chapter is to discuss epistemology in the context of ethics. We will start with major themes and issues in epistemology and then relate them to the topic of ethics. Let us begin with analyzing the notion of truth.

What Is Truth?

Our concern here is about what "truth" means. For example, the concern is not: *Is it true that child prostitution is wrong?* The concern is: *What does it mean to say that it is true that child prostitution is wrong?* The former question concerns justification for the belief that *child prostitution is wrong* and the latter question concerns what we mean when we report that *"child prostitution is wrong."* The philosophical problem of what truth means has been around since ancient times. In an elliptical way, Pontius Pilate (John 18:38) asked Jesus "What is truth?" This question has been studied more since the turn of the twentieth century than at any other previous time. In contemporary circles, there is no consensus as to what the word "truth" means, let alone whether truth exists at all. We will not explore that debate here. Needless to say, these divergent views on truth have seriously impacted our understanding of ethics. For example, when we talk about ethics, is the content of our ethical claims true, false, or neither? If ethical judgments are neither true nor false, doesn't this entail that ethical correctness reduces to whatever we or any speaker says is ethically correct? We will pick up this matter of the truth or falsity of ethical judgments in chapter three, but for now let us assume that when people speak of ethics they mean that it is true that some action is right or wrong.

Belief Formation, Justification, and Epistemic Myopia

Can two people reflect on the *same* evidence and yet infer two different judgments about what ethical truth the evidence suggests? Obviously the answer is yes. If they are making contrary or contradictory claims, then either both persons believe false beliefs or one of them believes a true belief and the other one believes a false belief. The reality of their disagreement should not lead either of them to embrace skepticism or relativism. Again, lack of consensus does not entail lack of truth. Truth is out there and it leaves a trail of facts to follow. The problem, of course, is that people perceive reality differently. With that said, if everyone sees reality the same way, this fact does not entail that everyone is in touch with reality or apprehends what is true, e.g., everyone could be misinformed. So consensus and truth do not go hand in hand. The awareness of truth requires only one apprehender, but apprehension is not *per se* an easy endeavor.

The divergence in judgment about what is true concerning some issue is obviously due to at least one person not seeing the *same* evidence the way it should be seen and understood because something is driving the person away from apprehending the truth. However, before we get into a discussion of the causes of blindness to truth, a discussion of a separate matter needs to be addressed: How to deal with disagreement regardless of who is right or wrong.

Conflict Resolution

Conflict concerning ethical matters like conflict concerning any disagreement can be encumbered by vices but can be resolved by virtues of character. Let us take a look at both. As far as virtues (i.e., a positive character trait) are concerned, at the top of the list is *benevolence* concerning a person's intent. Often barriers are erected when one interlocutor assumes something negative about the other interlocutor's intent, e.g., that he is driven by dishonesty, racism, sexism, selfishness, narrow mindedness, etc. The assumption here is that the other person is not interested in truth. However, if the interlocutors assume the best about each other's intention (e.g., that the person is seeking what is good or true), the assumption would at least grant misguidedness but with the intent to understand what is true. In politics, parties assume the worst of each other and thus shift to outmaneuver each other in order to maintain or secure power. Unfortunately, this may explain why American political parties talk past each other and never agree about nearly anything.

A second virtue is *empathy*. In nearly any ethical disagreement, it is important to put on the shoes of the other person as much as the imagination will allow. Doing so may help explain the person's intent and how the person may be interpreting a situation.

A third virtue is *humility*. If you are dealing with conflict, critically evaluate yourself before continuing the discussion. Expose yourself to the possibility of being in error.

As for vices, the following should be avoided. At the top of the list, avoid *disrespecting* the person of the view you do not agree with. Dislike the judgment, not the person who makes the judgment.

Secondly, avoid *mutiny*. Bringing other parties into the disagreement is not necessary and in fact is intended to imply the incompetency or error of the other person. The choice to "gang up" or to seek truth in numbers adds nothing to the truth or falsity of a claim. It is a cheap way to say, "Obviously all of us could not be wrong." To be sure, sometimes a third party is vital to discerning which of the two parties is wrong or barking down the wrong path. But in such cases, this third party is not a horde of other people and the third party is someone chosen by both interlocutors who they respect. The choice of this third person is based on her ability to be enlightening and objective (void of self-interest).

While instilling these virtues and ridding yourself of these vices will not determine who is correct in some ethical disagreement, but doing so will definitely construct a healthy doxastic environment for objective and critical reflection on the ethical issue being debated.

Sometimes, however, despite our virtuous character and attempt to be diplomatic, there are factors that we are unaware of that cause us to sway from the truth. In other words, there are things we are doing or not doing in conjunction with false beliefs that cause us to sway from the truth. These factors are under our radar. We are like the king who sincerely thought he was clothed in royal garb as he walked down the

ethics and epistemic myopia 27

streets of his kingdom. In reality he was completely naked. Let us call the unawareness of how things really are (viz., in our mind and in reality), *epistemic myopia*.

Epistemic myopia is not just a matter of having false beliefs; people have false beliefs all the time and don't know it. Rather epistemic myopia is essentially an *unawareness* that an internal or external barrier to our cognitive faculties stirs us away from we seeing reality accurately or "as it is." Theoretically, seeing reality accurately can simply be a matter of coming to terms with the falsity of a previously held belief or series of beliefs (e.g. a narrative) when the *dejure* or *de facto* defeaters[2] to the belief or narrative are understood; but myopia prevents this "understanding" from happening. A hallmark feature of humanity is the crowning jewel, rationality. Humans are quite insightful, articulate, and intelligent. However, myopia eliminates or confounds these features of rationality. When we are victims of myopia, we are like dreamers dreaming but not knowing we are in a dream. Only when we awake from a dream do we realize the bizarre and irrational nature of our dream thought processes and what seemed to be normal to us in the dream. Epistemic myopia, then, is analogous to an awake dream.

Consider the distinction between murder and killing. Killing is a necessary condition for murder but not a sufficient condition for murder. If murder and killing were bi-conditionals (where each is a necessary and sufficient for each other) then every instance of killing would be an instance of murder and thus wrong. But surely, as we will point out in chapter three, this is not the case. Killing someone by accident is not wrong. Any given person could see and make this distinction when thinking in abstraction and when no particular ethical issue is the focus. However, the minute this distinction is considered within the context of a specific ethical issue where emotions fly, myopia can enter the scene. Nevertheless, when myopia strikes a person, she is unable to see this distinction and thus unaware that she confuses murder with killing when she says killing is wrong. For some reason, this person cannot bring herself to believe that not all acts of killing are wrong. Providing argument after argument to convince her otherwise won't do, due to the resistive force of her myopia.

---

2. Borrowing language from philosopher Alvin Plantinga, de facto defeaters attempt to show a belief is false; a de jure defeater attempts to show that a belief is unwarranted even if it is true.

Consider another person who is emphatically opposed to abortions and holds a tight ship such that at every point of the prenatal development, her view holds that the unborn is considered to have the same value and ethical status as any adult human being. Holding a position like this makes the person's ethical position clear without having to figure out if there are any moments in the pregnancy when an abortion is permissible. The merit of stating an abortion is wrong at conception is not the issue here. However, the telling sign of myopia within this person is noted when the person says "Life begins at conception and it is wrong to kill a fetus since a fetus can feel pain and experience consciousness. It is really just an unborn baby." Notice how the person manipulated facts to fit her position against abortions. As pointed out, this person believes abortions at conception are wrong. To justify this claim she needs to argue why abortions are wrong at conception. However, when the person attempts to do so she shifts from the embryo (that exists at conception) to the fetus (that exists after the embryonic stage). Clearly what a fetus is capable of suffering and what an embryo is capable of suffering are different, but this person is driven by myopia and is unaware of her shift in what she is denoting in her argument. Put another way, this person wants to object to an abortion at conception but is unaware she uses reason that could only oppose abortions at the fetal stage of prenatal development.

Misguided Justification, Motivation, and Belief Formation

It is epistemic myopia that explains why two persons can derive completely different conclusions about the same ethical situation. Before we turn our attention to this issue, it is important to review the processes by which people form their beliefs, for belief formation along with the motivation and justification (or lack of) for beliefs is the source of myopia.

The beliefs that flash across our mind come to us either from our environment or from our own reflection. Our judgments of the truth or falsity of beliefs is a matter of what we know or what in philosophical circles is called justification. The competing models on justification take either a linear path to justification (known as foundationalism) or a circular path (known as coherentism).[3] Let us look at these models in order.

---

3. For an excellent discussion of justification and the distinction between foundationalism and coherentism, see Fumerton, "Theories of Justification," in *The Oxford Handbook of Epistemology*, 204–33.

ethics and epistemic myopia

Philosophers who are coherentists[4] take a circular approach to justification where every belief is justified by its coherence with some other belief. As a result, coherentism holds that no belief is foundational or self-justified. Here justification refers to a belief and its "hanging together" with a set of other beliefs. Moreover, coherentism is exhaustively doxastic, holding that no nonbelief states contribute to justification (this is called the *doxastic*[5] *assumption*). However, coherentism does not deny that sensory experience has a causal role in the manufacturing of beliefs, i.e., producing perceptual beliefs. Minimally speaking, what coherentists mean by "coherence" between beliefs is a matter of consistency, entailment or explanatory success of the "hanging together." Belief p is justified if it coheres well with q and r, e.g., if p is explainable by q and r. Alternatively, q and r are justified if they are able to explain p. As you can see, the justification is holistic.

Foundationalism[6] as a theory of epistemic justification states roughly the following:

> df: For any true belief P for S, S knows P if P is either a foundational or non-inferentially justified belief for S or a belief justified by foundational or non-inferentially beliefs.

In the former case, P is justified without appeal to any further belief. We can say P in this case is self-justifying. In some cases, the belief may be non-inferentially justified because it is directly caused by reliable sensory experience, e.g., perception.[7] Sensory experience is non-doxastic (not a belief or set of beliefs) and thus not needing justification.[8] In the latter case, P is justified because it is either entailed by some foundational belief (or by some other non-foundational belief) or inferred from some foundational belief (or some other non-foundational belief) via some

---

4. Philosophers who espouse some form of coherentism include Wilfrid Sellars, Keith Lehrer, and Laurence BonJour.

5 Doxastic is a term used in philosophy to refer to the discussion concerning beliefs. It is derived from the Greek word δόξα.

6. Philosophers who espouse some form of foundationalism include Descartes in his *Meditations*; among contemporary philosophers the list includes C. I. Lewis, Roderick Chisholm, Alvin Plantinga, and William Alston.

7. This form of foundationalism is called epistemic reliablism. For a discussion and defense of this view, see Goldman's *Epistemology and Cognition*, 58–121.

8. As we will see shortly, perceptual beliefs are not indubitable given the possibility of error due, for example, to drugs, organically induced delusions, or fanciful Cartesian demons. As a result, some philosophers hold what is called moderate foundationalism, according to which the foundational beliefs need not be indubitable but merely sufficient by itself to satisfy the adequate-justification condition for knowledge.

inductive probabilistic relationship. The inference from foundational to non-foundational beliefs is sometimes an inference to a best explanation.

Now I do not want to attempt a discussion on the merit of either set of theories. However, both approaches to justification do attempt to provide a warranted case of justification. When myopia occurs it is when a person holds a belief as foundational and justifies other beliefs by it but without a criterion for why the belief is foundational (e.g., where no reason is given for why the belief is self-evident) or commits to a narrative of beliefs and judge other beliefs by this narrative but without justification of the narrative itself (e.g., where no reason is given for why the narrative fits better with reality than another narrative or how the beliefs of the narrative themselves fit together). Let us call the former view quasi foundationalism and the latter view quasi coherentism. These two latter approaches to justification appeal neither to properly basic beliefs nor to coherence. Rather their proponents simply make an appeal to either their foundational beliefs as "certain" or to their narrative as "certain" because of (a) the psychological motivation driving it or because of (b) the naiveté behind it. When a person says he is certain "that X" (where X is a belief or narrative) he does not entertain the possibility that X is false because of (1) (i.e., he wants or needs it to be true) or because (2) (i.e., it is all he knows). With this attitude of certainty, it never crosses the myopic person's mind that their foundational beliefs or web of beliefs are false, and thus these beliefs are left unchecked and the myopic person categorizes them as unfalsifiable. Moreover, he proceeds to accept or reject incoming experiences and beliefs based on whether the experience or belief is supported by the foundational belief or the narrative. Now such conditions do not entail myopia; rather, they allow for it. Let us now look at four categories of causes of myopia: internal myopia, external myopia, normative myopia, and de facto myopia.

What Is Driving Your Beliefs: Just the Facts or an Internal Interpretation of the Facts?

Internal myopia is due to factors internal to a person's cognitive faculties. It is a person's (1) unawareness that his commitment to beliefs and values are biased by or guided by motivational factors internal to his cognitive faculties, e.g., fears, self-interest, desires, and intellectual limitations, (2) unawareness that these motivating factors present him with a false or *ethics and epistemic myopia* 31

skewed view of reality and (3) certitude that his beliefs and values are correct. (1), (2), and (3) result in myopia. Metaphorically, if our internal myopia were akin to a camera that does not take an accurate picture of the external world, we would take in sensory input and information like a camera with a broken lens or like a camera with a shutter that selectively discriminates what objects to focus on that are in its purview. Sometimes a person would confess to (1) but not to (2) and (3). Internal myopia does not result from a denial of truth when warranted de jure and de facto arguments are offered against what the myopic person believes. This scenario is reserved for what is later called normative myopia. The way the internal motivating factors work varies. For example, it is interesting to see a person who has suffered extreme abuse, or who felt guilty about an extreme offense, surround himself with a narrative or beliefs that function to eradicate or overcome the abuse or guilt, e.g., themes of penitence, themes of disassociation, beliefs that foster extreme positive self-esteem, etc.. When this extremism manifests itself among Christians, it can come in the form of hyper religiosity and absolutism. For example, the particular person may argue that medical treatment is a last resort after much prayer has not resulted in a cure for an illness. Having a hyper view of God's intervention in medical emergencies could make a person feel special or sufficiently worthy of God's praise. On abortions, the person may argue that abortions are categorically unethical even to save the life of the mother because they are convinced God will save both.[9] In fact, some extremism is responsible for explaining environmental and natural disasters as acts of an angry righteous God. Such beliefs could communicate total devotion to God and thus a recompense for past guilt and shame; they could also communicate a self-imposed ideal Christian identity of what God expects of them and thus an assurance of positive self-esteem. In all these cases, the myopic person is unaware of what is truly driving his religious devotion.

Internal myopia is responsible for the construction of a lot of theological ethics not founded on biblical text. For example, some Christians who have had no prior formal training in theology will often embrace, without justification, beliefs or narratives that describe God as beyond ethics and logic. When asked if God has any limitations, some Christians

---

9. Unfortunately guilt also works to enforce an attitude of legalism; on topics like abortion, the myopic person may have had an abortion in the past and felt extremely guilty of it and vowed as a means to atone for the abortion to be categorically opposed to any conceivable abortion.

feel called to express God's greatness in uncritical imaginative ways and in turn describe God in ways not supported by the Bible. Their God can send people to hell even if such people are free of any offense. Their God could condone rape, where the connotation of rape is not changed and no greater good is achieved by such rapes. In all the above cases, a hyper perfect concept of who God is, and what God does, is embraced despite the fact it is not based on the Bible and, just as important, the myopic person is opposed to a critical analysis or falsification of the belief in question due to their unawareness that they need their belief to be true.

The possible unaware rationales for embracing this hyper, non-rational religiosity vary. The motive could be out of gratitude towards God for pulling the person out of an extremely dark situation; nothing short of describing who and what God can do in unlimited terms would do. Let us include too a motive that is less God-centered and more self-centered; here the motive is existential in the sense that in the person's mind their well-being necessarily depends on there being a God and thus God must be beyond critical analysis or falsification lest God does not exist. Perhaps the same can be said about their interpretation (perhaps literal) of the Bible. Believing and expecting God to do very extraordinary things is seen as a way to impress God. After all, God does approve of those with much faith.

Outside of Christian circles a popular view of ethics in circulation is ethical relativism. Recall from chapter one, ethical relativism is the view that ethical rightness and wrongness depend on the beliefs of individual persons and cultures. A person who embraces ethical relativism as a foundational belief will embrace nearly any ethical belief as permissible. Among the possible motives unaware to the myopic person for embracing ethical relativism as a foundational belief or embracing a relativistic narrative are the following: the desire to see that everything has a right to live their life the way they want to, a desire to avoid confrontation, the need to be accepted by all, and the need to be free of guilt.

With internal myopia, the myopic person is not aware of arguments or narratives that are intended to be warranted or justified objections against their own belief or narrative. So if the internally myopic person is presented with a contrary argument or narrative, such evidence is packaged in a negative light to expose the alleged weaknesses of the evidence. That is, the evidence does not come with a label saying "on the contrary" unless it is also followed by a critique to nullify the objection. Not surprisingly, if the contrary evidence comes, the contrary evidence comes in the form of a straw man. However, when the internally myopic person is exposed to damaging evidence, he fails to see that evidence is actually damaging to his own beliefs. The myopic episode concludes when the person finds a way to integrate the evidence into his narratives or interpret it in such a way that it fits with what the person wants to be true (or false) or with what he is able to understand. So reflection on evidence in this case is discriminately aimed at proving unawarely what is desired to be true and disproving unawarely what is desired to be false. This is also called *confirmation bias*. During the reflection on "the evidence" the myopic person's "reflection" on and "search" for evidence involves confirming as true only evidence that appears to favor what he wants to be true (or false) and being indifferent or critical towards evidence that does not appear to him to favor what he wants to be true (or false). While he is unaware that he is biased he is highly critical and doubtful of evidence that appears to point away from what he wants to be true (or false) and naively embraces evidence that appears to point towards what he wants to be true (or false). In the background of *confirmation bias* or any other form of "conclusion driven" or "cart before the horse" reflection, the internally myopic person judges the value and truth of evidence relative to their narrative or foundational beliefs. In this case, so-called "critical reflection" is assumed to be taking place but it isn't. Sufferers of internal myopia are often on the hunt to find evidence that makes them feel better or less worse about what they already believe. The weight of guilt or comfort will drive a person on a life time campaign to champion an ideology that lessens guilt or increases comfort, respectively.

While internal myopia is due to internal motivational factors, it can be augmented by the limitations of a person's understanding and comprehension of a subject matter. So not only does a person desire that a belief be false, he does not understand it. In Prov 17:27 a person is considered wise when he constrains his words and does not freely state his beliefs without careful reflection. We do well to follow this proverbial truth. Let us be slow to dismiss others who disagree with us. Let us not speak before we have adequately familiarized ourselves with and comprehended the views of others. And when we cannot understand, stay silent.

Finally, imagination can be a not so obvious source of myopia. What any given person believes and makes a judgment about is ultimately based on given assumptions about the world. These assumptions cannot be challenged as false unless the person at least theoretically conceives how they could be false. This is where imagination is operative. Without a robust imagination, unshackled by dogmatism or volition, a person can be unaware of the falsity of her assumptions because she never critically assesses that they are less than self-evident. Thus she is blocked from the truth by her own imagination or lack of.

While several internal motivational factors have been offered to explain why myopia occurs, the last to mention is quite common. Here the internal motivational factor is ego or pride. It goes without saying that criticism can be hard to embrace. As such negative evaluations of ourselves are often rejected when they are in fact brutally true. Strategies to explain away the negative evaluations can come in the form of psychoanalytic responses like denial and projection or even a hyper criticalness of the evaluating criteria. Since the myopic person is "certain" that he has not failed (e.g., come short of perfection on an exam) or is guilty of some act (e.g., racism or sexism) he must deny culpability, project the imperfection on the accuser, or look for de jure and de facto defeaters against the source of the evaluation. Professors note this push back all too often when they assign less than perfect grades. Typical remarks from students are that the exam questions were not clear or the expectations of the professor were not clearly stated. These responses explain away the less than perfect score on an exam or paper. In business, managers rate themselves higher than where they are in management performance. In short, society at large suffers from what is called the Lake Wobegon Effect.[10]

What Is Driving Your Beliefs: Just the Facts or an External Interpretation of the Facts?

A second type of myopia is *external myopia*. External myopia is due to factors external to our cognitive faculties. It is a person's (1) unawareness that his sources of knowledge and values are derived from his environment (viz., his personal experiences, family, community, culture, or preferred media) and/or (2) unawareness that his sources present him

---

10. The *Lake Wobegon effect* is the tendency to exaggerate one's status, achievements, and abilities. It is named for the fictional town of Lake Wobegon in Minnesota from the radio series *A Prairie Home Companion*. According to the radio series' host Garrison Keillor, "all the women are strong, all the men are good looking, and all the children are above average." This myopic tendency affects people in various sectors of society, from managers and CEOs to college students. Despite the bell curve distribution among humans at large, people who suffer from the Lake Wobegon effect see everything they do as above average and any assessments that state otherwise must be flawed.

with a false or skewed view of reality and (3) certitude that his beliefs and values are correct. (2) and (3) or (1), (2), and (3) result in myopia. A person may be fully aware that her beliefs and values come from her religion but unaware that they are false. Metaphorically, if our cognitive faculties were akin to a myopic camera, we would take in sensory input and information like a camera when the environment of the camera is compromised due to such things as darkness or fog. It goes without saying that environment shapes how we see reality, but myopia comes into play when a person's certitude about their beliefs and values (which are in this case derived from the environment) prevents the person from forming true beliefs when the evidence for true beliefs is available.

Technically the environment does not cause myopia; rather a person's naiveté towards the certainty of his environmental beliefs, narratives, and values causes myopia. The reason for the naiveté and certainty is likely due to a lack of alternative or contrary sources of values and information. Prominent philosopher John Hick once claimed that "someone born in India is not only going to naturally be a Hindu, but also consider the Hindu-worldview normative (or normal) and all others wrong. For they simply have no way of seeing things any differently!" What Hick implies is that people in general do not adhere to a critical belief formation process. Warranted or not, corresponding to reality or not, people often embrace the narrative or beliefs that their personal experience, society, culture, religion, or peer group presents to them, no questions asked. In short, it is the lack of exposure to alternative viewpoints and narratives on their own terms, the lack of experience of alternative viewpoints and narratives on their own terms, and the lack of critical analysis from alternative beliefs and narratives that generates external myopia.

While some victims of internal myopia may suffer from abnormal internal states, victims of external myopia are often quite "normal" and "typically civilized." Consider the normative dehumanization of blacks in the United States during the nineteenth and twentieth centuries. Nearly 3,445 blacks were lynched between 1882 and 1968. The method of lynching was usually hanging and then being burned to death. So many blacks had been lynched by angry white mobs, that eventually the lynching of a black person became entertainment for many whites in the southern states. Often hundreds of spectators would gather to witness the execution, as if to attend a football game. Sometimes the spectators would take pieces of the dead black person's body as souvenirs! Today the typical, normal person would judge such acts as immoral, insane and abnormal.

Yet the perception of the lynchings was anything but immoral, abnormal and insane to the spectators and even those responsible for the lynchings. Many of the participants and spectators of these lynchings passively adopted as truth the racist mores of their society without the slightest critical counter reflection that such acts were wrong. The likely reason is that the participants and spectators were socialized from the time of their youth to see lynchings as permissible. The American society of today looks back at the past American society and asks, "How could many in American society believe such things? Surely we are more advanced and progressive then they were. We know better." It is almost certain that tomorrow's American society will look back at the present American society (no matter how enlightened they think they are) and ask, "How could they have believed such things?"

Similarly in Germany, Hitler managed to instill anti-Semitism into Germany's society during the 1930–40s. Children growing up during this time were told that Jews were "a problem;" this belief was accepted without exposure to pro-Semitic values. This anti-Semitism was not new to Germany; the reformer Martin Luther harbored such attitudes towards the Jews of his time. Islamic terrorists raise and socialize young children to believe that citizens of the United States are evil and need to be destroyed. These children grow up to be suicide bombers.

External myopia qua racist values of supremacy was strong enough to infiltrate science, a so-called purely objective discipline, during the nineteenth century. In the 1800s nationalism and racism flourished in scientific circles. In the 1830s a white professor of anatomy in Philadelphia, Samuel G. Morton, conducted "experiments" where he measured the interiors of Caucasian, Mongolian, Malayan, Native American and Ethiopian skulls.[11] Morton's conclusion was that the cranial capacity of the skulls varied according to race. At the top of the list were Caucasians with 87 cubic inches and at the bottom were Ethiopians with 78 cubic inches. Not surprisingly, it turns out Morton's experiments were confounded. Morton was selective in what skulls he used for each racial group. For example, he discharged small skulls from his Caucasian sample.

External myopia is also responsible for the racial divide in the justice system. The O. J. Simpson trial during the late 1990s is a paradigm example of external myopia along racial lines. Blacks and whites were polarized concerning the innocence or guilt of O. J. Many whites believed O. J.

---

11 For a discussion of Samuel Morton's myopia, see Nelson's "Men Before Adam," 167–76.

was guilty and many blacks believed he was innocent. With these results, obviously Americans formed their beliefs along racial lines. If Americans formed their beliefs objectively, there would not be such a strong correlation between race and the innocence or guilt of O. J. Simpson. One explanation of this polarization is that, despite the evidence clearly showing O. J. to be guilty, many whites and blacks were unconsciously biased towards or against O. J. Simpson because of how they viewed the American justice system and interracial relations. Other examples of subgroups and belief formation can be given. Blacks and other minorities tend to support affirmative action, while whites tend to oppose affirmative action. Evangelical Christians tend to be pro-life and anti-gay rights, while liberal Christians and most non-Christians tend to be pro-choice and pro-gay rights. These polarized tendencies, as a matter of fact, cannot be explained by individuals in each of these groups objectively drawing their own conclusions about these social issues independent of their group's cultural background.

Like internal myopia, external myopia often involves reflection of thought but not in terms of evidence labelled "on the contrary." Like internal myopia, a person suffering from external myopic can be exposed to arguments contrary to their status quo beliefs or narrative. However the arguments take on the form of a straw man and are usually accompanied with a rebuttal so as to maintain the status quo belief or narrative. Similarly, during the reflection on "the evidence" the myopic person will be highly critical and doubtful of evidence that points away from his environmentally acquired beliefs or narrative, and naively embrace evidence that points towards his environmentally acquired beliefs, or interpret the evidence so as to fit with what he already believes. Reflection is occurring but not in response to an argument. Reflection takes on the form of maintenance control where the cart is before the horse. Here the "party line" of society is heralded or used exclusively as a grid to analyze and interpret the evidence. For example, a person who sees a killer whale in captivity, say, at Sea World, may not see living in a tank for decades, rather than in the wild, as unethical. He may see the killer whale as part of the overall entertainment at Sea World. Such a person may even have loving pets at home in tanks or cages and thus, based on his personal experience with his pets, not see captivity of the whale as something to oppose.

A common external myopia that affects people in general occurs when people are asked to consider a foundational ethical question, viz., what makes an action right or wrong. All too often what happens is a conflation of the question of how one comes to the *beliefs* she has about what is right and wrong with the question of what makes an action right or wrong. When people are asked to state what makes an action right or wrong, often they present the party line championed in American culture:

> One's own personal experiences, upbringing and religious affiliations makes an action right or wrong; each person views what is wrong or right based on what they have learned or been taught throughout their life; what makes an action wrong or right is whether the person is able to sleep at night; what makes an action right or wrong is a person's gut feeling; and what makes an action right or wrong is a person's sociological and cultural upbringing.

Clearly these are answers to the question concerning why people have different beliefs about what is right and wrong or to the question how a person is able to discern that an action is right or wrong. So why do people provide answers to a questions they are not asked? Is it because the original question is not clear enough? Recall, the original question asked what makes an action right or wrong. There does not seem to be anything unclear in what the question is asking, yet people systematically interpret the question to be about epistemology. They conflate epistemology with metaphysics, i.e., they say what culture or individual persons believe is right and wrong is what makes actions right and wrong. Little reflection is needed to see that this conflation is incoherent, so why is it a common response among intelligent people in society? The answer is simple: external myopia does not discriminate against intelligence, and ethical/cultural relativism is ubiquitous. The proverbial story of the frog in a pot of warm water comes to mind. You could cook any frog that relaxes in a warm pot of water that slowly heats to the boiling point. Regardless of the intelligence of a person, if she passively embraces the beliefs and values of her culture and does not critically reflect on them in a "horse before the cart" sort of way, then over time she invites or opens the door to external myopia.

Consider one final example of external myopia on the topic of racial prejudice. Suppose, for example, a person holds the following two beliefs: (1) racial prejudice does not exist and (2) charges of racism are nothing more than an expression of paranoia or insecurity. Let us suppose further that (1) and (2) are foundational beliefs for him or part of a narrative he grew to adopt with a high degree of certitude. Naturally it follows that no matter what contrary evidence is presented to the myopic person against

(1) or (2) he will interpret the evidence as anything but indicating racial prejudice or, if he is an eye witness, view the event as a rare case of a dying pathology. To be sure, the person does not or would not literally claim that racial prejudice does not exist but when presented with another person's alleged eye witness testimony of racial prejudice, he categorically denies the testimony to be veridical. Such a person, but for the wrong reason, is akin to a person who rejects reports of a 2014 sighting of J. F. Kennedy playing poker in a Vegas casino. No matter how outlandishly the latter person explains away JFK in Vegas, he is assured that the claim JFK actually played poker in 2014 is impossible because such a belief is in conflict with his historical American narrative, with the foundational belief that dead people stay dead, and with the historical American narrative of nearly every other person, short of a few odd individuals. On the contrary, the narrative or foundational belief of a sufferer of external myopia does not have this assurity and thus not immune from criticism. There just are good reasons for why it is a bad idea for accepting someone's eye witness testimony that he saw JFK playing poker in Vegas. The myopic person, on the other hand, rejects the eye witness testimony because of his own environmentally acquired narrative or foundational belief that excludes the possibility of racial prejudice for no other reason than the lack of exposure to racial prejudice, if it exists. The defense for his narrative or belief would be that he has never experienced racial prejudice or been an eye witness to it. If it exists, he would claim, he would have experienced it or been an eye witness to it. What the externally myopic person fails to acknowledge in this case is that perhaps the demographics of his environment is homogeneous and thus not reflective of society as a whole. But because he is in the midst of this homogeneity he cannot see that the homogeneity is causing myopia.

What Is Driving Your Beliefs: Just the Facts or a Willful Rejection of the Facts?

Normative myopia is about culpability. Specifically, normative myopia is the state of being epistemically and morally irresponsible about what one believes. To be sure psychological states and environment play a causal role in normative myopia. However, the definitive element of normative myopia is exposure to de jure or de facto arguments presented for the purpose to be objections counter to a person's beliefs or narrative but where the person chooses instead to maintain his status quo belief or narrative. So we can define normative myopia in the following way: It is (1) either internal myopia or external myopia, (2) exposure to warranted de jure or de facto defeaters to the person's foundational belief or narrative, (3) the rejection of the defeaters qua defeaters, and therefore (4) where the person is without excuse for his rejection of the defeaters. A way to put this myopia in context is to say the person "ought to know better" because of his exposure to warranted arguments contrary to what he believes and where the arguments are presented as objections without accompanied rebuttals. Metaphorically this myopia is like taking a blurred photograph with a fully functional camera but without pushing the button or taking the lens cover off. In this metaphorical case, the photographer ought to know better than to take a photo under these circumstances since the instructions for the camera clearly state to do otherwise. A person with this myopia has a duty to dismantle his myopia because there are defeaters available to him, where he understands the defeaters as defeaters, but fails to consider them. A classic but sad example of normative internal myopia comes from the gifted and well informed Scottish intellectual and philosopher David Hume:

> I am apt to suspect the Negroes to be naturally inferior to the Whites. There scarcely ever was a civilized nation of that complexion, nor even any individual, eminent either in action or speculation. No ingenious manufactures amongst them, no arts, no sciences. On the other hand, the most rude and barbarous of the Whites, such as the ancient Germans, the present Tartars, have still something eminent about them . . . [This] could not happen, in so many countries and ages, if nature had not made an original distinction between these breeds of men. Not to mention our colonies, there are Negro slaves dispersed all over Europe, of whom none ever discovered the symptoms of ingenuity; though low people, without education, will start up amongst us, and distinguish themselves in every profession. In Jamaica, indeed, they talk of one Negro as a man of parts and learning; but it is likely he is admired for slender accomplishments, like a parrot who speaks a few words plainly.[12]

This is a classic case of normative internal myopia because there was sufficient evidence that the Jamaican was an intelligent human being; after all, anyone who graduates from Oxford University has to pass various examinations, which requires intelligence. Hume knew this! Despite

---

12. Hume, *Essays, Moral, Political and Literary*, 208.

the fact Hume knew the gentleman in question had graduated from the prestigious Oxford University and passed exams in order to graduate, Hume believed the best explanation of the evidence is that this Jamaican only seemed to be intelligent in the same manner that a parrot seems to manifest an understanding of language when it mimics human language. Unless Hume was speaking "tongue and cheek," his own racism blinded him from seeing the Jamaican scholar for what he was, a scholar.

Not to be outdone by Hume, Immanuel Kant had his own inexcusable beliefs. In Lectures on Ethics (27:346) Kant believed that sexual intercourse was degrading because he argued that humans engaged in such acts objectify each other. Also in the Lectures (27:347), he viewed masturbation as worse than suicide. Whether Kant was expressing Prussian Pietistic sexual mores or expressing his own sexual dysfunction, his morbid sexual beliefs were without excuse since any Bible he had access to clearly condemns his former attitude. Kant also had failings along racial lines as well. In *On the Use of Teleological Principles in Philosophy* (8:176) Kant argued that the "Negro" ranks at the bottom of the racial hierarchy of races although the Negro fairs better than the Native American at manual labor.[13] Finally, despite his limited travels, which did not extend far from his home in Prussia, he judged south sea islanders as being nearly savages and driven by a pleasure principle, i.e., where they "let their talents rest and resolve to devote their lives merely to idleness, amusement, and propagation of their species- in a word, to enjoyment."[14] Wherever Kant received his information on south sea islanders, it was false and offensive. Since Kant had no eyewitness evidence of their behavior and culture, Kant should have forgone any judgments about them.

Normative myopia is responsible for the construction of a lot of theological ethics that is based on an elliptical reading of biblical texts. For example, some Christian congregations embrace a material prosperity narrative and reject any beliefs or even interpretations of Scripture that would negatively critique or not cohere with the prosperity narrative.

---

13. Kleingeld argues that Kant's post-1790s view of race radically changed to the degree that Kant rejected his hierarchical view of race for a more egalitarian view. Kleingeld claims that Kant's shift was due to his new view of biology of humans. From conversations with a leading biologist of his time, Johann Friedrich Blumenbach (1752-1840), Kant's new view of race entailed only physiological differences and abandoned talk of a racial hierarchy of intellectual or moral virtues. So Kleingeld argues that Kant overcame his myopia. See Kleingeld, "Kant's Second Thoughts on Race," 573–592.

14. Kant, *Foundations of the Metaphysics of Morals*, 40–41.

Some biblical passages taken out of context are Mal 3:10, Phil 4:19, and 3 John 2. Now among the motives that could push some Christians to embrace and develop a prosperity narrative, one surely is having experienced extreme poverty. A likely story is that congregations that embrace a prosperity theology are stirred into a prosperity narrative by their pastors who for sure are culpable for the erroneous and irresponsible view of the Bible. Prosperity theology completely ignores St. Paul's account of his thorn in the flesh or even Jesus' birth in a manger. For that matter, prosperity theology ignores Jesus' concern about how difficult it is for a rich man to enter the Kingdom of heaven. The irresponsibility should not be extended to the congregations too since although objections to prosperity theology are not esoteric and concealed from anyone, the congregations unfortunately read them through the hermeneutical lens of their pastors' interpretation of these biblical objections from Jesus and Paul.

A person with normative myopia simpliciter is not intentionally resistive per se to being corrected or resistive to truth; however, he is irresponsible for holding a false belief or narrative because he has been exposed to defeaters sufficient to expose the falsity of his belief or narrative. In such cases, normative myopia is a result of, for lack of a better phrase, "intellectual laziness" to be informed. Persons who hold such false beliefs may not per se desire to hold these beliefs; nevertheless, they are guilty of not taking the steps to do their homework on current affairs. To be sure, unless such persons live in caves and do not have access to current affairs, they have an epistemic duty to dismantle this type of myopia. On the ethical front of culpability, ignorance is ethically neutral when the ignorance concerns others you are likely not to engage and have no prior knowledge of their culture and mores. In such cases ignorance would be offensive (see chapter 1) but not ethically culpable since the ignorance is due to no fault of the ignorant person, i.e., when the pertinent information is not accessible. However, ignorance is ethically culpable when it negatively impacts others and the knowledge of other cultures and mores is accessible. While no one can be culturally sensitive for every people group, being ignorant about some common categories of people is without excuse. In the United States, for example, constantly referring to a woman as "sweetie," an African American as "colored," Asians as "oriental," and believing Arabs and Muslims are coextensive terms even when due to ignorance is nonetheless offensive and also involves culpability since the information on the mores and cultural specifics of these categories of people is readily accessible to anyone living in the United States. However information on the mores and cultural specifics of some people group that has an obscured presence in the United States is not common knowledge to Americans. Being culpable for being ignorant of these former categories however is a far cry from walking on egg shells in the United States.

What Is Driving Your Beliefs: Just the Facts or an Unawareness of the Facts?

Finally, *de facto myopia* occurs when a person is unaware of her false beliefs but as a matter of fact or as a matter of principle, she can do nothing to see that she has false beliefs. Metaphorically speaking this type of myopia is akin to taking a blurred photograph of a person positioned very far away with a functional camera; however, the camera does not have a powerful lens to see clearly due to existing, current photographic technology and so the person is mistaken to be a friend but in fact is a stranger. Similarly, de facto myopia results when the person with it is unable to conceive of reality in any other way than in the way she perceives it. Alternative perspectives and evidence that count against her beliefs and narrative are not accessible to her either because they do not exist as yet or she lives in an environment void of them. When she is finally exposed to them, she greets them with hostility. So de facto myopia is: (1) an unawareness of the possession of false beliefs or narrative and (2) the absence of any evidence contrary to the false belief or narrative.

Centuries ago many people were mistaken to be demon possessed because they talked and behaved irrationally or even claimed to be a demon or some famous person of the past, like King Tut or George Washington. The fact of the matter is these individuals were not demon possessed but suffered chemical imbalances of the brain, like schizophrenia or bipolar disorder. However, centuries ago humans did not possess the science to know what the true culprit was for the irrational behavior and comments coming from these ill people. Similarly before the science was out to reveal the fact that cigarettes cause cancer, no person could have known that smoking was ethically wrong. The evidence, via studies and arguments, did not exist for anyone to know the harmful impact of cigarettes. When the person suffering from de facto myopia is finally presented with evidence or arguments contrary to his beliefs or narrative, out of ignorance, the alternative beliefs and narratives are treated as an unwelcome guest. Plato masterfully illustrated this negative goal of ignorance in Book VII (514a-520a) of his seminal work, the *Republic*:

> Next, said I, here is a parable to illustrate the degrees in which our nature may be enlightened or unenlightened. Imagine the condition of men living in a sort of cavernous chamber underground, with an entrance open to the light and a long passage all down the cave. Here they have been from childhood, chained by the leg and also by the neck, so that they cannot move and can see only what is in front of them, because the chains will not let them turn their heads. At some distance higher up is the light of a fire burning behind them; and between the prisoners and the fire is a track with a parapet built along it, like the screen at a puppet-show, which hides the performers while they show their puppets over the top . . . Now behind this parapet imagine persons carrying along various artificial objects, including figures of men and animals in wood or stone or other materials, which project above the parapet. Naturally, some of these persons will be talking, others silent . . . [The] prisoners so confined would have seen nothing of themselves or of one another, except the shadows thrown by the fire-light on the wall of the Cave facing them, would they? Not if all their lives they had been prevented from moving their heads. And they would have seen as little of the objects carried past . . . Now, if they could talk to one another, would they not suppose that their words referred only to those passing shadows which they saw?[15]

This is Plato's famous *Cave Analogy*. Through the mouth of Socrates, Plato goes on to claim that if any one of the prisoners escaped the cave and ventured outside the cave, he would see the sun, trees, water and other items in nature. It would take him awhile to accept that these items are real and what he formerly saw in the cave were merely shadows of these items. When the prisoner returns to the cave and reports his experiences to those still enslaved, they would judge him insane. They only had experiences of shadows and uncritically accepted the shadows and the interplay of the shadows as the totality of reality besides the cave itself. Ignorance is not *per se* a normative issue, in the sense that someone ought not to be ignorant. Ignorance often is beyond our control, given the absence of alternative information and experiences. When ignorance has had time to ferment and mature to certitude, alternative information and experiences are greeted as foreign bodies.

---

15. Plato, *Republic* VII.514a–15 (ed. Allen, 224).

Telltale Signs of Myopia

It would appear that a person cannot know that he is myopic since if the person knew he were myopic, he would not be myopic. While this is true introspectively, there are at least four tests a person can perform to look for signs of myopia in their own judgment or in that of another person. Three of the tests are objective in nature and a fourth one is subjective in nature. Let us consider the objective tests first.

One test determines whether inconsistency in judgment occurred. A second test determines whether anecdotal arguments where used to reach the judgment. A third test determines whether an appeal to minuscule or fallacious evidence was used to prove what a person wants to be true or to falsify what a person does not want to be true (either of the de jure or de facto sort). All three tests reveal an unknown bias. The first test determines a disregard for the universalizability principle.[16] If a person is myopic he would treat two situations differently that are actually similar and treat two situations similarly that are actually different. The second test determines that a judgment was based on an anecdotal argument. Anecdotal reasoning is hasty and reflects a rush to close the case on some matter or to pursue a particular end as if an agenda was behind the scenes. The third test determines if a person is guilty of the "cart before the horse" reasoning when faced with facts contrary to what she believes.

Let us address the first test concerning inconsistency. Clearly if a person interprets or judges similar situations differently, it is for at least two reasons. Either the dissimilarities are greater than the similarities or bias for some end in the person is the factor. For a person who honestly wants to be myopic free, an explanation of why the former state of affairs is the case rather than the latter is in order. Consider the following that occurred during the hearings for the presidential appointment of Susan Rice as Secretary of State. United States senator John McCain argued that she was not fit for the position because she denied and covered up the "lie" that the September 11, 2012 attack on the U.S. outpost in Benghazi, Libya was an organized terrorist attack. Whether or not the senator was myopic or not, one thing is certain and that is he made a distinctly different judgment in a very similar situation. Let's first see what he said about Susan Rice. According to the senator, "She's not qualified. Anyone who goes on national television and in defiance of the facts, five days

---

16. See chapter 3 for a discussion of the universalizability principle. Essentially the principle holds that similar situations require similar judgments.

later—We're all responsible for what we say and what we do. I'm responsible to my voters. She's responsible to the Senate of the United States. We have our responsibility for advice and consent." And in another interview he said, "I will do everything in my power to block her from being the United States Secretary of State. She has proven that she either doesn't understand or she is not willing to accept evidence on its face." However in a similar situation with a woman of the same ethnicity and last name as Susan, the senator said in 2005 of Condoleezza Rice that she was qualified to be appointed as Secretary of State, even though she testified that there were WMDs in Iraq. On the senate floor he said, "So I wonder why we are starting this new Congress with a protracted debate about a foregone conclusion . . . I can only conclude we are doing this for no other reason than lingering bitterness at the outcome of the elections . . . We all have varying policy views, but the President, in my view, has a clear right to put in place the team he believed would serve him best." Both women made similar claims about what they knew about the threat of violence in the Middle East, yet the senator did not judge them the same. When confronted by a news reporter with the similarities of the situations, he retorted in ad hoc fashion that the latter one was more serious because of the number of deaths that resulted. Clearly at this point the senator was guilty of normative myopia.

One more example should drive the point home that inconsistency reveals bias. Often when a natural disaster occurs, some Christian leaders assert that there was a divine cause behind the natural phenomenon. They evoke God as the ultimate cause of the disasters and they go on to add that the events are a display of God's judgment on particular humans. In Minnesota for example, a major bridge collapsed in 2007 and a few years later, a tornado damaged the steeple of a Lutheran church that was voting to ordain gay clergy. In both cases, some Christians held that citizens of Minneapolis and churches of the particular Lutheran synod were being judged by God because of sin. Now whether this is the case or not is not the issue. The issue is whether the Christians making these divine assertions on behalf of God are consistent, i.e., treating similar cases similar or dissimilar cases dissimilarly. Unfortunately the answer is no. It is doubtful that particular sectors of society have a corner on sin. However, the charge made against the Lutheran church is that God is in the business of judging sectors of the United States that approve GBLT agendas. Now either there are warranted reasons for holding this claim or not. A force of nature destroying one church would not suffice to warrant the claim. One would expect, from considerations of consistency, that proponents of this view would associate natural disasters with God's judgment of GLBT wherever there is a sector of the United States that condones GBLT agendas. One would also expect proponents of this view to be moved by the facts so that they would concede their view false if evidence did not support it. These expectations are not met. At the time the church's steeple was destroyed, the tornado also destroyed the roof of the Minneapolis Convention Center and a middle school in North Branch, Minnesota. As a matter of fact, a major sector of the United States that has a high incidence of tornados is the Bible Belt; a major sector that has a low incidence of tornado damage consists of liberal eastern states like e.g., Massachusetts, New York and Vermont. Proponents of the divine judgment view were not nor have yet to be moved by the inconsistencies or the falsifying facts. We have here a case of normative myopia. As for the bridge, both saints and sinner crossed it.

The second test looks at anecdotal reasoning. For various reasons (e.g., defensiveness or denial) people are often unconsciously compelled to reject a belief or embrace a belief simply because their own personal experience is inconsistent with it or supports it. At issue here is not the reliability of eye witness testimony. A white female who rejects the prevalence of racial profiling because she has never seen it or the woman who has had failed relationships and affirms that "all men are jerks" are guilty of myopia due to anecdotal reasoning. In such cases, the myopic person is content to stop investigating what is true and to settle uncritically with what her personal experience reveals.

The third test looks at whether a person is quick to dismiss evidence that is contrary to what she believes in the following way: appealing to miniscule or dubious evidence to support what a person wants to believe in a rather naive manner or being excessively critical of the evidence for what a person does not want to believe. In the former case, the person is quick to seek any evidence, whether hypothetical or factual, to support what she already believes no matter the sources or the sources' verifiability. For example, a person opposed to gun control reform may myopically argue that guns are not a luxury but a necessity since the Federal Government may one day attack its own citizens. Or an opponent of active euthanasia may myopically argue that despite successfully regulated euthanasia in Europe and successfully regulated physician assisted suicide in the United States, that one day physicians may start killing patients against the patients' will due to economic reasons. At the same time, however, the same *naivete* attitude is not taken toward the belief the person disagrees with. To be sure, in the latter case, the person objects to the opposing belief by appealing to ad hominems, red herrings, straw men[17], conspiracy theories, extremely improbable counter evidence, etc. Consider the polemic topic of euthanasia. A person who is opposed to euthanasia and who also suffers from myopia could appeal to very improbable evidence, no matter how obscure her "what ifs" are, to prove euthanasia unethical. She may suggest the following: "What if a doctor killed a person through active euthanasia and then a week later found out there was a cure for the patients' disease? Or possibly the relatives of the deceased found a tape of the deceased saying he or she wanted to be kept alive . . . but now it's too late." Of course fallacious reasoning is easily recognizable, but when the objective is to dismiss unwelcome evidence and beliefs, such reasoning can go unnoticed.

Finally the subjective test looks at introspection not directed at myopia but at non-cognitive conditions that may trigger the myopia. To detect myopia at the non-cognitive level, we ought to be sensitive to the moments when we are visceral about an issue, particularly with internal myopia. It is during these moments when internal factors like pride, fear, insecurities, and self-interest, may begin to guide us at the cognitive level and skew our perception of the world. This imperative does not also require that we become a skeptic and question the objectivity of our passionate beliefs. Instead it merely holds that we adopt the attitude that our beliefs, despite how obvious the beliefs may appear to be correct, can be flawed due to internal influences on us. As a matter of introspection, we can ask ourselves why we are so passionate about a belief being true or being false. Can we conceive and emotionally embrace the counterfactual, whatever it may be? If not, what are the reasons for not being able to do so? Are the reasons related to past harms we experienced? Are the reasons cloaking pride, fear, insecurities, and self-interest? Conceding an affirmative answer to these questions obviously reveals myopia but requires a strong degree of volition to do so.

So How Can We Guard against Being Myopic?

Now no one wants to be myopic, let alone myopic like the naked king. So what can we do to preempt myopia? As stated earlier, environment does

---

17. For a discussion on fallacies, see the appendix.

not cause myopia by itself. It is a given, each of us are in part or in whole a product of our community, personal experiences, social-economic background, ethnicity, religion, gender, age, nationality, etc.,. All these background conditions have binary functional roles in shaping how we perceive, feel, and evaluate our reality. They either lead us progressively towards a correct view of reality or act as a barrier to prevent us from seeing or adopting a correct view of reality. In the latter case, it is a challenge not to fall prey to the latter effects that environmental factors have on us. Essentially myopia can be curtailed by diversity of environment.

The lack of gender diversity is the source of many ethical problems, particularly sexual harassment. Since a man, for example, does not know what it is like to be a woman, he at least can diversify his experience to include platonic female relationships to approximate what it is like to experience life as a woman in terms of values, interests, fears, and perspectives. The lack of diversity along class is also a source of many ethical problems, particularly when it involves the treatment of poor people in health care and housing. Often times the poor are stigmatized with being lazy. It is said that a person cannot really understand the desperate nature of homelessness until he/she has become homeless or developed a relationship with a homeless person. Sure, we all know what homelessness means on an intellectual level, but the serious nature of it or the existential overcast of it can easily escape those who are not homeless. Personal experience often accounts for what a person values and how much they value it. This solution to myopia is simple: diversify your epistemology.

This diversification in epistemology has been noted by a number of feminist philosophers in what is called *standpoint theory*.[18] According to standpoint theory, societies are generally stratified along such categories as class, race, religion and gender. In these different ways that a society is stratified, different and conflicting epistemologies emerge. As proponents of standpoint theory argue, the epistemic positions of the oppressed groups in these categories are, per se, superior to the epistemic position of the oppressor groups. In order to survive in society, the oppressed group is forced to understand the oppressing group's ideology and thus take an outside, objective look at the oppressor's epistemology. A lesson learned here is that diversity of experience allows for a critical critique of our beliefs. From a practical stand point we should diversify our sources of media news

---

18. See Harding, "Rethinking Standpoint Epistemology: 'What Is Strong Objectivity?,'" 49–82; and Hartsock, "The Feminist Standpoint: Developing the Ground for a Specifically Feminist Historical Materialism," 283–310.

information, scholarly written books and journals, and most of all diversify our everyday lived experiences with people unlike ourselves in terms of race, ethnicity, class, religion, denomination, gender and other categories where humans vary. So while there is no sure way to know whether your beliefs are merely the product of your community on every occasion and issue, you can perhaps move closer to objectivity by seeing if other individuals outside your community share your beliefs (who have nothing personally to gain by agreeing with your beliefs). For example, with a polemic issue such as affirmative action, have you interacted and shared in the life experiences of African Americans and Latinos (particularly poor African Americans and Latinos) and read a defense of affirmative action? Or did you instead read about affirmative action but from material written with the intended purpose to deny white racism has become more subtle and that it continues its baleful influence through institutional structures? Having knowledge from both perspectives is needed to ward off myopia. It would make your judgment on this issue more objective and less conceiver dependent. To argue that affirmative action is just or unjust *a priori* places social justice in the abstract realm with mathematics and theoretical physics; surely it does not belong there.

Depravity, Spiritual Character, and Myopia

Some Christians hold that when all the facts of an ethical situation are accessible to a person, and the person makes a myopic judgment, the causal explanation is depravity. Such a claim makes myopia a spiritual or sin issue and leaves no room for environmental and confounding psychological variables. Passages like John 12:46; John 14:17, 26; and Romans 12:2 are used to support the spurious thesis that after regeneration, the believer's mind is transformed in such a way that the effects of depravity (e.g., myopia) are removed. A reasonable inference from this assumption is that myopia is more prevalent among those who are not Christians. It stands to reason that when disagreements arise between Christians and non-Christians on issues like abortion, euthanasia, gun control, and health care, Christians who hold this claim attribute the disagreement to the noetic effects of sin and that the non-Christians are the ones who "got it wrong" on these issues. Proponents of this view often hold to "the Christian narrative" and set it as the criterion of truth with the proviso that this narrative is the essence of the Bible and God. A champion passage for this spiritualized epistemology is Rom 1:21–25:

> For even though they knew God, they did not honor Him as God or give thanks, but they became futile in their speculations, and their foolish heart was darkened. Professing to be wise, they became fools, and exchanged the glory of the incorruptible God for an image in the form of corruptible man and of birds and four-footed animals and crawling creatures. Therefore God gave them over in the lusts of their hearts to impurity, so that their bodies would be dishonored among them. For they exchanged the truth of God for a lie, and worshiped and served the creature rather than the Creator, who is blessed forever. Amen. (NASB)

Supposedly this Romans passage is "proof" that non-Christians are void of any ethical insights.

Even if moral failure is ultimately a holiness issue, no Christian should naively believe with equal fervor that those who are "spiritually mature" or "seasoned Christians" are immune from the cognitive effects of depravity. The Bible and history does not support this presumptive view of epistemology. In Acts 15:36–39, for example, Luke reports that a disagreement developed between Paul and Barnabas concerning the prudence of having John Mark join them on a return visit to towns where they had preached the Gospel. Although the text indicates the reason why Paul objected to John Mark joining them, it does not indicate that Paul was correct. We are not told what Barnabas' reason was for recommending John Mark. Whatever the case is, Paul and Barnabas could not both be correct in their wisdom about whether John Mark should join them or not. This is true despite the godly character of Paul and Barnabas. On another occasion, the Holy Spirit used disciples in Tyre (Acts 21:4) and a prophet from Judea (Acts 21:10) to warned Paul not to journey into Jerusalem for the sake of his life. For unknown reasons, Paul did not discern these warnings as messages from God and eventually took the journey. As we see later in Acts, the journey caused great trouble for Paul which ended in his arrest. By the grace of God, Paul escaped death. Finally, we cannot forget Paul's confrontation with the apostle Peter in Gal 2:11–13. Paul opposed Peter to his face because Peter showed favoritism toward Jewish Christians over the Gentile Christians. Prior to their coming to Antioch, Peter ate with the Gentile Christians, but when the Jewish Christians arrived in town, Peter withdrew from eating with the Gentile

Christians. This should be surprising to the spiritualized epistemologist since Peter at this time in his life was a seasoned follower of Christ.

Unfortunately the Church has a reputation for lacking discernment and not heeding the Holy Spirit's voice. The copious doctrinal splits within denominations, the copious marital conflicts that lead to divorce among Christians and everyday conflicts between Christians on social and ethical issues are sufficient evidence to show that Christians often see through dark glasses. Being "in-tune" with God does not guarantee objective insight into truth. In fact, non-Christians oftentimes see just as clearly as Christians do on ethical issues. For example, the eastern sage-religious leader Confucius once stated that people should treat each other as they would want to be treated. This appeal to equality was not always recognized by many of the great evangelical leaders in the United States during slavery. Even when Christian leaders eventually opposed slavery, they sometimes supported or were indifferent to the issue of racial segregation. A spiritual icon like Billy Sunday was a victim of his cultural background of the early 1900s. Sunday was a Bible teacher with the Chicago YMCA and eventually an evangelist who toured the United States. He recognized the suffering and needs of minorities, particularly blacks. In 1917, during his Atlanta crusade, Sunday held meetings especially for blacks and even visited several black churches. However, Sunday took no steps to end segregation in his crusades. He believed that integration could tarnish his image as a national Christian leader among those who were segregationists. He left the social mores of the day untouched. Despite the prevailing pro-slavery mores of his time, Charles Finney was an outspoken abolitionist. In 1862, at Ohio's Oberlin College, he was responsible for Mary Jane Patterson becoming the first African-American woman to earn a bachelor's degree. Yet even Finney was opposed to integration of blacks and whites. Lewis Tappen, a leader in Finney's New York City church in the 1830s took issue with Finney about where blacks and whites were allowed to sit during service. He wrote to Finney: "Finding nothing could be done in a matter so near to my heart I left the church."[19] When Dwight Moody held revival meetings in the South, he did on a segregated basis. Billy Graham held integrated revival meetings but also held segregated revival meetings. In Jackson, MS., Graham told the press:

> I feel that I have been misrepresented on racial segregation. We follow the existing social customs in whatever part of the

---

19. Dayton, *Discovering an Evangelical Heritage*, 67.

country in which we minister. As far as I have been able to find in my study of the Bible, it has nothing to say about segregation or nonsegregation. I came to Jackson to preach only the Bible and not to enter into local issues.[20]

These are embarrassing moments in the history of the Church. They are also difficult moments to understand given the spiritual stature of the men in question. So why would God allow such prominent men like Graham, Moody, Finney and Lewis suffer normative myopia on racial issues where what is ethically wrong is quite clear? Apparently they are human and suffer the various forms of myopia, including normative myopia like everyone else. The lesson to take away from these embarrassing moments in Church history is that no matter how spiritually enlightened a person is, non-Christians are not the only ones in the dark. Myopia does not discriminate across spiritual lines. As Christians, the threat of myopia should increase the depth of our humility.

When equal criticism is applied to advocates of secularism, it can be pointed out that sure intelligence is not sufficient for ethical discernment. Intelligence has its place in ethical discernment; who could doubt this? However, humility is in order for anyone who entertains the notion that enlightenment is sufficient to free a person from ethical waywardness. It has already been shown that such is not the case when secular thinkers like Hume are taken into consideration. To be sure, not even a virtuous character (or even a godly character) will be sufficient so long as myopia is in the background. Nevertheless, as we will see in chapter four, virtues are essential for ethically sound judgments. However, for anyone considering enlightenment or simply high intelligence as sufficient for ethical discernment he needs to explain the odd enlightenment of one of the most intelligent persons in history concerning his marital relationship, Albert Einstein. Einstein was married to mathematician Mileva Maric for 11 years. The Einsteins had marital problems and Albert finally proposed to shift the marriage into a mere contractual relation for the sake of their children. Albert presented the following terms to Mileva:

Albert's conditions

A. You make sure:

1. that my clothes and laundry are kept in good order;

[20]. A quote from Billy Graham in Martin's *A Prophet with Honor: The Billy Graham Story*, 170.

2. that I will receive my three meals regularly *in my room*;

3. that my bedroom and my office are always kept neat, in particular that the desk is available to me alone.

B. You renounce all personal relations with me as far as maintaining them is not absolutely required for social reasons. Specifically, You do without:

1. my sitting at home with you;

2. my going out or traveling with you.

C. In your relationships with me you commit yourself explicitly to adhering to the following points:

1. you are neither to expect intimacy from me, nor reproach me in any way;

2. you must desist immediately from addressing me, if I request it;

3. you must leave my bedroom or office immediately without protest if I so request.

D. You commit yourself not to disparage me either in word or in deed in front of my children.[21]

While Mileva initially agreed to the terms. Albert eventually requested a divorce and she granted him his request. A man of Albert's intellectual stature failed to see that even a concern for the children would not have justified terms so extremely self-absorbed. Intelligence too succumbs to myopia. As you read the rest of this book, keep in mind the possibility of your own myopia when you agree or disagree with what is being presented and critically assessed as right, wrong, true, or false.

---

21. Reprinted in Neffe, *Einstein: A Biography*, 101.

3

A Construction of Formal Ethics: Reflections on the Phrases Moral Facts, Good, Right, Bad, Wrong, Inappropriate, Rude, and Offensive; and Reflection on the Implications of the Word Ought

IN CHAPTER TWO WE looked at pseudo-ethical views (MOTS), critically appraised them, and found them wanting. In this chapter we will begin our journey into what ethics is about or metaethics proper. This chapter constructs and discusses what is formally understood to be warranted positions on what ethics is in terms of what we can know and in terms of what makes an action right or wrong. In addition to this, we will look at the terminology of ethics in terms of the distinction between the words good, right, bad, wrong, inappropriate, rude, and offensive. But before we do this, it is worth distinguishing ethics from yet another matter, but this time the disjunctive subject matter is not problematic like the MOTS. Here I have in mind talk of right and wrong within a legal context.

Reflections on Normative Matters and the Law

Many people confuse talk of right and wrong within an ethical context with right and wrong within a legal context. For both ethical and legal judgments, it is appropriate to use the word "ought," such that we say: "You ought to do X!" However, the reasons for the "ought" differ for both. When ought is used in a legal context, generally speaking, it means one of two things. Either it means that certain guidelines for social behavior have been stipulated by the governing powers (e.g., elected official, dictator, king or parliament), and given a person's agreement to be ruled by the governing powers, the person ought to obey the given guidelines.

Thus "the law" or what is decreed by the governing power could essentially be whatever the governing power says it is. Or it means that certain guidelines for social behavior have been stipulated by the governing powers (e.g., elected official, dictator, king or parliament), not by caprice, but rather by principles of beneficence, non-maleficence and justice for the good of society. And given a person's agreement to be ruled by the governing power, the person ought to obey the given guidelines in light of certain second order considerations. Accordingly, under this description of ought, certain decrees may not be legal (i.e., a law) if the guidelines do not reflect beneficence, non-maleficence and justice. In other words, in countries ruled in this manner, what counts as a law is not *merely* what the governing power says, but rather what is just, beneficent, and non-maleficent. In the United States, when citizens do not think that specified laws reflect the principles of justice, beneficence and non-maleficence, then there are legal channels to change the laws. When legal channels have not worked (e.g., presenting an objection to the governing authorities like the Supreme Court, senators and congressmen) then civil disobedience is in order. Americans have exercised civil disobedience in their cry for civil rights and in their cry against war.

We do well not to settle for the "status quo" since those who make laws are not infallible and do not always rule in favor of justice, beneficence and non-maleficence. In the United States the Supreme Court has not always ruled according to these principles (e.g., "the separate but equal" Supreme Court ruling). Thus given the two senses of ought, a person who says "my position is correct because it is protected by the courts of the land" is question-begging.[1] Consider the following argument on the abortion issue:

> *A Question-begging and Is-Ought Legal Argument*:
>
> 1. Whatever the Supreme Court passes as a law ought to be obeyed as law.
> 2. The law says that a woman has a right to an abortion (via *Doe* v. *Bolton* and *Roe* v. *Wade*).
>
> Therefore, if a woman chooses to have an abortion, she ought to be able to do so.

---

1. See the appendix for a discussion on question-begging.

The problem with this argument is its first premise. It is stated as a given or as being true by definition. As has just been shown, there is an alternative sense of *ought* based on ethical and social principles of justice, beneficence and non-maleficence. You should appeal to this second sense of ought. It alone allows for critical reflection of a legal judgment. As a matter of fact, the Supreme Court had reasons why it legalized abortions before the second trimester; however, whether the Supreme Court made the right decision or not is a matter of critical reflection. We do well not to accept the Supreme Court's decision without such reflection. Failure to do so is to imply that a law ought to be a law because it is a law. Thus the failure of someone to seek justification for the Supreme Court's ruling is also guilty of the is-ought fallacy.[2] Let's take a brief look at the controversial Roe vs. Wade Supreme Court ruling on abortion.

In 1969, a Texas woman named Norma McCorvey (aka Jane Roe) became pregnant. Upon her discovery that she was pregnant, she wanted an abortion. However, she did not have enough money to travel to California, the nearest state where abortions were legal. With the help of two law students, McCorvey filed a lawsuit that challenged the Texas law. When the suit was brought before the U.S. Supreme Court in 1973, it ruled that a right to get an abortion was included in the right to privacy.

Despite a common belief, the 1973 Supreme Court ruling of *Roe v. Wade*, like many cases brought before it, was not unanimous. Let us look at the major and descent ruling, respectively:

> *Justice Harry Blackmun*: We need not resolve the difficult question of when life begins. When those trained in the perspective disciplines of medicine, philosophy, and theology are unable to arrive at any consensus, the judiciary, at this point in the development of man's knowledge, is not in a position to speculate as to the answer....If the State is interested in protecting fetal life after *viability*, it may go so far as to proscribe abortion during that period except when it is necessary to preserve the life or health of the mother.

> *Justice White*: At the heart of the controversy in these cases are those recurring pregnancies that pose no danger whatsoever to the life or health of the mother but are nevertheless unwanted for any one or more of a variety of reasons-convenience, family planning, economics, dislike of children, the embarrassment of

---

2. See the appendix for a definition of the is-ought fallacy.

illegitimacy, etc. . . . During the period prior to the time the fetus becomes viable, the Constitution of the United States values the convenience, whim or caprice of the putative mother more than the life or potential life of the fetus; the Constitution, therefore, guarantees the right to an abortion as against any state law or policy seeking to protect the fetus from an abortion not prompted by more compelling reasons of the mother.

With all due respect, I dissent. I find nothing in the language or history of the Constitution to support the Court's judgment.[3]

Which Justice was right? If we go back to premise one of the above question-begging argument, our question cannot be resolved since both men are members of the Supreme Court. So we can see that it is misleading to say that because the Supreme Court qua major ruling says something is a law (a first order issue) that it *ought* to be a law (a second order issue). So if you are going to address some issue within a legal context, then you ought not focus on what is *ipso facto* the law but rather focus on a more pertinent second order issue about what ought to be the law.

Metaethics Proper: the Terminology of Ethics

Let us move on to define common terms used in ethical judgments. These terms are good, bad, right, wrong, rude, inappropriate, and offensive. We will focus mainly on the terms good, bad, right, and wrong for now. The terms rude, inappropriate and offensive are derivatively meaningful in the context of these terms. Interestingly, the terms good and bad are often considered synonymous with the terms right and wrong, respectively. However, there is a distinction between the terms good, bad, right and wrong. An action could be right but entail a significant amount of bad consequences, and an action could be wrong but result in a significant amount of good consequences.

So what are good and bad actions? Let us first point out that the terms good and bad are asymmetrical. That is, doing an action that results only in some bad outcome is always wrong; but doing an action that results only in some good outcome is neither wrong nor right. This asymmetry sounds odd until we deconstruct the terms good and bad. Let us deconstruct good and bad by contrasting them to the terms right and wrong. Again, good and bad actions are different from right and wrong

3 *Rowe v. Wade*, 410 US 113 (1973).

actions. As for good actions, they are not couched in talk of obligations and duties. Actions classified as good actions are good because they are directly or indirectly valuable. Philosophers give various reasons why such actions are valuable: they are intrinsically pleasurable, they fulfill natural inclinations or they promote a person's or a group of persons' well-being. Drinking water, eating food, having sex, socializing, and reading are good actions in that they promote a human's well-being. Actions classified as bad actions are those actions that are directly or indirectly not valuable. Philosophers give various reasons why such actions are not valuable: they are physically or psychologically painful, they prevent the fulfillment of natural inclinations (e.g., violates the inclination to live) or they are detrimental to a person's or a group of persons' well-being. To be sure, the properties of good and bad actions are not isomorphically converse of each other. Good actions are simply identified by their value and are not prescribed ways of behaving. This lack of prescriptivity entails the following condition for good actions: the person performing them is not ascribed praise for doing them or ascribed blame for not doing them. So whether a person gives a friend a compliment or not, her giving the compliment or her refraining to do so should not be met with either praise or blame. This lack of prescritivity does not hold for bad actions. Bad actions are essentially and inherently wrong to do unless the following three conditions obtain: the person performing the action lacked freedom to do otherwise, a greater good was achieved by doing the bad action, or the person lacked knowledge of what she was doing. Notice that a person speaking in public never has to ask permission to shower another person with accolades nor has to speak such things in private. The same is not true of a person speaking in public who showers insults or criticism onto another person.

Let us now consider defining the ethical terms right and wrong. Right actions ought to be done and wrong actions out not to be done. By definition, then, these actions are normative in that they are actions that are binding on moral agents to do in the former case or not to do in the latter case. That is, to say that an action is wrong is, in part, to say we have a particular duty or obligation to avoid doing the particular action; and to say an action is right is, in part, to say we have a particular duty or obligation to do the particular action.

Let us first focus on wrongful actions. Philosophers vary over how they quantify the wrongness of a particular action, e.g., acting to reduce overall utility, acting against God's will, acting that devalues the sacredness of life, acting contrary to reason in abstraction or even acting against what natural inclinations dictate. With this much said, they agree that there are two common conditions true of wrong actions: (1) from a causal perspective, all wrong actions result with an intended bad event (in some cases this means preventing some good event from occurring) or in the failure to prevent some bad event from happening when, in both cases, no greater good is entailed by the bad event; and (2) from an epistemic perspective, all wrong actions require that the moral agent acting has the freedom to avoid the bad event (or what was referred to earlier as the freedom to do otherwise) and the awareness that the action should be avoided. Following Immanuel Kant's lead, 'ought implies can.' According to the first condition, we are not obligated to avoid the action in question if we are not *able* to avoid it (again this is the freedom to do otherwise). In fact, the action in question could not be identified as wrong for this very reason; it would merely be a bad action. According to the second condition, we are not obligated to avoid an action if we do not *know* we ought to avoid it. Finally a consequence of neglecting our duty to refrain from a wrong action is the ascription of blame and punishment to us for our failure.

As for right actions, philosophers similarly vary over how they quantify the rightness of a particular action, e.g., acting to promote overall utility, acting according to God's will, acting to promote the sacredness of life, acting according to reason in abstraction or even acting according to what natural inclinations dictate. With this much said, they agree that there are two common conditions true of right actions: (1) from a causal perspective, all right actions result in direct or indirect[4] promotion of something good where the failure to do so results in allowing something bad to happen. From an epistemic perspective, the rightness of the action also requires that the moral agent acting has the freedom to promote the right action and the awareness that the right action should be done. Unlike wrong actions, right actions lead to someone ascribing praise and reward to their agent. Finally, the thought that right actions are always entailed by the promotion of something that is directly good is not true. Married couples who are doing something good, like having

---

4. It may be thought that some right actions are just a matter of promoting the lesser of two evils. In such cases, it is argued, there is no good under consideration. This is not true, for in promoting the lesser of two evils, some good is indirectly achieved. In war, for example, casualties are sometimes unavoidable. A commanding officer may give a right command that sends troops to their death where an alternative wrong command would result in sending more troops to their death. While both commands result in death, the former command indirectly saved more lives.

sex, are not *per se* doing something right; or a healthy, hydrated person who does something good, like drinking a cup of water, is not *per se* doing something right. This is because the good obtain in both cases is not contrasted to preventing something bad occurring.

To make explicit the distinction between good, bad, right and wrong, consider the following examples. First, imagine a responsible driver who is driving during a snow storm. As a responsible driver, this person's car has new tires with plenty of good treading and he has recently installed new brakes. As fate would have it, a pedestrian jaywalks across the road just inches in front of the car. Our responsible driver tries earnestly to stop the car, but due to the snowy conditions, his car slides and runs over the pedestrian. The pedestrian dies as a result of the collision. While it is unfortunate that the pedestrian dies, the driver has not acted wrongly. We have here a case where the driver's action is bad but not wrong.

What is bad about the driver's action is that he has caused the death of a person. According to our account of bad actions, killing is ultimately detrimental to the pedestrian's well-being. However, the driver's action is not wrong, because there were not intelligible obligations for him to follow. We cannot intelligibly say what he ought to have done in this case since he could not have done otherwise. In his attempt to stop the car, the collision with the pedestrian was unavoidable due to the snow. Obviously the driver knew that he should not kill other persons without reason and nothing in his action indicates an intention to kill. Ultimately, the driver lacked the freedom to avoid killing. So in no way is the driver opened to an ascription of blame for his action however tragic the result was for the pedestrian.

Now consider a similar situation of a driver who is fully aware that his car needs new brakes very soon. Due to financial reasons, he prolongs the decision to have the car's brakes repaired and, instead, decides to drive his car slowly when he has to drive it. A month after making the decision to prolong the repair of the brakes, a pedestrian leaps out in front of his car while he is driving the car. While he is not driving fast, he cannot stop the car since now the car's brakes are useless. As a result he drives over the pedestrian and kills her. Unlike the other situation, this driver's action is not only bad in that he killed a person, but his action is wrong since he knew the ramifications of driving a car with failing brakes. If the driver argues that he tried his best to stop his car and thus should not be blamed, he has no case for his defense, since he could have done otherwise when the car's brakes began to fail months earlier.

It is not uncommon for some wrong actions to have good consequences or good features. In such cases, the act under consideration results in pleasure, utility of some sort or it may be conducive to a person's well-being in some sense. One such act would be having sex with another person's spouse which is clearly wrong but results, nonetheless, in physical pleasure. A similar action would be a parent who gives her child everything he wants but in doing so contributes to her son's spoiled character.

Finally let us address the terms rude, inappropriate and offensive. These terms can be classified as species of wrong actions. The term rude is generally defined as an insensitive, apathetic and inconsiderate act towards other persons. Let us categorize rude actions and comments into three categories: (1) rude by intent, (2) rude by impact and (3) rude by context. The rude act may not cause any harm but, again, it is wrong in sense (1) if it is an intentional disregard of another person's wishes and consent, e.g., when three employees are eating lunch together and then two of the employees decide to speak in a language that the third employee cannot understand. A similar rude act would be when someone makes a phone call but intentionally makes no attempt to identify himself by way of a greeting when the person who answers the phone is someone he knows but other than the intended receiver. Sometimes the rude act is intended to elicit anger in the other person, e.g., when a driver purposefully drives slowly because he knows the driver behind him is in a rush. However, due to cultural differences some acts may be rude in sense (2) where the rudeness was without intent, e.g., a guest from a foreign country who washes his feet in your kitchen sink because this is typical practice back home or where a person's cultural personal space is different from your cultural personal space. The act negatively impacts you as a "gross" act. Finally, in sense (3) an act may or may not be rude pending your relationship to the agent of the act. For example, in American society a person may unapologetically burp or display flatulent behavior without being considered rude at home with family, but in public with less intimate others, the same behaviors would be deemed rude.

The term offensive generally describes an action or comment that is disrespectful or demeaning towards a person. Often the way an action or comment is offensive is when it devalues a person in regards to her class, education, race, gender, nationality, politics, religion and similar identity markers. Let us also categorize offensive actions and comments into three categories: (1) offense by intent, (2) offense by impact and (3) offense by context. Obviously an action or comment is offensive if it is intended to be disrespectful or demeaning. However, a person's action or comment can be offensive in the second way even if she did not intend for it to be so. For example, a person may, unaware, use a term that was not historically racially derogatory but is currently racially derogatory (e.g., referring to an African American girl as a colored girl). In this case, due to personal or cultural ignorance, the offending person is oblivious to how the term "colored" is understood in contemporary society. Nevertheless, the deed is offensive because of the impact it has on its recipients, viz., an African American girl. This means that while the agent of the deed was not cognizant of the offensive nature of his deed, and for that matter was not intending an offense, the deed is nonetheless offensive and should not be cursorily dismissed. For the sake of the integrity of the agent of the offensive deed, its recipients should inform the agent of the impact of his offense. Once informed, the same person cannot be excused of the same offense if repeated. Thirdly, an action or comment can be offense by context. This is to say that an action qua offensive action occurs under certain circumstances depending on who does the act and who the act is intended to be directed at. Often the context is a matter of who the insiders and outsiders are. For example, there may be terms and expressions used by a particular group as a matter of jest that would be offensive for outsiders to use.

Finally, the term inappropriate refers to any actions or words that are condemned relative to a set of norms within a given professional, social or cultural context. Thus inappropriate actions and words are not *per se* wrong at the first order; they surely are wrong at the second order. To be sure, because they are condemned relative to a set of norms, they are not *per se* wrong in themselves. For example, using a cell phone while at work is not unethical in itself. After all, what is unethical about using a cell phone? But at a second order, because the corporation condemns the use of a cell phone during work hours, to use one regardless of this condemnation is to act out of disrespect for the corporation. Similarly a professor who lectures in the class room while wearing jeans would be dressing inappropriately if the university had a dress code policy against wearing jeans while functioning as a professor on campus. Wearing jeans is not unethical in itself, but to do so is unethical at the second level because it conveys disrespect and disregard for the authority of the university's norms. Other actions are inappropriate merely because of social norms of a given group. In many social settings, it is inappropriate for a couple to engage in passionate kissing while in public, say, at a restaurant or at a church fellowship hall. In some cultures, it is inappropriate to look into the eyes of an elder. It is important to point out that acts that are deemed inappropriate may also be rude since those who do them disregard the preferences of those in authority under discussion.

Some Broad Logical Claims about the Freedom of Choice and the Word "Ought"

Since ethics is about right and wrong, it entails a discussion about what we ought to do and what we ought not to do. To speak about what we ought to do or ought not to do necessarily restricts our freedom to act and to decide from a normative context. If ethics were a matter of "whatever we said is right or wrong is right or wrong" then it does not matter what we do. Right would be whatever we said is right and wrong would be whatever we said is wrong. The words *ought* and *ought not* would be meaningless. The normative nature of the restriction on our choices is primarily semantic and comes from what the words ought and ought not mean: to speak of an action as right, necessarily entails some other action is wrong, thus limiting or restricting the series of options opened to a person. Our freedom to choose in an ethical situation does not entail that our selected course of action is made correct by our choosing it. Recall that this was the main problem that plagued autonomism. To be sure, the semantic restriction that the word ought places on our choosing, or anyone else's choosing for that matter, holds even if all of our ethical beliefs are false.

Metaethics: the Ontology of Ethics

In the previous chapter we looked at moral epistemology in terms of belief formation and whether we can know our ethical judgments are unbiased and true. Let us return to the concern about truth and determine whether any ethical statements are true and whether they have truth-makers.

Not surprisingly, philosophers have given different answers to these questions. Some philosophers argue that ethical statements are neither true nor false. Proponents of this view are called non-cognitivists. For non-cognitivists, ethical judgments are about the internal attitudes or feelings of those who assert them. Non-cognitivism is a metaethical thesis since it defines the nature of ethical judgments, independent of what those who assert them take them to be. So a person may take her judgment to be true about some ethical matter, but a non-cognitivist would assert, nevertheless, that it is neither true nor false. David Hume and later A. J. Ayer championed this view. Riding off the dominant philosophical view of his time, logical positivism, Ayer wrote:

> [I]f I say to someone, "You acted wrongly in stealing that money," I am not stating anything more than if I had simply said, "You stole that money." In adding that this action is wrong I am not making any further statement about it. I am simply evincing my moral disapproval of it.[5]

For Ayer, propositions are meaningful if and only if they are matters of fact or are analytic (e.g., tautology). In the former case, Ayer and his logical positivists are referring to propositions that are verified by facts in the world. Beyond observing the fact that a person stole money, Ayer would argue, what more is there in the world that the word "wrongly" denotes? Ayer denies that there is any ethical fact in the world that "wrongly" denotes that is empirically verifiable. To be sure, "wrongly" denotes the feelings of the speaker of the proposition. But feelings are neither true nor false. So whenever we state that some act is wrong, we are simply expressing our feelings or in Ayer's words, emoting. Actions a person has negative feelings about, she judges as ethically wrong. Actions she has positive feelings about, she conversely judges as ethically right. This particular view of non-cognitivism is called emotivism.

In all fairness to Ayer, Ayer was not denying that ethical debates and ethical reasoning are unintelligible. Nothing could be further from the truth. For Ayer, what should be debated in ethics is whether or not our beliefs accurately describe facts in the world given how we feel about facts in the world. In ethical reasoning between interlocutors, Ayers says, the objective should be to successfully persuade the other that their perception of the facts is misguided. This rational persuasion to venture into greener pastures is normative, if not simply the rational thing to do, for both interlocutors. Ayer notes that people who are from the same society adopt similar values. Not surprising, this is because society cultivates or shapes what values its members adopt:

> And as the people with whom we argue have generally received the same moral education as ourselves, and live in the same social order, our expectation is usually justified. But if

5. Ayer, "Critique of Ethics and Theology," 107.

> our opponent happens to have undergone a different process of moral "conditioning" from ourselves, so that, even when he acknowledges all the facts, he still disagrees with us about the moral value of the actions under discussion, then we abandon the attempt to convince him by argument. We say that it is impossible to argue with him because he has a distorted or undeveloped moral sense; which signifies merely that he employs a different set of values from our own. We feel that our own system of values is superior.[6]

In Ayer's ontology, since values are not in the world but are simply features of our emotive lives that our society shapes, he concludes that ethics reduces to or is an extension of sociology. Obviously, then, when people who are socialized in the same society don't share similar ethical judgments, it is because one of them is mistaken about what the facts are. Conversely when the interlocutors are from different societies it is a waste of time to argue over ethical disagreement, given the values come from different societies. Consider an example like abortion as it is debated in the United States. Ayer would assert that a debate on this topic is rational to engage in despite the fact that terminating the life of an unborn is neither right nor wrong. Americans on either side of the pro-life and pro-choice side of the abortion spectrum feel the same way about the value of human persons. Both sides feel bad about the death of an innocent person because the American society is socialized to feel bad about the death of an innocent person. So, on this note, they agree across the board on value but disagree on the facts of the unborn entity as a person. As Ayer would have it, both sides could engage in rational discourse in so far as either side tried to persuade the other side that it is mistaken about the facts pertaining to the unborn. For example, pro-life proponents would try to persuade pro-choice proponents that they are mistaken about the unborn not being an innocent person. Pro-choice proponents would persuade pro-life proponents that they are mistaken about the unborn being an innocent person. Pro-life proponents would try to argue that "photos" showing an aborted unborn is an innocent human person and the converse would be true for the pro-choice proponents (claiming the unborn is just a collection of cells).

Other philosophers argue that ethical judgments are either true or false. Proponents of this view are called cognitivists. They argue that the criterion for meaningful propositions, Ayer and others propose, is itself

6. Ibid., 111.

neither a matter of fact or analytic (e.g., tautologies). Against the non-cognitivists, cognitivists hold that there are ethical matters of fact in the world or self-evident principles. As such, most cognitivists are classified as moral realists since these matters of fact or self-evident principles are objective realities independent of our conception of them.[7] The term "wrongly" then would denote some objective reality as opposed to any feeling of a speaker. Talk of an ethical fact or reality may sound suspect to some beyond what a person naturally observes like colors and sounds. Nevertheless, some moral realists simply account for ethical facts as being ontologically constituted by features in the natural world, as being the subject of the natural sciences, and as having causal powers to move a person for some normative end. As such, ethical facts can be constituted by sociological, biological and psychological facts in nature. For example, some moral realists refer to pleasure as the only thing that is intrinsically good and rightness as the maximization of pleasure.

Other moral realists account for ethical facts by appealing to non-natural facts of the world. These non-natural facts have what may be called a platonic nature in that they are not the subject matter of the natural sciences, not sensible, and do not have causal powers to move persons for some normative end. In either case, moral realism has come under much attack, even by supporters of moral realism. Moral realists who take moral properties to be platonic, object to the naturalistic version of moral realism and moral realists who take moral properties to be natural properties, object to the platonic version of moral realism.

The standard objection to the naturalistic version of moral realism comes from G. E. Moore.[8] As Moore saw things, being a naturalist about morality required thinking that moral terms should be defined correctly using terms that refer to and are reducible to natural properties. Historically, the obvious candidate would be pleasure and thus a moral realist of the naturalistic persuasion would define 'good' as 'pleasure.' For Moore, defining the former term by the latter commits what he called the naturalistic fallacy. For whatever natural property the moral realist appeals

---

7. Cognitivism is not equivalent to moral realism, for some cognitivists are "error theorists." Error theorists affirm that ethical judgments purport or affirm that something is true (e.g., it is wrong to kill innocent babes) but in fact are false because the ethical content of such judgments do not correspond to facts in the world. So for error theorists, non-naturalists are right that moral properties do not refer to or are reducible to natural properties but they are wrong in their assertion that moral properties exist.

8. Moore, *Principia Ethica*, 37–58.

to in order to account for goodness, it always made sense to ask, is that natural property good? If the two terms considered were identical in meaning and were the same property, then asking whether what was true of one was true of the other would not be an open-question, as in asking whether circles are round. But Moore's so-called naturalistic fallacy was directed at any position that tried to reduce goodness to some other property, including non-natural properties. So, for example, the view that reduces goodness to "what God commands" or to "God's nature" is also guilty of the naturalistic fallacy. For the same question could be asked of either of these reductions if they were good. For example, we can ask, "Is the will of God good"? Moore's naturalistic fallacy then is not an attack against naturalism or moral realism per se as it is an argument against reduction of good to any other property. Moore concludes that the irreducibility of goodness shows that goodness is a sui generis property and thus moral realism is not false.

Contra Moore, however, some have argued that Moore's open question is not as definitive as Moore thought against natural moral realism. The objection comes from a counter example to Moore's Open Question concerning the concepts "water" and "H2O." To be sure the former concept historically was not understood in terms of the latter until a basic understanding of chemistry was achieved in science. While water and H2O are metaphysically the same substance, Moore's open question could intelligibly be posed so as to inquire whether water is equivalent to H2O. Conceiving of water as being H2O is an empirical matter that requires more than an analysis of the concept water and H2O. In keeping with this distinction in our understanding of these concepts, some moral realists maintain that Moore's open question fails to make a distinction between semantic and metaphysical equivalence. In other words two concepts can have different meaning (a semantic concern) even though they refer to the same entity (a metaphysical concern).

Moral realism, however, of both the natural and non-natural kind have some problems to address. Non-realists and non-cognitivists charge moral realism with some or all of the following failures: failure to account for moral motivation and failure to account and explain how moral properties are knowable. Let us consider the alleged motivational failure. What critics point out is that moral claims are radically special and different from non-moral claims. Moral claims in their very nature motivate those who assert them to act a certain way unlike non-moral claims; thus moral claims are queer in this sense.[9] So for a person who asserts and believes that justice should be advanced in society, her judgment entails or implies that she be motivated to advance justice in society. If this person is not motivated to advance justice in society, then there is reason to think she is dishonest about her judgment or that she is utterly confused about what justice means. If the same person made a claim about the color of a tree, that it had brown leaves, there is nothing normative issuing from her judgment for her to act or be motivated a certain way, even if in fact she was motivated to touch the bark of the tree. To reiterate, this shows that there is an apparent distinction between moral and non-moral claims, where the former is essentially tied to a specific motivational response and the latter is not. Now how this distinction is explained is where the rub is between moral realists and their non-realist critics. Critics of moral realism claim that moral realists are essentially confused about what these moral claims are. That is, critics hold that among things internal to the speaker that the claim could be about, only her desires, fears, and preferences, not beliefs, have this power to make speakers of such claims respond a certain way. The way critics see the problem, it is not the normative nature of a moral claim (viz., that something ought or ought not to be done) that is the issue; rather it is the problem of how a normative belief alone could move a person to act. A person's value and desires for justice, apart from her belief that justice is valuable, is always what moves her to advance justice, other things being equal. On this reading of motivation, therefore, moral realists are forced to concede that moral claims are neither true nor false since moral claims are simply a matter of asserting desires and the like, which have no truth value.

Moral realists have offered responses to this objection. Some moral realists deny that this moral and non-moral claim distinction exists. They hold that not all non-moral beliefs are inert and that sometimes moral beliefs are inert. They say the charge that beliefs are inert or that beliefs do not motivate is a misleading claim. Whether or not a belief motivates action is based on the intentional content of the belief and other internal states within a person. Sometimes moral beliefs are inert. If a person says she believes that being courageous is a virtue but is not motivated to save a child in a burning building, we would conclude she is dishonest about her belief, confused about what courage means, or that she experiences a weakness of will that overpowers her to instantiate courage in this

9. Horgan and Timmons, "Troubles on Moral Twin Earth," 221–60.

instance. Her ability to act according to her belief would be due to other internal states in her, e.g., her fear of fire. If asked, the person could say she is genuinely honest about her belief and wanted to act courageously but admits to being a coward. Sometimes non-moral beliefs are essentially motivational for a specific end. The reason why the belief that a poisonous spider is near my hand causes me to retreat while the belief that a poisonous spider is near my hand in a concealed bottle does not is essentially a matter of the intentional content of each belief. If a person claimed that she believes jumping out of a plane in midflight is dangerous to do without a parachute and yet jumps out the plane without a parachute on her freewill, it is safe to conclude she is being dishonest or that she is confused about what she is saying. So not all non-moral beliefs pass muster without asking these questions of them. For both realists and non-realists alike, they do not disregard the doxastic status of non-moral claims because of their motivation component and regulate them to mere desires. The fact of the matter is, while non-moral claims like the claim about jumping out of a plane in midflight being dangerous essentially motivates the person who asserts it, it equally purports states of affairs in the world as being true or false.

A second problem moral realists face concerns the knowledge of moral facts. The non-natural moral realist has the task of explaining how we can know non-natural moral facts of the world that are not accessible to us via the natural sciences. The natural moral realist has the task of explaining how we can know natural moral facts of the world since science is usually in the business of describing the world rather than discovering normative features of the world or how it ought to be.

Let us consider the task for the non-natural moral realist. Since the non-natural moral realist holds that moral properties are not reducible or identical to any natural property, the truth makers of her claims, recall, have a platonic nature; they are not sensible. So just how are these moral properties apprehended if not by empirical observation? The obvious and traditional candidate has been a special moral sense faculty or intuition. The appeal to either form of apprehension is problematic. Talk of a mysterious moral sense faculty is intelligible but lacks any direct evidence unlike the typical sense faculties like the eye or ear.

As for the appeal to intuition, intuitions are not per se clouded in mystery. Perhaps the best way to understand an intuition is to consider it the direct, non-inferential apprehension and understanding of a belief or proposition, such as the axioms of mathematics. As such, what is understood by the mind is not a fact or feature in the world. While the application of mathematics may be about facts in the world (e.g., apples) the content or truth makers of mathematics are concepts, viz., numbers, sets, and their relationships. Similarly intuitions in ethics would be the direct, non-inferential apprehension and understanding of an ethical belief or proposition such as "good should be pursued and evil avoided" or "killing autonomous beings wantonly is wrong." The moral realist who embraces intuitionism thus described avoids a commitment to describing truth claims about moral properties in the world even if there are moral properties in the world.

Let us now consider the task for the natural moral realist. Critics like Moore et al. direct a similar open question toward natural moral realists like the question directed at their metaphysics of ethical properties. The difference here is that the concern is epistemological. For while moral properties may well be reducible to natural properties, what exactly do we come to know when we say good is "pleasure" or good is "what satisfies a desire we desire to have"? In either case there is nothing self-contradictory or incoherent in denying such properties as good. Critics argue that it is a hopeless task to seek some normative property in nature by use of the natural sciences or merely by empirical observation. Accordingly, pleasure or second order desires are easily accessible and are descriptive features of nature, but good is not something descriptive. Rather, good is prescriptive and normative and thus outside the confines of science. Moreover, as David Hume infamously asserted, good cannot be derived from an assertions of facts. From his comment about the relationship between "is" and "ought," he says:

> In every system of morality, which I have hitherto met with, I have always remarked, that the author proceeds for some time in the ordinary ways of reasoning, and establishes the being of a God, or makes observations concerning human affairs; when all of a sudden I am surprised to find, that instead of the usual copulations of propositions, *is*, and *is not*, I meet with no proposition that is not connected with an *ought*, or an *ought not*. This change is imperceptible; but is however, of the last consequence. For as this *ought*, or *ought not*, expresses some new relation or affirmation, 'tis necessary that it should be observed and explained; and at the same time that a reason should be given; for what seems altogether inconceivable, how this new relation can be a deduction from others, which are entirely different from it. But as authors do not commonly use this precaution, I shall

presume to recommend it to the readers; and am persuaded, that this small attention would subvert all the vulgar systems of morality, and let us see, that the distinction of vice and virtue is not founded merely on the relations of objects, nor is perceived by reason.[10]

In short, critics hold that there is not a place in nature for the normative qua normative. Before presenting how a moral realist could respond, let us explicate *normative*. Talk of what is normative refers to some standard, end, or obligation. In every use or sense of the word normative, the associated word "ought" is implied. When applied to science, normative tells us, among other things, what standards ought to apply for denoting what goes by the name "scientific" and what ought to be assigned non-scientific, e.g., what is mere opinion or sophistry. The ought is derived over time from experiments and confirmation of certain *explanans* that have high explanatory success in accounting for their targeted *explanandum*.

Put simply, a scientist ought not to appeal to supernatural causes like ancestral spirits to explain why a person has suddenly become ill. Rather an appeal to some hypothesis about a known or unknown virus or something of the sort is in order. Inductively scientists have come to discover that certain explanans generate knowledge of the natural order and these explanans are not spirits of ancestors. Our discussion of the normative nature of science can be put into the form of an argument: An appeal to natural causes has generated knowledge of the natural order. An appeal to ancestral spirits has not generated knowledge of the natural order. Science is the study of the causes and effects of the natural order. Therefore, a scientist ought to rule out spirits as a source of scientific knowledge. This is an inductive argument, but the ought is not derived arbitrarily even if not validly. When applied to the product of a creator, whether the product is biological (e.g., for theists this would be many things in the created order like trees and cows) or non-biological (e.g., a game of chess), normative tells us how the product ought to be treated or used in terms of its created end. The *ought* here is derived from the intended end for which the product was made. It is irrelevant to point out that a chess player's move of her bishop is purely arbitrary, for the inventor of chess could have easily intended the function and end of the bishop was to be moved one space to its left. But as a matter of fact, this is not the

---

10. Hume, *A Treatise of Human Nature*, 469.

end the inventor of chess desired for the bishop and thus a chess player ought not to move a bishop in this manner when she plays chess. Surely the person could move the bishop one space to the left, but she would not be playing chess. When applied to fiduciary relationships between at least two persons or parties, what is normative tells us what we ought to do or what our duties are toward the other person or party in terms of what we agreed to contractually or in virtue of the position the other person or party has toward us. The ought in "Jones ought not to steal X from Peter" can be derived from the fact that "Peter owns X." Stealing entails that the ownership of some X belongs to another party. Peter owns X and the meaning of "ownership" entails that Peter has the authority over the use and possession of X. Now of course talk of ownership such as "Peter is sitting in his car" is not as easily described as a fact in the world as "Peter is sitting in a car." What is needed is some appeal to work as described by John Locke or at least to granting that ownership of some sort is possible and that Peter in fact owns X.

In all these variations of the normative, there is a place for the word ought, but it does not have some mysterious origin nor is it a misplaced word. With that said, moral realists can explain, contra Hume, how an "ought" can come from "is" and more generally how talk of the normative is intelligible in an objective way in a natural world. This response to the humean objection was in order so that we can proceed with the assertion that there are ethical states of affairs in the world that can be assessed and discerned to be ethically right or wrong. Moreover, this response will allow us to assert that people have a variety of rights and non-human animals should be treated with care and humanely. Without this response, this book ends here.

4

Reflections on the Varieties of Normative Ethics: Discerning What We Ought to Do and How We Ought to Be

IN THIS CHAPTER WE turn to what is known as normative ethics. Normative ethics moves beyond ethical terminology (e.g., the discussion of what terms like "right" and "wrong" mean) and other ethical issues (e.g., whether there is any epistemological status to ethical judgments). Normative ethics looks at theories, algorithms, and principles applicable for making ethical judgments about what actions are right or wrong. Unlike metaethics which is essentially a descriptive analysis of the nature of ethics, normative ethics is essentially prescriptive and here the focus is on how those who are part of the moral community ought to act or be. Some of the main normative ethical theories in circulation, and the ones that have been historically appealed to, are natural law theory, utilitarianism, deontology, and virtue ethics.[1] Each of these theories comes with its on metaphysical claims about personhood, right/wrong action, and a notion of what is good (i.e., axiology). While the natural law theory is popular among Christians and Catholics in particular, it is not considered a thoroughgoing normative ethical theory outside these circles and for good reasons. The attention that natural law theory receives in this chapter will be limited and critical. However, this theory has its merits and one principle within this theory has popular appeal in applied ethics, particularly for medical or bioethics. This is the principle of double effect, which we will turn to later. Additionally, attention will be paid to the topic of rights, which is a discipline that encompasses the professional, ethical, social, and political well-being of living beings and their entitlements. In the end, no attempt will be made to argue for "the correct tool" or "the

---

1. These three theories do not exhaust the list of normative ethical theories, e.g., there is also ethics of care and social contract theory.

correct theory" definitive enough to warrant that title. Rather an eclectic, integrative approach to ethical decision making will be presented that encompasses the best components of the theories presented.

Normative Ethics

As we begin, a description of each of these theories will be presented, then some pros and cons of each as well. There is no order of preference or importance attached to these theories as they are presented. As stated, a major concern of normative ethics is about what makes an action right or wrong. Recall this concern was discussed in the previous chapter when the MOTS was critically assessed. There the answers of preference were "society" and "culture." Since ethics is evidence based in large part, any answer with warrant will point to factors external to mere beliefs. Any answer with warrant will make clear distinctions between epistemology and metaphysics. The following theories definitely do make it clear that the wrongness and rightness of an action is a matter of the structure and nature of the act itself and not a matter of our culture or personal beliefs.

Natural Law Theory

Natural law theory is essentially a theological ethics in so far as St. Thomas Aquinas structured it. For Aquinas, the universe as a whole and its parts are ordered by God in both functions and ends (*Summa Theologica* Ia IIae question 91, articles 1–2). This teleology or orderliness exists as an eternal plan of God or what Aquinas calls the eternal law. The natural law factors in for Aquinas in so far as it is the part of the eternal law that pertains to the affairs of humanity. In so far as humanity qua rational beings participates in the eternal law, we are able to violate it unlike the rest of creation. God's plan or laws for humanity are knowable empirically to all humanity by reflecting on how humanity flourishes in nature. The first law of natural law theory states that the good should be pursued and evil avoided. Aquinas follows Aristotle in thinking that an act is good or bad depending on whether it contributes to or deters us from our natural (proper) human end—the *telos* or final goal at which all human actions aim. That *telos* is ευδαιμονια, or happiness, where "happiness" is understood in terms of completion, perfection, or well-being. Obtaining happiness requires fulfilling what humans are naturally designed to do, i.e., what God ordered human inclinations and proper functions to be. Aquinas believed all humans have the same natural functions, and these functions can often be understood and known by considering what inclinations seem natural for humans to express and how human body parts are designed by God for some proper end and to express these inclinations. Humanity's ultimate function (or unique function when compared to other living beings) is contemplation. The identification of inclinations with proper functions has warrant for Aquinas because they cause humans to flourish. So a broad algorithm of natural law for considering an action good or bad can be stated as follows: Whatever act expresses or allows a human inclination is good or natural and whatever act forbids or frustrates a human inclination is bad or unnatural. Good, function, and natural inclination are coextensive terms and so are bad and unnatural. While it is true from a historical context that the natural law theory is couched in theism,[2] natural law theory does not entail theism. If you understand the theory, it essentially is couched in something called human nature, whether human nature as a universal essence is the result of God or natural selection. Formally natural law theory is quite intelligible as a normative ethical theory. How could it be argued that unnatural acts are anything but good and natural acts are anything but bad? Since ethics is based on human nature, according to the natural law theory, it will not be possible for humans to debate the dictates of nature so as to leave the verdict of right and wrong to culture and society.

Unfortunately the theological version of this theory loses credibility in the specifics. Can it be said that "natural" is equivalent to what is good? The answer is no. On a general level, inclinations that the social and behavior sciences discover to have their origin in nature tend to make humankind flourish as the natural law theory argues. For example, having encouraging and affirming parents make children flourish and verbally abusing children naturally makes children dysfunctional. Also, casual sexual intercourse among adults naturally leads to bad consequences when no care is taken to prevent pregnancy. This is because psychological studies have shown (not to mention common experience) that children naturally flourish psychologically and socially when they are raised in stable environments with the same mother and father. However, talk of "natural equates to good" runs afoul when abnormal but natural inclinations are taken into consideration. Sociopaths have inclinations to be antisocial and

---

2. For further discussion of natural law theory from a contemporary natural law theorist, see Finnis, *Natural Law and Natural Rights*, 100–133.

are not sympathetic. It would seem that a logical consequence of natural law theory is to affirm this behavior because it would be natural, but this would surely be wrong. However, it is not certain how natural law theory could condemn sociopath behavior. To be sure Aquinas does not per se define "natural" in physically or biological terms. What is natural necessarily is determined by God and we see what is natural by its good effects. Perhaps a natural law theorist could hold that only the inclinations that make humans flourish should have normative status in her theory. The obvious problem with this response is that natural would no longer be equivalent to what is good nor be biblically or divinely good.

Another problem to specify is the normative nature of sexuality. Sexuality is notoriously difficult for natural law theory to address in terms of what is right and wrong. For example, among the goods that humans could pursue is procreation. Procreation and sex are not equivalent acts, since the latter can occur without the former. An infertile couple could engage in sex, but to no fault of their own, they lack the natural ability to reproduce a child. However, Aquinas' emphasis on what counts as bad or unnatural is difficult to justify in the case of contraception options. Here the only ethically right way to engage in sexual intercourse with the intent of not reproducing a child is the rhythm method (with the exception allowed for couples who are not physically capable of producing viable sperms or eggs). For Aquinas, any attempt to frustrate what naturally occurs as the result of vaginal sex is artificial and unnatural.

> We must seek a solution from what has been said before: for it has been said (Chapp. XVI, LXIV) that God has care of everything according to that which is good for it. Now it is good for everything to gain its end, and evil for it to be diverted from its due end. But as in the whole so also in the parts, our study should be that every part of man and every act of his may attain its due end. Now though the *semen* is superfluous for the preservation of the individual, yet it is necessary to him for the propagation of the species: while other excretions, such as excrement, urine, sweat, and the like, are needful for no further purpose: hence the only good that comes to man of them is by their removal from the body. But that is not the object in the emission of the *semen*, but rather the profit of generation, to which the union of the sexes is directed. But in vain would be the generation of man unless due nurture followed, without which the offspring generated could not endure. The emission of the *semen* then ought to

> be so directed as that both the proper generation may ensue and the education of the offspring be secured.³

So any form of artificial contraception is ethically wrong. But given Aquinas' vaginal requirement, homosexual sex would also be ruled unnatural and thus unethical:

> Hence it is clear that every emission of the *semen* is contrary to the good of man, which takes place in a way whereby generation is impossible; and if this is done on purpose, it must be a sin. I mean a way in which generation is impossible in itself as is the case in every emission of the *semen* without the natural union of male and female: wherefore such sins are called 'sins against nature.' But if it is by accident that generation cannot follow from the emission of the *semen*, the act is not against nature on that account, nor is it sinful; the case of the woman being barren would be a case in point.⁴

Equally unethical would be anal sex between heterosexual couples since semen is wasted and prevented from its natural course and because the penis and vagina functionally fit together like hand and glove to make pregnancy possible.

Even when the natural law theory is shifted away from a theological context, the problems do not become less. What is natural from a secular, naturalist perspective is void of teleology and thus does not involve an over-arching design by God. As such we have no reason to think that what is natural is the result of one plan of one designer. Natural selection may produce several ends that make humans flourish. Even if it is argued that homosexual relationships do not promote the survival of the human species, such relationships do not also detract from it as well. They do, however, promote scalability and love, which are natural tendencies. Given that the basis of natural law theory depends on an ambiguous notion of what is natural and unnatural, many ethicists have rejected or abandoned the natural law theory.

However, contemporary natural law theorists like John Finnis have given natural law theory a new face and revitalized interest in it. He proposes a notion of the good that is couched in seven incommensurable basic goods. They are: (1) life, (2) knowledge, (3) play⁵, (4) aesthetic

---

3. Aquinas, *Summa contra Gentiles* 3.122.4 (trans. Rickaby, p. 283).
4. Ibid., 3.122.5 (trans. Rickaby; 283).
5. As Finnis notes, play is a "large and irreducible element in human culture" and

experience (of natural or man-made beauty), (5) sociability or friendship, (6) practical reasonableness, and (7) religion.[6] There is no hierarchy within the list. He appeals to anthropology to support the self-evident nature of these basic goods. Clearly each basic good is some sort of inclination humans naturally have for some end, that when instantiated, makes humans flourish.

With these basic goods in place, Finnis provides us with principles for discerning which goods a person ought to pursue in a given situation. These principles are derived from Aquinas' first ethical principle which is a good in itself: "*Good is to be done and pursued, and evil is to be avoided*" or what he calls basic good number (6), practical reasonableness. These principles are: (1) Have "a coherent plan of life": A person must view her actions in the wider context of her life. Don't live for the moment. Hence, the agent's action should be one that extends into and promotes her future. (2) Not having an arbitrary preference amongst the basic goods: The action should stem from the attitude that all basic goods are equally and intrinsically valuable. When choices are made to secure some basic good over another, the choice must not be done by devaluating of the good not chosen. (3) No arbitrary preferences among persons: The action should stem from the attitude that all persons are equally and intrinsically valuable. In the background here is the Golden Rule to treat others like oneself. (4) Have a sense of detachment from all the specific and limited projects one undertakes: In order to be open to any of the basic goods in "all the changing circumstances of a lifetime," a person must maintain a certain detachment from their goals or ends such that the goals or ends do not occupy the same importance or status of any of the basic goods. In other words, life goes on when goals and ends are not attainable. Failure to detach leads to fanaticism. (5) Do not abandon general commitments lightly: Basic goods are not always easy to acquire. Fidelity to one's goals and ends prescribes that one engages in these goals and ends beyond hardship. Otherwise, the basic goods, particularly in extreme cases, would be unattainable. Moreover, a person should seek out creative ways to pursue her goals and ends lest they needlessly waste

---

anyone anywhere could "see the point of engaging in performances which have no point beyond the performance itself, enjoyed for its own sake." See Finnis, *Natural Law and Natural Rights*, 87.

6. Finnis's notion of religion as a basic good is akin to Sartre's notion that, even with the death or non-existence of God, each person is responsible for their own destiny and actions toward self and others.

opportunities for fulfillment. (6) Act to bring about good with efficiency: This principle speaks to the need for efficiency in pursuit of definite goals. Consequences are important but not at the expense of any of the basic goods. (7) Respect for every basic value in every act: Respect every basic value in every act by never choosing against a basic good, i.e., act in such a way that no basic good is violated. (8) Favor and foster the common good of one's communities: A person should act in such a way that her action is not a result of ethical egoism but instead fosters the Common Good of her community. The common good refers to the interest all members of a community have to bring about a state of affairs where everyone can pursue the basic goods for their individual well-being.[7] Finally, (9) Follow one's conscience: A person must act in accordance with her conscience as opposed to what is expedient or convenient.

While the natural law theory like Finnis' could be allowed talk of objective basic goods, as a normative ethical theory, it remains to be seen if Finnis' natural law theory can provide a thoroughgoing and clear guide to ethical issues beyond the issue of the *ability* to form a life plan, and acting for the common good. It is a challenge to Finnis' natural law theory, with his strong stand that the basic goods are valued absolutely and for the sake of humans, to provide normative direction and guidance on a range of issues, e.g., the well-being of non-human animals, euthanasia, or same sex relationships without regurgitating traditional Thomistic natural law.

Finally, Finnis is emphatic that an appeal to consequences is important but not at the risk of compromising or negating a basic good. Like we will see with our next philosopher Immanuel Kant, Finnis is an ethical absolutist. This absolutism comes from Finnis' view that the basic goods have equal value. Thus a ramification of Finnis' absolutism is, for example, that lying is categorically wrong. Perhaps Finnis would prefer martyrdom to lying since lying would violate sociability and perhaps the common good.

---

7. As Finnis explains in *Natural Law and Natural Rights*, 303: "[E]very man has reason to value the common good—the well-being alike of himself and of his partners and potential partners in community, and the ensemble of conditions and ways of effecting that well-being—whether out of friendship as such, or out of an impartial recognition that human goods are as much realized by the participation in them of other persons as by his own."

Deontology

The word "deontology" is derived from the Greek words "deion" (meaning what must be the case) and "logos" (an account of). The thesis of deontology theories is that ethics does not depend on consequences of actions but on the inherent value of rational beings and the conformity of their wills to certain principals of rationality. One point not mentioned much about deontology is that these theories are internal in their focus. By this I mean they describe ethics as being about the nature of decision making, such that ethics is not about what happens in the world but about the rational and thus normative structure of the decision maker's judgment. Actions are only of secondary importance in that they are right or wrong in so far as they are logical extensions of our intentions, beliefs, and decisions. In light of these conditions, there are certain ways we ought to act, believe and form intentions. Contemporary proponents of deontology are John Rawls, Alan Donagan, Alan Gewirth and W. D. Ross. Let us begin our discussion, however, with the philosopher who is best known as a deontologist, Immanuel Kant (1724–1804).

Most of Kant's work on ethics is presented in *Groundwork for the Metaphysics of Morals* (1785), the *Critique of Practical Reason* (1788), and the *Metaphysics of Morals* (1797). In light of the woes of relativism, Kant wanted to make ethics akin to theoretical disciplines like physics and logic. If successful, Kant's ethics would share the objectivity and universality that these disciplines possess. Providing objectivity and universality is not always a matter merely of providing evidence to support a given judgment. To be sure, "evidence" is not always what makes scientists form consensus on scientific issues. Often times, it is the "nature" of science that leads to consensus in the scientific community. In science, and more so in logic, the issues discussed and reflected on do not impact humans personally and emotionally like the issues discussed and reflected on in ethics. It seems to be a truism that the more invested we are in an issue or the more we have to lose or gain given the truth of a matter, the more we become biased and myopic. This is certainly the case with the issues in ethics. Whether abortions are unethical or not, whether active voluntary euthanasia is ethical or not, and whether affirmative action is just or not, these issues impact those who reflect on them in a deep and personal way. There is the temptation for ethical inquirers to shift from *justifying* an act as ethical or unethical, to *wanting* an act to be ethical or unethical because of how such states of affairs would impact their lives.

The rare areas in science where this temptation also exists is where the ramifications of scientific judgments result in the affirmation or denial of beliefs we have on other subjects like nationalism, religion, politics, and race. We saw this when paleontology emerged as a science. Some European paleontologists eagerly searched for the remains of the earliest human fossils in Europe. Far be it from the truth, some paleontologists were steered by their zeal to find these fossil remains within their own nation or among their own race. Not to be undone, in 1948 Sir Fred Hoyle dismissed the Big Bang Theory because of the theory's theological ramifications. Historically speaking, the term Big Bang was coined by Hoyle. For Hoyle talk of a "Big Bang" (a finite and expanding universe) is "pure rubbish." Given this strong tug our passions can have on our discernment of truth, we can be free of this bias only if we abstract our passions from our decision making. For Kant this meant approaching ethics as a purely formal discipline where our ethical decisions were not motivated by circumstances and consequences in the actual world. Rather he believed ethics should be based on the very structure of reason itself and on the formal meaning of the words we use in our decision making process.

There are two main features of Kant's ethical theory. First, Kant held that actions are morally significant if they are done from the right intention. By right intention, Kant means doing something because it is one's duty to do so (viz., what Kant means by *acting from duty*). Here Kant points out that often we can do the right thing for the wrong reason (viz., what Kant means by *acting according to duty*). The moral agent should never do the right thing because of the positive consequences that her action produces for herself or others. She should do the right thing for the sake of doing the right thing. Later we will see that what Kant means by doing the right thing is doing what is in accord with formal rationality. Thus for Kant, right intention should not be confused with some emotional feeling about what course of action to take. The moral agent should feed the hungry not because of her emotional compassion but because feeding the hungry is right. A storeowner should return correct change to her customer not for the sake of having the customer return to purchase more items in the future; rather the storeowner should return correct change because it is right to do so.

The second main feature of Kant's theory is what he calls the categorical imperative, Kant's supreme principle of morality. When we act *from* duty, we are acting in such a way that our wills conform to the categorical imperative. Before we discuss the nature of Kant's categorical imperative, we need to discuss the nature of imperatives in general. For Kant, there are two kinds of imperatives, hypothetical and categorical. The imperative that is the basis of ethics is categorical. Kant's reason why the hypothetical imperative cannot be a basis for ethics is as follows. All imperatives are commands; they tell you what your duty is. All hypothetical imperatives, however, are conditional and exist in the form:

> If you desire/value X then do Y!

As such, they are binding only on those who desire or value X. For those who do not desire or value X, no such command follows. Now this is terribly disturbing since the command to act ethically now rests on whether the antecedent of the imperative holds true for everyone. Suppose X refers to "human life" and Y refers to "do not murder." If the antecedent concerning X is not true of you, then you have no duty not to murder. Kant was aware that rational beings very in their desires and values. Thus if hypothetical imperatives were the basis for ethics, then a form of ethical relativism would reign pending what one's desires and values are. Categorical imperatives, however, exist in the form:

> Do Y!

Who does or does not have a duty to do Y under this imperative is a misplaced question since the imperative is not entailed by an antecedent about what a given person does or does not desire or value.

Formulations of the Categorical Imperative

Kant offered several formulations of the Categorical Imperative. Let us consider two of them:

1. *Act so that we treat humanity, whether in your own person or in that of another, always as an end and never as a means only.*[8]
2. *Act only according to that maxim by which you can at the same time will that it should become a universal law.*[9]

The first formulation of the categorical imperative is based on the *respect for individual autonomy and the value of rational beings*. The second

---

8 Kant, *Foundations of the Metaphysics of Morals*, 47.
9. Ibid., 39.

formulation of the categorical imperative is based on logical consistency. Let us first consider how Kant develops a case for the first one.

A person's moral choices should consider the *autonomy* of other persons when such persons are affected by those choices. What is autonomy? This is a concept many people know all too well. For Kant, autonomy is the ability a person's will has to determine the moral law or ethics independent of constraints whether they be internal desires and impulses or forces external to the person. A person is neither free nor in control of her action if she lacks the ability to choose between her intended end and some other end under consideration. When a person is moved to act for some end by some impulse, desire, or external factor, then the person's will is not the cause of the action but the impulse, desire, or external factor that moves the will. Autonomy then is the ability of a person's will to intend for some end without constraint of any sort such that the will is ultimately moved freely by the person alone. Otherwise, the person intends according to the strongest desire or impulse. To be sure, it is not enough that the person's will to act is uncaused by desires and impulses, otherwise her action would simply be random. Rather her will is guided by some reason she self-selects upon reflection. Reason and freedom work together here to generate autonomy. Thus rational agents freely make choices or have preferences for what they consider to be good upon reflection in terms of what they want to do or want to happen to them. Since this is true of the very nature of persons (rational beings), Kant argued that any action a person takes towards another person should acquire the free consent of the other person being affected by the action. You will see this formulation of Kant's categorical imperative used in hospitals. Hospitals are required to obtain informed consent forms before surgeons perform any type of surgery on patients. The patients are not mere objects for experimentation and research. Failure to acquire informed consent is to treat the affected person as a mere object, i.e., to objectify the patient.

For Kant, persons are to be valued as both (1) ends and (2) intrinsically valuable beings. These two features can be overlooked since Kant only mentions explicitly talk of end in the categorical imperative. What does it mean to say persons are ends and possess intrinsic value? First, let's discuss Kant's notion of an end. He distinguishes between things that are ends and things that are means; and in order to talk about ends we need first talk about means. Things that are *means* are instrumentally valuable. They have value because they are a means to some other valuable thing.

That is, their value is always relational to the degree that their value is contingent on the existence of some other valued thing. For example, a dollar bill has *instrumental value*; it has value because it can acquire for us another valuable thing. It has value only because of its utility or what it can do for someone. Naturally then, things that have instrumental value acquire their value by being means to something that is valued for its own sake or what Kant called an *end*. Money is a means to an indefinite number of ends like a home, a car, or pleasure. However, to say something is an end only tells us that it is valued for its own sake and not for the sake of something else. Of course, knowing this feature of a thing tells us nothing about whether the thing's value depends on something else for its value. It is important to note here that Kant does not hold the view that ends exist independent of value givers. Value does not exist in the world as a mind independent reality; the value of some X (either as a means or as an end) requires a judgment that X is valuable as a means or valuable for its own sake. Thus the value of some X requires the *seeing that* X is valuable. Gold is valued for its own sake because value givers give it value for preferences they have. This leads us to talk of intrinsic value. To say that something has *intrinsic* value is to assert that the value depends on nothing else for its existence. Intrinsic value is not acquired or imputed. As such it is not circumstantial, conditional or relative. For Kant the only things that are intrinsically valuable are persons since they are necessary and sufficient for the value of all else. Persons are in the business of *seeing that* or *determining that* something is valuable to itself or, conversely, *seeing that* or *determining that* something is not valuable to herself. In short the rational person's capacity to ascribe value to things is what makes her intrinsically valuable. The capacity to see that or determine that something is valuable is the normative basis for autonomy in so far as persons ought to be able to live their lives based on what they freely value.

The value of a person cannot be overridden by the value of any non-person, e.g., a cat, a tree or a car. These latter things are not in the business of judging and ascribing value to things in the world (although a cat has desires for some end). However, one person's value can be overridden by another person's value.[10]

Let's look at an application of the categorical imperative. When a lie is told, the victim of a lie is stripped of her ability to self-determine her

---

10. This is not to hold that the value of a person is priceless. There are occasions when one person's life counts more than another person's life, e.g., the life of an elderly person who is near death and the life of a baby who has just begun life.

life since she is forced to respond to false information about her circumstances and objectified. Surely rape is also an instance of objectification, but it is often said that women who consent to sexual intercourse for profit are not being used as objects. While it is true that prostitutes freely consent to any number of sexual acts for a profit, Kant would still argue that women in these positions are objectified as objects since they are valued merely for their physical attributes and abilities:

> Sexual love makes of the loved person an Object of appetite: as soon as that appetite has been stilled, the person is cast aside as one casts aside a lemon which has been sucked dry.[11]

Only in the context of a monogamous married relationship is sex permissible; for only in this context, do the two parties come to a mutual agreement to accept the other person in that person's entirety, most of all the person's rationality. As a critique, Kant's position would seem to rule out many other bodily relationships since they too are based on physical features of a person, e.g., consenting to a game of tennis. Like a prostitute, the person is valued for his ability to play tennis. However, Kant would point out that the person's mental abilities are preconditions for the tennis match to take place and thus the whole person qua rational being is valued. Unfortunately for Kant, the same preconditions would not per se be absent in a sex act involving a prostitute. The argument could be made that a man who solicits sex from a prostitute could value her creativity and imagination in so far as such feats make the man feel more domineering or allow the man to descend more into his sexual fantasy. If anything, Kant's talk of treating others as ends is a necessary condition but not a sufficient condition for determining what is ethical.

In sum, the autonomy and intrinsic value of persons entail negatively that persons be treated not as *mere* objects (or as Kant puts it, as a means) unless they freely choose to be treated as such. Autonomy and intrinsic value entail positively that persons be treated such that actions affecting them take into consideration their freedom, preferences and desires (or as Kant puts it, sees her as an end). (So, again, lying is wrong for Kant because the person lied to does not get a chance to choose freely how to evaluate the real facts of the story he/she is told since he/she is given information not based in reality.) When a person is told "the building is on fire" when it is not, she is forced to leave the building for the sake of her life based on what she believes to be true. In this case, she does not

---

11. Kant, *Lectures on Ethics*, 163.

get the chance to choose how to act since she does not know what her real options are. Now supposed she was presented with the truth such that the building was not on fire. She may still leave the building, but at least in this case, she has a choice as to what she wants to do. Perhaps she leaves because she wants a change of scenery.

The second formulation of the Categorical Imperative captures Kant's concern that ethics should mirror mathematics' universality and logic's consistency. To reiterate, it states:

> Act only according to that maxim by which you can at the same time will that it should become a universal law.

Key words in this formulation of the categorical imperative are *maxim*, *will*, and *universal law*. Let's first look at the word maxim. For Kant, a maxim is any ethical rule or principle that a rational agent decides to live by. The nature and content of the maxim is broadly determined by the nature of the situation an agent is in as she contemplates what course of action to take. Ultimately each rational agent is free to decide for herself what maxim she will live by, but what maxim she has as a duty to follow or to avoid is determined by the categorical imperative. Kant does not define will and universal law in a technical way. The concept of "will" simply refers to wanting certain states of affairs to obtain and the concept of "universal law" refers to certain states of affairs being normative and applicable for every rational being. According to the categorical imperative, Kant holds that an agent ought not to act according to a maxim if it entails a logical contradiction or if it would be irrational to will into a law in light of its universal application.

Consider, for example, your contemplation of borrowing money from someone without the intent to repay the person. The maxim that guides your decision to do so would be something like the following: *whenever I am in need of money, I will borrow money and promise to repay it without the intent to do so*. Kant says that this maxim could never be made into a universal law; it contradicts itself. As a universal law, the maxim holds that everyone everywhere is allowed to make promises without keeping them. But in a world where people are free to make such promises, the instant the promises are made they self-destruct. For the notion of a promise requires that the promisee accepts the words of the promisor as true in order for the words to be declared a promise. When the promisee accepts the words of the promisor the words are then *defined* as a promise. So if there is a universal understanding that money borrowers never intend to pay back their borrowed money, then the promisee can never accept the words of the promisor as true. In other words, no one could ever make a promise because everyone knows that the promise will not be fulfilled. Now in this world where the above maxim is used, money can be transferred from one person to another, but on the basis of being nice not on the basis of a promise.

Consider a second example. Suppose you are returning to your car at a shopping mall car garage. Suddenly a person approaches you and asks if you can jump-start his car. You have jumper cables so you are physically capable of providing assistance. However, you decide to lie to the man in order to avoid inconvenience. Have you violated a duty in doing so? Kant would say yes. Let's see why. In this situation you acted according to the maxim: *let me live my life such that I am not inconvenienced by the needs of someone else*. According to Kant's categorical imperative the maxim does not self-destruct when made into a universal law, but you could never will that this maxim to become a universal law. As a rational being, you know that on some occasion you will need the assistance of someone else when your own efforts are inadequate. If the maxim were a universal law, then on that unfortunate occasion no one should help you out if they are inconvenienced.

Finally, consider one final example of the wrongness of an action based on its formal structure but this time with a critique. Affirming the Christian mores of his time, argues against suicide:

> A man reduced to despair by a series of misfortunes feels wearied of life, but is still so far in possession of his reason that he can ask himself whether it would not be contrary to his duty to himself to take his own life. Now he inquires whether the maxim of his action could become a universal law of nature. His maxim is: 'From self-love I adopt it as a principle to shorten my life when its longer duration is likely to bring more evil than satisfaction.' It is asked then simply whether this principle founded on self-love can become a universal law of nature. Now we see at once that a system of nature of which it should be a law to destroy life by means of the very feeling whose special nature it is to impel to the improvement of life would contradict itself and, therefore, could not exist as a system of nature; hence that maxim cannot possibly exist as a universal law of nature and, consequently, would be wholly inconsistent with the supreme principle of all duty.[12]

---

12. Kant, *Foundations of the Metaphysics of Morals*, 39–40.

Kant's objection to suicide is purely formal. Of course Kant's objection to suicide is warranted if in fact a contradiction ensues. But does he show this? He begins by affirming that there is only one maxim by which a person could commit suicide and it is based on the assumption that self-love entails self-preservation. Surly if this were the case, Kant would have a definitive case against suicide. Self-love so understood by Kant is the preserving of life but the goal of suicide is the termination of life; hence the contradiction. Pace Kant, the topic of suicide will not be taken up here, but it should be pointed out that the entailment Kant wants is contrived and invalid. Self-love is compatible not only with self-preservation but also, quality of life. As such, a proponent of suicide could argue that the maxim Kant challenges above is compatible with suicide for a person physically decaying from some disease.

Notice that in all the examples using the categorical imperative in the different formulations that we discussed so far, never was "duty" or what a rational person was obligated to do a matter of consequences. Rather duty and what a rational person is obligated to do were determined simply by an appeal to autonomy, logically impossible states of affairs and logical consistency. Having said this, it should be pointed out that the tool kit of deontology is couched in negative terms, viz., do not commit suicide, do not make false promises and do not objectify people. In other words, it provides guidance for what actions are wrong, but it is deficient in providing positive steps in deciding what actions are right.

Kant on Perfect and Imperfect Duties

Kant's call to act according to duty as opposed to consequences and interests is not as absolute as it may appear. While some duties to act are absolute and binding at all times and all places, Kant does not hold that all duties are obligatory in this way. He makes a distinction between what he calls perfect duties and imperfect duties. Perfect duties are the focus of much of his ethics and the only duties we have discussed so far. They are duties that are exceptionless, e.g., duties against murder, suicide and lying. (While it is less clear for lying, Kant holds that there does not exist a situation that allows for an exemption from these duties.) Imperfect duties are equally obligatory but the occasions to fulfill them are up to the persons who have them. Kant's classifies his two-fold division of duties into perfect duties to oneself, such as the prohibition against murder and suicide; perfect duties to others, such as the prohibition against false promises; imperfect duties to oneself, such as the obligation to perfect or develop one's talents and skills; and imperfect duties to others, such as performing acts of charity and compassion. As for these latter imperfect duties, Kant holds that the agents of these duties have freedom to choose the occasion and persons toward whom they have the duty. So these duties are obligatory towards humans, not towards any particular human.

Whether or not Kant was successful with his formal approach to ethics, his ethics had two substantial effects on Christian ethics. First, the categorical imperative allowed individual Christians to appeal to reason, rather than to the ethical dogmatism of either the Protestant or Catholic Church authorities. To be sure this gift of autonomy to the individual Christian was not intended to divorce Christianity from ethics, for Kant defended many of the mores of his Prussian religious background but with philosophical language and argument: prohibition against suicide; prohibition against prostitution; and a high regard for the value of human life where intrinsic value is the choice term rather than the *imago Dei*.

Utilitarianism

Utilitarianism is a very popular and efficient way to approach ethics. According to utilitarianism, what grounds ethical judgments and actions is a proper balance of their positive consequences over their negative consequences. Important philosophers who have argued for a utilitarian approach to ethics have been Jeremy Bentham, John Stuart Mill, Henry Sidgwick and J. J. C. Smart. Among these philosophers, British philosopher John Stuart Mill (1806–1873) has been selected to represent our discussion of utilitarianism.

Mill's presentation and defense of utilitarianism is found in his book, *Utilitarianism*.[13] For Mill, the principle thesis of utilitarianism holds that actions are right as they tend to promote happiness, wrong as they tend to produce the reverse of happiness. By happiness is intended pleasure, and the absence of pain; by unhappiness, pain and the privation of pleasure.[14]

For utilitarians in general, whichever action or rule *maximizes* utility over disutility is the right course of action or rule. By the same token, the right course of action or rule is the one that *minimizes* disutility over

13. Mill, "Utilitarianism," 260–81.
14. Ibid., 264.

other actions or rules. Mill goes on to specify that a person should choose the action or rule, in a given situation, that promotes the most known good for all those involved in the situation at hand. Thus, utilitarianism should not be confused with *ethical egoism*,[15] which holds that the right course of action is the action that best meets *only* your needs and interests. An often stated criticism of utilitarianism comes in the form of a straw man where utilitarianism is confused with ethical egoism. According to this straw man version of utilitarianism, "any act can be justified so long as a greater good is achieved in the end." This cursory account of utilitarianism neither reflects the spirit of utilitarianism nor the actual calculus of utilitarianism since it promotes the needs of the one over the needs over the many. Some Christians often opposed utilitarianism because utilitarianism is in conflict with an "absolutist" perspective of ethics. This absolutist perspective towards ethics considers ethics to consist of exceptionless principles (perhaps the 10 Commandments and other biblical prescriptions) that can be used exhaustively to address every ethical situation known to human kind. This perspective towards ethics goes under the guise as "biblical ethics." To be sure, this "biblical ethics" is foreign to the teachings of Jesus and more in line with the scribes and Pharisees of Jesus' day. Recall the *reductio ad absurdum* Jesus presented to the Pharisees in Luke 14:5? Christian scholars like William Paley also argued against holding the Bible to be a guide containing exceptionless principles for every situation under the sun.[16] Utilitarianism requires that we step into other peoples' shoes (i.e., their specific situation) and make an ethical decision based on some notion of achieving a collective greater good. In fact Mill holds that the "complete spirit of the ethics of utility" can be found in Jesus' declaration of the golden rule.[17] Specifically, a person should evaluate the foreseen utility (e.g., the physical

---

15. Ethical egoism should not be confused with psychological egoism. Psychological egoism is the thesis that humans in fact act only for their self-interest. This is Plato's argument in book 2 of *The Republic* where he talks about the invisible ring of Gyges. There Plato argues that, if any human wore invisible rings like Gyges's ring, both just and unjust men would act only for their self-interest because they know that whatever they do, none would see them do it. Both just and unjust men, among other things, would freely steal from the marketplace and sleep with any woman they chose. In response, psychological egoism does not fit with everyday experience. Often we do things for the sake of others.

16. For a detailed look at Christian scholars like William Paley, see Crimmins, *Utilitarians and Religion*, chaps. 1–6.

17. Mill, "Utilitarianism," 268.

and mental health of those affected and ultimately the sure happiness of those affected) gained by acting a certain way or following a specified rule and the disutility (e.g., physical and mental pain or pain) suffered from the same action or rule. Moreover, according to Mill, utility should be evaluated from a qualitative analysis of utility rather than a quantitative analysis of utility.[18] What Mill means is that some units of utility and disutility are more valuable or less valuable than other units of utility and disutility. Units of mental pleasure are more valuable than units of physical pleasure. In contrast to deontology, utilitarianism is what I call an external ethical theory in that ethics is concerned with the world and our actions in the world instead of our intentions, beliefs, and decision to act.

Again proponents of utilitarianism reject an "absolutist" approach to ethical decision making. They hold that no action is intrinsically right or wrong. This confession does not make utilitarians relativists. Utilitarians argue that an ethical approach to life that says "it is always right to do X" or "it is always wrong to do X" flies in the face of the complexity of life situations. Many life situations often force us to make decisions to do something that has both good and bad consequences. Contra the deontologists, we should reject the view that actions are right or wrong regardless of their consequences. Lying in general is wrong, but it may be right under given circumstances. According to Mill,

> [lying is right] when the withholding of some fact (as of information from a malefactor, or of bad news from a person dangerously ill) would save an individual (especially an individual other than oneself) from great and unmerited evil, and when the withholding can only be effected by denial.[19]

For example, Mill would agree that it is right for a missionary to be deceptive about his reason for being in a foreign country like Malaysia in order to further the Gospel. Surely a missionary operating under the disguise of "English teacher" in a country closed to the Gospel should say his only reason for being in that country is to teach English. He should not admit that he is ultimately there to spread the Gospel.[20] If Missionary Joe told Malaysian authorities what his main reason was for being in Malaysia, he

18. Mill's teacher, Jeremy Bentham, identified utility with pleasure, which is measured in terms of intensity, duration, certainty, propinquity, fecundity, purity, and extent.

19. Ibid., 275.

20. Barclay takes exception to this way of thinking. He believes that lying, except in absolutely necessary cases as in a just war, weakens a Christian witness. See Barclay's "Nature of Christian Morality," 45.

would not have the opportunity to further the Gospel. Or consider a missionary in a country that has just experienced a *coup d'e tat*, e.g., Rwanda. Suppose that missionary Joe is at home in the middle of a prayer meeting with Tutsi believers when Hutu militia knock on his door and ask whether he has Tutsi inside. Joe knows that Hutu militia systematically kill Tutsi and to admit the truth would result in the death of all the Tutsi women, men and children in his home. If missionary Joe were an absolutist about ethics as Kant was, he would hold the view that lying is always wrong and thus would admit that Tutsi are inside or refuse to answer the question. Either way, the Hutu soldiers would force their way in his home and kill everyone. From examples like this, the utilitarian argues that the way to maximize the most good in this situation is to lie and deny that Tutsi are inside. If our main ethical concern is the welfare of humanity, lying is the obvious course of action in this case. Many Christians are appalled by the thought that lying and deceit could be ethically permissible. But the examples just cited should curtail this negative attitude. If the biblical basis for this attitude is the 9th Commandment, it should be pointed out that the 9th Commandment actually is against giving false witness against another person, particularly in a court of law. Moreover, the writer of the book of Joshua in chapter 2 condones lying on some occasions (viz., in the case of Rahab lying on behalf of the spies in Jericho) and in Exodus 1:15-21 God blessed midwives Shiphrah and Puah for lying to the Pharaoh of Egypt. Rahab is later mentioned in chapter 11 of the book of Hebrews as a person of faith. From what we know from the biblical text, all that we know about Rahab is that she was a prostitute and lied to save the Israelite spies. Clearly she is not in the Hall of Faith for the former reason. Finally, if a case can be made that Christians should condemn lying and deceit without exception, then many practices that are common among Christians should be abolished: deceit used to arrange a surprise birthday party, telling children that Santa Claus exists, covering for a spouse who does not want to answer the telephone and pulling out of a weekly commitment that you no longer find interesting with the excuse that you suddenly became too busy or that God is calling you to do something else.

Rule Utilitarianism versus Act Utilitarianism

Even if utilitarians are right that consequences having top priority in ethical decision making, it is not at all clear what consequences are at issue. Some utilitarians hold that ethical decisions should be made after reflecting on the consequences that affect everyone in the situation you are facing. This view is called *act utilitarianism*. This view needs little discussion since it has been the form of utilitarianism we have referred to in our examples so far. Essentially it says the right action is the action that maximizes the most utility over disutility (or minimizes disutility when utility cannot be maximized) for everyone in the situation you are facing. Of course the wrong action is the action that does not maximize utility or minimizes disutility.

Other utilitarians hold that ethical decisions should be made after reflecting on the consequences of following each of the rules that prescribe ways of acting in your situation. This latter view is called *rule utilitarianism*.[21] Rule utilitarianism asks us to look beyond the consequences that may result from the situation we are in. Essentially it says that the right action is the action that follows the rule maximizing the most utility over other rules. Of course the wrong action is the action that does not follow the rule that maximizes the most utility. When the rule utilitarian speaks about a rule maximizing utility she is referring to the utility produced if everyone followed the rule. In short, it asks, "what if everyone in my situation followed this rule or way of acting"?

Consider a situation where a college student earned a D in a course he took during his last semester at his university. While the student will graduate, his GPA has dropped to 2.3 as a result of the D. It should also be added that the student applied for an entry-level job at a corporation during his last semester and the corporation's hiring personnel wants to hire the student if his GPA is at least 3.5. The student quickly brings the situation before the professor who assigned the D. The student pleads with the professor to change the grade to at least a B in order to get the job. The student explains that the job would provide quite a bit of income, more than he is making at his present job. Moreover, with the increased income, he can better provide for his wife and two sons. As the student ends his plea he tells the professor, "if it's any comfort, I won't tell anyone about the changed grade if you were to change it." As an act utilitarian the professor should change the grade because the B would produce more utility for all those affected by the professor's action, viz., the student and his family. Of course there may be disutility involved in this decision in terms of the guilt the professor may experience. As a result, it could be

---

21. Utilitarians like Bentham and Sidgwick are classified as act utilitarians. Matters are not that clear with Mill; however, many classify Mill as a rule utilitarian.

argued that an ethically better course of action is to offer the student extra credit to justify the changed grade. However, even here, the professor's guilt remains since other students in the class were not offered the same option for a better grade.

As a rule utilitarian, the professor should not make a decision based on the specifics of the situation; rather he should make a decision based on the rule that maximizes the most utility when followed by society or people in general. Basically the professor is faced with making one of the following choices: leave the grade as is or change the grade to at least a B. If the professor left the grade as it is, he is acting according to the rule that says *award grades based on merit*. If the professor changed the grade to at least a B, he is acting according to the rule that says *award grades based on need*.[22] If everyone in the professor's position (viz., other professors) followed the first rule then a lot of disutility would be avoided. Employers would not have to waste time investigating the academic records of potential employees to ensure that extreme grade inflation did not occur. The employer would not have to contact each of the potential employees' professors and ask, "look . . . we want to hire John Doe here at Acme Inc., because among other things he has a 3.7 GPA. But we want to know whether his transcript really reflects what he knows. Did you give him an A because of a personal issue he presented to you?" Moreover, if the first rule were followed students would be motivated to work hard for excellent grades, resulting in potentially excellent employees or productive members of society. As you can see, the first rule saves time and money. The second rule however produces a lot of disutilty if every professor followed it. Giving grades based on need would result in a decrease in motivation among students for excellent grades. They know that when personal matters become an issue, they can always rely on their professor to give them at least a B for the course. Unlike what happens with the other rule, employers would waste a lot of time and money to make sure they are hiring a competent person. Thus the professor in our example should follow the first rule and the leave the grade as it is.

Why is a distinction made between rule utilitarianism and act utilitarianism? One important reason has to do with problems noted with act utilitarianism. Opponents of act utilitarians have pointed out that act utilitarianism is sometimes incompatible with our moral intuitions about justice, human rights and the sanctity of life. Consider the

---

22. The number of rules considered for a given situation depends on how many rules could apply to the situation.

following example concerning the issue of justice. Suppose you are a sheriff of a small town where a woman has recently been raped. There is deep racism in this town. The majority group Y is racists towards the minority group X. The female victim was a member of X and witnesses of the crime say that the rapist was a male member of Y. Unless the rapist is found, members of X have publicly threatened to attack and possibly kill male members of Y as a means of retaliation. You have not found the perpetrator, but if you convict one innocent member of Y for the crime, you can head off the violence against several male members of Y. As an act utilitarian, what do you do? Obviously you would maximize utility for all those affected by your decision. In this case, punishing one innocent person is the choice to make. While utility is not maximized for the innocent person punished, it is for the rest of the male members of group Y. The utility of the many outweigh the disutility of the one. By punishing the one innocent male member of group Y, many other male members of group Y will not be attacked. Naturally this course of action is a tragedy of justice for the innocent person.

Or consider the problem utilitarianism has with human rights. Suppose you love to take showers with your bathroom window open. Unknown to you, your neighbor finds you attractive and one day saw you get in and out of your shower. Your neighbor is sexually aroused by viewing you and has found it enjoyable to view you naked like this on other occasions. It would seem that you would have serious reservations about him viewing you under such conditions. Nevertheless, the act utilitarian would see no problem with your neighbor viewing you naked because you are not physically or emotionally harmed. No disutility occurs. Nevertheless, your right to shower privately is being violated. So the act utilitarian has no clear way to protect your right to privacy.

Finally consider the problem utilitarianism has with protecting an individual innocent human life. Suppose you are a doctor working in the ER of a small country hospital that is miles away from any major city development. You have 5 needy patients, all of whom are in danger of dying unless you get suitable organs for them within the next 5 hours. One needs a heart, two need kidneys, one needs a lung and another needs a liver. A young man is rushed into the ER because he is losing lots of blood from a stabbed wound to his chest. It turns out that the lab results of a blood test performed on the young man indicate he is a perfect donor match for the five patients. Do you decide to forgo treatment for him because by letting him die and using his organs, you can save the other five patients? The act utilitarian says yes. Again, the needs of the many outweigh the needs of the one. Surely justification of this sort flies in the face of the sanctity of innocent human life.

These cheesy examples are supposed to show that act utilitarianism is problematic and unable to protect justice, rights and the life of innocent human persons. Rule utilitarianism is offered to avoid these problems. The rule utilitarian would argue that the sheriff should not follow the rule "convict the innocent person for the sake of saving more lives." If all sheriffs did this (viz., follow a rule that stems from this action), there would be no towns since no one would join a town to risk losing their right to a fair trial and justice in general. The rule utilitarian would say that any rule that allowed "Peeping Tom acts" would discourage anyone to take showers with their window open. But this leads to much disutility in that many shower takers in society who enjoy taking private showers with the bathroom window open must now do so with the window closed. The rule utilitarian would also argue that following the rule "the lives of the many outweigh the life of the one in a hospital" would lead to the closing down of hospitals since no one would enter a hospital knowing that he/she may not come out alive. However, act utilitarians like J. J. C. Smart rebut that what is ethically correct does not necessarily have to agree with our moral intuitions:

> Admittedly utilitarianism does have consequences that are incompatible with the common moral consciousness, but I intended to take the view "so much the worse for the common moral consciousness." That is, I was inclined to reject the common methodology of testing general ethical principles by seeing how they square with our feelings in particular instances.[23]

Whether you agree with Smart's point or not, it must be pointed out that our moral intuitions are sometimes biased by cultural and emotional factors. Consider our treatment of animals. While most humans are omnivores, we are selective as to which animals are ethically off limits for consumption. In some parts of Asia, for example, dogs are eaten, but as Americans we find the killing and eating of a dog difficult to swallow (no pun intended). Part of the difference between Asian and American attitudes toward dogs has to do with their feelings about dogs as opposed to the value of the dogs themselves. As Americans, we may say that dogs are too cute to kill. Now killing dogs may be wrong, but it has little to do

---

23. Smart, *Utilitarianism*, 68.

with how we feel about them and how cute they are. In the real world, sometimes what ought to be done or what is permissible is ugly and causes negative visceral responses. In his defense of act utilitarianism, Smart does more than pass intuitions about the correctness of common moral consciousness in a broad sense. In light of the examples of the sheriff, the peeping tom and the doctor cited against act utilitarianism, Smart's rejection of common moral consciousness is specifically, among other things, a rejection of justice, rights and the sanctity of individual human life. So if it is a matter of passing intuitions about whether notions like justice, rights and the sanctity of innocent human life trump the universal application of act utilitarianism, many ethicists side against Smart.

Nevertheless, it is an open question whether utilitarianism qua rule utilitarianism actually explains how justice, rights and the sanctity of innocent human life can be championed in specific cases merely by the maximization of utility. Rule utilitarianism can only tell us how justice, rights and the sanctity of innocent human life can be protected when the issue concerns the ethical rightness of policies and rules. In essence, rule utilitarianism and act utilitarianism are asking different questions and are concerned with different issues. If this is true, then they cannot be compared to each other in terms of their usefulness. Rule utilitarianism is concerned with providing the ethical principle that is best to adopt in so far as guiding ethical behavior in general or universally. It is not concerned with the overall utility of a particular action but with the utility of the particular action when it is done by people in general or society at large. Therefore, if this much is true, rule utilitarianism is not an improvement over act utilitarianism; it is a theory that addresses an altogether different normative issue. Consider the following two questions: (1) Should privately owned companies terminate sales persons who are marginally successful at selling the company's product and (2) Should Acme, a privately owned company, terminate a sales person who is marginally successful at selling the company's product? Notice these questions are addressing two different issues. The former is best addressed by rule utilitarianism and the latter is best addressed by act utilitarianism. The former question is concerned with the utility that results when most or many companies make the same decision to terminate or not terminate their marginal sales persons. The latter question is concerned with the utility that results when a particular company does or does not terminate a sales person. Rule utilitarianism would argue that termination of the salesperson is in order since privately owned companies would go out of business if *most* or *all* of them employed a marginal sales person rather than hiring a more competent sales person to replace these individuals. Act utilitarianism would argue that the right course of action depends on the specific circumstances surrounding the individual salesperson at the particular company. Is this salesperson a single parent and responsible for the livelihood of her children? Will it be difficult for the salesperson to land another job within six months or less? Is the company making profit gains such that the salesperson's contribution to the company is negligible? As the owner of the privately owned company you don't have shareholders that require you to fulfill a fiduciary responsibility to generate profit. So ultimately the decision is yours to make based on the overall utility for the company and the salesperson. So the right thing to do can vary for each individual company and sales person.

To return to the issue of protecting justice, rights and the sanctity of life, neither act not rule utilitarianism can do so. But as pointed out earlier, other theories like deontology have their shortcomings too. For example, deontology is useful in providing categorical and consistent grounds for what not to do, viz., what reason in abstraction forbids. It is also a useful theory in that it provides a basis for the intrinsic value of rational beings. However, it is not useful as a theory (the version Kant advocates) to provide guidance in terms of what positive actions we ought to take when an ethical situation is not merely "black and white" but more gray. Pace Kant, making a distinction between perfect and imperfect duties is not sufficient to account for every ethical situation, given some ethical situations seem to require exception from certain duties Kant classifies as perfect. According to Kant, a woman should not abort her unborn if it is a person because it has intrinsic value, but what should she do when the unborn person's growth threatens her own life to the degree that neither she nor the unborn person will live? Other perfect duties also seem suspect unless exceptions are made, e.g., categorically telling the truth. This tension between deontology and utilitarianism leads us to another ethical position that is a hybrid between these two theories. A middle position in normative ethics

W. D. Ross and *Prima Facie* Duties: Between Deontology and Utilitarianism

During the early part of the twentieth century a noted philosopher, W. D. Ross, proposed a middle position between utilitarianism and the classical deontology of Kant. In *The Right and the Good*,[24] Ross presents a perspective of ethics that criticizes utilitarianism for seeing ethics as a matter of consequences and Kant's deontology for its rigidity in holding that the command of an ethical principle is absolute or categorical. As a deontologist, Ross continues to use talk of duty but the duties we have as members of the moral community are *prima facie* rather than absolute. Contra Kant, Ross is a pluralist rather than a monist about the foundation of ethical principles. Where Kant couched ethics in the categorical imperative, Ross coaches ethics in a series of *prima facie* duties. Again a *prima facie* duty is a duty that is binding, other things equal, unless it is overridden by another duty or duties of greater ethical worth in a given situation. Ross lists at least seven such duties:

1. Fidelity. A duty to keep promises, to be honest, and to be truthful.
2. Reparation. A duty to repay wrong done to another.
3. Gratitude. We should be grateful to others when they perform actions that benefit us and we should try to return the favor.
4. Justice. We should try to be fair and try to distribute benefits and burdens equably and evenly.
5. Self-improvement. We should strive to improve our own health, wisdom, security, happiness, and well-being.
6. Beneficence. We should be kind to others and to try to improve their health, wisdom, security, happiness, and well-being.
7. Non-maleficence. We should refrain from harming others either physically or psychologically.

Because these duties are *prima facie*, they are not categorical duties in themselves, for there are occasions where they conflict with each other. The specifics of a given ethical situation would determine which *prima facie* duty is also categorical or actual in a given situation. As a deontologist, Ross is aware that ethical situations often involves conflict. Occasions to

---

24. See Ross, *The Right and the Good*, in *Ethics*, 362–79.

champion the value of "truth-telling," for example, are not always void of other values. Often such situations are often in conflict with beneficence or non-maleficence. The person who argues that lying is the ethically right thing to do when telling the truth would lead to the death of an innocent person is not championing lying simpliciter but is championing perhaps an unstated value, e.g., beneficence. So the actual debate for any given moral agent in this situation, according to Ross, is not about the virtue of truth-telling and lying but about the virtue of truth-telling verses beneficence. The moral agent's ability to make ethical sound judgments is due to what Ross calls intuition. Intuition tells us what the *prima facie* duties themselves are and which *prima facie* duty has priority over another *prima facie* duty when they are in conflict. To be sure, Ross is not advocating some early eighteenth-century "moral sense" theory like that of Francis Hutcheson, Lord Shaftsbury, Francis Hutcheson, or even that of Thomas Reid. For Ross we intuit ethical truths like we do mathematical truths only in the sense that such knowledge is not inferential or mediate. Our intuiting is a matter of previous experience and reflection of ethical matters. From a contemporary perspective, Ross offers a practical approach to ethics for anyone committed to deontology.

Normative Ethical Principles

Often times an ethical situation is so clearly understood in terms of what is expected as the normative responsive action, that a commitment to a robust ethical theory is not required to discern what to do. Equally so, a lack of wholesale commitment to a particular normative ethical theory does not entail a rejection of the entire normative ethical theory under consideration. People often speak of acting out of respect for someone without referencing deontology; and people speak of relieving the suffering of another person without referencing utilitarianism. With this in mind, the concern to make the right choice in acting may simply require an ethical principle rather than an entire theory. To be sure normative ethical theories are either the composite of various ethical principles or the justification of some ethical principle(s). Ethical principles (or values) are often commensurate with more than one normative ethical theory. The following is a list of some essential and frequently used ethical principles:

1. The Principle of Nonmaleficence

This is a principle of negation; it tells us what we should not do in itself. *Negatively*, a person has a *prima facie* duty not to harm self and others (physically, psychologically, spiritually and emotionally). Nonmaleficence not only includes a duty against harming someone but also against taking a risk that may lead to harm. This is perhaps the most essential ethical principle of any ethical principle and the reason is quite obvious if not self-evident. All things considered, there is never a justifiable reason to harm another human being or any living being as an end in itself. Across the board every normative ethical theory holds this. This is one of several sine qua non principles of ethics for those in the medical profession. Nonmaleficence, in conjunction with beneficence, is the foundation of the Hippocratic Oath.

2. The Principle of Autonomy

This principle is equally important as non-maleficence. There are very few occasions where autonomy is not to be respected. Nearly every ethical theorist has valued and argued for autonomy as essential to ethics. Most notable of these ethicists are Kant and Mill. Autonomy means self-ruled and is derived from the Greek word for self (autos) and rule (nomos). The essence of autonomy in terms of its use in ethics carries the sense of being one's own person in so far as each person ought to control the final and free determination of their well-being. The obvious antithesis of autonomy is slavery or objectification of a person or her will. Mill was concerned with and placed importance on the autonomy of the person in so far as he believed a person ought to be able to act or think as she pleases in every sense conceivable short of harming self or others, e.g., expressing her human rights. As stated earlier, Kant was concerned with and placed importance on the autonomy of the will of a person in so far as the person's will being the final determinant element for an ethical judgment. In either case, the expression of any given person's autonomy requires that others respect that person's autonomy. Autonomy is diametrically opposed to the idea that a person's culture or community determines her goals and life pursuits. In many cultures around the world, females are not respected to the degree that their human rights are violated; some lack opportunities to education and others are forced to live in an arranged marriage. Let's consider the practice of arranged marriages. There are about 60 million arranged marriages globally where the bride is under the age of 18 years as of 2015: in South Asia there are about 31 million arranged marriages, in sub-Saharan Africa there are 14 million arranged marriages, and in Latin America and the Caribbean there are 6.6 million arranged marriages. These teenage girls are married off to a much older man without their consent in any sense.

Often the rationale is that the girl's family, and father in particular, no longer needs to be liable for her. They no longer have to worry about the girl's welfare once she has been put in the financial care of her arranged husband. Nevertheless, whatever justification is offered, the young girl is not consulted and her autonomy is not respected, particularly when she is opposed to the arrangement. Often times, and in direct opposition to a concern about their welfare, these girls are impregnated by their husbands while their young bodies are unable to manage the pregnancy. As a result the young girls die along with their unborn. The lesson here in this example and in general about autonomy is that unless a person is expressing and exercising her autonomy against or in disregard to another person's autonomy, autonomy should be championed as a universal value over against any religion, culture, or ideology in general.

Respect for autonomy provides the lexical foundation for the following ethical principles: honesty, confidentiality, fidelity, and privacy. *Honesty* is the measure of how much truth a person reveals to another person. It is not equivalent to truth but presupposes truth. It follows then that a person can be fully truthful without being fully honest. An employee who tells her manager she took an hour lunch with someone would not be fully honest if she did not say that the lunch was also for an interview for another job. Full honesty is not per se obligatory since it could lead to restrictions on the autonomy of the person who is interested in pursuing her self-interest. If the employee were fully honest she would not be able to exercise her autonomy to seek a job change.

Confidentiality is the opposite of honesty where revealing is not the goal but concealing is. Confidentiality is a contractual matter because it arises only after there is a mutual consent of autonomy between two parties where one agrees to reveal some information and the other one promises to conceal it. By profession, a therapist is obligated qua therapist to *prima facie* conceal information concerning her client. The lack of confidentiality prevents a person from seeking psychological help.

Fidelity is the commitment to a promise of some sort. It is commonly understood in the context of marriage where the married partners agreed to be romantically and sexually monogamous but the meaning of fidelity extends far beyond this context. Confidentiality is an instance of fidelity in so far as a person agrees to conceal certain information. Fidelity includes other acts of allegiance to someone or to something. In so far as fidelity is an allegiance to some other person, it allows the other person to express her autonomy in so far as the other person is able to live out her role in the relationship. Lack of fidelity, therefore, is betrayal of the understood roles that both parties mutually agreed to and disrespects the wishes and autonomy of the one betrayed.

While there is no consensus as to the scope of *privacy*, it is primarily concerned with a person's control of the accessibility others have to her personal information, personal space, personal property, and personal choices. So while there is agreement a person has a right to privacy to her property, there is no consensus as to what denotes a person's property, e.g., a fetus or embryo. There is no debate that privacy extends to personal information, but there is debate as to when privacy to personal information should be suspended, e.g., surveillance of a person's social media and phone calls for the sake of national security.

3. The Principle of Beneficence

This is a principle of *Positive action*. *Positively*, a person has a *prima facie* duty to promote the well-being of self and others, and negatively to prevent harm in self and others (emotionally, psychologically, spiritually and physically). As Beauchamp and Childress put it: "the principle of beneficence asserts the duty to help others further their important and legitimate interests . . . confer benefits and actively to prevent and remove harms . . . [and to] balance possible goods against the possible harms of an action."[25] The acts of helping the needy by providing food and shelter count as instances of beneficence. It may appear that such acts require little reflection in terms of whether they should be done. Utilitarians, particularly Mill, developed various calculus matrices to show the best way beneficence can be maximized for the greatest good. Deontologists promote beneficence as well, but not from a position of personal interest or sympathy. The motive for beneficence comes from a duty of reason.[26] However, according

---

25. Beauchamp and Childress, *Principles of Biomedical Ethics*, 148–49.

26. Kant's presents a deontological perspective of beneficence. See Kant's *Doctrine of Virtue*, 115–22.

to Kant, the duty to beneficence is imperfect and thus no person has a particular duty of beneficence towards any particular other person. It can be argued, consequently, that it is unclear how far beneficence extends. For example, a logical consequence of beneficence could place an unrealistic demand on utilitarianism in practice. Motivated by beneficence a person may be required to sell most of his possessions in order to provide for the livelihood of some poor family. That is, the needs of the many outweigh the needs of the one. Given the impractical nature of this appeal to beneficence, it could be argued that no one has an obligation to do beneficent actions but should do so only as a supererogatory act. Bernard Gert takes this supererogatory stance towards beneficence. Gert limits obligations to the avoidance of harm. With the entire world as the context, Gert holds, all things considered, that each person has a duty to non-maleficence towards every person in the world she encounters. Conversely, he adds, each person cannot possibly have a duty to beneficence towards every person in the world she encounters. Gert's words are a hard pill to swallow, particularly for those who work in health care. Beneficence is another sine qua non principle of ethics for those in the medical profession. Pace Gert, he sees beneficence as a duty but only from a contractual, professional context. But if physicians and nurses have a duty to promote the well-being of patients, so why don't others in society have the same duty?

Peter Singer has argued that beneficence is obligatory only in the sense that persons have a duty to prevent harm as opposed to promoting some maximization of good, which is a distinct duty from non-maleficence. Some have argued that Singer's claim is a bit unrealistic. Giving away one's life savings to help starving people in Third World countries or to risk one's life to save a person drowning when your own swimming skills are deficient is unjustly taxing. Beauchamp and Childress take a more realistic stance on the obligatoriness of beneficence. They present the following necessary conditions for a beneficent duty:

> (1) Y is at risk of significant loss or damage, (2) X's action is needed to prevent this loss, (3) X's action would probably prevent it, (4) X's action would not present significant risk to X, and (5) the benefit that Y will probably gain outweighs any harms that X is likely to suffer.[27]

Beachamp and Childress give an example of such a situation that meets these conditions. A psychiatrist at no risk to herself has a duty of

27. Beachamp and Childress, *Principles of Biomedical Ethics*, 153.

beneficence to protect society against threats of harm that her patient expresses towards particular individuals.

4. The of Double Effect Principle

This principle is a hallmark feature of natural law theory. Thomas Aquinas developed the double effect principle in the *Summa Theologica* (II-II, Question 64, Article 7). It is a good principle to appeal to when faced with some action you know to be good but has obvious bad consequences. It asserts that a good action that produces a bad effect should be done only if the following conditions obtain: (a) the action is good in itself, apart from its consequences; (b) the bad effect cannot be avoided if the good action is to occur; (c) the bad effect is not a means to the good action; and (d) the consequences of the good action outweigh the consequences of the bad effect.[28] The 4 elements of the double effect principle are not arranged in order of importance, but all 4 conditions must be met for any good actions to be permissible that necessarily has a bad consequence attached to it.

This principle has been used to address a number of social and bioethical conundrums. On the topic of abortion, the double effect principle allows a pro-life advocate to regard an abortion as a bad act but yet permissible or obligatory, to produce for some good act of saving a mother's life in cases like a cancerous uterus or an ectopic pregnancy. The double effect principle, however, cannot be used to protect the mother's life if the abortion is intended, e.g., a rare procedure called fetal craniotomy. Of course if the fetus' head is not crushed both the fetus and mother will die, but the principle of double effect cannot provide justification for this procedure.

5. The Universalizability Principle

This last principal is Kantian in nature and is perhaps the most important principle in ethics; however, it is applicable to any normative ethical theory since it is purely formal in nature. Whether you take a deontological position, a utilitarian position or some other normative ethical position, this principle says that your moral judgments must be universal.

---

28. For a discussion of the principle of double effect, see Alison Hills, "Defending Double Effect, 133–52.

But in what way must they be universal? There are at least 2 possible ways a judgment could be universal: a) *Universal in its acceptance* or b) *universally in its application*. (a) concerns anthropological issues. Here we would simply visit all cultures and societies around the world and discover whether murder, rape and child abuse are *universally accepted* as immoral. However, moral judgments do not require this kind of universalizability. For if everyone in the world thought otherwise, murder, incest and child abuse would still be wrong. To be sure, ethical judgments require the universalizability of (b), where the application of consistency and objectivity are the issues. In other words, moral judgments presuppose the universalizability principle.[29] Harry Gensler has devoted much attention to the universalizability principle and formulates a positive and negative version of it in the following dictims:

> Positive formulation of the Universalizability Principle
>
> If TYPE A actions ought to be done or are permissible, then there is some universal set of circumstances F that make TYPE A actions right such that (1) TYPE A actions have F and (2) whenever an agent falls under F type circumstances he is obligated to do a TYPE A action.

And

> Negative formulation of the Universalizability Principle
>
> If TYPE A actions ought not to be done, then there is some universal set of circumstances F that make TYPE A actions wrong such that (1) TYPE A actions have F and (2) whenever an agent falls under F type circumstances he is obligated not to do a TYPE A action.

The universalizability principle holds even for hypothetical cases. The *Universalizability Principle* is similar to Leibniz's Law or *the indiscernibility of identicals*:

$$(x)(y)((x = y) \supset (P)(Px \supset Py))$$

According to Leibniz's Law, if it can be shown that what is on the left side of the '=' is equivalent (whether in fact or in theory) to what is on the right side, then there is no reason for treating what is on the left side differently from what is on the right side. That is, if x and y are identically

---

29. For further discussion of the universalizability principle, see Hare, *Freedom and Reason*, 7-50, 86-224.

constituted, then whatever is true of x is *ipso facto* true of y. What makes x and y equivalent are the properties they share. This is not an empirical truth; it is a formal matter of logic. This distribution of properties is the essence of the Universalizability Principle.[30] The Universalizability Principle does not determine what actions are morally right or wrong; it merely states what *logically* follows from any given judgment a person may make. In short it requires a person to "practice what he preaches."

Let us supposed that Hitler made a decree to have all Jews in Europe exterminated and it read: "Everyone who is Jewish ought to be exterminated." Now a decree like this is definitely immoral and unjust. What does the universalizability principle say about this decree? In terms of its moral permissibility, it says nothing. All that the universalizibility principle can say is that Hitler should be consistent. So, for example, if Hitler's physicians later told him a blood test indicated that he was 10 percent Jewish, then Hitler ought to be exterminated, given his *Jewishness*. For Hitler to exempt himself from the decree is for him to act inconsistent with his own normative belief system concerning Jews. If Hitler's response is that he is different from other Jews in light of his position as Fuhrer, he should still be exterminated. Hitler's leadership status could save him only if his original decree was: "Everyone who is a Jew in non-government positions in Germany ought to be exterminated."

Let us apply the universalizability principle to some very polemic topics. Consider the following judgment a person could make concerning abortion: *"A woman has a right to abort her unborn on demand"*! If someone made this judgment, then what logically follows from their judgment retrospectively is that their mother could have aborted him/her for the same reason. "What is good for the goose is good for the gander." It does not matter what reason, if any, the person's mother would have had for the abortion, she could have had one. If the person who made the judgment is a male, then his mother could have aborted him if, counter to fact, it were the case that she wanted a girl baby. The issue is not whether a mother has a moral or legal right to do such a thing. The issue is that such a choice is appropriate given the initial judgment that a mother has a right to abort on demand. Suppose a person made a contrary judgment about abortion to the previous one: *"The unborn has a right to life even if it has abnormal prenatal development problems"*! This judgment might not be too difficult

---

30. This principle is derived from Kant's ethical theory. According to another formulation of Kant's categorical imperative, "Act only on that maxim whereby you can at the same time will that it should become a universal law."

for the person to make if he or she were not expecting a child. But suppose the same person who made this judgment later discovers that he or she will be a parent. It logically follows that if that person's unborn had Down's syndrome, autism or any other abnormality, then that person must allow the unborn to be born. The necessity of the unborn's birth is an entailment of the person's judgment. If the person, upon discovery of their unborn's abnormality, decided to abort their unborn, then that person is acting inconsistently with their own judgment.

Consider one more example using the universalizability principle on the topic of the death penalty. Let us suppose the following judgment is made: *"The death penalty ought to be used when a person is convicted of a capital crime"!* What logically follows for the person who made this judgment is that their love ones should be executed if anyone of them is convicted of a capital crime. Moreover, the person who made the judgment should say, "Let me be executed if I am convicted of a capital crime!" To say or believe anything other than what logically follows from the initial judgment is to act inconsistent to the Universalizability Principle. Finally, suppose someone made the following judgment: *"The death penalty ought not to be used when a person is convicted of a capital crime"!* What logically follows from the person's judgment is that no matter how horrible a criminal's crime is, he should never receive the death penalty. Therefore given this person's judgment, for example, the case of two white racist men in Texas, who dragged a black man from the back of their pickup truck until his body was embedded into the road, ought not to receive the death penalty. This judgment logically follows from the person's judgment.

Rights

Much is made of talk of rights, such that ethical matters can be solved and discussed from the context of a person's right(s). In Thomas Jefferson's preamble to the Declaration of Independence, he speaks of civil liberties or what are also known as civil rights:

> We hold these truths to be self-evident, that all men are created equal, that they are endowed by their Creator with certain unalienable Rights, that among these are Life, Liberty and the pursuit of Happiness.

A contemporary reading of Jefferson's words would read as follows:

> We hold these truths to be obvious in themselves, that all humans are created equal, that they are born with certain rights that God granted to them, that among these are the right to live, right to autonomy and the right to pursue whatever they deem is good in life.

The first right that Jefferson speaks of is our right to life. Jefferson intends this right to involve protection from external harm from others, e.g., right from being murdered. The second right is essentially a reference to the various freedoms we have to express our autonomy in action, e.g., to be free to express our political or religious views or to be free to swim in a public swimming pool. The third right is an extension of the second right; it is our right to freely choice our own values and what we deem is good in life. Sadly Jefferson's intended audience or, to put it a different way, his reference to "all men" were white males. When Jefferson wrote the preamble in 1776, the colonies contained approximately 2.5 million people, with 500,000 of them slaves. However, taken in its literal, normative sense, the preamble refers to all humanity. In his *I Have A Dream* speech Martin Luther King referenced Jefferson and argued that African Americans have yet to realize the instantiation of these rights in their lives.

The Structure Types of Rights

The next order of business is to look at what rights are and their form. In general, rights are entitlements to be free to or free from some actions or states of affairs. These entitlements in either direction always require at least two persons, even if indirectly.[31] Nicholas Wolterstorff calls rights "normative social relationships" or "normative bonds between oneself and the other."[32] As an entitlement, a right entails that at least two persons are bonded (including even a bond of non-interference), whether welcomed or desired, by some action (or inaction) or state of affairs. In the field of rights talk, the standard classification of rights rests on an analysis of rights formulated by W. N. Hohfeld. Hohfeld formu-

---

31. If a person has a right to pick up and own a rock she discovers on an island and is not previously owned by any person B, then the rest of the world (person B and all other persons) have a duty or are bound not to interfere with person A's ownership of the rock.

32. Wolterstorff, *Justice: Rights and Wrong*, 4.

lated four categories of rights: liberty rights,[33] claim rights, power rights, and immunity rights.[34]

Rights qua liberties are rights person A has to some X (whether X is some action, inaction or state of affairs) where person A has no duty against some X. Not having a duty against some X can be couched in terms of the harm principle, such that a person is free to do whatever she wants so long as there are no other actual persons she has a duty not to harm by her action. Not having a duty against some X can also be couched in terms of there being no other person having the same entitlement. A person has the liberty to express herself in various ways so long as no one is harmed by the expression. The liberty to practice Christianity, read a book, or apply for a job at the post office are examples of rights qua liberties.

Rights qua claims are rights person A has for some X where at the same time person B has a duty to ensure that X obtains. Whereas liberties do not per se involve particular other persons, right claims do. Right claims are relational, requiring of some other person to do or not do something. Right claims entail a duty on the part of some other person to respect the right claim.[35] Rights of this sort are vast and extend from broad right claims at one end of the spectrum humans qua humans have toward each other, to right claims in the middle that humans have qua citizens which are called civil rights, to finally specific right claims at the other end existing in contractual private relationships, say, between employees and employers, and merchant and customer. There is no consensus as to what should be included on the list of right claims, either on a broad level of rights for all humans, on the level of citizenship, or even on a specific level of rights humans have in defined private relationships. Nevertheless, let us take a closer look at the three areas of the rights claim spectrum just outlined: human rights, civil rights, and private contractual rights.

To reiterate, right claims qua human rights are right claims all humans are entitled to in virtue of being a human being. This is at least what rights claims are connoted to be when described as human rights. The *universality* of human right claims is what essentially makes them distinct from civil rights, which we will later see are rights unique to and defined by a specified constitution of a given country. Both human rights and civil rights exact a duty on the part of governments to respect a given

33. Some writers use the term privilege instead of liberty.
34. Hohfeld, *Fundamental Legal Conceptions*, 35–64.
35. See also Feinberg, "The Nature and Value of Rights," 61–74.

right claim; however, with human rights, their correlative duties apply to all countries. It is important to point out here that human rights can include liberties. So while a person has a liberty right to breath air and to exist, she is entitled to hold her government to a duty to protect her right to this liberty. The universal, international recognition of human rights came about after the WWII. Prior to this time in many countries, if a citizen charged her country with a crime against her, she could not bring the charges before the judicial authorities of her country. However, this appeal to domestic judicial authorities is problematic.

First, the judicial authorities may be in cahoots with the part of government guilty of human right violations. Secondly, there may be nothing formally stated in the country's judicial system that recognizes the crime as a violation of a human right. The success of an Allied resistance and deployment of force against the crimes of Germany Nazism led to the call for an international tribunal. The result of this call was the formation of the United Nations in 1945. The UN describes itself as having four basic goals: (1) To keep peace throughout the world, (2) To develop friendly relations among nations, (3) To help nations work together to improve the lives of poor people, to conquer hunger, disease and illiteracy, and to encourage respect for each other's rights and freedoms; and (4) To be a centre for harmonizing the actions of nations to achieve these goals. A significant achievement of the UN is the *Universal Declaration of Human Rights* (1948). This document, in part listed various rights citizens of the world have and the correlative duties that all governments have towards its citizens.

These duties required all governments to protect the following rights classified as human rights: *equality rights* for all citizens such that they are treated with equal value and not discriminated against in terms of race, place of origin, language, sex, etc.; *security of personhood rights* for all citizens such that they are protected against slavery, murder, torture or cruelty, etc.; *due process rights* for all citizens such that they are not arbitrarily arrested, imprisoned without trial, and have access to a public trail; *liberty rights* as discussed above for all citizens that include right to privacy, right to certain freedoms like freedom of thought, self-expression, association, assembly, and movement; *political rights* for all citizens such that they have freedom to express political ideology and to participate in their country's political life by voting, being elected and serving in office, and assembling and protesting for some political end; and *social security rights* for all citizens that include rights to such social goods as education, employment, favorable wages, and protection against starvation; and finally *rest and leisure rights* for all citizens such that they are afforded rights to limited work hours and holidays with pay. While these human rights are understood to apply to all humans, unfortunately not all nations acknowledge them. Certain dictatorships and theocratic forms of government are instances where human rights are not acknowledged and protected.

Not all agree that the United Nation's charter is the final authority on human rights. Among the human right claims acknowledged by the United Nations, talk of social security or welfare rights has polarized thinkers along political persuasions. Advocates like Henry Shue argue that welfare rights or what he calls subsistence rights are not privileges but, as stated, rights for all humans. Shue says,

> By . . . subsistence, I mean unpolluted air, unpolluted water, adequate clothing, adequate shelter, and minimal preventive public health care . . . [The] basic idea is to have available for consumption what is needed for a decent chance at a reasonably healthy and active life or more or less normal length, barring tragic interventions.[36]

Surely libertarian advocates would disagree with Shue et al. For libertarians, any list of human rights and duties humans have towards each other must be minimal and include only rights classified as negative such that any corresponding duty is one of inaction or a duty to guarantee no interference of the negative human rights. On this short list would be a right against murder and theft while the corresponding duties would include the duty to protect innocent humans and the duty of non-interference. For libertarians the state exists as a necessary evil to ensure these rights. One particular positive right that libertarians champion is a right to property and the fruits of one's labor. Their justification for this right can be traced back to John Locke.[37] An obvious insight into this polarization of what is and is not a human right is that a person's political ideology shapes their view of what is on the list of human rights.

---

36. Shue, *Basic Rights: Subsistence, Affluence, and U.S. Foreign Policy*, 23.

37. Locke claimed that material items can be classified as property when we put our labor into the specified item, with the proviso that there exists no duty against owning the item in lieu of someone else possessing it. Supposedly, by working on some item we put ourselves into the item. See Locke, *The Second Treatises of Government*, 16–30.

Civil rights, as stated earlier, are very similar to human rights but are subjected, in terms of what they are, to the written words and interpretation of a country's constitution. Civil rights specifically refer to any rights that are required to ensure that every citizen of a country is equally entitled to all the rights that any other citizen of that country can claim as a right. Thus, civil rights take on the form of rights protecting against various forms of discrimination, e.g., racial, sexual, gender, religious, and disability oriented. Much has been made of civil rights talk in recent United States history due in large part to failure of African Americans living out the literal words of Jefferson's notion of "life, liberty and the pursuit of happiness." Since the civil rights movement in the 1960s, when the focus was on racial discrimination, talk of civil rights has expanded to concerns about discrimination against physical disabilities, gender, and sexual orientation. Without civil rights, such groups would not be guaranteed access to social and economic goods. With that said, the United States does not acknowledge economic equality per se as a civil right simpliciter. Only when economic inequality is attributed to discrimination of race, physical disabilities, gender, and sexual orientation is economic equality a question of civil rights.

At the other end of right claims are right claims pertaining to specific, private relationships that can exist among humans. Generally the nature of these private relationships is based on the transference of a good or service (e.g., wages, labor, information, education, counseling, merchandise, etc.); or it can be based on the transference of a penalty for some evil (e.g., lack of performance, violation of terms or of another person's right, etc.). Let's take a look at right claims existing in such relationships.

Right claims in these private relationships are just as important as any broad right claims. For example, without them employers and merchants could exploit, discriminate against, and violate employees and consumers. (For a description of these types of right claims, I will hereafter use employees/customers or employers/merchants as my examples.) To be sure, however, right claims are also had by employers and merchants, requiring employees and customers to honor their duty to them, e.g. to do the work they are paid to do or to write valid checks. Since the type of right-duty relationship that employee/customer and employer/merchant have involves the exchange of or agreement to something (e.g., labor, wages, merchandise, services, or penalties), right claims for employees/customers and employers/merchants necessarily involve a form of justice or what may be called equality. The equality here is not a matter of identity but of sameness. Equality so understood has historically had both a formal and proportional sense.

The formal sense of equality refers to the treatment individuals receive when they are similar in most relevant respects or what Aristotle affirms: "equals should be treated equally and unequals unequally" (*Nicomachean Ethics* 5.3. 1131a10–b15). This sense of equality is called formal because the ways in which two persons are being evaluated as equal is irrelevant. When two persons are similar in most regards (except in insignificant ways like eye color or skin color)[38] then whatever treatment or consideration one receives the other should equally receive it. The informal or proportional sense of equality is tied to or grounded in a particular concrete good (e.g., labor, wages, merchandise and services), evil, or penalty and its exchange from one person to another (Aristotle, *Nicomachean Ethics*, 1130b–1132b). What are considered "equal" are the proportions of the transferred items. That is, the exchange of a good, evil, or penalty for some other good, evil, or penalty is considered equal when they are proportionate to each other. The equality of the proportions is determined either by their quantity or quality. Let's take a look at right claims employees and employers are entitled to from the context of equality.

As employees/customers or employers/merchants, one type of right claims humans have are *procedural rights*. The possession of procedural rights requires that employees/customers or employers/merchants have equal and impartial access to procedures involving work situations, opportunities and treatment. So employees should have a right to due process involving hiring, termination, advancement, etc., and such rights should equally apply to all employees and potential employees. Hiring by means of nepotism would thus be ruled a violation of a person's procedural rights in publically owned companies and organizations. Procedural rights entail certain duties, particularly for employers. So, an employer has a duty not to terminate an employee without due process of an investigation by the human resource department regarding the charges against the employee, e.g., whether the evidence warrants that the employee is actually guilty of sexual harassment. To be sure employers have procedural rights as well. For example, an employer has a right to know in advance when a given employee is planning to resign. Usually

---

38. Even here, it can be argued that skin color can be justification for treating two persons differently when race or the skin color in a specific context produces some greater good.

the stipulated time frame is a two-weeks' notice. This equally entails that employees have a duty to notify their employers at least two weeks in advance before resigning. There are good reasons for this particular right. Employers need adequate time to find a replacement for the labor or services rendered by the employee.

Compensatory rights are a second type of rights claim that particularly applies to customers and employees. In so far as employees are concerned, these rights refer to just treatment when an employee is a victim of harm in the work environment. Again, justice is associated with this right in that it matters how much in terms of quantity and quality the evil (in this case harm) and the transferred good (in this case money or some other material payment for harm). When a male personal trainer sexually harasses a female sales person at a health club, the sales person is entitled some good. However, since justice qua equality is associated with compensatory rights, the quality and quantity of the sexual harassment determines the quality and quantity of the transferred good to her. The quality of physical sexual harassment (e.g., a touch or caress of her body) is qualitatively worse than that of verbal sexual harassment (e.g., a sexually loaded comment directed at her). The quantity of the sexual harassment would make matters worse if the trainer was guilty of it on more than one occasion. As far as the good transferred to her because of the sexual harassment, it must be proportionate to the quantity and quantity of the sexual harassment. Similarly, customers have a right to a refund or voucher when a product or service does not meet its stated promise. When a passenger's flight is canceled, the airline has failed to do what it promised in terms of flight arrival time. As compensation, the airline considers what good could be exchanged for their failure that would equal the harm to the passenger for arriving a day late. A free night stay in a hotel and a travel voucher are sometimes considered adequate exchanges when it is not caused by natural causes like storms.

A third type of rights claim employees/customers or employers/merchants are entitled to is a *contractual right*. These rights, and their corresponding duties, exist only when both parties freely enter into their contractual relationship. The content of the contractual rights and duties depends on the originator of the formal relationship and perhaps on formal notions of justice, sustenance, and well-being. Usually the originators of the relationship are employers, merchants, or some authoritative organization like the Occupational Safety and Health Administration. In the particular case of OSHA, it establishes the contractual rights and duties for the relationships that exist between other parties, e.g., relationships between hospital staff and patients or relationships between employees and employers. Contractual rights are not *per se* ethically normative but are normative and binding only because the parties of the relationship agree to be in the relationship and to the terms of the relationship. Obviously, if either party decides not to enter the relationship, then the rights and duties are void. The power of these rights and duties are granted by the autonomy of both parties. When a corporation hires an employee, the employee is told what rights and duties she does and does not have qua employee and what rights and duties the corporation does and does not have. Some of these rights are a matter of professionalism and cost-benefits; others are human rights since they are a matter of justice, sustenance, and well-being and are established and enforced by government authorities like the United States Department of Labor, e.g., rights against disability discrimination and a right to safety in the work environment. Some of these rights are established by the corporation itself, e.g., the right employers have to prohibit employees' access to the Internet, rights employers have to determine dress attire, the right the employer has to expect a specified amount of labor from its workers in exchange for wages, and the right the employer has to determine worker wages. Conversely corporations also determine what duties employees have, particularly duties against their rights qua liberties, e.g., duty not to wear blue jeans, a duty not to make private phone calls during work hours, a duty not to pray during work hours, and a duty to work the entire shift as opposed to leaving work early to catch a matinee movie. Organizations that provide health services like hospitals specialize in rights of justice, sustenance, and well-being. Through legislation, hospitals are required to provide patients with written documentation of their rights. When a person decides to receive services from a health organization, she contractually enters into the position of a patient. As such she is entitled to such rights as the right to courtesy and respectful treatment, right to information about treatment,[39] right to refuse care,[40] and right to confidentiality and personal privacy.[41] However, health organizations are

---

39. Here patients have a right to information concerning their diagnosis, treatment, alternatives, risks, and prognosis.

40. The prerequisite for a patient to have this right is mental competency.

41. The right to confidentiality includes the patient's right to refuse the release of their medical records to anyone outside the healthcare organization. Personal privacy rights often include the patient's right to every consideration of their privacy in regards

not limited to contractual rights of justice, sustenance, and well-being. They also participate in rights involving professionalism. For example, if a nurse wears her arm tattoo so that it is exposed to her patients, she has done no wrong in the act itself; she has a right to express herself. However, if the hospital she works for contractually stipulates no exposed tattoos, she is duty bound to forgo the exposure to the patients when she agrees to her employment contract.

Hohfeld refers to the last two rights as "secondary rules." They entitle a person to nullify a "primary rule" or primary right or to prevent a nullification of a "primary rule" or primary right. Rights qua power are rights a person A has to bring about change in a person B's claim rights, liberty rights, or even power rights (whether person B is one's self or another person). The power rights of person A essentially nullify the autonomy and a primary right of person B. Power rights are similar to claims rights in that they have correlative duties. The main difference is that the existence of a power right's duty is based on the authority of the right's possessor whereas the existence of a claim right's duty is based on the mutual consent of the parties or on some normative principle of human dignity or well-being. A police officer has the power right to nullify a person B's right to drive when the officer turns on his car's flashing lights. A psychiatrist has the power to hospitalize a person suffering bipolar disorder despite the person's delusional desire to commit suicide. A sergeant can nullify a captain's power right to command if the captain, for example, is guilty of human abuses or becomes incapacitated.

Finally rights qua immunities are rights person A has against person B when person B attempts to bring about some change X to person A. Converse to power rights, an immunity right nullifies a person with a power right to exercise the power over her. Moreover, they are the opposite of claim rights. Examples of immunity rights are human rights not to do some X. By contrast, human rights qua claim rights give a person freedom to do some X. A person has a claim right to vote and an immunity right to forgo voting for the incumbent President if the President attempted to force the person to vote for him/her. A private religious university has an immunity right to not hire atheist faculty if the state or federal government attempted to force it to hire an atheist.

---

to cultural, religious, and psychological well-being.

Justification and Function of Rights Talk

The justification of rights talk has much of its historical origins in the deontology of Kant. This is easily seen in Kant's focus on duty and its relationship to individual autonomy. However, rights talk is not per se limited to deontology. John Locke speaks of rights to life, liberty, and property.[42] Even prior to Kant and Locke, rights talk existed in the Middle Ages in Aquinas' development of Natural Law Theory in his talk of natural inclinations to flourish and the normative context in which natural laws exist. In fact, the argument can be made that rights talk can ultimately be traced back to the Latin term *jus gentium* (literally law of nations), a term that refers to Roman natural law (rather than Roman civil law) that stipulated just treatment to certain limited goods to non-Roman and Roman alike, particularly during times of war. The Romans adopted this notion from Greek stoic philosophy, which held that above any civil law of humanity existed a law for all humans and known by reason.

At any rate, in most rights talk discourse, the focus is on protecting and maintaining items that are either good in themselves or items that are deemed good by the subjective assessment of the individual who claims them. Goods of the former sort are good in an objective sense and have value independent of anyone's assessment of their value, e.g., an education or the preservation of life itself. Goods of the latter sort are goods minimally because an individual seeks them for her well-being, with the proviso that the obtainment or pursuit of such goods do not conflict with the rights and well-being of other persons. This distinction between objective and subjective goods leads to different viewpoints among ethical theorists concerning the function of rights in the first place.

On the issue concerning the function of rights, there are two common approaches to this concern: (1) the "interests theory" approach and (2) the "will theory" approach. According to interest (or well-being) theory the function of rights is to be conduits for expressing a person's interests. The nature of the interests is immaterial and inconsequential. The interest theorist is concerned rather with protecting a person's opportunity to fulfill her interests. Consider John Stuart Mill's concern about protecting individual interests: In *On Liberty*, Mill claims:

> [The] . . . only purpose for which power can be rightfully exercised over any member of a civilized community, against his

---

42. Locke, *The Second Treatise of Government*, 4–40.

> will, is to prevent harm to others. His own good, either physical or moral, is not a sufficient warrant. He cannot rightfully be compelled to do or forbear because it will be better for him to do so, because it will make him happier, because, in the opinions of others, to do so would be wise, or even right. These are good reasons for remonstrating with him, or reasoning with him, or persuading him, or entreating him, but not for compelling him, or visiting him with any evil, in case he does otherwise.[43]

To be sure interest theorists are not championing the deontological grounds for autonomy. For them, a protected autonomy is the means to which a person's interests can be maximized. For Mill, a person's autonomy, no matter how uninformed, should not be constrained or nullified by some greater good for that person (provided the welfare of others is not an issue). The Jehovah Witness who refuses a blood transfusion would be a paradigm case for Mill of a person who has a right to self-govern her life even at the cost of dying for an ill-formed religious reason. So for Mill the value of expressing and acting to fulfill an interest far exceeds the value of the interest's content.

But are all interests created equal and are all things that have interests, things that have rights? Surely jellyfish and ants have interests (e.g., to survive). Asking such questions brings to the forefront the ethical status of animals and whether they have rights on the interest theory model. Interest theorists would point out the capacity for interests is not sufficient for having rights. What is missing is the awareness of such interests and this awareness capacity requires minimally sentience and at most self-awareness. As Jeremy Bentham asserts:

> The day may come when the rest of the animal creation may acquire those rights which never could have been withholden from them but by the hand of tyranny. The French have already discovered that the blackness of the skin is no reason why a human being should be abandoned without redress to the caprice of a tormentor. It may one day come to be recognized that the number of the legs, the villosity of the skin, or the termination of the os sacrum, are reasons equally insufficient for abandoning a sensitive being to the same fate. What else is it that should trace the insuperable line? Is it the faculty of reason, or perhaps the faculty of discourse? But a full-grown horse or dog is beyond comparison a more rational, as well as a more conversable animal, than an infant of a day, or a week, or even a month,

43. Mill, "On Liberty," 135.

old. But suppose they were otherwise, what would it avail? The question is not, Can they *reason*? nor, Can they *talk*? but, Can they *suffer*?[44]

For Bentham and contemporary interest theorists like Peter Singer, a prerequisite for rights is at minimal, sentience. To be sure, the more interests something is aware of, the more rights it has. Since a pig has no interest in voting or even an awareness of what voting is, a pig obviously cannot have a right to vote. But as Singer argues, every sentient being (viz., non-human animals) should have a right for equal consideration of its interests, even if particular interests are more important than others.[45] Singer's Principle of Equal Consideration asserts: "we give equal weight in our moral deliberations to the like interests of all those affected by our actions."[46] He presents a *reductio ad absurdum* and argues that if we attempt to extend unequal consideration to the interests of animals because animals lack rationality, we will be forced to give unequal consideration to the interests of different human beings who are marginal cases and not equal to rational adult humans in terms of their interests, e.g., infants or adults who suffer from autonomy deficits like schizophrenia, Alzheimer's disease, or a coma.

Critics of interest theory point out that rights and interests are not per se normatively related. They claim a right can exist without an interest on the part of its owner and an interest can exist without a right. Suppose a professor has a romantic interest in one of his students, this hardly counts as an appropriate use of his power right to fail the student unless the student agrees to go on a date with the professor. Still yet, the concept of a person using her rights to act altruistically makes no sense when couched in an interest theory framework since rights here on this theory function to safeguard some self-interest of the person. Besides Mill, other interest theorists include Mill's mentor Jeremy Bentham and David Lyons.

According to will (or choice) theory the purpose of rights is to put a rational being in the position to exercise her autonomy in a purposeful way in the world over against or without interference from other rational beings. Talk of exercising autonomy here is not understood without normative parameters. Rather the context of autonomy is limiting to

---

44. Bentham, *Introduction to the Principles of Morals and Legislation*, 283.
45. Singer, *Practical Ethics*, 55–82.
46. Ibid., 21.

the degree that each rational being can equally express her autonomy without being objectified or positioned to be unfree. Surely if one person's autonomy is unconstrained then her actions toward other persons could on some occasions limit their autonomy and objectify them. To be autonomous, a person must be free to do as she pleases, but just as important for a will theorist, a person must be guaranteed control over what others may and may not do to her. Rights function to ensure this latter issue; that is, rights allow rational, autonomous beings to function as autonomous beings. Classified as a will theorist, Kant held the view that there is only one right humans possess by birth, "Freedom (independence from being constrained by another's choice), insofar as it can coexist with the freedom of every other in accordance with a universal law (6:237)."[47] The freedom that the will theorist endorses extends to the degree that persons have autonomy to relinquish a right on a given occasion, if they so choose. Other will theorists include H. L. A. Hart and Alan Gewirth.[48]

As a critique of the will theory, critics point out that some rights are beyond the control of our autonomy such that we have no control over our possession or use of them. For example, it is a strange state of affairs that a person can relinquish her right to be a free person as opposed to a slave or to be tortured. Equally problematic for will theorists is the intuition that all sentient beings have rights even if they cannot exert or possess autonomy. If this intuition is correct, will theorists cannot afford rights to marginal cases mentioned earlier (e.g., infants). Equally excluded from the possession of rights are non-humans like pigs, apes, and cows if the function of rights is to express purposeful autonomy. There are no reasons to think that any non-human animal has an understanding of a right (or even an awareness of its correlative duty if it exists) in order for it to use it, thus apparently nullifying the function of rights on the will theory model for non-human animals. Deontological animal rights theorists who employ the will theory would take exception to this criticism. According to deontologist Tom Regan, the basis of a living being's right to life is its being a subject-of-a-life. Regan outlines what he considers are the capacities of a subject-of-a-life. It will:

---

47. Kant, *The Metaphysics of Morals*, 30.
48. See Hart, "Are There Any Natural Rights?," 175–91; Gewirth, *Human Rights*, 11, 13.

have beliefs and desires; perception, memory, and a sense of the future, including their own future; an emotional life together with feelings of pleasure and pain; preference- and welfare-interests; the ability to initiate action in pursuit of their desires and goals; a psychological identity over time; and an individual welfare in the sense that their experiential life fares well or ill for them, logically independently of their utility for others, and logically independently of their being the object of anyone else's interests.[49]

What is wrong with animal experimentation and killing animals for meat isn't per se the pain and suffering, but the treatment of them as our resources (i.e., merely as our means). Regan emphatically makes the point that animals are deserving of rights as much as humans since they are also autonomous. He says, "It is highly unlikely that any animal is autonomous in the Kantian sense . . . But the Kantian sense of autonomy is not the only one. An alternative view is that individuals are autonomous if they have preferences and have the ability to initiate action with a view to satisfying them."[50] Regan calls this *preference* autonomy. It does not require the Kantian notion to will into law some universal maxim where the welfare of others is considered because they are seen as an end. It is, however, consistent with Kant's notion that autonomy requires the ability to make free, self-determining decisions. Fido, the dog, often makes decisions based on a preference he has for table food over his typical dog food. Fido's preference is intelligible only if he has memory of *himself* liking table food from a previous encounter with table food. Regan argues that in light of these subject-of-a-life features that Fido and other animals have, these features are sufficient for being autonomous. They do, after all, require self-awareness and freedom to choose, conditions Kant does require for being autonomous. Regan does not include all animals as subjects of a life but surely he includes mammals.

Justification of Rights

There is no consensus on the function of rights. In light of the criticisms posed to both the interest theory and will theory, the debate continues. There is equally no consensus on the justification of rights in terms of why they should be honored. Typically there are three positions taken

---

49. Regan, *The Case For Animal Rights*, 243.
50. Ibid., 84–85.

on the justification of rights: the natural rights theory, utilitarianism, and contractarianism views.

The natural rights theory appeals essentially to the cognitive features of a person: rationality, autonomy, self-determination to act on one's own preferences and ends. Here "natural" is taken to mean something intrinsic to the person. Some natural rights theorists present a deontological justification of rights. Accordingly, a person's rights have value and a person is in a normative position to exercise her rights because she is a self-determining being with ends she wants to pursue. Thus rights have value because they allow humans to pursue items they deem as valuable. Since persons are intrinsically valuable, so too are persons' rights. The value of rights on this view is the typical Kantian argument. The categorical defense of rights over their violability for some greater good perhaps was put best by Robert Nozick in the preface of *Anarchy, State, and Utopia*:

> Individuals have rights, and there are things no person or group may do to them (without violating their rights). So strong and far reaching are these rights that they raise the question of what, if anything, the state and its officials may do. How much room do individual rights leave for the state?[51]

Coming at natural law theory from a Thomistic perspective, John Finnis holds that there are certain intrinsic goods in life: life itself, acquiring knowledge, play, aesthetic experiences, sociability and friendship, practical reasonableness, and religion. Our ability to seek them as is what gives us value and the rights we have to pursue them.[52]

In stark contrast to a natural rights' justification of the value of rights is a consequentialist view of justification. According to proponents of a consequentialist view, rights have extrinsic value in so far as they produce or sustain a group or societal good. The group or societal good can be cashed out in utilitarian terms such that rights are valued because they maximize social utility, or even in egalitarian terms such that rights are valued because they ensure that the interests of everyone in society are equally considered.

A third view of the justification of rights values rights not because they are intrinsic features of human nature or because of the benefits of their consequences. Rather on this view, the value of rights is merely an entailment from agreements made between persons or by a person

---

51. Nozick, *Anarchy, State, and Utopia*, ix.
52. Finnis, *Natural Law and Natural Rights*, 198–230.

reasoning in abstraction. In a way, contractarian justification has its roots in deontology. A prominent proponent of this view is John Rawls. In *A Theory of Justice,* Rawls asserts that the best conception of a just society is one in which the rules governing that society are rules that would be chosen by self-interested rational individuals behind a veil of ignorance. The veil of ignorance is an epistemic tool Rawls appeals to in order to derive a notion of justice and co-extensive rights of a just society. Under this hypothetical veil, in what Rawls calls the "original position," individuals do not know any actual details about themselves in the real world, such as their sex, age, race, class, intelligence, abilities, etc. However, these individuals do know general facts about human society, such as facts about psychology, economics, human motivation, etc. From this state of awareness or "original position," self-interested rational individuals would choose the following two principles of justice:

> First Principle: Each person has the same indefeasible claim to a fully adequate scheme of equal basic liberties, which scheme is compatible with the same scheme of liberties for all;
>
> Second Principle: Social and economic inequalities are to satisfy two conditions:
>
> a. They are to be attached to offices and positions open to all under conditions of *fair equality of opportunity*;
>
> b. They are to be to the greatest benefit of the least-advantaged members of society (the *difference principle*).

The two principles are in lexical order such that the former principal guarantees liberties for all before inequalities of goods, offices and positions are allowed. From these two principles of justice Rawls lists the following rights a rational person would select under the veil:

- To powers of offices and positions of responsibility
- To income and wealth
- To self-respect
- To freedom of thought
- To freedom of conscience to religion, politics, and ethics
- To freedom of speech and the press, and freedom of assembly.
- To freedom of association
- To freedom from slavery

To be sure, it is not the intrinsic nature of these rights that give them their value; it is the mere fact that self-interested rational persons would choose them under the veil.[53] Rawls classifies these rights as ones championed by those in a liberal democracy.

Contractarianism has not received as much criticism as natural rights and consequentialism views on rights. Nevertheless, it has its critics. First, since contractarianism takes a formal approach towards rights, it does not afford rights a place in reality beyond our agreement to commit to them out of self-interest. Accordingly, then, contractarians are motivated out of self-interest rather than out of a compassionate concern for others. The motive for acknowledging rights is strictly non-moral. The expectation and hope for contractarianism to provide justification for rights for ethically normative reasons is just not there.[54] Secondly, for contractarians, rights don't exist outside of a contractual context; that is, individuals don't have inalienable rights prior to a mutual social existence. This ontological stance towards rights leaves contractarians in a difficult position to defend the rights, if there are any, for infants and mentally deficient adults. Their justification of a right has led some to argue that under Rawls' veil of ignorance, Rawls' notion of rights and justice would not protect non-human animals. Since under the veil, the contractors begin with the assumption they are self-interested "rational human beings," they forgo considerations and concerns for animals simply for self-interest sake. However, Rawls anticipates this charge against him and notes the distinction between morality and justice. There are duties of ethics and duties of justice. Rawls clarifies that just because animals cannot enter into a contractual relationship with persons does not entail that no ethical duties exist for their well-being. To be sure, Rawls acknowledges that animals are sentient beings and, for utilitarian reasons, rational beings are obligated to minimize their pain. Thus the ethical duty of non-maleficence comes from ethics, not justice.[55]

---

53. See Rawls, *A Theory of Justice*, 11–22, 60–65, 150–56.

54. See Sayre-McCord, "Deception and Reasons to Be Moral," 113–22; and Gauthier, *Morals By Agreement*, 221–22.

55. See Abey, "Rawlsian Resources for Animal Ethics," 1–22.

Applying Normative Ethical Theories and Principles

As stated, no normative ethical theory stands out as comprehensive to guide us in making ethical judgments for every ethical situation. Each has its value, in specific cases, in guiding us to make correct ethical judgments. As a rule, then, I suggest the following for decision making. I will call the approaches Plan A and Plan B.

Plan A

First, from the virtues of obedience and loyalty, as Christians we should do and believe what the Bible explicitly commands us to do and believe. From the virtues of obedience and loyalty, we should refrain from doing and believing what the Bible explicitly commands us to refrain from doing and believing. Secondly, we should seek ways to glorify God by advancing his righteous, just and benevolent character in our actions and attitudes toward humanity and nature. Thirdly, we should see humanity and nature as intrinsically valuable and seek ways to correct damage to humanity and nature. The nature of Plan A is to provide a prescription for an action rather than to provide justification for the rightness or wrongness of an action. The issue of whether or not God actually makes an action right of wrong will be taken on in chapter 5. Nevertheless, when ethical justification is your concern and when the Scriptures are silent on prescription or prohibition of an action, shift to Plan B.

Plan B

First gather all the facts concerning the ethical issue you are dealing with. This "fact gathering" involves questions of who is involved, what happened, and what the context is. (Facts like age, gender, race, diagnosis, prognosis, and culture of the involved parties of the matter are important.)

Second, consider whether you are determining the ethical nature of an action, practice or policy. Then enumerate and elucidate the various solutions, positions, practices or policies that are possible. Make sure you accurately describe the positions, practices and policies when you elucidate them. Thus, if euthanasia is a policy you are considering, are you referring to active or passive euthanasia? What is the issue that euthanasia is trying to address? What are alternative options that address the same issue? If you are addressing the ethical status of the death penalty, are you concerned with it in so far as it is practiced in the United States or are you concerned with it as a just concept for retribution? If a specific situation is your concern, then enumerate the various possible courses of action you can take in light of the situation. Whether you are concerned with solutions, positions, practices, policies or situations, at this stage you are not evaluating the ethical viability of the various options; you are simply enumerating them.

At the third stage of Plan B, you are to evaluate the various options you proposed. Here you evaluate each option in the following two ways: (1) for each option determine whether it *violated* any normative ethical principles and (2) for each option determine whether it *affirmed* any normative ethical principles. As a review, here is a list of the principles discussed in this chapter:

Principles of deontology

1. Autonomy/along with the duty to respect it
2. Fidelity: honoring your promise; follow through with your commitment, loyalty
3. Human, civil, and contractual rights: procedural, meritorious, contractual, substantive, compensatory rights
4. Universalizability principle
5. Privacy: Not being interfered with; or power to exclude
6. Confidentiality: self-imposed access to personal information
7. Honesty: be truthful
8. Dignity of humanity: Treat humans as nonexpendable; without a price tag

Principles of utilitarianism

1. Principle of greater good
2. Principle of lesser of two evils

Natural Law principles

1. Principle of double effect
2. Principle of forfeiture (discussed in a later chapter)

Generic principles

1. Benevolence: Do good, remove harm, and prevent harm
2. Nonmaleficence: Avoid the intent to initiate harm

The fourth stage is prone to much subjectivity because it is at the fourth stage that a choice is made for one of the options. There are no "meta rules" how this choice is made since it involves an appeal to various normative ethical principles and your preference for any given principle. If only two options were on the table and one affirmed beneficence and the utilitarian principle of a greater good while the other affirmed honesty and a contractual right to confidentiality, then there is no non-question begging meta rule that obligates the selection of one option over the other. Nevertheless, the choice made is objective in the sense that it is not based merely on personal preferences but on objective ethical principles that are preferred.

Virtue Ethics

Our final normative theory is a departure from the previous theories. Those who advocate virtue ethics emphasize motives and character as opposed to actions and decision making. An ethic of virtue centers on the claim that an agent's "being is prior to his doing." The logic behind this theory is that a virtuous person will do what is morally right because she/he is a virtuous person. One of the first Western proponents of this view toward ethics was the philosopher Aristotle (384–322 BC). In the *Nichomachean Ethics*, Aristotle says, "Every art and every investigation, and likewise every practical pursuit or undertaking, seems to aim at some good: hence it has been well said that the Good is That at which all things aim."[56] This end or good is what Aristotle referred to as ευδαιμονια (which can be translated as "happiness" but a better and more objective sense of what he meant is "flourishing").

---

56. Aristotle, *Nichomachean Ethics* 1094a (ed. Allen, 308).

In the background of Aristotle's view of ευδαιμονια is his commitment to *essentialism* concerning human nature and living organisms in general. All living things, in virtue of their life force or what Aristotle called their soul (ψυχὴ), have a proper function. The function of a living being varies according to the nature of its soul. Aristotle rejected the notion that God is the efficient cause of naturally existing things, since for him the universe is eternal. He did, nevertheless, maintain that living things have a purposeful essence determined by the type of soul it has just like a square has an essence[57] of being a four-sided figure. When living things behave and function well according to their natural essence they flourish. The better they function according to their nature the more they flourish. It is here that virtues enter Aristotle's view of *eudaimonia*. Virtues, or what Aristotle called an arête in Greek, are traits or dispositions that allow a living organism to function well according to its essence and thus flourish. A fish, for example, flourishes when it functions properly according to its essence. A virtue in a fish's case would be any trait that allows it to swim well. The same can be said of a tiger when, among other things, it has virtues that allows it to run fast. According to Aristotle, the same can be said of humans. When we function well according to our nature we flourish.

For Aristotle, the human soul has three elements or faculties. Like all living things, it has a vegetative faculty that functions to actuate nutrition, reproduction, and growth. A second faculty of the human soul is shared only with other sentient living beings. This is the appetitive faculty of the soul. It functions to actuate a living being's ability to sense, e.g., to hear, see, feel and desire. However, the uniqueness of the human soul is its rational faculty. For Aristotle reason has both theoretical and practical functions. In the former case reason functions theoretically to acquire knowledge and in the latter case it functions practically to conduct human behavior. When humans function well in both cases they flourish. Since ethics concerns human behavior, the particular virtues that ethics should foster are those that enhance the practical use of reason. For Aristotle there are 11 virtues for practical reasoning, e.g., courage, pride, temperance, truthfulness and generosity. Each of these virtues can be described as a means between excess and deficiency of some trait relative to each person.

---

57. While all things have essences, only animated things have souls.

Consider one virtue on Aristotle's list, courage. Courage is a correct estimation of and response to fear or danger in a situation. Underestimating and overestimating the actual danger are vices on either end of courage. The vice that underestimates the danger is called foolhardiness and the vice that overestimates the danger is called cowardness. How a given person expresses courage is relative to the person and her circumstances. For example, if you see a person attacking another person, expressing courage in this situation would be relative to you and the situation itself. Are you physically able to disrupt the attack? If not, maybe courage could be expressed by calling the local police on your cell phone. Virtues for practical reasoning impact and guide, as a charioteer does, the whole person. A virtue is a complex array of dispositions for a certain emotion, attitude, value, perception, and belief. Virtues as dispositions are acquired and take large amounts of time to develop. The practice of becoming virtuous comes from seeing virtuous behavior modeled and then acting likewise. As with any acquired skill, your mastery or proficiency of the skill develops over time. Many of us know what honesty is as a virtue, but the mastery and expression of it is another matter. Only the person who has mastered honesty is able to conceal and reveal truth at the appropriate times. Since virtue ethics is not about rules, no book could determine the appropriate honest act.

The Bible has its share of virtues. The word virtue is found in the New Testament in Phil 4:8; 1 Pet 2:9; 2 Pet 1:3, 5. A list of virtues in the New Testament can be found in Matthew's account of the Sermon on the Mount and, for example, in 1 Corinthians 13 with the well-known virtues of faith, hope and love. Jesus modeled virtues for his disciples. In fact, many of the stories and parables told in both the Old Testament and New Testament are in part told to inspire believers to imitate the virtuous character in them.

Over the centuries, there has been a departure from the focus on virtues in ethical theory. Part of the reason for this departure began in the seventeenth century with the Enlightenment's abandonment of the essentialism of Aristotelian metaphysics of human nature. Without a verifiable *telos* for all humans, it is difficult to talk about human flourishing. The criticism against ethics in general reached its height during the early part of the twentieth century with the rise of logical positivism.[58] However, in

---

58. Logical positivists rejected so-called objective ethical judgments, as meaningless. As a replacement, they introduced their non-cognitive version of ethics: emotivism.

1958 Elizabeth Anscombe wrote "Modern Moral Philosophy"[59] in which she revived the interest in virtue ethics. She points out that rule based or action focused normative theories of ethics are deficient in that they lack ethical discernment about how ethical rules ought to be used. They focus on the issues of ethical obligation and universal application of a rule. For Anscombe this focus is problematic because real lived ethical situations cannot be addressed by universal ethical rules and because they presuppose an authority or "law giver" that modern ethical theory no longer acknowledges.

Anscombe is on target with the insight that rule-based theories qua rule-based theories do not fare well in providing normative direction for every ethical situation. For example, as was pointed out, Kant's categorical commitment to truth telling requires us to tell the truth even in cases where tremendous harm may result when the truth is revealed. (However, her charge that ethical laws are incoherent without a law giver will be taken up in the next chapter.) Later in the twentieth-century philosopher Alastair MacIntyre in *After Virtue*[60] also contributed to the revival of virtue ethics. From a look at history MacIntyre notes that virtues vary from one social community and time to the next. Thus humans don't flourish according any given set of virtues. Contrary to Aristotle, MacIntyre claims that this is because the traditions that human communities happen to value and identify with, not some mistaken talk of human essence, determines what virtues lead to a flourishing life. These community traditions are determined by a continuous discussion and reflection on how the community identifies itself. Thus the virtues required to achieve the good for any given person are determined by "those traditions which provide both practices and individual lives with their necessary historical context."[61]

One objection levied against virtue ethics is that what to do in a given situation is left unaddressed. While this is a fair objection, the obvious benefits and appeals to virtue ethics are obvious. Our reflecting on and using ethical principles of utilitarianism and deontology do not occur in a vacuum. As humans we are beset with myopia and bias due in part to character flaws. A person of virtue is more likely to know when telling the truth and respecting a person's autonomy is more or less

---

59. Anscombe, "Modern Moral Philosophy," 1–19.
60. MacIntyre, *After Virtue*, 181–225.
61. Ibid., 207.

important than telling a lie in order to prevent harm or death to some other person. A person of virtue is more likely to know when she is using ethical principles to grind an axe and when she is using ethical principles to seek the good of someone. Moreover, given that ethical disputes are part of the trade of doing ethics, we fare better when our focus is on character development than when it is on convincing someone to do what we think is the right thing. Very few would debate the need for humans to be benevolent, compassionate, non-maleficent and self-less. As such we fare better in a society on issues like abortion when we try to implement these virtues into society than when we try to convince the members of society what choice they should make on abortion.

5

Swimming through the Murky Waters of Ethics and Religion: Ways Religion Does and Does Not related to Ethics

IN CHAPTER ONE THE following question was put forth: what makes an action right or wrong? The popular answer often given to this question is culture or society. For various reasons, this answer was shown to be extremely flawed and even incoherent. What is interesting, however, is that when the same question is altered and posed within a theological context a different answer emerges. So let us supposed the original question:

a. What makes an action right or wrong?

is altered to ask:

b. Does God make actions right or wrong?

What many people say when the question is framed as (a) is culture but when the question is framed as (b) they say God makes actions right or wrong. This is a bit puzzling since (a) and (b) are concerned with essentially the same issue: the grounding of ethical actions. Nevertheless, the same person is likely to say "culture" when responding to (a) and likely to say "God" when responding to (b). One plausible explanation for these puzzling divergent responses to the same issue is that people are confused as to what (b) is asking. Not that (b) is poorly written but for any number of reasons people confuse (b) with at least 5 other questions that are concerned with the relationship between God and ethics.

A Return to Metaethics: The Relationships between God and Ethics

In this chapter, we will take a look at six possible relationships between God and ethics, along with (b). To resolve these puzzling responses to (b) we will consider which, if any, of these 6 relations are warranted or are at least intelligible. Here are the six questions:

1. Does God make an action right or wrong?
2. Would life have purpose and value without God?
3. Can we know what is right or wrong without God's help?
4. Can we be motivated to act ethically without God or without the belief in God?
5. Does God make certain states of affairs or greater goods ethically intelligible?
6. Is God (or religion) related to ethics in some de facto way?

If we were to suppose that these questions can be answered with simple "yes" and "no" answers, a careful examination of these questions and the issues the questions grapple with would show that a "yes" or "no" answer to any of them does not entail a commitment to theism or atheism. For example, a theist can consistently answer "no" to all of them.

The *first question* is metaphysical and concerns the basis of *why* actions are right or wrong. For most Christians, if God did not exist, there would be no basis for what *is* right and wrong. In short, they claim that God provides the grounding for right and wrong actions. The *second question* is related to the first question. It is a question about axiology and meaning. Is there meaning and value to anything in the universe and, if so, what is the basis for this meaning and value? For some Christians, if there is no God, no life of any sort has meaning or value. The justification behind this belief stems from the assumption that a godless universe consists in nothing more than randomly arranged molecules with no purpose or significance. The *third question* is epistemic and concerns our ability to discern right from wrong. As far as this question is related to God, it is a question about whether ethics requires or benefits from a theistic epistemology. If the answer is yes, then the cognitive faculty of a human or what is often called the natural light of reason, is flawed by depravity and is essentially myopic. Without special revelation, we cannot or should not trust the deliverances of natural reason. Thus we should consult the Bible as either an exhaustive or foundational primer for ethical knowledge. The *fourth question* concerns the *telos* of our ethical motivation. Here the concern is whether God, self-interest, benevolence, etc. is what prompts us to act ethically. Some Christians take a nihilistic stance and affirm the following counter-factual: If God did not exist, then there would be no reason to care about right and wrong. The justification behind this belief is often the belief that in a godless universe, there is no transcendent being to whom anyone is accountable to. The *fifth question* is a broad concern about whether certain ethical beliefs and commitments that we have are intelligible only if there is an afterlife orchestrated by God. We can call this a transcendental question. Finally, the *sixth question* concerns whether God played a significant role in the development of ethics proper. This is primarily a historical rather than philosophical question.

Among these questions, it will be argued in this chapter that a case can be made for possible relationships (but no necessary *de re* relationships) for all but what question one is concerned with. To the disappointment of some theists, God may be *beneficial* to ethics but there is *no de re necessary* between God and ethics. Thus it will be argued that ethics exists as an autonomous discipline without the need for theism.

A *de re* Divine Metaethics

According to traditional theistic approaches to metaethics, God somehow grounds ethics in a deep if not exhaustive way. On this view, God is the basis of moral rightness and wrongness and/or the basis of moral value. Insofar as rightness and wrongness are concerned, some theists take the grounding to be based on God's will. Such a view is called the Divine Command Theory.[1]

Let us call the thesis that ethics depends on God in these two ways (rightness/wrongness and value) the *Divine Metaethics (DM) thesis*. Opponents of the DM thesis maintain that such a relationship entails a dilemma. This dilemma has its origin in Plato's *Euthyphro*, where Socrates asks Euthyphro, "For consider: is the holy loved by the gods because it is

---

1. For contemporary defenses of the DCT, see Adams, "Divine Command Ethics as Necessary A posteriori," 109–19; Swinburne, "Duty and The Will of God," 213–27; and Quinn, *Divine Commands and Moral Requirements*, 23–65.

swimming through the murky waters of ethics and religion

holy? Or is it holy because it is loved by the gods?"[2] Accordingly, either way Socrates' question is answered precludes any hope that a grounding relationship exists between God and ethics. Generally the dilemma is described as follows:

a. If the theist answers that the relationship obtains in so far as the grounding and meaning of morally right/wrong actions and moral goodness/badness *is* God, then ethics would be arbitrary.

or

b. If the theist answers that the relationship obtains in so far as God *informs* us of what is morally right/wrong and of moral goodness/badness via his decrees, then God is redundant.

Let us call the above dilemma the *DM dilemma*.[3] Supposedly the dilemma follows given the theist's commitment to the antecedent of either (a) or (b). Taking the offensive, the critics claim that the consequent of (a) and (b) are unacceptable.

The First Horn of the DM Dilemma

The first horn of the DM dilemma is an *ontological* assertion about the grounding of ethics insofar as God grounds or is the source[4] of ethics (in virtue of God's will or nature). Accordingly, actions and values are morally right/wrong and good/bad solely because God wills them to be so or because they are grounded in his being. It is interesting to note that the claim God is both a necessary and sufficient condition for the objective moral realm can be found in the works of both theists and non-theists alike. Jean-Paul Sartre, for example, asserted that if there is no God there can be only descriptive facts in the world, no normative facts:

> The existentialist, on the contrary, thinks it very distressing that God does not exist, because all possibility of finding values in a heaven of ideas disappears along with Him; there can no longer be an *a priori* Good, since there is no infinite and perfect

---

2. Plato, *Euthyphro* 10a (ed. Allen, 65).

3. This dilemma is broader than the one against the Divine Command theory; here the focus is on moral values and not just on moral rightness and moral wrongness.

4. As I will try to argue, it is unclear what exactly *ground* or *source* means insofar as it explains God's relationship to ethics.

consciousness to think it. Nowhere is it written that the Good exists, that we must be honest, that we must not lie; because the fact is we are on a plane where there are only men. Dostoievsky [sic] said, "If God didn't exist, everything would be possible." That is the very starting point of existentialism. Indeed, everything is permissible if God does not exist, and as a result man is forlorn, because neither within him nor without does he find anything to cling to. He can't start making excuses for himself.[5]

The contemporary atheist Kai Nielsen remarks:

Perhaps there are human purposes, purposes to be found in life, and we can and do have them even in a godless world, but without God there can be no one overarching purpose, no one basic scheme of human existence.[6]

Representing a contemporary theistic perspective, William L. Craig similarly remarks that "if God does not exist, then in a sense, our world is an Auschwitz: there is no absolute right and wrong; all things are permitted."[7]

Theists who hold the first horn claim that God makes certain types of actions and things be morally constituted. This view of ethics is continuous with moral realism in that the moral features of the universe are just as much the effect of God's creation as are physical properties and objects.[8]

The DM Dilemma and Question One

Let's first critically assess question one in light of the DM dilemma. Accordingly, critics claim, if the DM thesis regarded actions, then God could have decreed or caused actions in the actual world, such as rape,

---

5. Sartre, "Existentialism," in *Existentialism and Human Emotions*, 22.
6. Nielsen, "Ethics Without Religion," 556.
7. Craig, *Reasonable Faith: Christian Truth and Apologetics*, 67.
8. On this view, it is not enough to say that God describes certain actions and things to be morally constituted a certain way. This would suggest that actions and things are not objectively morally constituted. For actions and things to be morally constituted, they must genuinely have moral features within them. This claim is true by definition; nothing can be morally constituted unless there is something about it that makes it that way. This is analogous to saying a red pencil is red because it really has the property "redness" in it. For moral realists, these moral features of actions and things are not reducible to descriptive physical features of the universe. See Mavrodes, "Religion and the Queerness of Morality," in *Rationality, Religious Belief, and Moral Commitment*, 213–26.

to be morally right as opposed to morally wrong. Since on the DM view of ethics, God's will or act of creating is the sole arbitrator for determining what is ethically right or wrong in the actual world, God can have no constraints (even logical ones) on his willing or creating the way he does. Accordingly, in some logically possible world, instances of rape are morally right because there is nothing intrinsic to the nature of rape that makes it wrong independent of God; on this view something God does in some mysterious sort of way is essentially the only reason why rape in the actual world is in fact wrong.

If, however, rape is equivalent to and defined as forced sex upon one person against that person's will by another person (unfortunately this may need to be augmented that no greater good is also achieved), then it seems that, contrary to the DM view, there could be no world where God could cause or decree rape to be right. The nature and supervenience of the property "morally wrongness" does not seem to be a property God has power over, particularly such that he could determine what actions in his created universe have these properties and which ones do not. Surely God could create a universe in which no one ever complained or offered resistance to a request for sex by a stranger (or any other person). In such a world, necessarily, no sexual request would violate anyone's autonomy. Nevertheless, if people expressed their autonomy in this manner, rape would still be wrong but would not be *instantiated* in this possible world (i.e., there would never be a case of rape in this possible world). The only power God could have in this world is the power to determine whether to instantiate this world or not. Thus we see that relating God to ethics according to this first interpretation of the first horn is undesirable for the theist.

Not moved by this objection, a theist who holds this view of the DM thesis may appeal to a certain vague and albeit convoluted subjunctive claim. She may assert the following: "God could command and will that rape be right, but he would never do so. This decision not to will rape as right is why I serve God." What is so convoluted about this claim is that it is not a true subjunctive claim. Its proponent fails to acknowledge that notions of *could* logically precede notions of *would*. We cannot talk about what possible state of affairs would occur unless we first state what possible states of affairs are logically possible in the first place. The theist who holds this quasi subjunctive claim must first show that it is possible God *could* will that rape is right before she entertains the thought that she serves God because he *would* never do something he could do. Theists of this sort beg the question about the very nature of what is logically possible for God to do. Until it can be shown how God could logically perform such a task, this rejoinder is not worth further consideration.

Now another route the DM proponent could take regarding the creation of moral properties is to hold that God creates the moral features by necessity. Here God was not free to make rape or any other action, like murder, ethically right. She could argue that as far as actions are concerned, God would not command that rape be morally permissible because as a loving God, God necessarily commands loving actions. Here God's will is constrained by God's benevolent character and thus love necessarily flows from God's character. On this second reading of God determining ethics, actions are not arbitrarily morally right or wrong; they are morally right or wrong because they are necessarily prescribed, forbidden or commanded by a benevolent God. Christian theists Robert Adams and William Lane Craig hold this attitude. They assert that our moral duties are "determined by the commands, not merely of a supreme potentate, but of a just and loving God. God is essentially compassionate, fair, kind, impartial, and so forth; His commandments are reflections of His character."[9] Theists like Adams and Craig make this move in order to establish a non-arbitrary basis for ethics and to ensure that the status of moral judgments is not determined independently of and above the sovereignty of God. The charge of arbitrariness may evaporate if this route is successful. However, on further analysis, it does not. This route does not adequately respond to the DM dilemma for the following reasons.

Theists like Adams and Craig make the common mistake of confusing (1) *what motivates God to give his commands* with (2) *what makes God's commands true*. Consider the following analogy from what I call the *benevolent parent example*. Suppose a small child enters the kitchen of her home and motions toward a hot pot of water on the stove. Suppose also that the child's parent is in the kitchen to respond to this situation. The parent would be benevolent if he gave the following command to his child "do not touch the pot." If the child asks, "why should I not touch the pot," the parent could simply say, "because I said so." Of course, the parent does not literally mean that her command is capricious or conventional. The justification of the parent's answer to the child's question does not directly refer to the act of touching the pot but to the act of obedience. So touching the pot is extrinsically wrong, or at least not wise. Independent of the child's question and the parent's response to the child's question, it

---

9 See Craig, *Does God Exist?*, 172–73. See also Adams, "Divine Command Metaethics Modified Again," 66–79.

turns out that there are reasons why the benevolent parent's command is true (e.g., touching the pot causes physical pain and damage to the child's body). So if we want to know why the parent's command is true, it is because of what happens to the child if she touches the pot of hot water. If we want to know what motivated the parent to give the command, we look to the parent's benevolent character. So the reason why touching the pot *is* wrong[10] has nothing to do with the benevolent character of the parent. Touching the hot pot would still be wrong even if the parent were evil and gave the command to touch the pot. This example merely shows that benevolent parents would never command their children to do what they already know to be wrong. By analogy it illustrates two points about God's commands.

First, it illustrate that certain actions are right or wrong independent of God's command to do or not to do. The reason God commands us not to do certain things is because he knows that the acts in question are immoral and, as a benevolent being, he could not command that we act immorally. However, God commanding in this benevolent way in no way leads to or is identical to the ontological assertion that God is benevolence-itself and causes actions to be either right or wrong.

Secondly the story notes the distinction between some action being wrong and some wrong action being prohibited. Actions that are prohibited merely exact obedience whether or not performing them entails doing something wrong. A child who disobeys her parent's prohibition to eat food for a week is actually doing what is right although she acts from disobedience. Thus disobedience is not intrinsically wrong, particularly when starvation is a threat. Moreover, when an action is neither right nor wrong, to fail to do it can be wrong at a second order level if it is done out of disrespect. This is an important point to mention since the Bible is filled with commands from God to do things that are neither morally right nor wrong in themselves (e.g., the command or prohibition against eating meat mixed with milk or the command to follow the copious dietary laws) and commands to do or refrain from doing things that are morally right or wrong in themselves (e.g., do not rape or murder).

In the end, by admitting that God's will is constrained by His benevolent character, the theist would also be admitting that actions are intrinsically morally right or wrong, independently of God. After all, why would a theist be troubled by and object to God willing that rape be

10. The term *wrong* is being used in a prudent sense, but the analogy holds for ethical situations as well.

morally right unless she understood that rape is an action intrinsically wrong, independent of any determinations on God's end? That is, she understands that rape is simply a wrong action. It is abhorrent to think God would even think that rape could be right. God would not be a loving God if he commanded rape since desires issuing from a loving character are logically inconsistent with the desire that rape be right.

Other DM proponents have tried to resolve the arbitrary objection another way. They will proclaim that God *is* "benevolence" or "goodness itself." A noted proponent of this view, Greg Bahnsen, provides us with the following clear description of it:

> Certain behavior is good because God approves of it, and God approves of it because it is the creaturely expression of His holiness—in other words, it is good. To be good is to be like God, and we can only know what behavior is good if God reveals and approves of it. The important point is that good *is what God approves* and cannot be ascertained independent of Him.[11]

Consistent with a presuppositionalist worldview, this proclamation simply begs the question as to what goodness is. What is good is replaced by what God approves, which in turn is replaced by what is good.

To highlight the circularity of this view another way, consider what those like Bahnsen consider to be the basis of rightness and wrongness, viz., what a benevolent God wills. We can ask what they mean when they say God is benevolent. The obvious response is that God is benevolent because he always does what is right. With this reply in hand, we should now see the DM proponents' circular logic. As we saw earlier, they equate "what is right" with "what God wills." So to say God is benevolent is to say God does what he wills. If we are looking at what God does in order to discern his benevolence, then short of admitting to an independent

---

11. Let us restate Bahnsen's claims by replacing the word "it" with what he identifies as "good behavior": "Certain behavior is good because God approves of good behavior, and God approves of good behavior because good behavior is the creaturely expression of His holiness—in other words, good behavior is good. To be good is to be like God, and we can only know what behavior is good if God reveals and approves of good behavior. The important point is that good *is what God approves* and cannot be ascertained independent of Him." If one thing is clear from Bahnsen's words it is that God approves of good behavior, but we are left wondering what defines behavior as good. We can make the circularity in Bahnsen's claim more obvious by connecting other identity claims he makes to something like the following: "good behavior" eqauls "what God approves" and this expression is equal to "the creaturely expression of God's holiness," which is equal to "good." See Bahnsen, *Theonomy*, 284.

standard of benevolence, theists like Bahnsen must say that benevolence is whatever God does or wills. It is no compromise of God's glory to hold that his benevolence is measured by his actions, which in turn are measured by an independent standard of beneficence.

To deal with these kinds of problems, William Alston in his essay *Suggestions for Divine Command Theorists* makes a distinction between moral obligation (rightness) and moral goodness. Moral obligations apply only to humans who have the ability (freedom) not to meet moral obligations:

> On [my] view, moral obligations attach to all human beings, even those so saintly as to totally lack any tendency, in the ordinary sense of that term, to do other than what it is morally good to do. And no moral obligations attach to God, assuming, as we are here, that God is essentially perfectly good. Thus divine commands can be constitutive of moral obligations for those beings who have them without it being the case that God's goodness consists in His obeying His own commands, or, indeed, consists in any relation whatsoever of God to His commands.[12]

Alston makes this distinction so as to avoid identifying moral rightness in some circular fashion that says X is morally right iff God obligates X and adding that God is good if he does what he obligates (or what is right). So a moral obligation or what is right, being distinct from moral goodness, does not apply to God since God's nature is perfect, not allowing for the possibility to not do what is morally obligatory of God's will. In other words, God is good without having any obligation to do what is right. Obligations or actions deemed right apply only to beings that have the causal power not to do them. While Alston avoids presenting a circular notion of moral goodness in that moral goodness is prior to and distinct from moral rightness and avoids an arbitrary ethics in that God cannot command cruelty because God is morally good, can he avoid presenting a vacuous notion of moral goodness? In other words, what does it mean to say God is good? Alston says the following:

> We can think of God himself, the individual being, as the supreme standard of goodness . . . Lovingness is good (a good-making feature, that on which goodness is supervenient) not because of the Platonic existence of a general principle or fact to the effect that lovingness is good, but because God, the supreme

12. Alston, "Some Suggestions for Divine Command Theorists," 315.

standard of goodness, is loving. Goodness supervenes on every feature of God, not because some general principles are true but just because they are features of God . . . Note that on this view we are not debarred from saying what is supremely good about God. God is not good, qua bare particular or undifferentiated thisness. God is good by virtue of being loving, just, merciful and so on.[13]

So God is good because God is loving, just, merciful, and so on. But now we are back to posing the DM dilemma: Is God good because he is loving, just, merciful, and so on or is being loving, just, merciful, and so on good because God possesses these features? To avoid this return to the DM dilemma, Alston holds that predicates are either Platonic predicates or particularistic predicates and that love, justice, and mercy are of the latter type. Alston explains the distinction between the two types of predicates in the following way:

a. "Platonic" predicates, the criterion for the application of which is a general "essence" or "Idea" that can be specified in purely general terms,

and

b. "particularist" predicates, the criterion for the application of which makes essential reference to one or more individuals.[14]

The former predicates provide identity for some X in virtue of being necessary and sufficient conditions for X to be an X. The latter predicates provide identity for some X in virtue of similarity or conformity X has to the concrete paradigm. Identifying some X as a triangle is to say it has the following abstract properties: three sides and being two dimensional. Identifying some X as a meter is to say it has the same or nearly the same length as the standard meter stick in Paris. So like the meter stick in Paris is the standard of a meter, God is the standard of goodness. It is not at all clear that Alston has added any insight to the dilemma or any reason to reject Platonism. Is it the case that:

---

13. Alston, "What Euthyphro Should Have Said," 291–92.
14. Ibid., 292.

a. love, justice, and mercy are good because they are "features of God"

or

b. God is good because God is loving, just, and merciful?

As with the stick in Paris, it generates the notion of a meter in virtue of the de facto length it is. The notion of a meter does not determine that the stick in Paris is a meter. So Alston would accept (a) and reject (b) since (b) is Platonism. In other words, God makes these predicates good; these predicates do not make God good. Alston gives no answer as to why (a) is preferable to (b) other than saying the foundation of Goodness has to stop somewhere. Pace Alston, this is special pleading for a divine grounding of ethics and those who take a non-natural or natural realist position will have much to say that differs from Alston's conclusion. Why couldn't moral goodness simply be the platonic predicates of love, justice, mercy, and so on and the instantiation of love, justice, mercy, and so on be what makes any concrete thing be good whether or not it is God? Alston does not have an answer to these questions.

THE DM DILEMMA AND QUESTION TWO

Our discussion of goodness turns our attention to Question Two which is about the relationship between God and axiology. Our concern here is whether there can be purpose and value that does not come from God or requires God. Notwithstanding problems of what makes actions right/wrong, DM proponents hold that God is the basis of axiology. Theists of this sort traditionally have held that God is the source of all values. As the "source" of values, God is intrinsically valuable and anything reflecting God's image is likewise valuable. In this "platonic" way, God represents the eternal, maximum Good-itself, and anything participating in His nature in any degree likewise has value, though to a lesser degree. For example, many theists hold that humans have value and that the basis for this value is the presence of the *Imago Dei* in human nature. Accordingly, human nature is qualitatively similar to the divine nature. Perhaps this is taken to mean that humans are valuable because of their possession of, or potential for, various forms of rationality that God possesses for such capacities as self-determination, moral reflection, social discourse, and personal preference formation.[15] God's role in axiology then is twofold: (1) He functions as a maximum, objective standard of value and (2) He creates humans who reflect this intrinsic value. At face value, I do not dispute these two claims for (1) is not *per se* a metaphysical claim but an epistemological claim and (2) is a teleological claim. Neither claim *per se* makes any explicit reference to God being the "source" of value in the robust way DM proponents affirm. To be sure, the DM proponent's robust view of value holds that God is not only our standard of value but God is also a necessary condition for our being valuable.[16] Here things in the universe have value only if God exists, for without God the universe is a conglomeration of amoral entities and properties. Championing this position, theist J. P. Moreland writes:

> On an evolutionary secular scenario, . . . [human] beings are nothing special. The universe came from a Big Bang. It evolved to us through a blind process of chance and necessity. There is nothing intrinsically valuable about human beings in terms of having moral non-natural properties. The same process that coughed up humans beings coughed up amoebas; there is nothing special about being human. The view that being human is special is guilty of specie-ism-an unjustifiable bias toward one's own species . . . There is no point to history[17]

William L. Craig similarly augments this assertion about a godless universe:

> But if there is no God, what reason is there to regard human flourishing as in any way significant? After all, on the atheistic view, there's nothing special about human beings. They're just accidental by-products of nature that have evolved relatively recently on an infinitesimal speck of dust called the planet Earth, lost somewhere in a hostile and mindless universe and doomed to perish individually and collectively in a relatively short time.[18]

---

15. In chapters 1 and 2 of Genesis, the Bible says that God created humans in God's image. A being of God's nature cannot lack significance and value, and if we are made in God's image we likewise have value. For a biblical discussion of this issue, see Grudem, *Systematic Theology*, 442–50. For a theological and philosophical discussion of this issue, see Yandell, *Christianity and Philosophy*, 260–61.

16. Craig, *Reasonable Faith*, 57–72.

17. Moreland and Nielsen, *Does God Exist?*, 112.

18. Craig et al., "The Debate: Is Goodness without God Good Enough?," 31.

Not only does this theistic driven axiology find a godless system of axiology to be incoherent and arbitrary, its proponents attempt to elucidate what they mean when they assert that God is *the* standard of value. As Craig does:

> The question might be pressed as to why God's nature should be taken to be definitive of goodness. But, unless we are nihilists, we have to recognize some ultimate standard of value, and God seems to be the least arbitrary stopping point . . . [because] God is a being worthy of worship.[19]

I reject this robust theistic axiological claim for two reasons. First, Moreland and Craig fail to explain why valuable things in this world require a transcendent foundation. Surely naturalists would hold that all things are constituted by randomly organized molecules, but they would not be required to hold that they are identical to them. Even some theists hold this form of non-reductionism. On naturalists' and theists' accounts, rationality[20] is in part or in whole the content and foundation of human value. While naturalists and theists differ primarily[21] over the mechanism responsible for human rationality, upon reflection, we see that humans are not valuable per se because of the *mechanism* responsible for their possession of value; rather humans are valuable because they are *rational*. This is particularly clear from the perspective of natural selection as a mechanism for our rationality. It works blindly and has no goals or purposes. Moreover, the emergence of rationality may be improbable from natural selection. So when Moreland and Craig say that humans are not special from a naturalistic evolutionary point of view, they surely are correct to point out that humans are not significant in terms of our arrival, since our rationality and existence was not intended. We would never have been missed since we would have never been anticipated. But we must ask rhetorically, what difference does it make what *kind* of causal factor(s) are responsible for producing self-awareness, rationality, and the like? Whether God or naturalistic evolution is responsible for our having such features, it does not matter. If it does, what is the

---

19. Craig, *Does God Exist?*, 173.

20. By rationality I am referring to, among other things, self-awareness, consciousness, and self-determination.

21 It must be granted that causal factors in the existence of value are not irrelevant, for surely a splash of paint on canvas is valuable merely because of its arrangement. However, it is more valuable when the arrangement is the result of a designer rather than chance.

argument? Our concern here boils down to a de facto matter. The fact is we have these features. If there is no God, then naturalistic evolution, perhaps, is the only alternative modus operandi to account for our having the features. It would be *ad hoc* for a theist to admit that humans are valuable in light of these features but then deny this claim if it turns out that these features were the result of blind Darwinian forces. Naturalists would agree with Moreland that there is nothing special about being human if "the same process that coughed up humans beings coughed up amoebas." But here the naturalist would simply mean that humans were not expected or intended to come about by natural selection. In other words, they obviously embrace the resulting consequences of naturalism that there is nothing special in the emergence or arrival of human beings; humans came into being by chance. However, the naturalist would reject the notion that humans lack value. This is wholly a different affair. Thus theists like Moreland and Craig confuse the *causes of our value* with our *being valuable*.

But let us return to the standard of value simpliciter. Craig specifically addressed this issue, and it is unclear what Craig means by standard. The word "standard" in the context of determining value asks for a definition of value as Craig correctly points out. This much is clear, but why is a non-arbitrary definition of goodness difficult to come by? If God is required to define goodness, how is it that God does so? It is not at all clear that the non-existence of God entails nihilism as Craig claims. If God did not exist, is it not conceivable that a definition or concept of goodness could exist such that having cancer is recognized as not fitting that definition or where drinking clean water to stay alive can be recognized as fitting that definition? In this case, Aristotelian and Thomistic considerations about flourishing come to mind. But suppose God is definitive of goodness, we can always ask the question, "Why is God definitive of goodness?" Craig's answer is that "God is a being worthy of worship." But this answer simply places us back where we started since God would be worthy of worship *only* because he is good. A more telling criticism of Craig's claim is the problem of identity. If God is identical to goodness then whatever is true of God is true of goodness. Recall Leibniz's Law or *the indiscernibility of identicals*:

$$(x)(y)((x = y) \supset (P)(Px \supset Py))$$

Surely God is not identical to goodness. An appeal to the Thomist view of simplicity won't assist in this matter either for it has its own can of worms to deal with.[22] If there is such a thing as goodness which all good things and all good actions reflect, participate in, or simply are, there are other ways the theist can account for it. She could accept goodness as something earthly or non-supernatural. If we make the latter move, we could simply take goodness as some unanalyzable non-natural property that certain actions and things possess[23] or we could take goodness as some analyzable natural property of actions (e.g., psychological and physical pleasure) that is teleologically oriented towards some entity's well-being. In either case, an ascent to God is not *per se* required.

Now Craig, Moreland, and other DM proponents would object that no argument has been offered for my last claim. And on this note, I am not convinced that an argument needs to be offered. They are the ones who hold the view that goodness cannot be conceived independent of God. This is a rather dubious claim. Surely to ask whether there are any intelligible reasons for saying "feeding the poor" in a naturalistic/atheistic world is good is an ill-placed question; it is not an intelligibly opened question. What makes such an action good is that it promotes a human's well-being. In whatever way we cash it out, our account of goodness in this case would be very earthly. What is not ill-placed is the question why God is needed as a standard to describe these types of actions as good. Calling God or anything good requires that God first do something worthy of this title. If God never did anything, in what sense could he be called Good? To retreat to the position that seeking the well-being of humans is a good thing to do because humans are good in virtue of being made in God's image is another instance of confusing the cause of something's value with its being valuable.

Finally in agreement with DM proponents, naturalists would further add that there is no ultimate purpose to life if life's value comes exclusively from some transcendent source. Contra Aquinas, the naturalist holds that the purpose of human existence is not to love God since there is no God. Nevertheless, naturalists would contend that the purpose or meaning of life comes about by engaging the world or nature itself on its own terms. To be sure, this is not a call to the existentialism of Sartre

22. One problem with simplicity is that it makes God the summation of his properties or a collection of abstract ideas.

23. For example, G. E. Moore held that, like the color yellow, goodness is a natural feature of the physical universe, but neither yellow nor goodness can be semantically reduced to any natural features of the physical universe. See Moore, *Principia Ethica*, 6–16.

and Camus. Nature itself presents us with a litany of temporal goods to pursue that are quite valuable in themselves. Fathers, by seeking the well-being of their children, have a purpose to live. A sprinter finds meaning in winning a gold medal at the Olympics because the gold medal is the expression of being the fastest sprinter. There is something meaningful in being better than one's competitors. There is something meaningful in receiving a rose on your birthday because the rose expresses to the recipient that the bearer of the rose values and cares for the recipient. All such states of affairs are what they are even in a godless universe. Even stepping beyond the community of *homo sapiens*, naturalists can make talk of value and purpose intelligible on a much broader scale. For surely rectifying harms done to planet Earth or even to sentient life affords a description best called good because the presence of life over and against no life is a more valuable state of affairs. The attitude that a godless universe is full of facts but void of values is quite dubious.

However, human persons would be qualitatively more valuable in a theistic world since human persons would, in a theistic universe, have the additional property of being designed and made for a purpose. According to Christian theism, humans were created by a perfect and loving God to be in an ethical and loving relationship with him- in Christian theism, humans aren't just the random effect of processes in an amoral and purposeless world.[24] So while natural selection can produce valuable beings like ourselves, it is incapable of purposely doing so. This inability of natural selection (more properly natural destruction) is no sleight against value being possible under naturalism. Rather the point being made is that Christian theism makes our value more significant and robust given the fact that our value is intentional in its instantiation than it is under naturalism where its instantiation is a random occurrence.

The Aftermath of Questions One and Two: an Ethically Autonomous World

When the metaphysics and axiology of ethics is the issue, accepting an ethically autonomous world is not difficult for the theist to do. To be sure, our option for relating God to ethics in the way that the second horn does will not lead to ethical nihilism, relativism, and skepticism. As we saw in the chapter on normative ethics, we had good reasons for considering ethics objective and intelligible, even though God was not part of that

---

24. I am grateful to Harry Gensler for his helpful comments on this paragraph.

discussion. We can take a deontological view of ethics and argue that child abuse and rape are wrong (regardless of culture, location, or time) whether or not God exists, simply because such acts violate the autonomy of their victims. Or one can appeal to empirical considerations and take a utilitarian ethical view. Here such actions as child abuse and rape are wrong (regardless of culture, location, or time), whether or not God exists, because of the amount of disutility (in terms of pain or psychological damage) such acts inflict on the child and the rape victim.

Either way, the ethical judgments or true propositions corresponding to such actions (e.g., that it is wrong to cause pain for pleasure's sake or that it is wrong to restrict a person's autonomy irrespective of the person's goodwill) are necessarily true and do not depend on God in any way since they are true in every possible world. Some theists, however, charge that the truth-makers of these truth-bearers are hard to comprehend when considered to be Platonic ethical properties or abstracta. This is the position that William L. Craig takes:

> It is difficult . . . even to comprehend this view [non-theistic Platonism]. What does it mean to say, for example, that the moral value justice just exists? It is hard to know what to make of this . . . it is bewildering when in the absence of any people, justice itself exists . . . it is hard to know what it is for a moral value to exist as a mere abstraction.[25]

As a conceptualist, Craig holds that abstracta do not exist independently of the concrete particulars that they instantiate or of the mind of God.[26] For theistic conceptualists like Craig, an abstractum like the number 2 exists as an idealized abstraction from two concrete objects and is a necessary feature of the divine mind. Pace Craig, if justice "is bewildering . . . in the absence of any people" then justice is bewildering prior to creation itself. For how can justice be less bewildering if it is an abstraction in the mind of God? Craig's question of how there can be justice without just people begs the question against alternative accounts of moral values. Is there anything incoherent in Platonism or even

---

25. See Moreland and Craig, *Philosophical Foundations for a Christian Worldview*, 492. This quote is likely William Lane Craig writing since Moreland has written in defense of universals in *Universals*, 1–184. While Craig and Moreland wrote *Philosophical Foundations for a Christian Worldview*, it is my opinion that the quote represents only Craig's view of conceptualism.

26. See Moreland and Craig, *Philosophical Foundations for a Christian Worldview*, chap. 10.

a naturalized ethics committed to nominalism (where value is reducible to but not conceptually identical to pleasure)? What is so bewildering about Platonism and nominalism? Some mathematicians, whether they are committed to theism or not, hold that numbers exist even if they are not instantiated in concrete particulars. Nevertheless, even if Craig is correct that justice does not exist apart from just concrete states of affairs, his objection to Platonism is no argument in favor of the type of conceptualist grounding of ethical abstracta (or ethical truths) that Craig wants to defend. The naturalist who says value is constituted by pleasure, for example, would agree with Craig that moral values do not exist as Platonic abstractions (viz., the naturalist is a nominalist), but again this admission does not entail by default an ontological grounding of ethical truths *in* God's mind.

Finally, as we have also seen in our discussion of normative ethics, able ethicists have historically been able to comprehend axiology either in part or in whole without couching axiology in theistic metaphysics. Again, for example, when we look at the deontology of Kant, the intelligibility of valuing a self-reflecting rational being as an end deserving respect, or the value hedonists place on sentient beings, do not depend on the existence of God but on the very nature of the agents or patients we are engaged with.[27]

The Second Horn of the DM Dilemma

With this said, there seems to be no cogent reasons to adopt the first horn even though ethics is intelligible without God. But our concern has not been whether ethics is intelligible without God, but whether a relationship between God and ethics is required at best or is possible at worst. So when we move from the first horn to the second horn the question is: is adopting the second horn equally problematic? Of course the age old objection has been that the second horn leaves God redundant. However, on a closer, critical level, there is ambiguity in the charge that an acceptance of the second horn entails a redundant relationship between God and ethics. For according to the Oxford dictionary, for example, redundant is defined

---

27. This is certainly the case for Immanuel Kant and John S. Mill. In general, moral realists posit moral facts and values in the world that are either natural or non-natural. Recent ethicists who champion ethical realism without theism are not few. See Boyd, "How to Be a Moral Realist," 181–228; and Brink, *Moral Realism and the Foundations of Ethics*, chaps. 6–7.

as "no longer needed or useful; superfluous; able to be omitted without loss of meaning or function." Theists who take the second horn admit that God is not strictly *needed* to ground ethics. (Recall this is about our metaphysical question.) So God is redundant in this metaphysical sense but God is not redundant if redundant is taken to mean superfluous. All the theist needs to do is show how the following claims are compatible:

1. Ethical judgments are autonomous and true independent of God.
2. For any ethical judgment that is true independent of God, God does in fact know it to be true.
3. Therefore, given the truth of (i) and (ii), God does not occupy a superfluous relationship to ethics.

There are several ways the theist can do so. All such ways require the theist to channel her energy away from her concern about the metaphysical question and to some degree the question about axiology. Rather the theist would focus her energy and concern on the third and fourth questions about epistemology and motivation with the proviso that no *de re* relations between God and ethics are championed. The theist can even point to God being non-superfluous to ethics even in ways not involving God's knowledge as we will see when we entertain question five. However, before we consider what these relationships can be, let us first consider positions some theists have taken who consider God to have a *de re* relation to ethics in light of the epistemic and motivational questions.

The DM Dilemma and Question Three

Let's consider the third question about the epistemic relationship between God and ethics. Again this is an issue about whether moral agents like ourselves can *know* what is right or wrong without God. Obviously an answer asserting an absolute negative reply to this question welcomes the second horn's challenge. Some DM proponents hold that a *de re* relationship exists between God and ethics such that the notion of a moral universe makes sense or is intelligible only in relationship to God. Accordingly God supplies humans with esoteric knowledge concerning the rightness and wrongness of an action that is not discernable merely to the faculties of human reason. Here knowing what is right or wrong requires knowledge of the Bible, e.g., the imperatives of the 10 commandments. The claim here is human inquirers could not know that murder and rape are wrong if the Bible did not inform them that these acts are wrong. This is a peculiar claim, for it is not at all clear why God is needed as a precondition to our ethical belief formation. I am not aware of any ethical theorist who holds this view, but it is by far a popular view among Christian laity.[28]

Like any modal claim, it affirms that actions like rape and murder could not be known as wrong in a godless universe since it is necessarily the case that God is a prior condition in our knowing and appropriately responding to such acts as wrong. Also, like any modal claim, it affirms that actions like rape and murder cannot *be* or be *conceived* as wrong in a universe without God (or even a universe conceived without God). Taken as a modal claim, it is quite dubious and question-begging. If it were true, no amount of ethical insight on our behalf could allow us to discern the ethical wrongness of the most horrific of acts. In the absence of God this claim entails that we necessarily find ourselves, say, standing before a man killing another man for pleasure and be unable to know that his action was wrong. On a much larger scale, we would also be unable to point out why the Jewish holocaust was unethical or why any genocide is unethical. It is absurd to think that human minds could not know these acts are wrong by their own light of reason. Women who have been victims of rape can conceive, express, and affirm the wrongness of their rape without reference to God in any direct or indirect way. In fact, they can even quantify their unfortunate incident as wrong. In either case, they can do so because of the physical and emotional pain they incurred and the violation to their personhood. Stated in a slightly different way, the DM modal claim entails that the experience of the physical and emotional pain along with the violation of autonomy are not sufficient epistemic markers to know the wrongness of rape. As a matter of common experience, it is doubtful that victims of rape would agree with this claim. Rather horrific acts like rape or even murder and child prostitution do not require God's insight; humans are well equipped to discern the wrongness of such acts. So for reasons embedded in the second horn, God is redundant as an informer in regards to these particular acts. But

---

28. To be sure, presuppositionalists argue that God and God's word are the standard of ethics; however, they do not hold the extreme epistemic claim that a person cannot know what is ethically right and wrong unless she reads the ethical commands in the Bible.

there is a warranted way God is not redundant when the relationship is epistemological.

For the theist who does not hold this *de re* position on ethical knowledge, God could play an occasional, but important, role to justify her ethical beliefs that are not undoubtedly true and perhaps polemic. As previously mentioned, many ethical beliefs are known to be true with a fair degree of certainty, e.g., that rape is wrong and that boiling human beings in hot oil merely for pleasure's sake is wrong. We can say such ethical beliefs are properly basic. However, when it comes to taking a position on such polemic issues like abortion, the death penalty, affirmative action, embryonic stem cell research, and euthanasia, God's objective discernment could be crucial. While normative ethical theories can provide sufficient reasons for which actions are right or wrong concerning these issues (our metaphysical concern), our *actual application* of these theories often falls short of being objective and impartial(our epistemic concern) since humans often fall prey to epistemic myopia of various kinds in the use of normative ethical theories. That is, humans are fallible, at times unconsciously biased, and sometimes lack pertinent information and the virtuous character to make objective ethical judgments. Many theists attribute some of this myopia to Adamic depravity. Looking to what an omniscient and benevolent God knows would be crucial in such circumstances.

However, we do well not to put all our marbles in a biblical epistemology unless we are willing to concede the inevitable fact that doing so, beyond broad biblical principles about how to treat humans, comes with a price. That is, using biblical texts to discern the ethical nature of specific albeit polemic issues may be beyond our reach. Discerning what God's perspective is on issues like the death penalty, reproductive technologies, war, and euthanasia involves hermeneutical correctness that we might not have. This is evident by the fact that on their best day, Christians derive various divergent views on the same ethical issues from the same specific biblical texts.

Even when hermeneutics is not an issue, it is not always clear that God's perspective on a polemic ethical issue is itself an ethical perspective. All too often God's condemnation or prescription of an action is for theological reasons, not ethical reasons. For example, the condemnation of sexual immorality in the New Testament states the following: Our body is the temple of the Holy Spirit (1 Cor 6:19) and that sexual immorality violates the believer's relationship with the Trinity (1 Cor 6:12–20). The ethical reason against sexual immorality is not given. As Christians we do well just to obey God for the theological reasons he gives. However, such obedience is dubious and less obvious to the lifestyles of non-Christians. We can't just say to them, "Thus sayth the Lord . . ." They are not concerned with how sex affects their relationship with God. We need to be able to explain ethical prescriptions from the Bible without the appeal to theological explanation and justification. A person working in youth ministry will find it difficult to explain to an inquisitive non-Christian youth why pre-marital sex is unethical if the explanation is based on the Trinitarian concerns of 1 Cor 6:12–20. They are likely to be concerned, and for good reasons, with the implications of these actions for themselves and other humans.

Even when an ethical issue is explicitly addressed *qua* ethical issue in the Bible, theists have not always formed a consensus about what ethical implications to draw from them for issues not explicitly addressed in the written word. For example, there is a consensus among Christian theists that God affirms the equality of all human beings. As such, we should act in a manner that treats human beings as equals. But this is where Christian theists part company on what they take to be God's perspective on, for example, affirmative action. Theists who oppose affirmative action would say they do so because God is opposed to treating human beings as unequals and affirmative action does just that. For them, affirmative action is essentially reverse discrimination against whites and white males in particular. After all, if human beings are equal, then the skin color of the humans applying for a position of employment or applying for entrance into a university should not matter. When persons of color are selected over whites, this is treating whites like African Americans were once treated during Jim Crow days. On the other hand, theists who support affirmative action would say they support it because God is opposed to treating human beings as unequals. In an ideal world, all humans would be treated as equals, but in the historical, real world, people of color have not been treated as equals, particularly African Americans due to slavery, Jim Crowism and the effects of these discriminatory practices in contemporary society. In order for us to realize the equality that God knows to be just, affirmative action is a means we could use to bring about the equality.

Finally we have the unnerving passages, particularly in the Old Testament, that condone the slaying of innocent of babies, e.g., Ps 137:9; and 1 Sam 15:3. It is not at all clear that these *herem* passages have a straight forward interpretation about justice and God's command to Israel to kill on God's behalf. As far back as Origen, the literal interpretation of these passages was called into question.[29]

The DM Dilemma and Question Four

Let's take a look at the fourth question about ethical motivational. Again, this question is about whether humanity can achieve ethical excellence or at least behave in an ethically appropriate way with or without God. For theists who take a *de re* position on God's relationship to ethical motivation, they hold that humanity would lack the motivation to do what is ethically right if God did not exist. Accordingly, in a godless world humanity would lack the desire to do the right thing. If anything, humans would do whatever is in their self-interest to do. This "anything" is often identified as evil or at least as lacking in ethically appropriate content. Again, this is a position popular among the laity. For those who hold an extreme account of this position, they envision mass chaos obtaining in a godless universe, where humans behave very suspiciously of each other, or act in a very "cut throat" manner. To explain why it is that atheists can and have modeled appropriate ethical behavior, the explanation offered is that God instilled even within atheists a motivation to seek the good of self and others from altruistic considerations. Talk of a "God created" ability in humans supposedly derives scriptural support from St. Paul's epistle to the Romans:

> For when Gentiles who do not have the Law do instinctively the things of the Law, these, not having the Law, are a law to themselves, in that they show the work of the Law written in their hearts, their conscience bearing witness and their thoughts alternately accusing or else defending them. (Rom 2:14–16, NASB).

This talk of divine ethical enabling is similar to what British sentimentalist philosophers like Francis Hutcheson, the Earl of Shaftesbury, and Hume called a moral sense,[30] which allows us to respond correctly, emotively, and volitionally to ethically right and wrong situations. Unfortunately, God's motivational role does not afford the DM proponent what she

---

29. See Origen, *Homilies on Joshua* 15.144.

30. For the British moralist, this moral sense was simply an ability, not a per se faculty like an eye for seeing. Accordingly, this ability allows us to feel a sense of pleasure for actions that are right and a sense of displeasure for actions that are wrong.

wants. The historical layman's interpretation of the Pauline text is that God plays a causal role in ethics by imprinting the very content of the Hebraic Law (e.g., the 10 Commandments) onto the human heart or mind. From this perspective, the implication for the DM proponent is that, short of having this divinely given Law, humans would not be capable of ethical motivation, i.e., to be moved to do the right thing or to be convicted of doing the wrong thing. To be sure, Paul never says the Law is written on our heart; he says "the work of the Law written in . . . [our]hearts."

For those who have the Law (in this case the Jews) the effect of the Law or what Paul calls "the work of the Law" is threefold. It first serves as an end in that it is an epistemic tool for prescriptions of both community and personal ethical conduct. The Law in this sense allows the Jews to make ethically appropriate decisions concerning what is right and wrong behavior without having to know the justification behind these ethical decisions. Secondly because the Jews aim to please God, the Law has the effect of convicting the Jews once they understand what God prescribes or forbids through the Law. Thirdly, it serves as a means to measure the obedience of the Jews, regardless of the content of the measurement, viz., the Law. In this sense the Jews' obedience to God is strictly based on their categorical commitment to the Law, without exception. When they do not measure up to its standards in the most insignificant way, they fall short of God's obedience and approval. Here the content of the Law is not as important as is absolute conformity to it, and this is what God expects. So once understood, these three effects take place. The Gentiles or non-believers do not have the Law, yet they experience the effect of the Law such that they are capable of doing actions that the Law would prescribe. Thus they are a law to themselves. So how is this possible?

According to one view, the Gentiles in Romans 2:14–16 are *Christians* and, as a result of their conversion, do the work of the Law. Augustine understood Paul's reference to Gentiles to be Gentile Christians.[31] On this view God supernaturally instructs them to perform ethically appropriate actions. This view is highly improbable beyond asserting God's role as a supernatural convictor. For to be convicted, the Gentiles need to also know what particular actions they are convicted of. Does this come by divine illumination or intuition? Moreover, without the Law, the Gentiles would need an alternative epistemic tool apart from God for making decisions, where they take matters into their own hands and

---

31. Augustine, *The Spirit and the Letter* 26.43—28.49, 177–182. For further discussion of who these Gentiles were, see Kruse, *Paul's Letter to the Romans*, 136–40.

provide objective justification for their ethical decisions. But once this is granted, there is no need to refer to the Gentiles as Christians since the basis of their ethical decision making are their natural faculties of reason, which are employed by all humans. Pace Augustine, Paul makes it clear that the Gentiles do the Law or are obedient to it by nature (φύσει), not by some divine illumination or intuition.

A more plausible view of the text is that Paul is making a distinction between Jews and Gentiles simpliciter and that his use of "work of the Law" is in reference to the first and second sense of "work of the Law." Accordingly, the Gentiles equally have the ability to make ethically appropriate decisions for both community and personal conduct, are convicted when they violate these prescriptions, and are equally responsible for their shortcomings. What causes the Gentile to be convicted is not the Law or God but their conscience. The Gentile's conscience convicts her (or alternatively defends her) concerning her ethical behavior. So Paul is merely asserting that the requirements of the Law, or at least the ability to behave consistently with it, are not an esoteric affair that places the Jews in a privileged position before God.

Of course, whether God instills within all humans a sense or intuition of right and wrong, and a desire to do what is right (for both atheists and theists), is mainly a theological issue; such a thesis cannot be confirmed empirically and philosophically. The fact of the matter is, atheists can and often do live ethically virtuous lives as much as any theist does. Contrary to popular belief, atheists need not be motivated from self-interest in order to do what is right. To be sure, as David Hume pointed out, humans are often motivated to act from sympathy and empathy. Once we put ourselves in the shoes of another person, we recognize what is conducive to that person's well-being or harmful to the person (what we may call empathy). From this vantage point we have the ability to feel positively or negatively about those states of affairs obtaining for the other person and to be sympathetically motivated to ensure that they obtain (if conducive to their well-being) or don't obtain (if harmful to their well-being).

It is an open question whether empathy and sympathy originate from egoistic or altruistic considerations. An egoistic perspective takes a means view of empathy and sympathy. Here the moral agent who empathizes is able to see that sympathy prevents feelings of guilt and social condemnation. Conversely, empathy allows a moral agent to see that sympathy leads to ascriptions of praise and other positive outcomes that sometimes have existential import. An altruistic perspective takes an end view of empathy and sympathy. Here the moral agent who empathizes is able to see the gravity of the other person's plight and to be moved simply for that reason. Conversely, on the same view, the moral agent who sympathizes is able to feel the gravity of the other person's plight and the benefits that lay in store for the other person if the moral agent were to assist or help. Whether the egoistic or altruistic perspective is correct is a moot point in the context of the discussion concerning humanity's ability to be sympathetic with or without God since both accounts grant that humans can be sympathetic. To be sure, an egoistic account of sympathy makes complete sense of morally noble behavior and motivation in a godless universe. With emphasis on "ego" humans can easily be motivated to embark on a lifestyle that ensures their own legacy, given the finality of their existence. In a godless universe, whether our lives are significant depends on what we do with them in the brief years we have since there is no life beyond the grave. So upon reflection, we should expect humans to live noble lives in a godless universe unless humans believe their existence extends beyond the grave.

Nevertheless, while ethical motivation is possible in a godless universe, we need not abandon any attempts to forge a relationship between God and ethical motivation. An ethics couched in Christian theism is not motivationally superfluous *to the theist* for at least two reasons. First, whether or not God exists, the concept of God qua creator and benevolent Lord of our lives provides a qualitatively greater motivation to act ethically than the concept of what George Mavrodes calls a Russellian world,[32] where God is conceived to not exist. So, for example, while ethics can exist in a purely naturalistic world, ethics understood from a Christian theistic world or merely theistic world would prompt greater motivation to be ethical, e.g., to respond in gratitude to a loving God. Specifically, despite their own potentially selfish desires, Christians would have as their over-ridding modus operandi, unconditional love, as found in Luke 10:27:

> And he answered, "You shall love the Lord your God with all your heart, and with all your soul, and with all your strength, and with all your mind; and your neighbor as yourself." (NASB)

---

32. Mavrodes's description of a Russellian world comes from Bertrand Russell's description of a world without God in his 1903 essay, *A Free Man's Worship*. In such a world the following are true: a) minds and mentality are produced accidentally by blind evolutionary forces; and b) human life ends at the grave. See Mavrodes, "Religion and the Queerness of Morality," 561–69.

Plato notes this motivational element in the *Apology*. He quotes Socrates as saying: "Gentlemen of Athens, but I shall obey the God rather than you ... For the God commands this, ... and I believe that you have yet to gain in this City a greater good than my service to the God."[33]

If we return to the debate about whether sympathy originates from self-interest or altruism, surely actions originating from the latter are morally superior since they are done merely for the sake of some other (whether to please God or the recipient of the sympathy). Nevertheless, the debate is not about whether all actions are altruistically motivated but whether some are or whether all are not. No one disputes that some actions are selfishly motivated. To be sure, some egoistic ends do not consider the well-being of others; in fact, they require an absolute disregard for the well-being of others. Much can be said about this debate, but this much is sure: persons are motivated to act from self-interest only when there is a self-interest end to obtain. Now when no self-interest end exists, and granting that persons can be sympathetic, surely what other reason would a person have to be sympathetic in a sympathetic-conducive situation other than to do good merely for the sake of some other? While this is a rhetorical question, it is an empirical matter whether such situations exist much at all. Since selfishly motivated actions readily occur, perhaps on average or more than average, people have some self-interest end in mind that they desire and less likely have some altruistic ends available to pursue.

Nevertheless, while the verdict is still out, I am putting forward an intuition that selfless, unconditionally loving, and compassionate acts are indeed rare. If this intuition is true, then the theological claims of Christian theism in particular suggest a significant role between God and ethics. Here God's role in ethics would be to provide humans with supernatural power to overcome the trappings of their selfishness, for the sake of some altruistic motivation. The consensus among most world religions is that human nature is neutral or good in regards to the egoistic/altruistic debate. Among the world religions, Christianity is unique in casting humanity neither as intrinsically good or neutral, but as fated with a disposition for self-centeredness.[34] According to the Bible, a main role

---

33. Plato, *Apology* 29d–30a (ed. Allen, 86).

34. I do not want to give the false impression that the doctrine of depravity is universally embraced by all branches of Christianity. The issue of whether humans are naturally good, bad, or neutral is debated by Catholic and Protestant branches of Christianity. For purposes of this book, by "Christianity" I am referring to those branches of Christianity that endorse the view of depravity.

the Holy Spirit plays in the life of a human is to counteract the natural tendencies to act from self-interest. The Holy Spirit overcomes a person's selfishness that results in what the Bible calls the fruit of the Spirit when the person yields to the Holy Spirit:

> But the fruit of the Spirit is love, joy, peace, patience, kindness, goodness, faithfulness, gentleness and self-control. (Gal 5:22–23, NASB)

The apostle Paul provides personal testimony of the struggle between the selfless tendencies that the Holy Spirit provides and the selfish tendencies that his own nature provides:

> I find then the principle that evil is present in me, the one who wants to do good. For I joyfully concur with the law of God in the inner man, but I see a different law in the members of my body, waging war against the law of my mind and making me a prisoner of the law of sin which is in my members. (Rom 7:21–23 NASB)

With God at the helm, humans are able to prefer selfless acts of unconditional love and compassion over competing acts driven by desires to do something for self-gain. Accordingly, God provides humans, the ones God indwells, with an altruistic impetus (perhaps selfless desires or intentions) to overcome what comes naturally for humans to do most of the time, viz., to act from self-interest.

While this is a theological assertion, there are reasons to believe it is true.[35] If any religion is other-centered, it is Christianity. For members of Christian ministries that seek to meet only spiritual needs of people with the message of Christ, they do so without any expectation of salvific merit for themselves. And for members of Christian ministries that seek to meet both the physical and spiritual needs of people they minister to,

---

35. Christian relief organizations seek to set up operations in countries where there are various religions, one dominant religion, or no religious dominance among the indigenous population. What drives them to work in these countries is not the presence of other Christians in those countries, but the presence of humans with physical needs. Christian organizations operate in countries as religiously diverse or secular as China, Sudan, Myanmar, Kosovo, Cambodia, Niger, Indonesia, Pakistan, Vietnam, Jordan, and Afghanistan. It is somewhat dubious to speculate that the motivation for the Christians of these organizations to be in these countries is purely self-serving. One fact that counters this speculative move is the reality that in many of these countries the Christian workers face many risks that endanger their lives or at least their livelihood.

they do so not for achieving their own eternal life or heavenly rewards. While this may not be standard in practice among Christians, it is in principle. Thus, citing examples of unconditional love and compassion among Christians should not be stalemated by the copious examples of atrocities in the name of Christ by Christians over the centuries. The world over knows about the Atlantic slave trade, the Crusades of Europe, and the reluctance of German churches to confront Nazism in WWII Germany. These are not trivial instances of evil and demand an explanation. But the body of Christians is diverse in perspective and action. Surely the existence of these atrocities does not entail the falsity of the claim that God works and has worked through Christians.

The failures of some Christians do not entail the failure of all Christians. It should be noted that for each of these atrocities, there were Christians who opposed them. During the slave trade, Christians abolitionists opposed slavery in the United States and Britain; the Crusades occurred during a time in Europe when Christians unfortunately did not question the orders of the papacy; and Christians like Dietrich Bonhoeffer who, as a pastor of the Confessing Church in Germany, opposed Nazism during Hitler's reign. In fact the unconditional love and compassion for all humans, if exhibited in the lived experiences and mission work of non-Christian believers, would negate the charge that only Christians are those known by their love and compassion for humans unconditionally. But history has not shown this. And this is truly the case with the history of Christian work in the world over the centuries. While much stains the face of Christian history, we need only point to those many instances where those Christians operating under the control of the Holy Spirit have lived out unconditional love and compassion towards all humans around the world.

Making this claim about the noble deeds of Christians should not be taken as an ascription of Christian pride. The agape love that is the hallmark of Christianity is and should be ascribed to God's activity in humanity. The only recognition of honor humans qua Christians can receive is and should be ascribed to their willingness to be vessels or conduits of God's love.

The DM Dilemma and Question Five

Let us turn to the fifth and transcendental/utilitarian question. Are there greater goods or states of affairs that are intelligible only if God exists? A look back at one of the criticisms of utilitarianism is that even if the consequences of an action determine that an action is right or wrong, no human can foresee all or the most important consequences of an action. Consequences are not nomic, so a calculation of a particular action is not always possible. So while a decision we make may be ethically right, we are not always in an epistemic position to know that it is right. These unknown great goods can come from great evils, but their obtainment requires God. To be sure, from a teleological perspective, some greater goods cannot or are not realized in this life. Such goods, according to Christian theology, obtain in the afterlife. Conversely, the pursuit of any action that does not maximize earthly utility, given the falsity of theism, would be wrong. Truths that affirm this latter claim are the series of counterfactuals in Paul's first letter to the Corinthian church:

> and if Christ has not been raised, then our preaching is vain, your faith also is vain. Moreover we are even found *to be* false witnesses of God, because we testified against God that He raised Christ, whom He did not raise, if in fact the dead are not raised. For if the dead are not raised, not even Christ has been raised; and if Christ has not been raised, your faith is worthless; you are still in your sins. Then those also who have fallen asleep in Christ have perished. If we have hoped in Christ in this life only, we are of all men most to be pitied. (1 Cor 15:14-19, NASB)

Surely Paul and the other disciples were not maximizing utility if their earthly existence was the totality of their existence. If anything, they should be pitied. The self-less life Christ endorsed, in itself, requires a person to avoid self-gain. As Jesus bluntly states in his dictum:

> For whoever wishes to save his life will lose it; but whoever loses his life for My sake will find it. For what is a man profited, if he shall gain the whole world, and lose his own soul? or what shall a man give in exchange for his soul? (Matt 16: 25-26, NASB)

Christ and Paul encouraged a selfless, sacrificial lifestyle. The consequences of a self-sacrificial life are positive when the person's post-mortem existence is calculated into her overall utility. As Christ puts it better than any hedonist, if it were possible to acquire all the utility of the world for one's self, the consequences would not be as valuable as a life that gains an eternal amount of utility with Christ.

The finite and infinite distinction of the utility is further discussed by Jesus when he says:

> Do not store up for yourselves treasures on earth, where moth and rust destroy, and where thieves break in and steal. But store up for yourselves treasures in heaven, where neither moth nor rust destroys, and where thieves do not break in or steal. (Matt 6:19–20, NASB)

Here Jesus points out that earthly utility has a finite duration (his metaphor of moths and vermin) and heavenly treasures have an eternal duration. Surely living a self-sacrificial life has its rewards in this life, but these rewards are for others. For example, forgoing material gain as a surgeon in an industrialized country in order to provide surgical services for humanity in a third world country clearly benefits those who were not able to pay for the benefits of the surgical treatment they received. Equally is it the case for those who spend their entire lives providing relief for victims of natural disasters in third world countries. Mother Theresa is such an example. In all such cases there is a greater good achieved in that one person forgoes personal utility for the sake of others. But greater goods are achieved for the sake of the agent of such actions and for the sake of those the actions impact when the context of the actions is the afterlife. The greater goods being considered here are desirable things that can obtain only in the afterlife and can only be instantiated by God. The range is many, but the particulars include a loving union with God and a loving union with those sacrificially impacted by such actions.[36]

If these eternal goods are merely fictional ends (and done for the sake of others), then a life of sacrificial living that results in no gain in the temporal life of others is total foolishness. Paul declares this point in his letter to the Corinthians:

> Otherwise, what will those do who are baptized for the dead? If the dead are not raised at all, why then are they baptized for them? Why are we also in danger every hour? I affirm, brethren, by the boasting in you which I have in Christ Jesus our Lord, I

---

36. Carson describes these treasures as "love undiluted, a way of life utterly sinless, integrity untarnished, work and responsibility without fatigue, deep emotions without tears, worship without restraint or disharmony or sham, and best of all the presence of God in an unqualified and unrestricted and personal way." See Carson's *Sermon on the Mount*, 76–79.

> die daily. If from human motives I fought with wild beasts at Ephesus, what does it profit me? If the dead are not raised, let us eat and drink, for tomorrow we die. (1 Cor 15:29–32, NASB)

Paul is not advocating some sort of ethical egoism here. It is not clear what he means by gain made for "human reasons," but in rhetorical fashion, he is arguing that the gain is less than the resulting injuries from the encounters. Most likely the human reasons he is referring to are the beliefs in Christ's resurrection and the resurrection of the dead, but taken merely as constructs of the human imagination. That is, the resurrection of Christ and the resurrection of believers from the dead are assumed false realities. Thus whatever self-sacrifices he makes when he fights wild beasts from this subjunctive counter-factual are foolish endeavors. Under such circumstances, it would be better to pursue one's own good and live out an epicurean life. While the end to which Paul aimed was couched in theological language (viz., the salvation of the Roman world), it can equally be couched in the language of utilitarian and *eudiamonian* ethics. In other words, what greater good is achieved if there is no eternal life for those risking their lives to spread the Gospel and for those who accept the Gospel?

The DM Dilemma and the Sixth Question

Finally, the sixth question asks whether "Christian theism" in particular, plays a non-redundancy role in the conceptual development of ethics from de facto considerations. It can be argue that it does. That is, we can draw attention to the historical roles Christianity has played in the metaphysical and epistemological development of a global ethics. There are several claims unique to Christianity for how it plays these special roles. These historical roles do not entail that God is needed metaphysically or epistemologically for ethics. Nor for that matter, in most of the reasons to be presented, does the God of Christianity have to exist for ethics to be impacted and developed in this manner.

Christianity's role here is twofold: (1) Christianity introduced humanity to an understanding of ethics not limited either by self-interest or theological ends, and (2) via the *imago Dei*, Christianity introduced humanity to the concept of the intrinsic value and equality of *all* human persons (what we may call the brotherhood and sisterhood of humanity).

Let's look at the first role. A common narrative in circulation about ethics is that its goal should be to seek the greatest good (where "good' is simply utility, flourishing, or well-being) for all humans (and perhaps even other non-human beings) involved in a situation or to respect all involved in a situation. In either case, what is rejected is ethical egoism; that is, rejecting that what is normative is the self-interest of the agent of the action in the situation. Two observations should be made about this narrative. First, the narrative is primarily "other-centered." Secondly, the narrative values "other centeredness" as an end as opposed to as a means. (Surely an ethical egoist could champion the needs of others so long as her utility is maximized.) This narrative, however, does not object to an exclusive focus on the agent of an action so long as the agent is the only person to gain or lose from the action. It can be said that this narrative embraces or takes as intuitively correct certain features or principles of no one normative ethical theory but of several of the standard normative ethical theories, viz., deontology, utilitarianism, and natural law. This same narrative rejects and prohibits as ethically wrong the following actions: rape, slavery, murder, child abuse, racial and similar forms of discrimination, etc., With this said, the following question comes to mind: how did rational agents like ourselves come to this narrative?

In what follows, I will attempt to answer this question. I will attempt to show that Christianity was a sufficient condition in the development of this ethical narrative. To be sure, I will not attempt to show that Christianity was a necessary condition for this narrative. To do so would be to reject most of what has been argued in this chapter so far. As a sufficient condition for this narrative, the modest claim will simply assert that Christianity was a de facto cause of this narrative, thus providing yet another relationship God has to ethics.

A brief look at history shows that the golden rule and prohibitions against murder, rape, adultery, and stealing can be found in the annals of many civilizations' ethical codes. Such condemnations are correct, and arriving at such truths is not hard to come by with minds functioning from the perspective of rational self-interest. Philosophers like Thomas Hobbes saw this and argued this very point. In the *Leviathan*, Hobbes begins with a thought experiment in which he describes humans as driven primarily by self-interest and living initially in a non-historical state of nature. A state of nature is an existence without a government or cooperative living, where everyone seeks their own well-being without concern for others. Unfortunately if everyone focused on acquiring the goods (e.g., food, land, spouse, clothing, and shelter) essential to their own well-being this would lead to a "constant state of war, of one with all." Hobbes writes, "The life without rule of law is the life of every man against every man which is solitary, dull brutish, nasty and short." [37] This is true for at least four reasons. For one, the goods essential for our well-being are scarce. This leads to fierce competition to acquire these scarce items. Secondly, some humans are more gifted than others or have more material goods than others, but even these individuals need the assistance of others to obtain their well-being, e.g., even those who possess a lot of material goods need to sell those goods to others to be rich and need others to process those goods into usable items. Thirdly, those who are less gifted than others or have less material goods than others will not allow those with more gifts and goods to dominate and exploit them. Finally, those who possess much material goods will likely invade or preemptively attack those who do not have these goods in order to defend their goods and to persuade those they attack that they are a force to be reckoned with. Essentially then, whether a person possesses material goods or not, everyone in the state of nature has something to lose.

In order to escape from these unfortunate states of affairs, rational individuals operating from self-interest contractually agree to live cooperatively under a set of rules. The rules agreed upon are rules that mutually benefit everyone under the contract. It is rational for each member of this community to condemn murder because doing so safeguards each of the persons in the community a right to life; also the mutual agreement not to steal allows each person in the social group a right to keep her material goods without the threat of a takeover from another person in the social group. As Hobbes would add, the community establishes a governing body called the state to ensure by force or penalty that each citizen in the community fulfills her obligation to this mutually agreed upon contract of ethics.

However, a commitment to not commit such acts as murder, rape, and theft captures many of our moral intuitions about what ethics is about, but not all of them. The common ethical narrative referenced earlier would judge this Hobbesian ethic as deficient due to the fact that it is couched in ethical egoism. To be sure, an ethics generated out of self-interest can only muster so much. Such an account of ethics is ontologically sterile in that ethical obligations are maintained only out of a concern for

---

37. For a review of the social contract theory, see Hobbes *Leviathan*, chap. 13.

collective self-interest within an identified contracted society. An ethics of mutual collective self-interest, while arriving at correct ethical truths, fails to capture what many ethicists consider to be a normative feature of ethics, viz., "other-centeredness" as an end. There is nothing in the Hobbesian account that entails or implies "other-centeredness" as an end. Nor for that matter is there anything about a Hobbesian account that would prompt those in the contracted society to value "other-centeredness" as an end. While members of a social contract may flourish ethically with the Leviathan in place to ensure the contract's implementation, the members are merely called to value each other as means and not as ends. This particular problem or sterility of the Hobbesian account is clearly seen by its inability to apply an ascription of dignity to humans qua ends outside a socially contracted society. A Hobbesian ethics explains well why and how humans come to justify the prohibition against acts like murder, rape, and stealing *within* a society, but it does not explain well why humans would also condemn murder outside its particular boarders towards another society. From a social contract perspective, it is conceivable that one society can justifiably flourish at the expense of another society and thus be ethically oblivious and indifferent toward the society it vanquished. In fact, this has been the approach to ethics that civilizations have worked from since the dawn of time in light of the copious wars and exploitation of others that humans have engaged in.

In short, noting that a given society flourishes within its own boundaries does not immune that given society from ethically exploiting other societies. Advanced European countries enslaved Africans to provide free labor for the Americas. Ironically they attempted to justify the atrocity. It is also important to point out that the Africans transported to the Americas as slaves owe their enslavement in part to neighboring African tribes who participated in the slave trade out of self-interest. As painful as it is to break up and sell a family, the conquering Africans involved in the slave trade did not concern themselves with the well-being of their fellow African victims as long as the Africans sold were outside their socially contracted community.

This lack of "other-centeredness" in the Hobbesian account also fails to capture what many[38] ethicists consider to be another essential

---

38. There is no universal consensus here. As noted earlier, some ethicists, for example utilitarians like Peter Singer, argue that humans do not have a privileged position in the moral community of life. As noted earlier, Singer attacks the views of those who wish to give the interests of animals less weight than the interests of

normative feature of ethics, viz., the intrinsic, egalitarian value of *all* human persons such that the value of each human person is not based on social/economic status, ethnicity, usefulness to others, gender, age, religion, nationality, etc. History has shown why ethicists deem this feature of ethics to be essential. For example, a contrived European view about a hierarchy of race (race qua species) allowed countries like Great Britain, Portugal, and Belgium to conceive of their African victims as less than fully human, i.e., belonging to another species. In recent times the Japanese imperial army expanded into the rest of Asia to, among other things, acquire raw material for its industrialized society. Shintoism teaches and thus provided justification for Japanese conquerors to see themselves as sons of heaven ruling over the rest of Asia. But these case studies are consistent with a Hobbesian ethics.

While the beliefs that human persons are and should be treated as ends (or intrinsically valuable) and that all human persons equally possess the same amount of value constitute the core features of most ethical narratives in current circulation, it is worth noting the historical origin of our embracing and coming to know these normative features of ethics. By investigating this origin we will see that Christianity has a de facto relationship to ethics in that the metaphysics of Christianity introduced these features to the Western world.

Specifically Christianity holds that all humans are created by the same God and that, in terms of what humans are, they are all equally valued before God regardless of any conventional or non-conventional category humans may belong to. As the apostle Paul states in Gal 3:28:

> There is neither Jew nor Greek, there is neither slave nor free man, there is neither male nor female; for you are all one in Christ Jesus. (NASB)

This theme is also explicit in Col 3:11:

> [T]here is no distinction between Greek and Jew, circumcised and uncircumcised, barbarian, Scythian, slave and freeman, but Christ is all, and in all. (NASB)

---

human beings. He argues that if we attempt to extend such unequal consideration to the interests of animals, we will be forced to give unequal consideration to the interests of different human beings, e.g., those with defects. However, doing this goes against our moral intuitions. Singer concludes that we must instead extend a principle of equal consideration of interests to animals as well. See Singer's argument for this claim in *Practical Ethics*, 55–82.

While this metaphysics has a theological context, the theology behind it merely functions to strip away from our understanding of humanity the conventional categories we place on each other in terms of hierarchies based on race, religion, gender, class, national origin, or any other form of distinction and discrimination. To be sure, the Pauline texts place our equality in Christ, but this is Paul's modus operandi to show that any distinctions among humans are either man-made or at least lacking in any value before God. In these passages Christ is meant to delete the value humanity places on the conventional and even naturally existing categories humans belong to. With such a metaphysics in hand we would not embrace the Golden Rule in some Hobbesian fashion, as a means to achieve the good life for ourselves. Rather we would see the Golden Rule as an ethical end of behavior in so far as we are motivated to value the good life of others as much as we value it for ourselves since the "other" and ourself are of equal value, independent of a shared society and even at the expense of our own justice and rights. In short, this is what the New Testament refers to as agape or unconditional love. Again the underlying assumption of this Christian metaphysics is that each human should ultimately be concerned with the well-being, transformation, and improvement of *all* other humans, e.g., in their social, psychological, spiritual, and physical nature, as if all humans were one and the same person. Since the care and concern we have for ourselves is unconditional, ipso facto the Christian metaphysics calls us to care for any particular human in unconditional terms as if any other particular human person were our self.

This collapsing of the other into ourselves ignores any categories each human actually belongs to via class, ethnicity, gender, or even if the human is our enemy or has caused offense. In a time and in a Jewish culture that did not embrace this unconditional ethical dictum, Jesus introduces it and explicitly points out that the love he has in mind is not prompted by self-interest:

> You have heard that it was said, "You shall love your neighbor and hate your enemy." But I say to you, love [$\alpha\gamma\alpha\pi\alpha\tau\varepsilon$] your enemies and pray for those who persecute you, so that you may be sons of your Father who is in heaven; for He causes His sun to rise on *the* evil and *the* good, and sends rain on *the* righteous and *the* unrighteous. For if you love those who love you, what reward do you have? Do not even the tax collectors do the same? If you greet only your brothers, what more are you doing *than others*? Do not

even the Gentiles do the same? Therefore you are to be perfect, as your heavenly Father is perfect. (Matt 5:43–48, NASB)

Matthew is not asserting that the rewards are the incentives or motivation for why Jesus says we should love our enemies. After all, he uses the Greek word for unconditional love, αγαπατε. To be sure, Jesus' theological focus on rewards and adoption as sons of God is mainly to provide us with a standard by which we can measure up to God as much as it is possible to do so. It is clear from this text in Matthew that the prescribed intent of our good will toward others is not self-gain. We have here an imperative to ethical behavior that is essentially "other-centered" qua an end as opposed to "other-centered" qua a means. This end is the well-being of the other for the sake of the other. The agent's self-interest would only be a secondary end or not an end at all.[39] This imperative is counter-intuitive to the natural mind where self-interest rules.

More importantly, it would not emerge from a mind that processes ethical reasoning from the perspective of self-interest since the goal or purpose for acting ethically is for the sake of the stipulated enemy. In these cases there would be no net self-gain for the agent of the act (i.e., the one who is called to love his enemy[40]) by forgoing as an end, say, justice. Moreover, the imperative is not required by communal or corporate self-interest either since a society can be functional without the imperative, by merely committing to various forms of alternative justice, e.g., retributive or compensatory justice.

---

39. A principle like the Golden Rule doesn't *per se* capture these ethical intuitions since its imperative for us to treat others like we want to be treated is ambiguous. Social contract theory entices us to treat others like we want to be treated because our own survival requires us to do so. According to social contract theory if we failed to treat others like ourselves, others in turn could equally fail to treat us like they would like to be treated. The application of the Golden Rule here is simply self-serving. However, the application of the Golden Rule could be from formal considerations. That is, if we see ourselves as possessing the properties of being a human person and of being intrinsically valuable, then anything else that instantiates those same two properties should also be treated as such. Notice the Golden Rule can be interpreted in both ways. Moreover, it is not clear whether the Golden Rule is informative for ethical action toward those outside of our social context, viz., those who are not our neighbor or in far proximity. Finally, the Golden Rule also is perspectival; it operates from our individual cognitive limitations of how we prefer to be treated. To be sure, we are not always the most objective discerners of what is best for us.

40. I take it that Jesus' reference to enemy is not per se someone who is in conflict with another person, but to include someone who is neutral or provides no gain for the agent.

Seeing people as ends in themselves may be an obvious intuition and require nothing more than what many call the light of reason, but its introduction as a belief into history was no small feat by Jesus over two millennia ago. His dictum as seen in the Matthew passage and Paul's dictum in his epistles were and are a counter measure to the metaphysics that couches ethics merely in self-interest or convention. Jesus' and Paul's ethical view of the human person was a radical departure from the worldviews of their time and of worldviews prior to their time.[41] Contrary to the hierarchical views of the human person as conceived by their Jewish countrymen and of the Romans who ruled Palestine, Jesus and Paul revealed to humanity a view of the human person that excluded caste and other distinctions of value.[42] This Christian metaphysic was a radical departure from the Greco-Roman world of their time. Let's take a look at the ethical attitudes and values of the ancient world of their day.

From what we know, the Greco-Roman world did not value all human life equally. Despite Greece's great achievements in philosophy, science, art, and literature or Rome's claim to cultural greatness in such areas as politics, military power, and technology, the mores of these civilizations were nothing to be desired or applauded. In fact, the newborn, the sick, and those in slavery in the Greco-Roman civilizations were treated with conditional worth at best and were mere commodities at worst. Among the tragedies done to newborn infants was infanticide. Greek historian Lucius Mestrius Plutarchus (c. 46–20 AD) stated:

> No, but with full knowledge and understanding they themselves offered up their own children, and those who had no children would buy little ones from poor people and cut their throats as if they were so many lambs or young birds; meanwhile the mother stood by without a tear or moan; but should she utter a single moan or let fall a single tear, she had to forfeit the money, and her child was sacrificed nevertheless; and the whole area before

---

41. It should be noted that Paul is not without controversy concerning his view of women. However, such matters as women being responsible for transmitting depravity and their role in the liturgical function of the church do not rule out Paul's view that all humans are ontologically on par when axiology is the issue.

42. Again, there is some debate about whether Paul discriminated against women. From my assessment, Paul's imperative that women should not speak in the assembly of the church (1 Cor 14:34–36), that women are the weaker vessel, and other such comments are to be taken functionally and not metaphysically.

the statue was filled with a loud noise of flutes and drums took the cries of wailing should not reach the ears of the people.[43]

Even Plato made some surprising comments about the value of a human being. He stated that "a poor man who was no longer able to work because of sickness should be left to die" (*Republic* 3.406d–410a). Those who were not blessed with Roman citizenship found life unbearable and lived life as an instrument of entertainment for those who were Roman citizens. Rome is infamously known for its gladiatorial games that began in 264 BCE. As Alvin Schmidt points out, the gladiatorial games were a morbid form of entertainment in the Roman world:

> Gladiators were usually slaves, condemned criminals, or prisoners of war, all of whom were considered expendable . . . Sometimes a hundred or more gladiators fought on a given day . . . Whether fighting beast or men, thousands upon thousands of gladiators were slaughtered during the seven centuries of this cruel institution . . . When Emperor Titus inaugurated the Coliseum in Rome in AD 80, five thousand wild animals were killed in one day, along with the numerous gladiators whose blood saturated the sands of the amphitheater.[44]

To be sure, the ancient Greco-Roman world was not without its virtues. Recall from chapter 4 the reference to the stoic concept *jus gentium*. However, *jus gentium*, like social contract theory, emerged from the minds of ancient Greeks and Romans not because they saw and valued the welfare of the "other" for the sake of the "other" as an end in itself, but *jus gentium* was a practical means of operating a civil society and for maintaining civil and peaceful relationships with foreigners. For example, *jus gentium* required Romans to treat prisoners of war decently and award them the basic human necessities for survival like food and water. If a prisoner of war was abused to the point of death, the person responsible would be prosecuted. However, despite its humanitarian spirit, *jus gentium* did not condemn the practice of slavery. In Rome a person became a slave under several circumstances, e.g., if convicted of a crime like murder or if the person's mother was a slave. At any rate, slavery is slavery and Roman slaves were not awarded the status of a person but were rather relegated to the status of property.

---

43. Plutarchus, *Superstitiones* 171d (ET, 2:495).
44. Schmidt, *How Christianity Changed the World*, 61–62.

Finally, much can be said about Christianity's introduction of certain virtues that, prior to the advent of Christianity, were not endorsed.[45] When we look at the list of twelve virtues Aristotle endorsed, what we find absent are such virtues as mercy, compassion, and humility. We see these virtues introduced in Jesus' Sermon on the Mount discourse, but they are also found throughout the New Testament. Mercy (ἐλεήμων) (e.g., Matt 5:7) as it is described in the Bible does not entail releasing someone from a deserved debt but has a more broad sense of rendering someone free from bondage. Compassion (ἐσπλαγχνίσθη) is mentioned in the New Testament (e.g., Matt 9:36 and Col 3:12) and is equivalent to the combine use of the terms empathy and sympathy. Compassion expresses the emotive reaction of seeing someone or something in dire need of help, feeling bad about their situation, and doing something to alleviate the pain or to meet the need. The paradigm New Testament passage for compassion is Jesus' reaction to the needy crowd in the Gospels: "When He went ashore, He saw a large crowd, and felt compassion for them and healed their sick." (Matt 14:14, NASB)

The New Testament does not just give us an introduction to compassion simpliciter, but rather a sense of compassion for persons unconditionally. The early Christians took to heart Jesus' modeling of unconditional compassion and expressed it as a virtue that ended in death. For example, as far as compassion towards the sick is concerned, Pope Dionysius of Alexandria makes a significant contrast between the early church's attitude and behavior towards the sick and the Greco-Roman world's attitude and behavior as depicted in Alexandria:

> Certainly very many of our brethren, while, in their exceeding love and brotherly-kindness, they did not spare themselves, but kept by each other, and visited the sick without thought of their own peril, and ministered to them assiduously, and treated them for their healing in Christ, died from time to time most joyfully along with them, lading themselves with pains derived from others, and drawing upon themselves their neighbours' diseases, and willingly taking over to their own persons the burden of the sufferings of those around them. And many who had thus cured others of their sicknesses, and restored them to strength, died themselves, having transferred to their own bodies the death that lay upon these . . . But among the heathen all

---

45. I am referring specifically to the Western tradition of ethics. To be sure, the notions of mercy, humility, and compassion can be found in non-Western religions or ethical traditions, e.g., Buddhism and Hinduism.

was the very reverse. For they thrust aside any who began to be sick, and kept aloof even from their dearest friends, and cast the sufferers out upon the public roads half dead, and left them unburied, and treated them with utter contempt when they died, steadily avoiding any kind of communication and intercourse with death; which, however, it was not easy for them altogether to escape, in spite of the many precautions they employed.[46]

Humility (ταπεινοφροσύνη) is mentioned in various places in the New Testament. Not only is it mentioned in the Sermon on the Mount Discourse in Matt 5:3 but also in Luke 14:11, Col 3:12, James 4:6, 1 Pet 5:6, etc. Humility, as a virtue, requires a person to seek and maintain an objective perspective of her abilities, position, and privileges, among other things, and to avoid boasting about these objective features she possesses. As a negative consequence of humility, a person acquires a perspective of who she is not: she is not omnipotent, she is not self-sufficient, and she is not more important than any other human. Among other things, humility leads to community, benevolence, and equality. Contrary to popular opinion, humility is not equivalent to self-debasement, self-hate, or pity. The Apostle Paul provides us with an exemplary example of humility and showcases it as a main feature of Christ's ministry on earth:

> Do nothing from selfishness or empty conceit, but with humility of mind regard one another as more important than yourselves; do not *merely* look out for your own personal interests, but also for the interests of others. Have this attitude in yourselves which was also in Christ Jesus, who, although He existed in the form of God, did not regard equality with God a thing to be grasped, but emptied Himself, taking the form of a bond-servant, *and* being made in the likeness of men. Being found in appearance as a man, He humbled Himself by becoming obedient to the point of death, even death on a cross. (Phil 2:3–8, NASB)

When all is said and done, we see on the horizon of the first century AD a new and radically different metaphysic that entailed a radically progressive ethics. Both were a de facto product of the Christian worldview. For the first time in history, we see a community of people whose ethical actions and character are not limited either by self-interest or theological ends and who treat *all* human persons with equality and intrinsic value. The scholars of the Greco-Roman world seemed unlikely candidates to posit this metaphysics or ethics. I say this, given the worldview they

---

46. Dionysius the Great, *Epistle 12—To the Alexandrians* 6.108–9.

worked from. While it was a matter of time, perhaps, before humanity adopted an altruistic ethics and saw the value of treating all humans equally and with intrinsic value, Christianity can take credit for being the first Western worldview to do so and in an environment foreign to such ethical notions.

Is a Divine-Based Metaethics Equivalent to Ethical Relativism?

The basic assumption behind the DM thesis is that ethics is a matter of some authority figure, in that ethics requires the declaration of someone's thoughts to ground or make true what is right and wrong. DM proponents imply that without God's declarations that we find in the Bible, there could be no ethics since someone has to *say* what is right and wrong in order for there to *be* right and wrong. Consequently, without God and God's word, humans are left to decide for themselves what *is* right and wrong. It is unclear what is at stake here. Notice nothing is problematic in asserting that humans can decide for themselves what they *believe* (or think) is right and wrong. Surely humans are fallible creatures and their declaration of what is right and wrong is fallible as well. And surely God is infallible, and his declarations of what are right and wrong are infallible. In neither case, however, do God's declarations or humanity's declarations of what actions are right and wrong make any action right or wrong. To suggest otherwise is to affirm that actions are right or wrong simply because some authority said they are right or wrong, whether the agent is God or some human. This move is a conflation of epistemology with metaphysics such that "what is believed" and "what is" are one and the same affair. This move is nothing more than relativism discussed earlier with a divine twist.

Contra divine relativism or cultural relativism, I have argued that ethics is not in the mind of God or in the mind of the members of a given culture or society. Ethics is in the acts committed, and correct beliefs about right and wrong are made true by properties or descriptions of the ethical acts themselves (granting the possibility of nominalism) or are true in a platonic sense. Saying they are true because they are the necessary thoughts of God is question-begging. As I have tried to show, proponents of the DM thesis have failed to show how rightness/wrongness and value depend on God's declarations or volitions in a *de re* manner. What we have seen is that this type of grounding to ethics makes ethics arbitrary, question-begging, or non-cognitive. Until these theists provide a theistic basis for ethics without these problems, the criticism of the DM thesis stands.

The Bible, God, and Ethics: A Return to Normative Ethics

Despite the objections posed against the Divine Command theory, many Christians still hold that doing ethics according to God's will as reported in the Bible is the correct and only way to know what is ethically right and wrong. Any approach to ethics that does not acknowledge God is, on this view, a device of spiritual and biblical compromise. The Bible, on this view, rather than the categorical imperative, maximization of utility, or any other reasons is the basis for how we know what is right and wrong. *Ipso facto* anything the Bible directly or indirectly commands is necessary and sufficient for having a Christian normative ethics. Since reasoning is forbidden and biblical commands are taken at face value, this view requires us to take biblical commands as non-contextual, categorical, and exceptionless. In the end, the biblical commands are not to be interpreted as situational to fit the needs of humankind. Human behavior, or more specifically human flourishing, must conform to and be couched in a literal interpretation of the biblical commands. A consequence of this view is that if God commands us not to steal or lie, then if we stole or lied, our action would literally be a sin even if it resulted in saving the life of another human.

Let's call this approach to normative ethics the *Biblical Absolutism Theory* (BAT). Suppose that a natural disaster destroys a small town. Most town people evacuated before the disaster hit, including owners of many businesses like grocery stores. However, some people did not manage to leave and are trapped in the town until outside help arrives. These same towns' people have not eaten for days. Some of them manage to find food in a nearby grocery store. Not knowing when help will arrive, they steal and eat the perishable items for nourishment. According to the BAT, these people acted wrongly and are in sin since they violated God's command not to steal as found in Exodus 20 and Deuteronomy 5. It is not a dispute that the Bible condemns stealing, but are we to take the condemnation in an absolute sense? Does God forbid stealing categorically, or is the condemnation *prima facie*? According to rabbinical hermeneutics of first-century Judaism, the Mosaic Law was prescribed without exceptions. Jesus reveals this view of the Law in his dialogue with the Pharisees:

> And it happened that He was passing through the grainfields on the Sabbath, and His disciples began to make their way along while picking the heads *of grain*. The Pharisees were saying to Him, "Look, why are they doing what is not lawful on the Sabbath?" And He said to them, "Have you never read what David did when he was in need and he and his companions became hungry; how he entered the house of God in the time of Abiathar *the* high priest, and ate the consecrated bread, which is not lawful for *anyone* to eat except the priests, and he also gave it to those who were with him?" Jesus said to them, "The Sabbath was made for man, and not man for the Sabbath. So the Son of Man is Lord even of the Sabbath." (Mark 2:23–28 NASV)

Jesus makes clear that laws and principles serve the good of humankind and that the good of humankind is not held hostage by laws and principles. Essentially then, any form or system of rules are *prima facie* binding.

With all that has been said in this chapter, many perhaps will dismiss the arguments put forward to make ethics an autonomous discipline. With that said, a reflection on the nature of myopia and what actually is the "beef" with these arguments is in order. We do well to avoid the charge made by the Pharisees who argued from tradition rather than the Word.

6

Some Polemic Social Issues in Applied Ethics: Affirmative Action, the Death Penalty, and Abortion

Applied Ethics

IN CHAPTER 4, WE discussed ethical affairs from a theoretical context, by surveying several normative ethical approaches to making ethical decisions in general. With this in hand, we are ready to move on to applied ethics. The topics that we can apply ethics to are copious. If we are concerned with the application of ethics in the business and corporate world, we are engaged in and studying business ethics. If we are concerned with the application of ethics in medicine and health care, then we are engaged in bioethics (or what is called medical ethics). If we are concerned with the application of ethics to policies, affairs, and actions about aging and the elderly, we are engaged in applied ethics to gerontology. Some topics cross over into several topics. For example, social ethics deals with ethical issues and problems that society faces. So the death penalty, affirmative action and abortion would fall under social ethics qua applied ethics. But unlike affirmative action and the death penalty, abortion also falls under bioethics.

In this chapter, we will focus our attention on these three latter issues: affirmative action, the death penalty, and abortion. We will take a look at affirmative action and its relationship to a parallel problem of racism insofar as these are existing problems in the United States. The various pros and cons of affirmative action will be discussed. It will be argued that affirmative action, when practiced as a means (there are several of them) rather than as an end, is not reverse discrimination but rather an appropriate form of justice to eradicate social and economic inequalities that exist along racial lines, and is a public good because of its diversity agenda. Next we will take a look at the ancient practice of the death penalty and its relationship to religion. The death penalty is unique as an ethical issue in that it is commanded by God in Christianity and other religions. This association with ethics and religion will allow clarity in whether the death penalty is ethically right or even theologically right. In the end, it will be argued that as a theological practice, the death penalty had its place in time as a hyperbolic decree from God for certain theological infractions; however, as an ethical practice, it is not ethically warranted and never was intended to be practiced by Jews and Christians. Finally, we will take a look at abortion and its relationship to metaphysics. By definition, an abortion is the termination of a prenatal life. So contrary to popular opinion, an abortion is not the termination of part of a woman's body. There are strong biological facts about the unborn in the womb to buttress this claim. Unlike affirmative action and the death penalty, it is an open question whether abortions terminate a person, a proto-person, or merely a non-person human being (biologically classified). As such, the ethical wrongness of abortion is a gray issue. Unlike affirmative action and the death penalty, the metaphysical correct view of a person and a human determines whether or not abortions and other reproductive procedures (e.g., IVF and the indefinite freezing of embryos) are permissible. So neither the traditional pro-life position nor the traditional pro-choice position will be defended.

Race, Society, and Affirmative Action

Former President Kennedy coined the term "affirmative action" in 1961. The origins of affirmative action began with President Roosevelt in 1941 when he issued an executive order to prevent defense contractors from discriminating against minorities. However, it was after President Lyndon Johnson's *Executive Order 11246* that required contractors working for the Federal government to take "affirmative action to ensure that applicants are employed without regard to their race, creed, color, or national origin." Over the years, to reduce gender and racial discrimination and disparities, affirmative action was augmented to the degree that preferences toward racial minorities and women became the focus not just for employment but also for admission in educational institutions.

As far as a defense of affirmative action is concerned, the arguments come in two varieties. One variety is often called "backward-looking" arguments. They argue from the perspective that affirmative action is justified from considerations of justice for past racial and gender related harm to women and people of color. Seminal work by Judith Jarvis Thomson is representative of such arguments.[1] Thomson's backward-looking argument defends affirmative action as a form of compensation for past harms against minorities and women for exclusion from educational institutions and places of employment (because of such practices as Jim Crowism and sexism). Thomson suggests that standard notions of merit, as the basis for employment and education acquisition, be suspended for the sake of this greater good of rectifying past harms. The other variety is often called "forward-looking" arguments. They argue from the perspective that affirmative action is justified from utilitarian considerations by (1) eradicating presently existing racial and gender disparities and (2) providing enriched education benefits and effective work environments through diversity. Work by Thomas Nagel and James P. Sterba are representative of such arguments.[2] While the intentions behind affirmative action are good, in recent times affirmative action has been looked at with scorn without regard to its intentions, particularly when it is raced based. Let us take a look at some of the objections posed against race based affirmative action.

Objection One: Reverse Discrimination

The first objection we will consider is the frequent charge that affirmative action is essentially reverse discrimination. In fact, this is the most common, popular charge against affirmative action. Accordingly, affirmative action discriminates against the rights of whites in that it takes away their rights to educational and employment opportunities. A sizable percent of the evangelical Christian community even argues in this fashion. For these Christians, the Bible calls for equality of all humans in that all humans have inalienable rights. Since affirmative action is based on racial and gender preferences, they argue that it violates the rights of whites

---

1. For a backward-looking argument in favor of affirmative action, see Thomson, "Preferential Hiring," 364–484.

2. For a forward-looking argument in favor of affirmative action, see Nagel, "Equal Treatment and Compensatory Discrimination," 348–63.

and white males in particular. Some go as far as saying affirmative action is an intrinsically unjust policy. In agreement with this objection, rights are serious issues and the violation of any right is a *prima facie* problem. Before the issue is addressed as to whether affirmative action is in violation of anyone's rights, it would be important to take a historical look at just how some opponents of affirmative action have proceeded with this charge and whether their charge against affirmative action was merely about rights violations or about their own views regarding race and entitlements.

In his book, *Affirmative Action*, Tim Wise writes about the *Gratz v Bollinger* case which was brought before the Supreme Court in 2003. This case involved a white female applicant named Jennifer Gratz who applied to the University of Michigan undergraduate school of Literature, Arts and Sciences in 1995. She was rejected and she cried reverse discrimination because she "knew" people of color were selected over her who were not as qualified. How Getz knew about the qualification of the other applicants is a mystery. For sure, her belief was not based on a review of the other applicants' files. The facts speak otherwise. For example, in 1995, when she was rejected, over 1000 other white applicants were accepted to Michigan even though they had lower test scores than she did. However, she did not complain about the "unfairness" of the University for their admission. Wise adds that there were several thousand other white applicants who also were rejected despite having had higher scores and grades than she did. So with this context in hand, there are some interesting questions to consider. From the facts alone, Gratz was not passed over on behalf of people of color, so much as she was by other whites, who had lower test scores than she did. Moreover, if anything, the 2000 other whites who were rejected were in a more justified position to cry discrimination than Gratz. Even in the absence of affirmative action at Michigan, Gratz would have still been rejected since there were one thousand other white applicants who were accepted into the University despite their lower test scores using the straight grade and SAT formula that she used. So would Gratz have complained against these other whites and what would be the basis of her complaint?

In another case, a white male named Tom Woods also cried reverse discrimination when he lost a university teaching position to an African American female at San Francisco University. His public protest of alleged racial discrimination led to Proposition 209, a California initiative that made affirmative action illegal in education, employment and contracting in California. Later Woods admitted that he did not know of the qualifications of the African American female. It turned out that she was far more qualified than him, having published several books and articles. Woods also did not mention that he was unpublished for the first 15 years after receiving his doctorate.

The belief or perception that affirmative action takes employment and education opportunities away from whites is very common among those who oppose affirmative action. Unfortunately this belief is maintained among the populace just as much as the belief that the discipline of philosophy is merely about speculative ideas and opinions where truth is never the goal. The fact of the matter is that statistics do not support this highly popular belief about affirmative action. Nearly 90 percent of faculty members at United States universities are white; less than 6 percent are black. If the fear of reverse discrimination were based on actual reverse discrimination, we would expect the employment of minorities to be much higher than this.[3] Several studies of court cases have shown that the number of racial discrimination cases filed by whites and sex discrimination cases filed by men ranges from 2 percent to 5 percent of all discrimination cases. The remaining cases involve charges of discrimination reported by people of color, women, the elderly, the handicapped, etc. Another study of complaints filed with the Equal Employment Opportunities Commission between 1987 and 1994 revealed that only 4 percent of racial discrimination cases involved charges of reverse discrimination.[4] The instantiation of affirmative action is not as rampant as the rhetoric would imply; nevertheless, affirmative action has conjured up existing attitudes of some who have used affirmative action as a scapegoat.

While Gratz and Woods apparently had an ax to grind, given the shallowness of their accusations, criticism of such behavior does not rule per se in favor of affirmative action. The question still remains whether affirmative action violates the rights of whites. We will return to the Gratz v Bollinger case, but let us take a look at the very first Supreme Court case involving affirmative action in academia hiring and admissions in order to begin answering this important question. This would be the famous Regents of the University of California v. Bakke case. The case involved the University of California, Davis, Medical School and Allan Bakke, a white applicant. UC Davis had two separate admissions pools, one for

3. Wise, *Affirmative Action: Racial Preference in Black and White*, 69, 70.

4. Burstein, "Reverse Discrimination Cases in Federal Courts," 511–28; Reskin, *The Realities of Affirmative Action in Employment*, 73.

general applicants, and a second pool for minority and economically disadvantaged applicants. The former pool was opened to anyone but the latter excluded whites. The medical school reserved 16 of its 100 slots for applicants enrolling through the second pool. Bakke applied, both in 1973 and 1974, and was rejected both times despite the fact that his test scores were higher than applicants in the second pool. Bakke complained because he believed he was a victim of reverse discrimination in light of the 16 slots reserved for minority and economically disadvantaged applicants. Bakke argued that his rejection was in violation of Title VI of the Civil Rights Act of 1964 which essentially asserted: *No person in the United States shall, on the ground of race, color, or national origin, be excluded from participation in, be denied the benefits of, or be subjected to discrimination under any program or activity receiving Federal financial assistance.* Bakke argued that he was better qualified than the minority applicants who were accepted, and since they were accepted over him, the only reason for their acceptance was based purely on their skin color, which he asserted was racial discrimination. The court ruled in favor of Bakke because it agreed that he was a victim of reverse discrimination. In the ruling, Justice Powell argued that UC-Davis Medical School was involved in an illegal assignment of admission slots based on racial quotas.

But as Ronald Fiscus argues, the court's decision was problematic.[5] Fiscus takes a historical look at the present status of one particular group of minorities, African Americans. If African Americans were not subjected to the ills of slavery and racism, we would expect them to be represented in educational and employment circles relative to the percentage of the population they represent, viz., 13.4 percent. "In a more perfect world those minority applicants would have achieved superior high school records and MCAT scores in proportion to their percentage of the general population."[6] A person's denial of this counter-factual smacks of racism in so far as the person attributes the educational and employment failures of African Americans to features intrinsic to the very nature of African Americans. At any rate, in a world free of racial and other forms of discrimination, there would be no need to set aside 16 slots for enrollment at institutions like UC Davis; all applicants would have access to the skills needed to perform well on placement tests. So, argues Fiscus, affirmative action is a means of compensating for the lack of skills needed

---

5. Fiscus, *Constitutional Logic of Affirmative Action*, chaps. 1, 3.
6. Ibid., 75.

to perform well on tests caused by racism and other discriminatory factors. Fiscus' argument leads to the claim that in the absence of affirmative action, whites are reaping the benefits of quality education due to past practices of racism against minorities like African Americans. Moreover, Fiscus argues, in an ideal world without past discriminatory practices in place and where affirmative action would not be needed, "Bakke's so-called objective record would have placed him below the top hundred candidates [regardless of race]. [Contrary to Bakke's complaints and expectations, he] apparently would have ranked among the top hundred whites applicants, but he would not have ranked among the top hundred of *all* candidates."[7]

When we look at the person, Allan Bakke, we see a similar tale to that of Jennifer Gratz's cry of reverse discrimination. Like Gratz, we have reason to question the motive for Bakke's assertion that his rejection at UC Davis was an instance of reverse discrimination. Like Gratz, we have reason to suggest that the charge of reverse discrimination was Bakke's ad hoc modus operandi for overturning his rejection to the University of California Medical School at Davis. Bakke was 37 years old when he applied and may have been rejected because of his age; Bakke was rejected at ten other schools, one of which had no slots set aside for minorities; and Bakke never complained about the 36 whites who were accepted over him despite having lower scores than him. In light of the confounding variables surrounding Bakke's rejection, we are left puzzled as to why Bakke specifically focused on UC Davis and was specific about which particular variable was responsible for his rejection. As we will see later, while the Supreme Court ruled in favor of Bakke, the question of race in the Bakke case eventually leads to support for affirmative action.

Unmoved or unaware of the shortcomings of the Bakke, Gratz, and Woods cases or of the other facts just mentioned, the sentiment of many people in society still insist that affirmative action is reverse discrimination because it violates rights. Obviously no one simpliciter is for violating anyone's rights. So whether or not affirmative action is wrong or not, its wrongness won't turn on the intended goal to violate someone's rights as an end. Independent of the Courts' decisions, this popular rights violation argument has the following form: (1) affirmative action violates one person's rights for another person's rights and (2) in principle it is wrong to violate one person's rights for another person's

---

7. Ibid.

rights. (3)Therefore affirmative action is wrong. Proponents of this argument hope to cover every instance of rights violation and declare them wrong. To speak in such absolute terms is problematic. However, in their defense of (2) often an appeal to Jim Crow laws is made in a *reductio ad absurdum* fashion. Surely Jim Crow laws were wrong. Thus opponents of affirmative action claim that affirmative action is one wrong used to compensate for another wrong.

From 1876 until the Civil Rights Act of 1964, Jim Crow laws[8] and their perennial racist spirit flowed through the veins of nearly all Southern states' structures and institutions. Jim Crow laws allowed for public schools, public transportation, washrooms, and restaurants to have separate buildings or locations for whites and "coloreds." During WWII, for example, captured German soldiers that were transferred to the United States were allowed to eat in American restaurants wherever they wanted to sit. African American soldiers, on the other hand, who fought for the United States against these Germans were not afforded the same privileges and rights. They, unfortunately, were either not served, ordered to selected seating, or forced to order "carry out" in these restaurants because of the state sanctioned Jim Crow laws. According to critics of affirmative action, if racial discriminating against African American soldiers because of racial preferences for whites was wrong during Jim Crow days, then it is now wrong in any form toward any human, particularly as it is expressed in the implementation of affirmative action policies that impact whites.

---

8. In 1890 Louisiana put into law the "Separate Car Law," which required blacks and whites to ride in separate train cars under the guise of equal accommodations for both. In 1892, in protest to the Jim Crow Law, Louisiana blacks set the stage for Homer Plessy to sit in a white train car in order to get arrested. He was arrested and his lawyer took the matter to court. Judge John H. Ferguson upheld the law, and Plessy's attorney took the case to the Supreme Court in *Plessy v. Ferguson*. On May 18, 1896, the U.S. Supreme Court, ruled in favor of Ferguson and the "equal but separate" law in a seven-to-two decision. The term "Jim Crow" has its roots in the 1832 derogatory depiction of blacks by white actor Thomas D. Rice in what he called Jump Jim Crow. Jim Crow Laws quickly spread throughout the South. In fact, discriminatory laws were in place well before Jim Laws became the order of the day. Denying African American men the right to vote through legislating laws similar to Jim Crow Laws began as far back as the beginning of the 1890s. These laws required literacy tests, poll taxes, and all-white Democratic Party primaries to ensure the exclusion of black men because of the deficiencies of their social/economic background.

What is happening here is that critics are describing affirmative action as equivalent to Jim Crowism.[9] This is a gross misunderstanding of what affirmative action is even if instances of affirmative action turn out to be unjust. Taking a perspective that ignores history and sociology, those who describe affirmative action as equivalent to Jim Crowism believe affirmative action is an end rather than a means policy about racial preferences. As such, according to this misunderstanding of affirmative action, people of color are selected over whites or white males *merely because* of race. Therefore, affirmative action like Jim Crowism is blatantly unjust. If this is a fair and accurate description of affirmative action then ipso facto it is reverse discrimination. So let us take a look at affirmative action to see if it is equivalent to Jim Crowism (or at least analogous to it). If they are equivalent or analogous, whatever is true of one is true or likely true of the other.

Let us look at Jim Crowism as our first analogue. It has the following features:

- Discrimination based solely on race.
- Discrimination out of contempt for a race.
- Discrimination to maintain a race based economic monopoly

Jim Crowism clearly violates the most fundamental human rights and civil rights afforded to any human (see chapter 3). As a series of policies, Jim Crowism held that racial preference for whites was an end in itself. So are the same features true of affirmative action? Is racial preference for persons of color an end in itself for affirmative action policies?

First, when we look at affirmative action, we see that it is mainly employed where race is a main, but not sole, component for discriminating between races. What many opponents of affirmative action are saying when they equate it with Jim Crowism is that affirmative action is in the business of preferential treatment for individuals solely because of their ethnicity and color as an end, even when the individuals were unqualified. This is a common belief among many opponents of affirmative action, particularly among disgruntle whites who were looked over by a hiring committee in favor of a minority, like Tom Woods. It is unreasonable to assert that a Hispanic American who is selected over a white male for a university teaching position is unqualified and selected solely because of his race. If he were selected merely because he is a person of color, then the selection

---

9. Glazer, *Affirmative Discrimination: Ethnic Inequality and Public Policy*.

process would be reverse discrimination and equivalent to Jim Crowism as an end policy. But surely he isn't unqualified since the announcement for the position he applied to stipulates that the potential candidate needs a PhD. Whereas with Jim Crowism, the reason why the black child could not drink from a water fountain during Jim Crow days was solely because she was black; the Hispanic male is not selected solely because he is a person of color. It is irrational to think a hiring committee would hire an unqualified Hispanic to teach physics if he is unqualified to teach physics.

Secondly, unlike Jim Crow Laws, affirmative action does not discriminate out of contempt for a race. Jim Crow Laws were established and maintained to discriminate against persons of color merely because of distain and hatred for persons of color. During the days before and during Jim Crow Laws, many whites perceived African Americans as intellectually inferior, physically unpleasant to the eyes, and among other things, hygienically filthy. Jim Crow Laws allowed a de jure buffer for whites who wanted a comfortable distance from African Americans and who wanted to establish a public and legal way of life that affirmed white superiority. Whereas with affirmative action, when a person of color is preferred over a white person for a job or for admission to a school, clearly the motivation to establish and maintain this racial preference is void of distain and hatred for whites. Thus again the exclusion of whites in affirmative action policies is not desirable as an end. Affirmative action, unlike Jim Crow Laws, as a means policy, can be concerned with equalizing the playing field of opportunity or undoing past harms; it is not focused on or fueled by racial contempt for whites.

Thirdly, Jim Crow Laws and similar Southern laws that legally prohibited African American political power or simply intended to provide de facto limits to African Americans' political power allowed whites to maintain a monopoly over the political and financial institutions in the southern United States. The most widespread Jim Crow Laws mandated racial segregation in schools and in public accommodation such as railroads, restaurants, buses, and street cars. As much as Jim Crow Laws in writing were based on the so-called "separate but equal clause," virtually nowhere in the South were affairs equal. Most accommodations in the South were not only separate but also unequal and inferior for African Americans. To be sure, sitting in the back of a bus, sitting in the balcony of a theatre, or not being able to dine in a restaurant could hardly be based on equality. Such segregation resulted in inferior education and inaccessibility to political power for African Americans. In some southern states, it was illegal to provide housing to African Americans in an all-white community. Now the reason Jim Crow Laws could be implemented into American society was because the authors of such laws were white and controlled the legislative power to allow such laws to be put into law. Simply put, affirmative action policies cannot function this way. The clear reason for this is that ethnic minorities (e.g., African Americans) do not have an economic and political power base to establish and maintain this reverse ethnic monopoly, even if they were assisted by sympathetic white supporters.

As has been shown, to muster the charge that affirmative action violates the rights of whites in an equivalent way that Jim Crow did is a difficult task to perform if at all possible. Obviously then affirmative action policies are not equivalent to Jim Crow Laws but if affirmative action violates any rights, what rights are supposed to be the target of this violation?

The answer to this question is not at all obvious. Usually when this objection is raised, the key concern is that affirmative action discriminates against a white person's right to be judged by a color blind policy of individual merit. So apparently what is at stake here is the right to be judged by individual merit either for academic achievement or work performance. Merit generally connotes an individual's earned right to some desired good based on her self-effort. Merit is generally quantified by highest GPA, highest test scores, sales made, generated revenue, etc. Thus opponents of affirmative action charge that affirmative action denies individuals, with the greatest merit, their right to the goods they earned a right to and, in turn, rewarded those without merit access to these same goods. In a way, then, theft is perceived to have occurred. Among those who champion this objection to affirmative action they may also champion a relatively recent epistemology that Edwardo Bonilla-Silva calls *color blind racism*.[10] A significant portion of society and academia embraces this en vogue form of racism. It consists of one or all of the following four:

1. *Abstract liberalism*: uses concepts of political and social liberalism (e.g., equal opportunity, individualism and egalitarianism) to explain racial problems or explain them away (e.g., rejecting affirmative action and embracing color blindness)

---

10. Bonilla-Silva, *Racism Without Racists*, 25–52.

2. *Naturalization*: asserts that humans have a natural tendency towards homogeneity and hemophilia

3. *Cultural racism*: interprets social-economic disparities within an ethnic group to be dysfunctional culture

4. *Minimization of racism*: maintains the attitude that racism is rare and when it occurs it is due to individuals rather than to institutions.

Proponents of color blind racism appear "'reasonable' and even 'moral,' while opposing almost all practical approaches to deal with de facto racial inequality."[11] They flirt with a nostalgic perspective of the Civil Rights Era and its leaders. Their most notably favored Civil Rights leader is Martin Luther King Jr. In 1967, the April edition of *Life Magazine* referred to King's anti-Vietnam position as "demagogic slander" and "a script for Radio Hanoi." Later, former president Ronald Reagan described King as a near-Communist. In recent times suddenly King has become the poster boy for those who espouse abstract liberalism in their charge against affirmative action. Bracketing out everything else King said on racial equality, they quote a single phrase in his 1963 *I have a Dream* address about his children not being judged by "the color of their skin..." Thus, they hold, King was affirming his disapproval of affirmative action and his affirmation for individual merit. The African American conservative scholar Shelby Steele, in his *The Content of Our Character* interprets King this way. The East Indian conservative Dinesh D'Souza in his 1995 book *The End of Racism* says affirmative action "seems to be a repudiation of King's vision, in that it involves a celebration and affirmation of group identity [as opposed to individual merit]." We have myopia showing its face here. What King actually remarked was that he was against his children being *valued* because of their skin color; his speech made no reference to his children being *selected* because of their skin color. Even if King's comment was intended to blast racial preferences, the context of his speech then would be a day when Americans live in an ideal society where racial discrimination and racial economic inequalities did not exist. No one who advocates affirmative action argues for affirmative action under these ideal circumstances. Proponents of affirmative action defend affirmative action as a *means to* this ideal America, not as an *end in* this ideal America. Again though, King's comment was about the respect his children should receive from society as humans,

---

11. Ibid., 28.

not their job and educational opportunities. Institutions that implement affirmative action do not judge the value of people in light of their skin color nor do they select people, in many cases, because of the content of their character. When a person applies to a law school, he is minimally banking on his academic merit to contribute to his acceptance, not on the respectable nature of his character. Bakke did not object to his rejection from UC Davis' Law School because his character was not considered!

Moreover, King was actually in favor of affirmative action. In his 1963 Why We Can't Wait speech, King argued:

> Whenever this issue of compensatory or preferential treatment for the Negro is raised, some of our friends recoil in horror. The Negro should be granted equality, they agree, but he should ask for nothing more. On the surface, this appears reasonable, but it is not realistic. For it is obvious that if a man enters the starting line of a race three hundred years after another man, the first would have to perform some incredible feat in order to catch up.[12]

It is obvious from this speech that King is arguing for a backwards-looking approach to affirmative action. Nevertheless, apart from this historical discussion of King's actual words and their relevance to affirmative action, talk of merit as an objection to affirmative action makes false assumptions about who has merit and how important merit is.

First, affirmative action policies generally consider the index by which merit is measured to be important in selecting individuals. As was pointed out during the discussion of Jim Crowism, affirmative action is not merely about racial preferences; merit is important too. Proponents of affirmative action look at GPA's, test scores or experience as either a pre-requisite or as one of several factors for the selection process. Among these factors, merely being a minority is not a sufficient condition for the application of affirmative action. To reiterate, it is not rational or prudent to select individuals that are unqualified. Businesses that select unqualified employees cannot compete, from the perspective of profit making, with businesses that hire qualified employees. Ramifications would also be detrimental for organizations that are non-profit, but primarily focus on revenue, e.g., universities. Graduation rates would be low and students would be set up for failure if they are selected without qualifications.[13]

---

12. King, *Why We Can't Wait*, 124.

13. While some would argue that this in fact is what results from affirmative action, this objection is confounded. If a university admits minorities that are academically challenged, then the obligation falls on the university to provide remedial

Secondly, if individual merit trumps racial preferences it should equally trump all preferences in selections. Ironically, though, proponents of the merit objection say little to nothing against these other preferences. Consider alumni and athletic preferences. Alumni preferences account for 25 percent of the student body of United States universities and colleges. Harvard University's admission rate for the children of alumni has been between 35–40 percent![14] Moreover, Harvard admits children of alumni who are less qualified than children of non-alumni. Former vice President Al Gore's son, Albert Gore, was admitted to Harvard with lower than normal admission qualifications. Preferences for children of alumni have been in practice since shortly after World War I. They began in part to reduce Jewish American enrollment. However, since the inception of preferential admissions, complaints have mainly focused on racial preferential admissions for African Americans. Ironically a 1991 report by Berkeley's Institute for the Study of Social Change reported that more whites have been admitted to the top 10 elite United States institutions via alumni preferences than the combined total of African Americans and Latinos via affirmative action.[15] In the 1980s when there was an increase in highly qualified Asian Americans applying to universities there was not also an increase in their enrollment. This was not due to quotas for African Americans as some feared. Rather Asian Americans were being overlooked and displaced by sons and daughters of white alumni with lower test scores. Most hypocritical along these lines is the discovery that many opponents of affirmative action on the University of California board of regents used their position of privilege to "curry favor in the admissions process for" sons and daughters of friends and relatives.[16]

Thirdly, proponents of affirmative action have pointed out that the gravity of merit is lessened when it is put in a historical context. Accordingly, talk of white male merit in terms of earned degrees, test scores, etc., cannot be quantified in a vacuum. Some white males have superior GPA's and test scores because they benefited from a superior primary and

---

courses or programs that would bring the students up to standard. Students who are unqualified for college are not unqualified by nature but by their inadequate primary and secondary education. An adequate affirmative action program should include not just preferences for minority admission but also for minority retention. Universities do have such retention programs.

14. Busenberg and Smith, "Affirmative Action and Beyond," 170.
15. Woo, "Belief in Meritocracy an Equal-Opportunity Myth."
16. Lawrence and Matsuda, *We Won't Go Back*, 96.

secondary education which they in no way were responsible for. As with any individual born or raised in a fortunate environment, their success in life is just as much a matter of luck as it is merit. Conversely, many people of color, particularly African Americans, are born into poverty and thus inherent substandard education that their white male counter-parts generally do not inherent.[17]

Fourthly, the objection falsely assumes that talk of most deserving is never in conflict with other values such as social utility, where social utility trumps individual merit. That is, proponents of affirmative action have argued that when individual merit is continuous with talk of who is most qualified, sometimes the terms of who is most qualified is a matter of social or over all utility. Thus medical schools can choose applicants who will be the most useful and effective doctors in light of a community's most pressing needs. So an applicant's *blackness* may make a difference in being the most effective doctor in treating black patients in black urban settings. To be sure, it wouldn't be *per se* because black doctors can relate better to black patients, but because historically they have usually set up practices in black communities where non-blacks have gone elsewhere. If there is a shortage of doctors in the black community, the existence of an affirmative action policy seeking black medical students could make the shortage diminish. As Bernard Boxill argues, even if *some* white doctors are more likely to practice in black ghettos than black doctors, considering race as a criterion for admission to medical school is not undermined. The appeal to affirmative action to ensure that black doctors set up practice in black ghettos is based on the generalization that black doctors do set up practice in black ghettos. But as with any generalization, exceptions are allowable without compromising the truth of the generalization.[18]

Finally, in a rather tongue and cheek way, sometimes opponents of affirmative action appeal to the NBA draft selection to charge proponents of affirmative action with inconsistency in so far as they downplay the importance of individual merit. Let us call this the "NBA Draft Objection." Proponents of the NBA Draft Objection point out that since the time African Americans were allowed to play in the NBA, African Americans have dominated the NBA for the simple reason that they merit this dominance based on their hard work, developed skills, and performance. So, the argument goes, if proponents of affirmative action want

---

17. Rachels, "What People Deserve," 150–63.
18. Boxill, "Equality, Discrimination and Preferential Treatment," 340.

to downplay the importance of individual merit where individual effort, skills and performance are front center, then they should consistently downplay individual merit for being drafted into the NBA. But there are two problems with the NBA Draft Objection. First, recruiting less skilled non-African American players would be in order if there were an overall social utility of preference for doing so. But surely no one, particularly proponents of affirmative action, would suggest doing this. Sports fans want their teams to win regardless of the team members' skin color. If this were not the case, the fans would complain that the team members were mainly African American despite the fact the team had a winning season. So there must be something wrong with appealing to overall social utility over individual intrinsic merit in the NBA.

Secondly, what proponents of the NBA Draft Objection fail to factor into this comparison between individual intrinsic merit in education/employment and individual intrinsic merit in the NBA are the prerequisites for acquiring merit for either one. Entrance into a university that is based on individual intrinsic merit is assessed by entrance examinations (e.g., ACT and SAT). However again, to perform well on any entrance exam, a person needs adequate primary and secondary education. Adequate educational institutions, at any level, require adequate financial backing. The following are some alarming facts about primary and secondary education. Less than 10 percent of public school revenue comes from the federal government and the remaining 90 percent comes from the state and local sources. While states have taken up some of the burden from individual districts, local sources of revenue perpetuate a static source of discrimination against the poor. That is, property taxes that are determined by and collected at the school-district level accounts for 34 percent of funding for public schools. If a school is in an affluent area with a lot of money, the local property taxes will be high. As a result, the funding that schools receive varies according to the economic base of the communities they are located in. Public schools in wealthier communities receive more funding and public schools in poorer communities receive less funding. These varying economic circumstances in turn lead to a variation in school expenditures and quality of education. For example, high quality teachers are more likely to apply to schools with higher salaries, best facilities, and latest in learning technologies. Conversely teachers less qualified will trickle down to public schools offering less money and having fewer resources. In the end, the quality of the students produced will clearly not be determined by their individual merit but by the financial base of their school.[19]

The relationship of these findings to African Americans should be clear. Over 27 percent of African Americans live in poverty and over 39 percent of African American children, less than 18 years old, live in poverty. African Americans growing up in low-income communities, due to no fault of their own, are thus bound to be deficient in the skills needed to perform well on the entrance examinations to a university. Persons not growing up in poverty neighborhoods, due to no effort of their own, thus have access to skills needed to perform well on the entrance examinations. Such is not the case with entrance into professional sports. Basketball is usually used as the paradigm in this anti-affirmative action objection to social merit, but this is unfortunate since acquiring skills to perform well in the NBA does not require financial backing. Whether a person is born into poverty or riches, the opportunity to acquire the skills for the NBA simply requires hard work on the court. The poorest of the poor can manage this requirement. All that is needed is a basket and a ball; the latter can be found in any park in any poor neighborhood. Merit here is simply an individual affair. To reiterate, skills to perform well on entrance exams require adequate education and anyone born into poverty does not have access to this kind of quality education. Proponents of affirmative action are aware of the obvious differences between merit for professional sports and merit for higher learning at a university. This is why proponents of affirmative action do not demand its implementation in cases where the playing field is equal among all competitors, e.g., such as it is in many professional sports.

Objection Two: Unjust Compensatory Rewards

A second objection to affirmative action argues against affirmative action's backwards-looking justification of *compensatory justice*. According to the objection, affirmative action intends to rectify the harms of, say, African Americans, at the expense of white males who supposedly had little or nothing to do with the past harm of African Americans. Moreover, the actual recipients of preferential treatment are often middle and upper class minorities who have suffered little to no harm. This is because, as the objection goes, only middle and upper class minorities would have the skills

---

19. Friedman, *Measure of a Nation*, 99–130.

and abilities needed to fill job positions or excel at the college level.[20] In all likelihood, the objection continues, the African Americans' possession of these skills and abilities is an indication that they did not suffer from a deficient education. So while these middle and upper class minorities may not be the most qualified or have the best test scores, they had equally comparable education to that of their white counterparts. These middle and upper class minorities are equivalent to the middle and upper class minorities in Fiscus' ideal world scenario. This all goes to argue that a need for affirmative action is redundant at best and unjust at worst. Moreover, the objection adds, affirmative action overlooks many individual Appalachian whites who are actually harmed due to a deficient education. This objection is wrong for several reasons.

First, the objection fails to address the benefits of affirmative action for lower class minorities who are skilled or as intelligent as middle class minorities independent of them having first rate education. Sure, economics contributes greatly to the quality of education a person receives, but even under depleted conditions, some intelligent persons can excel educationally in impoverished primary schools. Paradigmatic examples are minorities like Ben Carson, who had a humble, poor beginning but now is head surgeon of pediatric neurosurgery at John Hopkins; Booker T. Washington, who was born a slave and lived in impoverish when freed but when on to help develop what s now know as Tuskegee University; or Oprah Winfrey who also had origins in poverty but went on to become a billionaire. However, these are exceptional individuals that the general population of African Americans should not be measured by. But for the majority of individual persons, if they grew up in poverty conditions they are likely not to excel, regardless of ethnicity. Very few people of any ethnic background could achieve the success of either Carson, Washington, or Winfrey without quality education. With that said, the point is that skills and abilities can be acquired or possessed without quality education. So let's not throw the baby out with the bath water. Even if most beneficiaries of affirmative action are middle class, this does not warrant the opposition to it for impoverish African Americans who have raw talent but not the quality education. But according to the objection, the needed quality education cannot come from affirmative action since affirmative action also benefits middle class minorities as well. Truth be told, the absence

---

20. Simon, "Preferential Hiring," 315–19; Sher, "Reverse Discrimination, the Future, and the Past," 81–87; Goldman, *Justice and Reverse Discrimination*, 65–102.

of affirmative action benefits the middle class of any ethnic group at the expense of those without the quality education.

Secondly, the objection assumes that affirmative action is only for highly skilled jobs. This is not true. Even if lower class minorities are not generally as educated and skilled as middle class minorities, their economic status does not necessarily depend on such prerequisites. There are plenty of jobs that do not require college degrees, viz., semiskilled, blue-collar, craft, police and fire fighters jobs. Affirmative action policies have benefited minorities in such cases.[21]

Objection Three: Racial Prejudice Is Outlawed and a Relic of the Past

Without affirmative action in place, critics of affirmative action hold that racial discrimination would go away, since affirmative action, they argue, is the only form of discrimination in practice and is de facto against white males (with the exception of gender based affirmative action). Specifically, the argument goes as follows: Affirmative action allegedly is supposed to eradicate racial discrimination against minorities and women. However, racial discrimination is the result of racial prejudice and racial prejudice does not exist against minorities and women except in rare cases. Racial discrimination does exist against whites and white males in particular when affirmative action policies are used. Therefore, affirmative action is unjust against whites or redundant because racial discrimination does not occur against minorities and women.

Unfortunately, although discrimination against minorities and women is no longer legal, laws against racial discrimination are not sufficient to control the existence or amount of racial discrimination against these groups. This is in part true because racial discrimination does not entail racial prejudice. It is very conceivable that a corporation can implement (even if not intentionally) a practice of hiring primarily white males.[22] On this point, what this third objection fails to acknowledge

---

21. Leonard, "Antidiscrimination of Reverse Discrimination," 145–74; Leonard, "Employment and Occupational Advance under Affirmative Action," 381–84.

22. This is an instance of what is called institutional racism. Institutional racism can be defined as practices and policies in institutions that sustain racial discrimination, such as in places like schools, work places, and agencies that provide education, healthcare, criminal justice, and employment. A specific institution (i.e., a particular corporation) may sustain racial discrimination without the practices at the corporation

is the perennial problem of institutional racism via *networking* which can exist without racial prejudice. Studies have shown that new job opportunities are often advertised by word of mouth-by family, neighbors and friends.[23] It saves publicity costs and it garners job applicants for whom a reliable worker has vouched. Moreover, Katheen Parker of the National Center for Career Strategies reported in 1990 that 80 percent of executives find their jobs through networking.[24] Networking is not illegal so long as the jobs are announced to the general public. How is this related to discrimination? Well it is common knowledge that America is a racially segregated country and relationships seldom cross racial lines. Ninety percent of whites claim that they have no problem with blacks moving into their neighborhood; however, when their neighborhood reaches 7 percent black, whites begin moving out massively.[25] This "exodus" indicates that for whatever the reasons are for the *white flight*, whites lack black relationships. This is unfortunate since networking is generally relationally based and thus race-specific. Whites occupy more white collar jobs than persons of color. If networking occurs, it will likely be a white person in a position of power who vouches for their friend. While this white employee would not harbor much racial prejudice, the friend she vouched for is likely to be white. In this unfortunate "racial" polarization, minorities have the most to lose since whites occupy the position of power by being the employers who in turn are the ones who determine who is hired. For ill or for good, this ensures that those who are in power (in this case, employed) stay in power. It turns out that 95 percent of top corporate executives are white males despite the fact that Asian Americans on average have higher percentages of bachelor's degrees than whites. Under the practice of "networking," even poor whites benefit more than middle class Asians. While Asian Americans represent just over 5.1 percent of the United States population, whites represent about 78 percent of the population, not 95 percent. Without affirmative action, perhaps the demographics of social/economic status would be worst off for minorities, let alone Asian Americans. Thus the belief that anyone in America, regardless of race or gender, could be hired merely by merit is not a present reality.

being intrinsically racist.

23. Feagin and Feagin, *Discrimination, American Style*, 43–84.

24. Ezorsky, *Racism and Justice*, 15.

25. Farley et al., "Stereotypes and Segregation: Neighborhoods in the Detroit Area," 750–80.

Objection Four: Argument from Individualistic Justice

The fourth objection argues from a strong American tradition. This tradition values individual freedom and mere individual responsibility. As such none of us should be morally culpable for anyone's plight but our own. What is assumed in this tradition is a lack of communal or collective moral responsibility to community, unless the responsibility is a result of individual culpability for some act of irresponsibility. To be sure benevolence and kindness are valued in this tradition but only if they are self-determined, freely chosen as some sort of supererogatory act.

So what is the fourth objection to affirmative action? All too often opponents of affirmative action argue that whites as a group are not responsible for the injustice done to African Americans currently or in the past (of course the claim extends to a rejection of responsibility to African slaves in the past). So the argument goes, why should whites collectively suffer for the present economic plight of African Americans unless they qua individual whites were responsible for some sort of racial discrimination? The strength of this objection turns on whether affirmative action is understood as unjust towards an individual or towards a group.

An analogy would help to illustrate this point. Imagine a family with two healthy children. As a family all the members seek the good of each other. The parents in particular ensure the economic and social well-being of the children by providing shelter, food, and the financial means for the children to express themselves socially in activities like sports. Eventually the parents decide to have another child. Unfortunately the new born child is dealt a bad hand. He is born with a childhood disease that requires the parents to make major adjustments in terms of the distribution of their time, labor and money towards individual members of the family. No longer can the parents afford to pay for tennis lessons for their older children, nor do they have the time to drive the middle child to soccer practice. Instead, the parents shifted their time, labor and money in such a way that their new born has the best quality of life that they can provide in light of a disease no one had any control over. However, the older and middle child reach a point where they feel exhausted and unfairly treated. They complain to their parents that they had nothing to do with their younger sibling's disease and exclaim that they qua family member should not be punished or responsible for the disease. They add that justice requires that their parents' time, labor and money be redistributed equally to them as individuals. The parents reply by noting their older children's hardship. But speaking from a communitarian mode, they point out that if their children's ethical concern is about justice, then justice needs to be understood for what it is, viz., a *relational* concept of fairness and equity. Recall from chapter 4, this requires treating equals as equals and unequals as unequals. Justice is intelligible only when the entities are related.[26] Thus for the parents to treat the next door neighbor's children on par with their own in terms of how they dispense their time, labor and money towards the neighbor's children would be a misuse of the term justice. This would be an instance of treating unrelated children (or unequals) as equals (the parents own children). The children next door do not have the same relationship to the parents as the parent's own children do to them. By contrast, for the parents not to redistribute their time, labor and money among their children for the sake of their ill child would be unjust. In the end, unless the older siblings could argue a case that they were not related and part of the same family, their complaint is unwarranted. The children in the household are related to the parents qua their own children; however, they occupy unequal relationships among themselves as the parents' children.

In like manner, unless white Americans do not see themselves as fellow citizens alongside Americans of color, e.g., African Americans, then this objection against affirmative action is unwarranted. Like the ill child, sacrifices are made for the good of the American family, i.e., the citizens who do not fare well due to historical and presently existing barriers to economic/social success. This communal attitude for equity is particularly true for Christians. We have a biblical edict to eradicate social inequalities (see Jas 2:14–16 and 1John 3:17). However, Scripture does not condition this eradication such that it is trumped by self-interest and personal rights. Jesus is quite clear that Christians should not be concerned about their own rights being violated when someone's greater good is at hand:

> You have heard that it was said, 'An eye for an eye, and a tooth for a tooth.' But I say to you, do not resist an evil person; but whoever slaps you on your right cheek, turn the other to him also. If anyone wants to sue you and take your shirt, let him have your coat also. Whoever forces you to go one mile, go with him

---

26. I will not attempt to argue the point here, but it is apparent that on a broad scale we have relationships with all of humanity but the degree of our commitment to any particular human varies and increases according to the degree and depth of the relationship.

two. Give to him who asks of you, and do not turn away from him who wants to borrow from you. (Matt 5:38–42 NASB)

Jesus describes the life of those who follow him to be a life of sacrifice. When Jesus talks about taking up their cross and then to follow him, he does not condition the task to be one of convenience or choice. At times Christians back out of an opportunity to act, simply because they are mandated to act. A common adage rings throughout some Christian communities: "Christians should care for the poor, down trodden, needy, and victims of injustice but not if they are forced to do so. It is a violation of my rights for the Federal Government to force me to be benevolent." According to this adage, individual freedom and autonomy have a higher and absolute status that trumps benevolence for others and any other value that is community oriented.

Christians do well to avoid elevating individual political values over biblical values that concern the welfare of the poor or masquerading political values as biblical values. The United States' Declaration of Independence is not canon. The Jeffersonian rights contained there are not absolute entitlements, particularly when the welfare of others is involved. There is much in Christian circles that described God as a "God for me" rather than a "God for us or them." While the focus on racial or gender preferences may exclude individuals who are not persons of color or women, affirmative action gains by opening opportunities that did not or may not exist for persons of color or women. When a Christian complains that a person of color or a woman benefited from their exclusion from some admission or hiring process, the complaint itself implies individual freedom, autonomy, and self-interest outweigh the welfare of others.

Objection Five: The Results of Diversity Are Negative

Another forward-looking argument that appeals to social utility argues that diversity in the university (among the student body or faculty) makes for the best learning environment. As a general rule, diversity in any group setting functions as an epistemic compensator to derive objective predictions of some collective good. It also generates more insight and understanding of some collective problem or issue. In either case, multiple paths to some end are more productive than a single path. Conversely, diversity discourages inferior predictions and faulty understanding of some problem or issue. As David Orentlicher points out, the very structure of the United States national government is a composite of judicial, legislative, and executive branches. Even the United States capitalist economic system is based on diverse competition in the free market.

Before we look at the specifics of the diversity argument, a look at a glaring straw man of the diversity argument is in order. In an unpublished article titled *Affirmative Action: The New Racialism*, Eric Mack of Tulane University argues that the diversity argument is actually a form of racism. He describes the diversity argument in the following way:

> Although it comes in a variety of versions, the key idea here is simply that, within every institution or aspect of American society, the distribution of positions ought to match the racial, ethnic, or gender composition of American society has a whole. The irony is that this aspiration is *not* based on the liberal vision that all people are ("under the skin") fundamentally alike so that, when discrimination is banished, there will be a natural tendency toward proportionate "representation." Rather the Diversity demand for the selection of people on the basis of their race, ethnicity or gender is based on the belief that the members of any given racial, ethnic, and gender group are fundamentally different from members of other groups. According to this Diversity argument, the differences among people are perceived as matters of individual talents, aspirations, efforts, choices, and character. Rather, people differ from one another on the basis of biological groupings. What matters is not who you are as an individual or what you have made of yourself as an individual but what group you *represent*.[27]

Eric Mack is obviously expressing another objection from the position of color blind racism. Clearly Mack misrepresents the diversity argument given his abstract liberalism perspective. For Mack, all humans are the same beneath skin differences, when he says all humans are "fundamentally alike." This assertion flies in the face of well-established sociological facts that cultures exist and people vary according to their culture. There are Irish, German, African American, Native American, and Chinese cultural ways of seeing reality through such epistemological prisms as values and past history. Such can be said along gender lines as well as Sandra Harding explains in her criticism of the term Cartesian epistemology. It is uncertain which proponent of the diversity argument Mack has in mind when he asserts that diversity proponents see diversity

---

27 Mack, "Affirmative Action: The New Racialism?"

to be a matter of "biological" variation. It is clearly a straw man to assert that proponents of the diversity argument see such groups as Chinese or African Americans as being biological different racial groups. To be sure, even when opponents of the diversity argument do not target the diversity argument on this faulty biological basis, they still manifest an abstract liberal perspective. The rhetoric against the diversity argument in this case appeals to liberal notions of individualism by insisting that talk of a collective consciousness of African Americans or Asian Americans smacks of racism. While not all African Americans think alike, and in the spirit of social and political liberalism, African Americans are as individual as members of any other ethnic group, there are common experiences and common values in the African American culture. Ethnic cultures, like any culture, are fluid and internally identified by their "family resemblance" or traits. With this said, it is an empirical matter whether African Americans or any other ethnic group has a perspective. On this note, public polls often show this to be the case when political, religious, and social issues are the topic.

The historical origin of the diversity argument goes back to an unexpected view point of Supreme Court Justice Powell in the *Regents of Univ. of Cal. v. Bakke* case. While Judge Powell argued in favor of Bakke because he deemed racial quotas were unconstitutional, he surprisingly argued that race or ethnicity could be used as a factor in a university's application and admission process in order to promote and achieve diversity in thought and education among students.

> This clearly is a constitutionally permissible goal for an institution of higher education. Academic freedom, though not a specifically enumerated constitutional right, long has been viewed as a special concern of the First Amendment. The freedom of a university to make its own judgments as to education includes the selection of its student body... The atmosphere of "speculation, experiment, and creation"—so essential to the quality of higher education—is widely believed to be promoted by a diverse student body.[28]

It was not until 2003 that the Supreme Court reviewed its second case involving affirmative action in regards to education admissions in *Grutter v. Bollinger*. The facts of this case involved a white female, Barbara Grutter, who applied unsuccessfully to the University of Michigan Law

---

28. Regents of Univ. of Cal. v. Bakke, 438 US 311 (1978).

School in 1997. The Law School denied her admission despite the fact she earned a 3.8 undergraduate GPA and an LSAT score of 161. Appealing to *Regents of Univ. of Cal. v. Bakke*, U of Michigan Law School stated that their admission policy factored race into their selection process in order to achieve diversity. Grutter filed a suit against the university, charging it with racial discrimination. The point of contention between Barbara Grutter and the University of Michigan Law School stems from what is called the "Michigan Mandate." The University of Michigan's president, James Duderstadt, introduced the Michigan Mandate in March of 1990 as a plan to increase the representation of under-represented minority faculty, staff and students at the University of Michigan so that there were a proportionate representation of under-represented minorities in the State of Michigan and the United States as a whole.

The rationale for this diverse representation is the basis of the University's diversity argument:

1. The future United States will be diverse and pluralistic like the rest of the World.

2. Universities have an obligation to meet the challenges of a diverse and pluralistic future, both nationally and globally.

3. Therefore, universities need to cultivate future leaders who understand and reflect this pluralism and diversity.

4. Therefore, the creation of a diverse and pluralistic campus environment at the University of Michigan is critical to the University's ability to produce future leaders who understand and reflect this pluralism and diversity of the United States and the World.

The Michigan Mandate established the following objectives: 1) To seek, nourish, and sustain a culturally diverse campus community and 2) To recruit, support, and develop members of under-represented minority groups among students, faculty, staff, and key leadership. With these objectives met, the University of Michigan expects to produce diverse leaders who are themselves diverse or are prepared to understand a diverse and pluralistic world. When the Supreme Court ruled on the *Grutter v. Bollinger* case, Justice O'Connor delivered the opinion of the Court and sided with Bollinger and the University Of Michigan. She narrowed the issue of broad diversity from the Bakke case down to ethnic diversity. In the decision O'Connor stated:

> The [Law School's] policy aspires to "achieve that diversity which has the potential to enrich everyone's education and thus make a law class stronger than the sum of its parts." [...] The policy does not restrict the types of diversity contributions eligible for substantial weight in the admissions process, but instead recognizes "many possible bases for diversity admissions." [...] The policy does, however, reaffirm the Law School's longstanding commitment to "one particular type of diversity," that is, "racial and ethnic diversity with special reference to the inclusion of students from groups which have been historically discriminated against like African-Americans, Hispanics and Native Americans, who without this commitment might not be represented in our student body in meaningful numbers. [...] By enrolling a critical mass of [underrepresented] minority students, the Law School seeks to ensur their ability to make unique contributions to the character of the Law School."[29]

While appearing to be at odds with Justice Powell's ruling in Bakke, O'Connor argued that the Law School's admissions program broke no law in its aim to be highly diversified. The Law School treated ethnicity as an essential factor that would generate diversity campus-wide but not at the expense of racial quotas for members of certain racial groups.

There are two criticisms of the diversity argument that come to mind. Both criticisms argue that affirmative action as a tool to promote diversity does more harm than good. First, some critics point out that faculty and students on predominately white campuses hold the attitude that diversity decreases the best learning environment for them.[30] A research study by Stanley Rothman and et al., sampled 140 American colleges and universities. The data collected for the study consisted of responses from students, administrators, and faculty members at U.S. colleges and universities. The list of institutions covered the span of institutions from the least to the most prestigious. Interesting, none of the questions from the survey tested for the effectiveness of affirmative action. The study found that students, faculty, and administrators were *dissatisfied* with the quality of education and work ethic of their peers in institutions with more black students than in those institutions with less. That is, as "the proportion of black students enrolled at the universities rose, student satisfaction with their university experience dropped, as did assessments of the quality of

---

29. Grutter v. Bollinger, 539 US (2003), 3.

30. Rothman et al., "Does Enrollment Diversity Improve University Education?," 8–26.

their education . . . the higher the enrollment diversity the more likely students were to say that they experience discrimination."[31] The study did not indicate that the administrators, faculty, and students found affirmative action *lowered academic standards.*

At any rate, whatever merit the Rothman study allegedly had for pointing out the negative impact diversity policies have on universities, it is far from conclusive in light of conflicting results from another diversity study published around the same time. Patricia Gurin et al. showed that diversity actually promotes learning.[32] The databases for the Gurin study came from the Michigan Student Survey (MSS) and a survey that the Cooperative Institutional Research Program (CIRP) started. The MSS database consisted of answers to questions that 1,129 white, 187 African American, and 266 Asian American freshmen from the University of Michigan answered in 1990. A follow-up survey was conducted four years later. The CIRP survey consisted of 184 institutions and included 10,465 white, 216 African American, 496 Asian American, and 206 Latino students. The initiative to investigate the effects of diversity came from the researchers' optimistic ideology about diversity, i.e., diversity causes breaks in normal routines of thinking and disrupts habitual thinking. A racially diverse student body creates the environment for disruptive thinking and thus mental growth.

The Gurin study wanted to know diversity in terms of (1) "classroom diversity" or formal instruction in the classroom on race and ethnicity as they are integrated in politics, history, and sociology and (2) "informal interaction diversity" outside the classroom. What the Gurin study looked at was whether (1) and (2) types of diversity lead students to become more intellectually proficient as interactive members of a racially diverse society. The study found that "informal interaction diversity was especially influential in accounting for higher levels of intellectual engagement and self-assessed academic skills for all four groups of students."[33] Classroom diversity had a significant impact on white and Latino students. Gurin et al. concluded that "The actual experiences students have with diversity consistently and meaningfully affect important learning and democracy outcomes of a college education."[34]

31. Ibid., 15.
32. Gurin et al., "Diversity and Higher Education."
33. Ibid., 351.
34. Ibid., 358.

When the effectiveness of diversity was brought to the attention of the Supreme Court in the Grutter v. Bollinger and Gratz v. Bollinger cases, the Michigan Association of Scholars argued in its brief concerning scholars that:

> However strong the evidence of its benefits, men and women of principle would insist that segregation by race, imposed by the state, is simply unacceptable. The advantages that may flow from it (MAS would say) could never begin to justify a policy that is intrinsically immoral and unjust. And so it is with this case at bar. It is unjust to give advantages or impose burdens on the basis of skin color –even if doing so had some benefits, and even if that racial discrimination were honorably motivated. Racial discrimination is wrong; no benefits alleged to flow from diversity on the campus or in the classroom can make it right.[35]

It is unfortunate the Michigan Association of Scholars made this comment since it misses the point. The call for diversity is not categorical but a matter of promoting utility.

The goals of the diversity argument on university campuses are to (1) erode away racial biases by diversifying the different viewpoints presented in the class room and (2) better equip future leaders to understand the racially diverse world in which they live (e.g., the Michigan Mandate). Again, the assumption of such goals is that students, left to their own sensibilities and epistemic backgrounds, would graduate with their biases with a limited education experience and not be as well prepared to lead and engage a racially diverse world. If such is the case, any study that addressed the impact of a diverse educational experience should either reveal that there is a positive impact on students or no negative impact on students at all. It is puzzling and troubling to find that studies actually reveal a *negative* impact at least in the preferences of students and faculty as opposed to a positive or neutral impact. It is interesting also that part of the Michigan Association of Scholars' point is not a point many if any would contest, viz., that universities graduate productive and educated students in the absence of diversity measures. As James Sterba put it, unless the subject is physics, math, or logic, it is difficult to see how anyone could think that faculty and students of color do not contribute significantly to class room discussions, particularly on the topic of race.[36] Even on topics where there

---

35. Grutter v. Bollinger and Gratz v. Bollinger, *Brief of Amicus Curiae, The Michigan Association of Scholars in Support of Petitioners*, 21.

36. Sterba, *Affirmative Action for the Future*, 72.

may be little room for an ethnic perspective (say from an African American perspective) like mathematics and physics, this lack of a perspective does not entail "no" contribution to learning from this ethnic perspective. As David Boonin points out, "part of the reason that diversity might prove important has to do with its ability to foster innovative approaches to things other than the subject matter of a discipline itself: things like alternative approaches to teaching, to do collaborative work with others, to resolving disputes with colleagues, to connecting the university to the larger community beyond, and so on."[37]

Interesting, the reverse is not true of historically black colleges. That is, intentionally enrolling and boosting the enrollment of white students at historically black colleges like Morehouse, Spelman and Howard would not increase the best learning environment of the students already there. African American students, generally, live diverse lives already and this is true of many students of color. They live diverse lives in the sense that they live in the dominant white culture and must contend with the dominant culture to be heard and to express their own cultural identity.

At any rate, using affirmative action to diversify a white campus environment can increase the future representation of minorities that have high-level careers. One reason why many minorities are not highly skilled professionals (e.g., doctors, lawyers and educators) is because they do not pursue high level careers in light of their belief that such careers are not credible options for them. Law schools and medical schools can use affirmative action policies to admit minority applicants with the long-term goal of increasing the number of professional minorities. In this case, affirmative action would be used to admit and graduate minorities to function as optimistic images or "role models" for future professional minorities. Consider what Japanese American anchor person Ann Curry said about broadcasting: "When you're a child and you don't see people like you doing something, it doesn't enter your mind you could do it. . . . It's like looking through a shut glass door into a room that seems so tantalizing, but the door isn't open to you."[38]

The second objection to the diversity argument is that it does more harm to the students of color than good. According to this objection, affirmative action harms students of color when they are recruited to attend very prestigious universities that are too demanding for them.

37. Boonin, *Should Race Matter?*, 161.
38. An interview with Ann Curry by Jeffrey Zaslow in his "Straight Talk" column in *USA Weekend Magazine*.

This objection is also called the "mismatch" hypothesis. In the *Grutter* Supreme Court ruling, Justice Clarence Thomas appealed to the mismatch hypothesis in his dissent. Justice Thomas stated, "The Law School tantalizes unprepared students with the promise of a University of Michigan degree and all of the opportunities that it offers. These overmatched students take the bait, only to find that they cannot succeed in the cauldron of competition. And this mismatch crisis is not restricted to elite institutions." Whether or not the mismatch hypothesis is warranted is an empirical matter.

Is Justice Thomas' dissent based on obvious data to support it? On the contrary, while some studies indicate that the mismatch theory is warranted,[39] most studies indicate just the opposite.[40] For example, African American male students who went to prestigious universities graduated at a higher rate at prestigious universities than did similar African American male students at less prestigious universities. William G. Bowen et al. tested the mismatch hypothesis by grouping African American men by their high school GPAs and then looked to see if those with low GPAs who enrolled in more selective, elite institutions graduated at a lower rate than those with the same GPAs who went to less selective and less elite institutions. Their findings showed just the opposite.[41] They go on to add, "contrary to what the . . . mismatch hypothesis would lead us to expect, the relative graduation rate advantage associated with going to a more selective university was even more pronounced for black men at the lower end of the high school grade distribution than it was for students with better high school records."[42] Even if the mismatch hypothesis were validated and conclusive, there are serious ramification lingering. Given Prop 209 students would be sorted along various slots and thus recruited and admitted according to what slot they fit in. Elite institutions would admit elite students, average institutions would admit average students, and less than average institutions would admit less than average students. While this sorting out may increase graduation rates, it systematically slots out cultural capital and career success for all but the elite students.

---

39. See Bowen et al., *Crossing the Finish Line*, chaps. 5–6; and an unpublished paper by Arcidiacono et al., "Affirmative Action and University Fit: Evidence from Proposition 209."

40. See Bowen et al., *Crossing the Finish Line*, 207–13; Bowen and Bok, *Shape of the River*, 53–90.

41. Bowen et al., *Crossing the Finish Line*, 209–10.

42. Ibid., 209.

There are great benefits of attending and graduating from an elite school like Harvard or Yale that are just not there at less elite schools. So, if Prop 209 is sorting students into various levels of schools, and if this sorting is at least partially linked to ethnicity, it seems that opportunities and levels of success are also being sorted along those lines.

Objection 6: Affirmative Action Increases Racial Tension and Generates Inferiority

A sixth objection to affirmative action asserts that affirmative action instigates racism and increases tensions and conflicts among society's different racial groups. It is unclear just how this objection is supposed to be an objection. Is the objection supposed to show that affirmative action policies are unjust? If so, it is a non sequitur. To rephrase the question, are the supposed unfortunate consequences of increased racism and tension sufficient to dismiss affirmative action as unjust? It seems not. Consider the many slave revolts and the nineteenth-century abolitionists' attempt to abolish slavery; the revolts and efforts of the abolitionists obviously met with resistance and contempt. Asking rhetorically, would this obvious consequence be sufficient to consider the abolitionists' actions unjust? Or consider Moses' attempt to free the Israelites from Pharaoh. When Moses angered Pharaoh such that Pharaoh required the Israelites to make bricks without straw, are we to conclude that Moses' request for Pharaoh to "let the people go" was wrong simply because of Pharaoh's anger? Given that the ends of both the forward-looking and back-ward-looking arguments for affirmative action are noble, it is unclear why opponents of affirmative action would become consumed with hatred and tension against minorities. This type of visceral reaction is expected only if affirmative action was literally equivalent to Jim Crow discrimination.

This sixth objection to affirmative action also holds that affirmative action demoralizes its recipients. Accordingly, this objection charges that minorities are selected merely because of *being* a minority. Thus, the objection holds, the negative psychological impact on minorities is demoralizing when the particular minorities in question realize that their ability and skills were not adequate or were not considered in the hiring and admission process.

In response, it should first be pointed out that empirical studies do not support this objection. Evidence to the contrary has been that affirmative action has a positive psychological impact on African Americans. African Americans working in corporations that have affirmative action policies are just as content as African Americans working in corporations that do not have affirmative action policies. The former "demonstrate greater occupational ambition and are more likely to believe that people are helpful than the latter . . . [In fact, African Americans] who believe that affirmative action played a part in their hiring or promotion have no less confidence in their ability to do their job than do other workers."[43] It is puzzling how an African American could be demoralized because of affirmative action, given she knew prior to applying for a position that affirmative action would play a part in her hiring or admission. It is not rational for a person to place herself into a situation she knows will create a demoralizing environment for herself.

The demoralizing objection requires the hidden assumption that affirmative action policies select unqualified applicants, otherwise why would the person feel inadequate? If a person of color, who has earned a PhD, for example, applies for a position at a university, and is knowingly selected in part because she is a minority, why should she feel inadequate upon being selected? Was not a prerequisite for the position a PhD degree? Surely she was not selected merely because of her skin color (as discussed earlier in this chapter).

Even the suggestion that the person of color feels demoralized because she was selected over more qualified applicants is a non sequitur. How would the person of color have access to information concerning the qualifications of other applicants? Even if she did, the objection implies that her earned degree has value relative to the degree of those she is in competition against. Suppose a qualified person of color was offered two different positions at two different institutions. Suppose also she is aware that the qualifications of the other applicants at one institution are less than her qualifications and the qualifications of the applicants at the other institution are greater. In both cases, her qualifications are the same, yet the demoralizing objection holds that she would be demoralized only in the latter case. We are left puzzled and wondering why a person of color would be demoralized at all when she is qualified. Perhaps she feels the better qualified applicants could do a better job, but this does not entail that she cannot do a competent job at what she is hired to do given she is qualified. Surely if the two places of business that she applied to

---

43. Hochschild, "Affirmative Action as Cultural War," 350. See also Hochschild, *Facing Up to the American Dream*, 98–102, 290–92.

required her to do the same work in both, she would generally either be incompetent in both or competent in both.

Perhaps rather a person of color could feel demoralized if she believes that services her position offers should be maximized for the recipients who receive them (e.g., the recipients being customers and students). Thus while she could perform her job well, there would be someone who could do so better and thus shortchange the recipients of the services offered. Unfortunately this way of self-reflection leads to a pessimistic slippery slope. It goes without saying that there will always be someone who can "do a better job." This concern about who does a better job is intelligible, ceteris paribus, if the applicant who is demoralized is not competent and provides less than competent services to customers or students. But this is true with or without affirmative action.

The Second Side of the Social/Economic Inequality Coin

If the question were asked whether affirmative action is sufficient to eradicate social and economic disparities at least among people of color, the answer is, it depends. The social and economic success of any person depends on both internal and external factors. (This is particularly true of persons of color.) So far we have looked at external factors that play a part in the success of persons of color, e.g., the absence of institutional racism and racial prejudice. When such factors are absent and there are no existing internal or psychological barriers, then the answer to the question just posed is, yes. However, when deep internal detriments are present, factors like low individual motivation and low self-esteem, the answer is not so clear. Even with affirmative action in place, both for hiring and admission purposes, a person cannot be forced to enroll into a university or apply for a job. The idiom "you can lead a horse to water, but you can't make it drink" comes to mind.

The causal factors for shaping both low or high individual motivation and self-esteem are complex since the will of the individual plays a contributing role. Nevertheless, a person's psychological constitution is not developed in a vacuum or independent of an environment or community. Unlike most communities in the United States, the African American community has been shaped and victimized by racism, deep poverty and the unwelcomed gifts that come with these forces. In his book *Race Matters*, philosopher and black activist Cornel West argues that the institution of slavery had a profound impact on African slaves during the founding of the United States. Not only were African families separated and exploited as property by their slave masters, their psyche, as a result, also was gravely impacted. West refers to this psychological impact as nihilism. For West:

> Nihilism is to be understood here not as a philosophic doctrine that there are no rational grounds for legitimate standards or authority; it is, far more, the lived experience of coping with a life of horrifying meaninglessness, hopelessness, and (most important) lovelessness.[44]

As West notes, the major enemy against African Americans at that time was not the former of these evils (viz., slavery and its exploitation), but the latter (the ensuing nihilism). This is no surprise. Anytime a person is separated from his/her children or parents without the possibility of a future reunion, hope and meaning are annihilated. With the collapse of the African family came the collapse of the various African cultures. This resulted when Africans were separated, sold and forced to labor on plantations with other African slaves who came from unfamiliar regions in Africa. Few people in history have endured this kind of pan psychological trauma.[45] Any people under such a nihilistic threat are bound to seek a refuge. This refuge came in the form of religion that their white masters embraced. As West adds:

> The genius of our black foremothers and forefathers was to create powerful buffers to ward off the nihilistic threat, to equip black folk with cultural armor to beat back the demons of hopelessness, meaninglessness, and lovelessness. These buffers consisted of cultural structures . . . [viz.,] black religious and civic institutions.[46]

Black churches in particular became the flag ships for the development and success of the Civil Rights Movement during the days of Jim Crow. During the Civil Rights Movement, many African Americans held education, hard work, the nuclear family, and individual contribution to society as virtues and values. The black church pushed and promoted these

---

44. West, *Race Matters*, 14.

45. When the ancient Jews were under Egyptian slavery or when they were exiled to Babylon in 585 BC under Nebuchadnezzar II, they maintained their culture and still do so till this day.

46. West, *Race Matters*, 15.

affirmative action, the death penalty, and abortion

virtues and values. In recent times since the Civil Rights Movement, there has been a shift away from many of these virtues and values. This is not a matter of armchair philosophy but a matter of empirical fact. At the fiftieth anniversary commemoration of the *Brown vs. Topeka Board of Education* Supreme Court decision, social activist Bill Cosby was one who courageously pointed this shift out. It is worth citing excerpts from his speech:

> ... in our cities and public schools we have fifty percent drop out. In our own neighborhood, we have men in prison. No longer is a person embarrassed because they're pregnant without a husband. No longer is a boy considered an embarrassment if he tries to run away from being the father of the unmarried child. Ladies and gentlemen, the lower economic and lower middle economic people are [not*] holding their end in this deal. In the neighborhood that most of us grew up in, parenting is not going on. In the old days, you couldn't hooky school because every drawn shade was an eye. And before your mother got off the bus and to the house, she knew exactly where you had gone, who had gone into the house, and where you got on whatever you had one and where you got it from. Parents don't know that today. I'm talking about these people who cry when their son is standing there in an orange suit. Where were you when he was two? Where were you when he was twelve? Where were you when he was 18, and how come you don't know he had a pistol? And where is his father, and why don't you know where he is? And why doesn't the father show up to talk to this boy? ... 50 percent dropout rate, I'm telling you, and people in jail, and women having children by five, six different men. Under what excuse, I want somebody to love me, and as soon as you have it, you forget to parent. Grandmother, mother, and great grandmother in the same room, raising children, and the child knows nothing about love or respect of any one of the three of them. All this child knows is "gimme, gimme, gimme." These people want to buy the friendship of a child ... and the child couldn't care less. Those of us sitting out here who have gone on to some college or whatever we've done, we still fear our parents (clapping and laughter). And these people are not parenting. They're buying things for the kid. $500 sneakers, for what? They won't buy or spend $250 on Hooked on Phonics.[47]

The internal side of the success story for African Americans, then, is a return to the virtues and values of the black church and other civic and

47. Cosby, "Pound Cake Speech."

cultural institutions. The external side of the coin is affirmative action. Focusing on one side more than the other can result in shift blaming and scapegoating. It is unfortunate that many Americans of all persuasions fail to see this. They either look to structural changes in society, like affirmative action policies, as the cure all to the plight of African Americans, or they idealize the United States as a post-racist country such that failure to succeed in life is essentially a matter of individual choice.

The status or lack of status of the African American is perhaps the one fact both sides agree on. As Michael Fletcher notes: "Over the past 100 years, perhaps no slice of the US population has been more studied, analyzed and dissected than black males . . . [They] have been the subject of at least 400 books."[48] For example, only 15 percent of African American males in the 25–29 age range have a bachelor's degree. The reasons identified as the causes for this low rate are a low high school graduation rate, a low college enrollment rate, a low college graduation rate, below average parental graduation rates, low income, and single parent family structure. Surprisingly, with all the research and analyzes Fletcher talks about, there is no consensus that there is a relationship among these internal and external factors.

As we reach near the end of the discussion of affirmative action, it has been argued that affirmative action is a *justifiable* means of advancing the social and economic success of people of color, particularly African Americans. No attempt was made to argue that affirmative action is ethically mandatory, again only that it is justifiable. No attempt was made to argue for affirmative action for the sake of meeting stipulated racial quotas. Quotas are an easy prey for opponents of affirmative action. Affirmative action does not entail quotas. Quotas always involve hiring and admitting a fixed percentage or an exact number of persons of color (or women) whether the former are qualified or not to avoid sanctions (this is reverse discrimination). This has the unfortunate effect of selecting persons who are unqualified and hence the perception most people have of affirmative action.

Affirmative action policies merely involve an attempt to hire or admit persons of color (or women) without the attached required numbers, percentages, and sanctions. Affirmative action policies merely search for candidates with specified qualifications (race being just one of them). If the candidates are not found, the search continues or anyone with the

---

48. Fletcher, "At the Corner of Progress and Peril."

affirmative action, the death penalty, and abortion 217

specified qualifications is selected (short of being a person of color or a woman).[49] Numbers and percentages are used but merely as guides or estimations. For those who are opposed to race based affirmative action, by asserting it is "ethically unjust," should keep in mind the goals behind affirmative action policies. Any opposition to affirmative action should share some of these ethical goals and provide a *Plan B* that addresses the same problems affirmative action in principle attempts to solve. Without a *Plan B*, those who oppose affirmative action are themselves guilty of perpetuating injustice in terms of doing nothing to reduce social and economic disparities among racial minorities. How can opposing one form of alleged injustice (what they call reverse discrimination) without opposing another form of injustice (viz., social and economic racial disparities) be just? Similarly those who support affirmative action should see affirmative action as a (means) process, not an event (end) if the recipients of affirmative action have deficient qualifications. This is particularly true of affirmative action in education. Admitting students of color to a university who have lower test scores than their white counterparts without monitoring and mentoring the students of color, at least until they are capable of competing and performing as well as their white counterparts, is a tragedy. Failure to do so defeats the purpose of affirmative action. Affirmative action in this guise is unjust to its recipients, other white students, and to the greater good of society at large.

Moreover, no attempt was made to argue for affirmative action as an end, where race preferential treatment was the ultimate goal. Nor for that matter should affirmative action end someday. Affirmative action is not a program that has an expiration date attached to it. Rather it is a mechanism to maintain or issue into society a certain set of conditions that reflect Thomas Jefferson's idealized United States. In summary these conditions are the following where (1) all Americans, regardless of race have an education that is minimally competitive with the education of the most economically advantaged Americans,[50] (2) all Americans, regardless

---

49. On a personal note, I made the final cut for a teaching position at an institution of higher learning. I was told that the institution was seeking to diversify and so it was clear I was being pursued because of my race, in part. However, I did not specialize in a certain area of philosophy the institution wanted and so the institution selected another candidate who was a white male. If the institution was set to select a person of color regardless of merit, I would have been chosen merely because of my degree and race. This is not affirmative action.

50. Of course the consequence of (1) is that class-based affirmative action is justified along similar lines as race-based affirmative action.

of race are not racially discriminated against intentionally or unintentionally by institutions and practices that determine their social and economic well-being, and where (3) corporations and educational institutions promote hiring and admitting that reflects the diversity that already exists in society. The need for affirmative action would vary according to *when or if* the mentioned conditions cease or discontinue.

Unfortunately, the likely responses from opponents of affirmative action to the six defenses of affirmative action presented here would be to reiterate in part assumptions about racism already made: that (1) and (2) are not idealized future states of affairs but are present realities and thirdly that the pursuit of color blindness, not diversity, should be normative. If (1) and (2) are present realities, then the success of any American would be a matter of self-determination or pulling herself up by boot-strapping. According to this common belief, gone are the days when social and economic disparities are the result of intentional racial discrimination. Civil rights laws are in placed to prevent this type of discrimination. Moreover, as Stephen and Abigail Thernstrom are quick to point out, "Whites with a pathological hatred of African Americans can still be found, of course. But the haters have become a tiny remnant with no influence in any important sphere of American life."[51]

It is unfortunate that many like the Thernstroms see individual racial prejudice as the essence of racial discrimination. According to the logic of this attitude, since racial prejudice no longer exists on a large scale basis as it did during the Civil Rights and pre-Civil Rights Era, the only plausible explanation for social and economic disparities is due to factors internal to racial minorities themselves. The charge of victimization lurks in the background of this attitude. Minorities like Bill Cosby are heralded as prophets of truth in so far as shining light on the belief that social and economic disparities have an internal mechanism.

But for those like the Thernstroms who see only the internal factors, they have a lot to explain in so far as making their image of a one-sided coin an intelligible concept. Why is it that so many people of color, and most African Americans in particular, are not living Jefferson's idealized American life style? The logical conclusion to draw from the Thernstroms' perspective is that this unfortunate reality can be explained sufficiently by the victims themselves. This means that poverty stricken and poorly educated minorities have decided out of a sheer act of will or indifference

---

51. Thernstrom and Thernstrom, *America in Black and White*, 500.

affirmative action, the death penalty, and abortion 219

not to do anything about their plight, or they suffer from a battery of vices stemming from their culture that Bill Cosby pointed out, viz., laziness, poor parenting skills, self-esteem issues, and lack of a protestant ethic. This one-sided coin imagery implies that most qualified persons of color are successful in life since they have not suffered from racial discrimination. After all, what qualified person of color would choose not to be successful? Of these earlier three assumptions the first one is absurd, the second one is simplistic and the third one is a classic case of begging the question.

The Death Penalty

The death penalty is the retributive sentence used in some states for murder and other capital crimes. According to the Supreme Court, the death penalty is not necessarily a violation of the eighth amendment (not *per se* an instance of "cruel and unusual" punishment). However, in the 2002 *Atkins v. Virginia* case, the Supreme Court ruled that the use of the death penalty on mentally retarded criminals is "cruel and unusual punishment" and thus is a violation of the eighth amendment for such persons. And in the *Roper v. Simmons* case, the Supreme Court ruled that the death penalty is not permitted for convicted juvenile.

In this section of the chapter, we will look at the ethical status of the death penalty strictly as an ethical form of retribution. It will be argued that the death penalty is not an ethically warranted form of retribution. We will not focus on the pro and con arguments that address the death penalty as it is practiced in any particular country, particularly the United States. This approach is taken since the ethical warrant of the death penalty turns more on its theoretical structure rather than on its objective success or failure when implemented. Any objections to the death penalty because of flaws in how it is executed or "sentenced out" are actually not objections to the death penalty but objections to its current use. If anything, these objections should call for the discontinuation of the death penalty until such flaws are eradicated. Moreover, it will be shown that these objections to the death penalty as a practice actually call for, by logical consequence, a discontinuation of retributive justice of any sort. In order to make a case for this focus on the theoretical structure of the death penalty, a discussion of the objections to the death penalty as a practice is in order. Finally we will look at the death penalty from a biblical context and determine whether the Bible condones the death penalty. It will be argued that the prescription for the death penalty in the Bible is made for theological and hyperbolic reasons rather than ethical reasons.

The Death Penalty in Practice versus the Death Penalty in Theory

The justness and ethical nature of the death penalty is currently an issue only for the United States as far as industrialized nations are concerned. Other industrialized nations like Germany, France and Great Britain have outlawed this form of response to capital crimes. Nevertheless, the just and ethical nature of the death penalty does not turn *per se* on *de facto* considerations in the United States or other countries. Moreover, a distinction needs to be made between the death penalty as a practice in the United States or anywhere and the death penalty simpliciter. This distinction in theory and practice allows clarification in why the death penalty is or is not unethical and clarification in what way it is or is not unethical. We therefore turn our attention to arguments in favor and against the death penalty as it is practiced in the United States and arguments in favor and against the death penalty in theory or simpliciter.

The arguments supporting the death penalty come in two varieties. One takes the form of a backward-looking argument and justifies the death penalty directly from retributive considerations. Arguments in this category are deontological in nature. We will apply this argument to the death penalty in theory and in practice. The other argument takes the form of a forward-looking argument and justifies the death penalty indirectly from deterrent considerations. Arguments in this category are utilitarianism in nature. We will apply this argument to the death penalty in theory and in practice. These two arguments are not *per se* linked; the failure of the former does not entail the failure of the latter. So, a rejection of the death penalty requires a rejection of both arguments.

A Backward-Looking Argument for the Death Penalty: Punishment

Is it the case that the death penalty is a justifiable means of retribution? The justification of the retributive argument is sometimes stated as follows: (a) from a normative perspective, criminal behavior entails punishment, and (b) from equitable considerations, punishment should be measured out according to the quantity and quality of the criminal behavior. The basis of (b) can be *lex talionis* (law of retaliation) or what is called "an eye for an eye" or it can be the *principle of forfeiture*. *Lex talionis* is an ancient form of retribution that has roots in oriental texts, respectively:

> If a builder builds a house for someone, and does not construct it properly, and the house which he built falls in and kills its owner, then that builder shall be put to death. If it kills the son of the owner, then the son of that builder shall be put to death.
> *Law of Hammurabi*

> But if there is any further injury, then you shall appoint as a penalty life for life, eye for eye, tooth for tooth, hand for hand, foot for foot, burn for burn, wound for wound, bruise for bruise. (Exod 21:23–25, NASB)

Lex talionis is a bit ambiguous in meaning at least in quantity and quality. For example, if a serial killer is captured and sentenced to death, his death would not equal in quantity the deaths of his victims. Also, should the state implement a form of death for the convicted person equal to the quality of death, i.e., the form of death the convicted person used in murdering his victim? Surely not. The state would be as equally criminal in stabbing to death a convicted criminal who stabbed to death his victim multiple times.[52] Therefore it is important to classify what crimes warrant the death penalty and important to classify what form of execution is warranted as well, other than by appealing to *Lex talionis*.

Since *Lex talionis* is considered a bit barbaric, a different sort of justification is needed that avoids the ambiguities of quantity and quality. The ethical justification needed comes to us from a component of Natural Law theory called the *principle of forfeiture*. According to the principle of forfeiture, human life is valuable and all humans have a *prima facie* right to life. In light of this right, no human may destroy the life of another human. However, a given individual human forfeits this right to his own life when he violates the same right to life of another human. The principle limits retribution to crimes resulting in death and unlike *Lex*

---

52. For further discussion of *lex talionis*, see Mikliszanski, "The Law of Retaliation and the Pentateuch."

talionis it does not require exacting punishment that is equitable to the crime committed in quantity and quality. The *principle of forfeiture* fits with the current practices of the death penalty in the United States. To date, murder is the crime the United States justice system has declared warranting the death penalty. Some states did allow the death penalty for the rape of a child, e.g. in 2007, the Louisiana Supreme Court upheld the death sentence for Patrick Kennedy who was convicted of raping his step-daughter, *Louisiana v. Kennedy*. However, the U.S. Supreme Court on June 25, 2008 declared this decision unconstitutional. It is not the purpose of this chapter to debate the merits of the Court's decision in light of the constitution. From ethical considerations, it stands to reason that death would be a justifiable basis for a state sanctioned death in light of the *principle of forfeiture*; however, this is not the case for other crimes, like rape of a minor, treason, espionage or kidnapping.

As to the ethical concern about the manner in which the execution is carried out, not all forms of the death penalty are equal. The 8th amendment's language of "cruel and unusual punishment" provides a standard and warrant for considering the well-being of the convicted criminal. In writing the 8th amendment, Justice William Joseph Brennan, Jr. provided an operational definition of cruel and unusual punishment, He included the following: punishment that is degrading to human dignity (especially torture) and punishment that is clearly and totally rejected throughout society. Contemporary means of execution by lethal injection as opposed to electrocution are consistent with the 8th amendment. Similarly, if, according to the principle of forfeiture, the execution is the nullification of a criminal's right to life, a concern to meet his crime with an equal measure of punishment would be to go beyond the forfeiture of his right. Thus, electrocution, beheading, and hanging would be extreme measures of execution.

Some have argued that retribution alone does not warrant punishment. This objection is based on a rather question-begging claim that retribution must aim, in addition to a just desert, toward bettering society. We have here the view that punishment is odd when stripped of its teleological social good.[53] Gertrude Ezorsky presents a thought experiment where "punishing criminals has no deterrence effects worth achieving." In this world suppose punishing the criminal has no further effect, the imaginary criminal is ready to go out and commit his crime all over

---

53. Ezorsky, "The Ethics of Punishment," xi–xxvii.

affirmative action, the death penalty, and abortion 223

again, and victims have no desire for retaliation. Despite these counterfactual dispositions, deontologists are obligated to punish the criminal.[54] Again, Ezorsky sees this as odd.

There is nothing odd here according to deontologists if retaliation is a measure of the value of the victim, otherwise a wrongful act could be left ignored and the message would be that the life of any victim has no value. Perhaps Ezorsky's thought experiment would deal a devastating blow if the criminals were also sado-masochistic. At any rate, what we can see so far is that there is nothing incoherent or unethical in the concept of punishing a criminal by death. It remains to be seen whether the death penalty practiced by fallible human beings is ethical or not.

Let's turn our attention to the retributive argument when applied to the death penalty in practice, specifically in the United States. The arguments against the death penalty in practice are several. At the top of the list are charges that the death penalty as a practice is racially discriminatory, costly due to appeals processes, and errs on putting to death innocent persons. The import of the distinction we made earlier between the death penalty in theory and practice is particularly made obvious with these particular charges. Let us look first at the argument from racism.

The Death Penalty in Practice: An Objection from Racism

Opponents of the death penalty in the United States point out that the death penalty is flawed due to the racist discriminatory attitudes of attorneys, jurors and judges in the criminal justice system. Specifically, evidence has shown that blacks are sentenced to death more often than their white counter parts. For example, in the United States from 1930-1990, 4,002 people were executed and over 50 percent of them were black despite the fact that blacks represent only 12 percent of the United States population.[55] Also, there exists a large "race gap" between the attitudes of whites and blacks in their support for or against the death penalty. One study found that blacks are likely to support arguments that opposed the death penalty when the arguments show that most executed criminals are black or when too many innocent people are executed. The same study found that whites are more likely to support the death penalty because

54. Ibid., xviii.
55. Conklin, *Criminology*, 415.

of the same arguments (anti-death penalty arguments) when whites discover that the criminal justice system discriminates against blacks and sentence them more than whites.[56] Nationwide, blacks and whites are victims of murder in roughly the same numbers; however, 80 percent of those executed murdered white people.[57]

Over the years there have been three waves of studies on the relationship between race and criminal justice.[58] The first wave occurred during pre-civil rights days. It indicated that there was indeed racial discrimination towards blacks in the criminal justice system. A thorough study by Swedish social scientist Gunnar Myrdal and associates called *An American Dilemma* indicated rather unsurprisingly that more racial bias existed in the South. Their research indicated that blacks were sentenced for criminal activity more often when their victims were white. One horrific example dates back to the electrocution of a fourteen-year-old African American George Stinney on March 24, 1944, in South Carolina. George was convicted of murdering two young girls, eleven-year-old Betty June Binnicker and her eight-year-old friend Mary Emma Thames. George was the youngest person to be put to death in the United States in the last one hundred years. George's trial lasted just two hours, and his defense attorney presented no defense. The all-white jury took only ten minutes to find George guilty. George's family was not able to speak to him or see him prior to the trial nor defend him in court. His father was fired from his job at a lumber mill. The family was eventually run out of town.

With the progress made from the Civil Rights Era, such atrocities decreased. In fact the second wave of research, which took place during the 1970s and 1980s, argued that race was no longer a factor in the sentences of the convention of criminals. The second wave researchers argued that the first wave did not control for the degree or severity of black offenses. The first wave simply looked at the disproportionate number of blacks convicted of crimes. The second wave took into account both black and white prior criminal records. Research done by Alfred Blumstein at Carnegie-Mellon University and Michael Tonry at the University of Minnesota Law School argued that the reason for a higher incarceration rate for blacks over whites was due to blacks having a higher imprisonable crime rate. However, the final, third wave of research pointed to

---

56. Peffley and Hurwitz, "Persuasion and Resistance."
57. Dow, "Death Penalty, Still Racist and Arbitrary."
58. Brown et al., *Whitewashing Race*, chap. 4.

methodological problems with the second wave; this third wave began in the 1990s. This third wave acknowledges higher imprisonable rates among blacks, but added that the second wave did not point out the racial ties to this crime rate. The racial ties in this case were not per se intentional or overt; rather they were subtle, cumulative, incremental and institutional. Among the methodological problems with the second wave is what is called "over-aggregation" of data about black and white incarceration. Third wave researchers Robert Crutchfield and associates point out that Blumstein's data obscured variations in black arrests and incarceration rates between different states. When the data is looked at by state, some states reflect a match between arrest and incarceration and in other states blacks are incarcerated at a higher rate than their arrest rate.

Moreover, the third wave looks at what happens after offenders are arrested, e.g., detaining, diverting, and sentencing. As blacks progress (or digress) through the criminal justice system, overrepresentation increases. Research indicates that this is due to differential treatment of juveniles by race.[59] For example, juvenile authorities institutionalize youth who come from families they think are unable to provide parental support for them in the community. While the intent here is race neutral, black youth from single parent homes or from homes without an employed parent are more likely to be institutionalized and many blacks as a matter of fact fall into this category.

While this reflection on racism and the criminal justice system focuses on crimes in general, two points about the death penalty are worth noting. First, if it turns out that blacks are committing a disproportionate number of capital crimes, it is not surprising that institutional factors contribute to producing criminals of this sort by first incarcerating them. Secondly, since research indicates that incarceration rates among blacks are higher than their arrest rates, due to racial discrimination in some states, it is likely to follow that blacks would receive the death penalty in the same manner by state.

It is a non-sequitur, however, to conclude from these facts that the death penalty as an abstract judicial procedure against criminal behavior is *ip so facto* unethical, for the force of this objection is grounded in racial facts about a given society, not in the notion of sentencing a criminal to death. We need only point out that this objection deflates when applied to countries that practice the death penalty like Saudi Arabia but yet have

---

59. Ibid., 141.

no race problem. Nevertheless, when the charge of racial discrimination is applied to the death penalty in practice in the United States, the death penalty is a de facto unethical form of retribution. Advocates of the retribution argument should aimed at a moratorium in states where racial discrimination is noticed unless racial discrimination is wiped clean from the slate in those states or becomes an negligible factor in prosecuting criminals for capital crimes.

The Death Penalty in Practice: An Epistemic Objection about Convicted Innocents

This second objection is not per se independent of the first objection. It also focuses on the judging process of who is and who is not sentenced to death. However, the focus of this objection is on innocent victims who are charged with a capital crime. While the first objection opposed the severity of the sentence of death for a convicted criminal, this second objection objects that a sentence should have been made in the first place because the person charged was innocent. Of grave concern is the finality of the sentence for the innocent person. There have been more than a handful of cases where innocent persons were sentenced to death but fortunately were released. What would be worst are cases where the accused were actually executed. In either case the wrongness of the death penalty in practice is due to errors of insufficient evidence. The force of this objection is that the errors are irreversible. If for no other reason, the argument goes, life imprisonment is morally obligatory for a capital crime since ending an innocent person's life is the gravest of crimes.

A rejoinder to this objection affirms the imperfection of the United States criminal justice system. It argues by analogy that if the sentence of an innocent person to death is a basis for discontinuing the death penalty, then why not dismantle life sentences too since innocent people are sentenced to life in this imperfect criminal justice system? But since it is absurd to rule for the complete dismantling of the criminal justice system, then any argument from imperfection should be rejected. This rejoinder is flawed because it assumes a close analogy between the injustice of a life sentence and the injustice of a death sentence in cases where the persons charged are innocent. Surely requiring an innocent person to spend the remaining years of his life in prison is an awful state of affairs, but it is *a* life that is better than *no* life.

The Death Penalty: A Forward-Looking Argument from Deterrence

Proponents of the death penalty may appeal to a utilitarian argument based on the forward-looking consideration of deterrence. The justification would be similar if not identical to the justification offered for punishing an innocent person for any crime if a greater good could be achieved. The argument here justifies the death penalty, even if a few innocent people are sentenced to death, if the death penalty maximizes the greater good of deterring future murders against more innocent people. In short, the argument goes, lives saved because of the "deterrence effect" that the death penalty has on potential murderers outweighs the deaths of innocents who are falsely accused of committing a capital crime. The attitude behind this argument seems akin to the attitude behind military campaigns, viz., a few dead soldiers is a better state of affairs than a lot of dead soldiers; they are collateral damage.

There are at least two empirical problems with the deterrent argument. First, there are no definitive case studies that show the death penalty actual deters crime. Studies have shown that the crime rate is about the same in states that have the death penalty and in states that do not have it.[60] Secondly, like all utilitarian arguments that violate the principle of justice, this argument does not respect or secure the right to life of innocent humans. Its sole concern is that fewer innocent people than more innocent people are killed. It is less concerned that *any* innocent people are killed. This is a bit troubling if a right to life and just treatment under the law are intrinsic values.

The Death Penalty and the Bible

As we have seen, there are no definitive theoretical arguments against the death penalty when used for retribution. If anything is certain, there exist problems with the practice of the death penalty in so far as the principle of justice is violated for innocent and racial minorities (e.g., African Americans). However, matters are not so definitive against the death penalty for someone who follows the prescriptions of the Christian Old Testament. To be sure, Christians of all persuasions have to come to terms with Old Testament edicts that endorse the death penalty. Some

---

60. Bedau, "Capital Punishment and Social Defense," 302.

Christians could argue that since there are biblical passages where God commands the death penalty, that any other form of retribution would violate God's command and his authority. Thus if God commanded the death penalty during biblical times, surely the death penalty is obligatory posterior to biblical times since ethical commands are trans temporal.

While it is clear that the Bible commands the death penalty, what is not clear is whether the command is for ethical reasons. First, let us reference some of the cases for which God commands the death penalty: Adultery (Lev 20:10–21), rape (Deut 22:22–21), idolatry (Deut 13:6–11), murder (Gen 9:6; Exod 21: 12–14), breaking the Sabbath (Exod 35:2) and disrespect towards parents (Lev 20:9). To recall, ethical commands require universality, and so if each of the above uses of the death penalty were justified on ethical grounds, then the universal application of the death penalty would not be restricted by temporal considerations. Thus the command in Exod 21:12–14, for example, to execute murderers should apply to the execution of murderers in contemporary societies. As an ethical command to execute murderers, the justification of this command as an ethical judgment could be granted by the principle of forfeiture.

Unfortunately, matters become murky when explaining God's command for the death penalty, as an ethical imperative, for the other offenses. That is, if in the Bible God commanded the death penalty for offenses like idolatry, rape, disrespect towards parents, and breaking the Sabbath, then persons guilty of the same offenses in contemporary times should also receive the death penalty. This sentencing follows logically if God's command for the death penalty in these cases is for ethical reasons. Recall from the universalizability principle, the rightness or wrongness of an action does not change over time. Similar cases require similar judgments. But can you imagine sentencing your children to death and then executing them if they became disrespectful? Moral intuitions run deep in affirming the negative to this question and they should. It is difficult to establish an ethical basis for the obligatoriness of the death penalty for these odd cases in the Old Testament. In light of these problems, there are several possible solutions.

According to the first solution, the threat of death was God's method to exact holiness from Israel. It is a solution that is foundationally based on the incompatibility between God and sin. This solution holds that while these cases of the death penalty in the Old Testament were ethically wrong and required retribution, God's choice for the degree of retribution was based on non-ethical reasons. Naturally taking such a position begs the question as to what the non-ethical reasons were. The context for most of these offenses was the upholding of holiness and sanctified social life in the midst of pagan societies. The Israelites needed to be shown how serious sin was to God and how much he detests it. The punishment of death is surely a clear and distinct way of modeling how all sin, regardless of type, is not acceptable behavior for anyone committed to a relationship with God. We see this point expressed in Lev 20: 22–26 and Deut 13:6–11. In these passages, God makes it clear what his plans were for Israel. He set them apart to be his own holy people and to provide for them a land. The people previously in the land could not be his people because of the gravity of their sin. So if Israel wanted to be a part of this plan, certain expectations had to be made clear; a holy life was categorical. As an incentive, the penalty of death ensured that Israel would be "afraid, and no one among you will ever do such an evil thing again."

Such was the Mosaic Law. Unfortunately, the Israelites, and humanity as a whole, suffer from depravity and thus are unable to follow God's commands exhaustively. However, as Rom 8:1–4 points out:

> Therefore there is now no condemnation for those who are in Christ Jesus. For the law of the Spirit of life in Christ Jesus has set you free from the law of sin and of death. For what the Law could not do, weak as it was through the flesh, God did: sending His own Son in the likeness of sinful flesh and as an offering for sin, He condemned sin in the flesh, so that the requirement of the Law might be fulfilled in us, who do not walk according to the flesh but according to the Spirit.(NASB)

The requirement of holiness, though still a goal for a follower of God, is no longer a *basis* for the believer's relationship with God. Christ's death on the cross functioned as a vicarious price for our offenses and thus allowed us to have a relationship with God despite our offenses. So even if followers of God do not meet God's high standard of holiness found in the Mosaic Law, their relationship with God is not jeopardized.

Notice this solution's appeal to the death penalty for theological reasons[61] does not undermine the ethical significance of the offenses committed. God was not merely concerned with establishing holiness and sanctifying the nation of Israel. Scripture is clear that God's

---

61. Further evidence of this dual condemnation of offenses can be seen in Lev 18:21. Here God condemns child sacrifices as a divine offering because the sacrifices honor Molech, and are thus guilty of idolatry. The secondary, and unstated, condemnation of course was that such acts kill innocent life.

retributive response to the offenses considered the well-being of the innocent victims of the offenses. For example, the Bible makes a distinction between a female victim of a sexually impure act (Deut 22:25, 28) and a female voluntary participant of a sexually impure act (Deut 22: 23). In the former cases, only the male who initiates the sexually act is sentenced to death unless the virgin is not engaged (verse 28); in the latter case, both the male and female are sentenced to death. So retribution is required of every unethical act even if death is not justified as a means of the retribution.

So according to this solution, what should be the Christian's ethical attitude toward the death penalty? If we return to the theological reason for the death penalty, Jesus Christ put an end to the need for the death penalty for that reason. We are now justified before God because of Christ's work. However, we can go a step further. Not only are we positionally justified before God because of the work of Christ, we also stand in a position to become like Christ in his character and image once we enter into a relationship with him. Jesus implies as much in John 8:1–11:

> But Jesus went to the Mount of Olives. Early in the morning He came again into the temple, and all the people were coming to Him; and He sat down and began to teach them. The scribes and the Pharisees brought a woman caught in adultery, and having set her in the center of the court, they said to Him, "Teacher, this woman has been caught in adultery, in the very act. "Now in the Law Moses commanded us to stone such women; what then do You say?" . . . [J]esus stooped down and with His finger wrote on the ground. But when they persisted in asking Him, He straightened up, and said to them, "He who is without sin among you, let him be the first to throw a stone at her." Again He stooped down and wrote on the ground. When they heard it, they began to go out one by one, beginning with the older ones, and He was left alone, and the woman, where she was, in the center of the court. Straightening up, Jesus said to her, "Woman, where are they? Did no one condemn you?" She said, "No one, Lord." And Jesus said, "I do not condemn you either, Go From now on sin no more." (NASB)[62]

---

62. There is a question of this passage's canonicity. It is not found in any significant Greek text (e.g., in neither Bodmer papyrus). There are no comments on it by first-millennium Greek writers. Eusebius does mention a story of an adulteress in the *Gospel according to the Hebrews* but the certainty that the two women are the same is an open question among contemporary scholars. Evidence for it comes exclusively from the Western Church. Augustine and Ambrose were aware of it.

affirmative action, the death penalty, and abortion

In this Johannine text, Jesus dealt with an offense punishable by stoning according to Lev 20:10–21. When we connect this story to Jesus' view of adultery in Matt 5:27–30 we see that he considered adultery in thought and adultery in action to be equivalent in offense. Most if not all morally responsible humans (including the Pharisees before him) are guilty of the former offense but not the latter offense. If the two acts were equivalent in moral standing then whatever judgment Jesus held for one act should follow for the other act as well. What we see in John 8:1–11 is Jesus' judgment of forgiveness for the latter act. This leads us to believe he advocated forgiveness for the former as well. Following this reasoning, if adultery is met with forgiveness so are the other acts from the Old Testament requiring death. We have here then a case against the death penalty or at least a cessation of the death penalty.

While a main theme of this passage is about forgiveness, another equally important theme here is restoration of a broken person. Jesus commands the woman to no longer be adulterous. He calls her to change. While rabbinical law would call for her death, Jesus did not. In no way did Jesus condone her behavior. This is clear from the fact he said to discontinue adultery. We see here Jesus' call to restoration of the woman over the call to exact retribution. To be sure, retribution (qua justice) and restoration are not in opposition to each other although to pursue retribution to the degree the woman is put to death makes restoration and retribution together impossible. Rather, from Jesus' perspective, restoration of the woman was a higher ethical concern. Perhaps restoration should be a higher priority within the Christian community where restoration surely is possible. The shift to retribution would be in order where Christ's authority did not reign. We have reason to think this shift in emphasis from restoration to retribution or vice versa was a matter of authorial context when we read Rom 13:1–5. Paul resurrects the retributive side of offenses but not *per se* at the exclusion of restoration. Paul writes:

> Every person is to be in subjection to the governing authorities . . . Do what is good and you will have praise from the same; for [the governing authorities are] a minister of God to you for good. But if you do what is evil, be afraid; for it does not bear the sword for nothing; for it is a minister of God, an avenger who brings wrath on the one who practices evil. Therefore it is necessary to be in subjection, not only because of wrath, but also for conscience' sake.

It must be admitted that it is a matter of debate whether Paul has in mind the death penalty when he refers to "the sword" or merely to the authority and power of the state to punish. Reformers like John Calvin and Martin Luther understood Paul in the former way. However, in keeping with Jesus' prescription against the death penalty, the latter is a better reading. There is a good case that this is Paul's intent.[63] But even here restoration is not incompatible with retribution. What is certain is that talk of restoration is not the goal of the Roman secular authorities. So in this context, Paul explains that retribution is the next best response to criminal or sinful acts. Moreover, for severe crimes like rape or murder, the guilty person cannot be restored when the death penalty is applied. Only a life sentence or imprisonment of some sort allows for the possibility of restoration. Restoration obviously is not guaranteed during or after a prison sentence; restoration occurs only when the guilty freely opens up *to* restoration. However, for any Christian to have a chance to imitate Jesus' offer of restoration, to criminal or sinful acts of an offender within a secular authorial context (e.g., a prison), the offender has to remain alive. When we return to our discussion of the adulterous woman, Scripture is silent on whether she actually departed from an adulterous lifestyle. Nevertheless, we should follow Jesus' lead in at least offering restoration independent of the guilty person's desire to be restored.

A second solution to the problem of biblical capital punishment is to treat passages like Lev 20:10–21; Deut 22:22–21; Deut 13:6–11; Gen 9:6; Exod 21: 12–14; Exod 35:2; and Lev 20:9 as hyperbolic. In terms of the written Law, the form of execution for the death penalty was stoning. The witness of the offense is called to throw the first stone (implying a previous trial). However, there is reason to think the Jewish legal community applied a hyperbolic interpretation to these texts. Doing so would drive home to the Jewish layperson the serious nature of the offensive. In the various cases of offenses, with the exception of first-degree murder (Num 35:31), it was possible to have the offense commuted by a "*koper* that a judge would determine."[64] In this case *koper* (money or some other material item) was used to compensate for the offender's life. Now this is a plausible and ethically coherent reading of these passages, but it begs the question why the Pharisees in John 8:1–11 actually were ready to stone the woman. A possible explanation to ease this tension is to recall

---

63. See Hobbs and Hobbs, *Contemporary Capital Punishment*, 466.
64. Kaiser, "Leviticus," 1142.

that the Pharisees were always ready to trap Jesus in some inconsistency. Whether a *koper* was being demanded or the request to actually stone the woman, in either case, Jesus had authority to forgive the woman. Thus his response, in conjunction with pointing out the hypocrisy of the Pharisees, explicitly stated no retribution was required. This was because of the greater good that could result from forgiveness within a Jewish community that looked to God as the final judge.

Some Christians will not be satisfied with the conclusions taken here on the death penalty. Charges of compromising the text or "liberalizing" the Bible are to be expected. However, these ad hominems do not contain a consistent and warranted objection to the conclusions drawn here. At issue here is how to embrace the Bible in its entirety without selecting, in a question-begging manner, some prescriptions in it as universal/transtemporal and others as merely historical. If in fact the sentence of death is *en vogue* for murder so too is the sentence of death *en vogue* for adultery, disrespect for parents, and for dishonoring the Sabbath.

The Ethical Status of Abortion

Among the various ethical topics that can be debated, the abortion issue is perhaps the most visceral of them all. A person's association or personal relation to an instance of an abortion is more common than that of affirmative action or the death penalty. Because of the visceral nature of the abortion issue, it should not be surprising that the rush to ambiguity or certainty is often intentionally factored into the discussion of its ethical status in order to allow persons on both sides of the abortion debate elbowroom to maintain his/her own position in the face of defeaters to their own view. The discussion of abortion in this chapter aims to weed out any ambiguity and to chip away at any claims to certainty proponents on either side may have. We will first begin with a discussion of what the various positions are on abortion. From there we will define terms essential to the discussion of abortion that turn on certain biological, conceptual, and metaphysical commitments about being a person and being a human being. Since this is an ethical issue rather than a theological issue, no attempt will be made to defend or attack the act of an abortion on theological grounds. With that said, particular biblical passages that address abortion (and they are few) will be discussed. Moreover, the discussion of abortion here will not venture down the path of the law and constitutional rights or rights violation, e.g., the 14th Constitutional Amendment or Roe v. Wade (1973) beyond cursory remarks. Finally we will look at various arguments posed for or against the permissibility of an abortion.

There are essentially two camps on the ethical status of abortion. Both camps see the core of the abortion debate to center around the issue of rights and who or what has rights. Rights are (1) claims or entitlements persons have to do or not to do some actions, or they are (2) claims or entitlements persons have for certain treatment from other persons. In the latter case (2), the specified treatment is often referred to as a duty others have to the person affirming or having the right. Broadly understood, the camp that affirms that the unborn has a *prima facie* right to life (except when the pregnant woman's life is jeopardized) falls under what is classified as the pro-life position.[65] Conversely, the camp that upholds the pregnant woman's right to an abortion as absolute is essentially what is classified as the pro-choice position. Proponents of pro-choice are not pro-abortion. They do not conceive an abortion as good simpliciter. They take the position that an abortion should be a safe and legal option for all pregnant women; whatever the ethical status is of the unborn, the mother's right to her body categorically trumps the unborn's ethical status.[66] In fact the pro-choice position is not *per se* even a position on the rightness or wrongness of an abortion. As I will later show, it is rather a position about the primacy of the woman's right to decide the fate of her pregnancy, whether she has an abortion or not. Nevertheless, we have here, on the one hand, the view that the unborn has a right to life, and on the other hand, the view that the mother has a right to her body.

It should not escape one's notice that talk of a right to life is highly controversial. First, does the existence of a right require or entail that what has the right affirm or claim the right? If so, this requires and expects the possessor of the right to have certain abilities. Minimally it would require that the possessor of the right be self-conscious and even more so requires that the possessor be aware she has the right. But then this requirement would nullify any embryo and even a new born a right to life since in either case, they are not self-conscious and do not make

---

65. A person can be pro-life without justifying their objection to an abortion from the stance of rights the unborn has.

66. Notable exceptions to this view would be that of pro-choice advocates like Judith Jarvis Thomson who grants the right to an abortion only in cases where the pregnancy is involuntary whether or not the unborn is understood to be a person.

claims on the treatment they receive from persons. Secondly, do only persons have rights or do rights extend to non-persons (see chapter 4 on rights)? Thirdly, if rights apply only to persons, then we are led to ask whether an embryo or a fetus is a person? Fourthly, while no one questions whether an adult human being is a person, it remains to be seen if a human embryo or human fetus is a person. Now we are asking whether there is a distinction between being a human being and being a person. To answer these questions, it is better, perhaps, to shift the focus from abortion and talk of rights, to talk of terminology about what an embryo, fetus, human being, person, and other related terms are.

So What Is a Human Being?

Let's begin with a discussion of the term human being. This term has a biological classification in the sense that what it connotes falls under the category of things studied by biology. It is an undeniable fact that the unborn entity in the womb is a human being. While there is debate about when a pregnancy begins (either at fertilization or implantation),[67] most physicians without much hesitation would admit that the embryo is a human being. In his book embryologist Clark Edward Corliss writes:

> It is the penetration of the ovum by a spermatozoan and resultant mingling of the nuclear material each brings to the union that constitutes the culmination of the process of fertilization and marks the initiation of the life of a new individual.[68]

Keith Moore echoes this claim when he writes:

---

67. There is a debate over when life begins. Some claim that life begins when syngamy occurs or when the maternal and paternal chromosomes merge and form a diploid set. Others hold that life begins when the fertilized egg implants in the uterus. This latter view seems to be an arbitrary starting point since the embryo clearly is alive before implantation takes place. Implantation is merely a sufficient condition for the embryo to continue to live; implantation is what allows the embryo to develop due to the nourishment from the mother. So while it is unquestionable that a woman cannot be pregnant unless she is biologically responsible for the life of another, it does not follow that this state of affairs is also a necessary condition for the embryo to remain alive. Arguing this way would be like saying that an adult human being is not alive unless it is connected to its sources of nourishment, viz., sources for respiration and other essentials for continued existence. Surely a human is alive even if it is submerged momentarily under water or stranded in the Sahara desert.

68. Corliss, *Patten's Human Embryology: Elements of Clinical Development*, 30.

> A zygote is the beginning of a new human being (i.e., an embryo) ... Human development begins at fertilization, the process during which a male gamete or sperm (spermatozoo development) unites with a female gamete or oocyte (ovum) to form a single cell called a zygote. This highly specialized, totipotent cell marked the beginning of each of us as a unique individual.[69]

And finally two other scientists Ronan O' Rahilly and Fabiola Miller write:

> Although life is a continuous process, fertilization... is a critical landmark because, under ordinary circumstances, a new genetically distinct human organism is formed when the chromosomes of the male and female pronuclei blend in the oocyte.[70]

The following facts are true of this "new individual," "distinct human organism," or what we may call a human being:

1. As a necessary condition for having a separate existence, the embryo has its own genomic sequence of 46 chromosomes.[71] If the mother scraped cells from the inside of her mouth or *anywhere* in her body, the DNA of these cells would be identical with other cells in her body except for the cells identified as the embryo.

2. The embryo is not merely a collection of cells capable of multiplication. Cancer cells have the ability to multiply so multiplication is not a sufficient condition for separate existence. Rather the embryo also has the ability to develop, differentiate and mature. Such abilities are not true of something that is merely a collection of cells.

3. No other "collection of cells" has these features that allow it to be classified as a life.

---

69. Moore, *Developing Human*, 2, 16.
70. O'Rahilly and Miller, *Human Embryology and Teratology*, 8.
71. It was a common belief that unique DNA was not sufficient as a marker of separate existence since twins were thought to have the same DNA. Recently scientists from several countries proved this to be false. That is, scientists from the University of Alabama at Birmingham and at universities in Sweden and the Netherlands found that twins do not have identical DNA. See Bruder et al., "Phenotypically Concordant and Discordant Monozygotic Twins Display Different DNA Copy-Number-Variation Profiles," 763–71.

These facts concerning the embryo rule out the popular belief that the embryo is merely an extension of the woman's body.

Beginning as an embryo, the human being develops into a fetus, infant, toddler, adolescent and finally into an adult. Terms like "embryo" and "infant" should remain distinct for they mean different things. They refer to different biological developmental stages of the same human being. The following is a description of the stages and capacities of a human being from conception to birth during the human's prenatal journey in the womb. When a single sperm enters the mother's egg cell, the resulting cell is called a zygote. The term 'zygote' comes from the root Greek word 'zygotos' meaning "joined." This process is called fertilization and it occurs within two weeks after the previous menstrual period. At the moment of fertilization, the human being's genetic make-up is complete, including its sex. Within 24 hours after fertilization, the zygote travels to the Fallopian tube and begins cell division, forming what is called a blastocyst. Five days after fertilization, the blastocyst reaches the uterus and implantation occurs 8 to 10 days to 2 weeks. The blastocyst consists of two kinds of cells. One set of cells are the inner cell mass (or what will develop into fetus). The other set of cells surround and protect the inner cell mass cells from the outer environment. The uterus is the human's source of food through the mother's bloodstream. When the blastocyst begins to divide into specialized cells, it transforms into what is called an embryo. The word embryo comes from the Latin word 'embryum' meaning "that which grows." The embryonic stage begins on the 15th day after conception and continues until about the 8th week. The entire period the human is in the womb developing is called gestation age. It is measured in week time slots or in three-month periods called trimesters.

The following list describes some significant developments in the human being while it is in the womb:

- Week 3 of pregnancy (gestational age): The brain, spinal cord, and heart begin to emerge.
- Weeks 6 to 7 of pregnancy (gestational age): Brain waves can be detected and recorded and the heart continues to develop and now beats at a regular rhythm.
- Week 8 of pregnancy (gestational age): The lungs begin to emerge.
- Week 9 of pregnancy (gestational age and beginning of fetal period): All essential organs have begun to form.

- Weeks 11 to 14 of pregnancy (gestational age): The sex of the human is identifiable because the genitals are differentiated.
- Weeks 15 to 18 of pregnancy (gestational age): Sucking the thumb occurs.
- Weeks 19 to 21 of pregnancy (gestational age): The human can hear and makes more movements (quickening).
- Week 22 of pregnancy (gestational age): Heartbeats can be heard with a stethoscope.
- Week 24 of pregnancy (gestational age): Point of viability for the unborn human.
- Weeks 31 to 34 of pregnancy (gestational age): Rhythmic breathing movements occur, but the lungs are not fully mature.

As an embryo, the human being does not have the capacities it will have when it develops into an infant. The genotype of a human being remains the same throughout its life while its phenotype matures over time. The genotype of a human being (or any living organism for that matter) is its entire genetic information, even if the instantiation of most of this information exists only potentially and unobservable at the embryo stage. The phenotype of a human being consists of the instantiated features of its genotype that gradually manifest themselves over time, e.g., its shape, behavior and internal functions. This distinction between genotype and phenotype is important because it is easy to falsely denote a human being in terms of how it looks as opposed to what it is. For example, an embryo does not have fingers, a head and legs; thus, it is easy for someone to suggest that it is not a human being. This failure to make the genotype/phenotype distinction allows some to devalue the embryo qua human being because it does not look like human beings that exist qua infants or toddlers. Unfortunately it is a true and common dictum that humans value things the more such things look like them and even more so when such things look like things they love (e.g., pets).

Human Beings: Moral Patient or Moral Agent

While it is an undeniable fact that the unborn at conception is a human being, it is another matter whether it is also a moral agent at conception. Moral agents are entities in which the following conditions are true of them: (1) they have the ability to understand what they ought or ought not to do in an ethical sense (in so far as understanding a given ethical principle or set of principles), (2) they can freely choose to do or refrain from doing what they ought to do in an ethical sense and (3) they can freely choose to do or refrain from doing what they ought not to do in an ethical sense. Moral agency is essentially an ethical concept about moral responsibility. Human beings that exist as embryos, toddlers and even as comatose human beings, cannot be morally responsibility for their actions; hence they are not moral agents. However, they are nevertheless human beings. So are they also part of the moral community that children and adults belong to?

This question turns on some feature or set of features that tie children and adults together as deserving of ethical consideration, such that it matters what is done to them (as opposed to what they do).[72] Traditionally philosophers have considered this feature to be sentience, i.e., the ability to feel pleasure and pain. It turns out to be the case from granting this claim about sentience that any living being that possesses it is ipso facto a member of the moral community, deserving of moral consideration and care to the degree that it should not suffer wanton harm at the hands of a moral agent. The range of such living beings is vast, e.g., mammals, reptiles, birds, and for our purposes, the human fetus. The same is true of human beings who are born with anencephaly; while they will never become conscious beings due to the absence of a cerebral cortex, they have the ability to experience pain. All sentient beings of the moral community have a position in the moral community not as moral agents but as *moral patients*. In addition to being able to experience pain, a moral patient is unable, because of its lack of cognitive abilities, to understand and act according to moral principles. This is certainly true of a fetus. While a moral patient is thus unable to do anything wrong, a moral patient is capable of doing something bad. That is, moral patients can cause harm to other living beings. A baby or mentally ill human adult qua moral patient is capable of harming another human being but is not also morally responsible for such an act.

It should be noted at this point in the discussion on moral patients that not all human beings are sentient. Consider an embryo; it is capable neither of consciousness nor sentience. For this reason, embryos qua

72. The concern here is not on what children and adults do, and it should not be. Children are not capable of the same actions as adults in regards to the mental content of such actions.

human beings would seem to fall outside the moral community. As such, the argument to forgo causing it pain would seem not to be applicable here. On the contrary, however, to end an embryo at this stage of biological development would prevent it qua human being from acquiring the capacity to experience future pleasures. Most embryos go on, if they are not aborted, to develop into conscious[73] and sentient beings that are capable of experiencing 70 plus years of mental and physical pleasure. From a utilitarian perspective then, the greatest amount of utility is maximized if the human being is allowed to progress through the full range of its biological development. As a rejoinder to this concern is the fact that untold thousands of embryos exist in frozen liquid nitrogen tanks; they are leftover from previous attempts at IVF. There are over 500,000 embryos currently frozen in storage at American clinics. They represent the population of a city the size of Atlanta. As a matter of fact, the fate of the embryos is either to remain frozen, be donated to scientific research, or adopted by someone who is infertile.

What Is a Person?

We now turn our attention to personhood. Personhood is a difficult concept to connote. In fact there is no consensus on the connotation of person. Personhood could be connoted functionally and metaphysically. Let us begin with a functional connotation of personhood. Some propose the view that a person is a self-conscious and self-aware entity that has the ability to make rationally free choices.[74] Philosopher Mary Ann Warren holds the view that the following 5 functional conditions are sufficient for personhood:

1. Consciousness (of objects and events external and/or internal to the being), and in particular the capacity to feel pain;
2. Reasoning (the developed capacity to solve new and relatively complex problems);
3. Self-motivated activity (activity which is relatively independent of either genetic or direct external control);

---

73. Whether it is conscious or the soul is conscious through the body as dualists argue is contested.

74. See Warren, "*On the Moral and Legal Status of Abortion,*" 333–43.

affirmative action, the death penalty, and abortion 241

4. The capacity to communicate, by whatever means, messages of an indefinite variety of types, that is, not just with an indefinite number of possible contents, but on indefinitely many possible topics;
5. The presence of self-concepts, and self-awareness, either individual or racial, or both.[75]

Condition one is true of a fetus and a newborn, but not the other four conditions. Self-awareness does not present itself in infants until the end of the second year.[76] As for an embryo, it fails to function in any of the five ways. Warren's functional view rests on the actual possession of these features. So Warren does not consider a newborn to be a person. As such the death by infanticide of a newborn is not per se ethically wrong on her account. Warren is aware of the visceral reaction many will have to her account. In light of these concerns she says

> A newborn infant is not a great deal more personlike than a 9 month fetus . . . In this country, and in this period of history, the deliberate killing of viable newborns is virtually never justified. This is in part because neonates are so very close to being persons that to kill them requires a very strong moral justification as does the killing of dolphins, whales, chimpanzees, and other highly personlike creatures. It is certainly wrong to kill such beings just for the sake of convenience, or financial profit, or "sport." Another reason why infanticide is usually wrong, in our society, is that if the newborn's parents do not want it, or are unable to care for it, there are (in most cases) people who are able and eager to adopt it and to provide a good home for it.[77]

It is not clear what Warren means by "virtually never justified" since she only gives two reasons why it is wrong to kill newborns. These two reasons taken together imply that killing newborns is wrong when (a) others are disturbed by their death and (b) their death prevents infertile couples or interested adults from adopting them. What Warren implies here is that there are some hypothetical occasions where killing them is not wrong or at least ethically neutral. What occasions these are is not stated. However, it is clear that she classifies newborns merely as moral patients. The fact that Warren is concerned about infanticide suggests she

75. Ibid., 339.
76. Levene and Chervenak *Fetal and Neonatal Neurology and Neurosurgery*, 25.
77. Warren, "On the Moral and Legal Status of Abortion," 342–43. On the ethical status of infanticide, see also Tooley, "*In Defense of Abortion and Infanticide.*"

is not indifferent to the well-being of infants. However, her functional view of personhood invites criticism, particularly the one concerning infanticide she anticipated.

First, Warren does not make a distinction between dispositional and occurrent capacities or functions. Making this distinction places infants back into the category of persons. Some capacity Y (whether Y is a property like self-consciousness or an activity like having a desire to experience the future) is *dispositionally* true of some X (whether the X is an embryo, infant, or adult) just in case X merely has the potential for Y and actually has the causal powers or properties to bring about or manifests Y. Some Y is *occurrently* true of some X just in case X actually brings about or manifests Y. So an adult named Paul possesses a brain that allows or causes him potentially to speak Russian (in a dispositional sense) even though he actually does not speak Russian (in an occurrent sense). Similarly, an infant named Paul possesses a brain that allows or causes him potentially to be self-conscious (in a dispositional sense) even though he actually is not self-conscious in an actual sense. With this distinction made, Paul the infant can be a person and thus infanticide is wrong not because of his death disturbs others or because his absence creates a shortage of adoptable infants, but because his life is morally significant enough to the same degree any other human's life is morally significant.

Secondly, Warren unintentionally provides occasions for when it is unjust to kill a fetus, viz., (a) and (b) above. It is interesting to point out here that Warren considers a fetus and newborn to be virtually equivalent in their constitution. Recall she says, "A newborn infant is not a great deal more personlike than a 9 month fetus." Even if the distinction between dispositional capacities and occurrent capacities is not warranted, at least on Warren's account, the same reasons for why killing an infant should also apply to the fetus. As a matter of fact there are people who are applauded by the death of a fetus or who would want to adopt the fetus upon delivery.

While Warren's account provides sufficient conditions for functional personhood, another account proposes a necessary condition for personhood. On this view, an entity is not a person if it is not a viable human being, where existing *ex utero* is a necessary condition for personhood. Viability, however, is not a property intrinsic to the fetus; it is determined by biological capacities of the fetus and by currently existing technology. Of course, technology varies over time and from place to place. Hence there is no universal gestational age that defines viability. What is viable at 6 months may with future technology be viable at 3 months. In the United States viability is 24 weeks into gestation. If anything is certain about this functional view is that an entity may or may not have the necessary conditions for personhood relative to the advancement of technology. A functional connotation of personhood does not allow for talk of an entity being potentially self-conscious, self-aware, and able to make rationally self-determined choices. Functionality is a matter of how a thing actually functions, not how it could function. Functional connotations of personhood thus can only tell us when some entity *functions* in part or in whole as a person; they cannot tell us when some entity *is* a person. So as much as Warren may want to argue that an infant is not a person, she could only hold, on her view, that the new born does not function like a person. In principle, functional accounts of personhood are neutral on what persons consist of. That is, functional accounts are compatible with materialism and immaterialism. Let us turn our attention to metaphysical connotations of personhood.

Metaphysical Connotations of Personhood within Christian Theology/Philosophy

The ancients used the term soul to refer to personhood. Historically, the earliest metaphysical account of unborn personhood in Christian writings comes from the second-century writer, Clement of Alexandria in his *Excerpts from Theodotus*.[78] He speculates that the soul has a pre-earthly existence. Accordingly, God directly creates the soul and it is implanted into the womb by angels. To be sure, Clement's speculation does not allow him to reiterate the view of the soul Plato advocates in the *Meno* and *Timaeus*. The soul, as Clement conceives it, is finite and enters the womb qua *tabula rasa*; he does not conceive of the soul as eternal and possessing a cognitively repressed awareness of the forms or any other object of knowledge.

A more earthly origin of the soul originates with another second-century Christian writer, Tertullian. Tertullian claimed that God indirectly creates each soul in that each soul is an extension of the previous soul that produced it. Specifically each person's soul is an extension of its father's soul in some mysterious way and this continuity among souls goes back to the first soul of Adam. Tertullian's notion of the production

---

78. See Jones's discussion of Clement of Alexandria in *Soul of the Embryo*, 112.

of human souls is analogous to the sexual reproduction of human bodies, in that each person's body is an extension of its parents' bodies. This continuity among human bodies (from parent to children) goes as far back as the first humans. For Tertullian, this continuity via sexual union includes the extension of the father's soul to his offspring soul. That is, part of the father's soul becomes the soul of his offspring. Tertullian conceived of the soul as corporeal and during sexual intercourse, part of a male's soul enters the womb of a female along with the male's seminal fluid (or as the ancients called it, "seed." He writes,

> So far as the philosophers are concerned, we have said enough. As for our own teachers, indeed, our reference to them is *ex abundanti*—a surplusage of authority: in the Gospel itself they will be found to have the clearest evidence for the corporeal nature of the soul. In hell the soul of a certain man is in torment, punished in flames, suffering excruciating thirst, and imploring from the finger of a happier soul, for his tongue, the solace of a drop of water. Do you suppose that this end of the blessed poor man and the miserable rich man is only imaginary? Then why the name of Lazarus in this narrative, if the circumstance is not in (the category of) a real occurrence? . . . For unless the soul possessed corporeality, the image of a soul could not possibly contain a finger of a bodily substance; nor would the Scripture feign a statement about the limbs of a body, if these had no existence . . . For an incorporeal thing suffers nothing, not having that which makes it capable of suffering; else, if it has such capacity, it must be a bodily substance. For in as far as every corporeal thing is capable of suffering, in so far is that which is capable of suffering also corporeal . . . The soul, then, we define to be sprung from the breath of God, immortal, possessing body, having form, simple in its substance, intelligent in its own nature . . . the soul proceeds from human seed.[79]

Clement and Tertullian represent the two main Christian theological positions taken on the nature of the unborn and on the soul in general. Clement's view is known as *creationism* and Tertullian's view is known as *traducianism*. Both men understood that conception was the moment when the soul was present in the womb. While time and focus will not allow us to explain why, since the time of Christian theologians like Augustine and Jerome to the twentieth-century, creationism became the dominant Christian account of the origin of the soul.

---

79 Tertullian, *Treatise on the Soul* 7, 22, 25 (ANF 3:186–87, 202, 206).

affirmative action, the death penalty, and abortion

As far as creationism is concerned, it comes in two varieties. One view holds that the unborn qua person is present in the womb at the moment of conception by being *causally related* to the embryonic tissue in the womb. This was the view of Clement. The other view holds that the unborn is present in the womb at conception; it *informs* and *animates* the embryonic tissue in the womb. After a man's seed (again, what modern biology calls a sperm) enters a woman, her menstrual material becomes animated by what Aquinas calls a vegetative soul (which animates her menstrual material to possess properties like growth and the ability to receive nutrients). Next this soul morphs into a sentient soul which animates the now living being in the womb to have new properties such as sensation and locomotion. Finally Aquinas asserts that the human rational soul replaces the sentient soul and is infused into the body by a direct act of God. In one place Aquinas follows Aristotle in saying that the rational soul is infused at 40 days for males, and at 90 days for females. Modern Thomists hold that God creates the rational soul at conception and dispenses with the vegetative and sentient soul altogether. This is why Catholics are opposed to abortion at conception. While both views are specifically theological, they are couched in philosophy, particularly ancient Greek philosophy. Those who hold the former of these two subdivisions are Platonic/Dualist and those who hold the latter are Aristotelian/ Thomist.[80] Let us shift the focus from theology to philosophy to allow us to address abortion at a more broad level and to be inclusive of other worldviews not per se Christian.

Philosophical Connotations of Personhood Within and Outside of Christianity

Among philosophers, Plato and Descartes held this view. It asserts that the body and soul are separate substances. At some point in time, God creates the soul and connects it to the body (at conception or sometime later). See Plato's *Meno*, *Republic*, and *Timaeus*; for Descartes, see his *Meditations*. Many think Jesus affirmed this view when he said,

> "Do not fear those who kill the body but are unable to kill the soul; but rather fear Him who is able to destroy both soul and body in hell." (Matt 10: 28, NASB)

---

80. Both views are called creationism because they assert the view that God directly creates the soul or person.

Dualism and Personhood

The dualist view of personhood holds that a person is an immaterial substance that is essentially consciousness (or at least has the deposition for consciousness). In some unexplained way, this consciously existing entity is causally connected to the developing non-conscious human in the womb. The non-physical substance (person) will eventually manifests itself through the medium of the human body when the body becomes a fetus and acquires the biological complexity to house conscious states in the fetal brain. Thus this view conceives of the developing unborn as a host for the soul. The destruction of the body does not entail the destruction of the soul. It is for this reason that brain stem babies for dualists would not be classified as persons, but merely as human babies.

Now it is telling that dualism is perhaps the dominant folk view of personhood in the world, yet many of those who hold it identify the embryo or fetus with the person. Many pro-life proponents defend the right to life of the embryo or fetus on grounds that they believe an abortion is the termination of a person. If truth be told, dualism entails that an abortion is not the termination of a person, but rather the termination of a human being. Since dualism holds that the person is only causally connected to the body qua human being, an abortion cannot be the termination of a person. Interesting that pro-life dualists who would refuse to concede this point about what abortions terminate actually agree with it despite themselves. While they say an abortion is the termination of a person, they also say that only souls qua persons pass on into a post mortem existence in heaven. Basically the problem is this: If the body that is buried in the ground after death is not the person that journeys on to heaven, then this same body earlier at conception qua embryo was not the person either. But this type of dualist does not see this inconsistency.

On a consistent view of dualism, what would make any death of a human being unethical is the separation of the soul and human being, or to put it differently, the death of a human body that is causally interacting with a soul. With this said, does the termination of a human being rather than the termination of a person make an abortion less unethical? The answer should be yes since the soul has higher value than the body in virtue of the soul being equivalent to the person on this view. This is particularly true for an embryo since not even an embryo can be classified as a moral patient; it is not capable of sentience.

So is an abortion of an embryo ethically wrong for dualism? Since dualism with its talk of post mortem existence is essentially a philosophical view that grounds the existence of the soul in God, this question is a concern requiring an answer from a theist. Whatever answer the theist could provide, the answer would be mere speculation since there is no verse (at least for Christian theists) or any detectable way to affirm the moment when God would causally connect a soul to a human being. For all we know, the soul may not be united to the body until the human being becomes a fetus. This epistemic conundrum leaves the dualist with a very serious ethical problem concerning abortion. Since the dualist cannot know when the soul is united to the body, it is conceivable that an abortion is the termination merely of a human body, not a soul/body unity. The dualist also faces an additional problem of a metaphysical sort. Again since we know the dualist places a higher value on the soul because it is what a person is, the dualist still needs to state what value, if any, the embryo has since it is neither conscious nor sentient. It would be a grave mistake for a dualist to respond that embryos are made in the image of God since they identify personhood with the soul rather than the body.

Thomism and Personhood

The Aristotelian/ Thomist conception of personhood conceives of a person as a hylomorphic union of matter (viz., the developing prenatal body) and form (viz., an immaterial rational soul).[81] Contra the Cartesian view, the Aristotelian/ Thomist conception of the soul is unique in two ways. First, the soul is not identical to the mind. On this view, the mind is an actualized property of the soul. As an actualized property of the soul, it does not require matter for its existence and activities. Secondly, the soul and the body are not distinct substances. On this view, the body is an actualized property of the soul. The body is merely a biological structure that depends on the soul for its essence or organization. Both the mind and the body depend on and exist ontologically posterior to the soul. As such, for Aquinas, what has the most significant value is not the soul, body, or mind, but the composition of these elements in what he calls a human being. The term "human being" or what Aquinas refers to as a person is reserved for a substance that can actualize the capacities of thinking,

---

81. For a contemporary Aristotelian/Thomist conception of the soul, see Moreland and Rae, *Body and Soul*, 121–228.

sensing, feeling, occupying space, growing, etc. It is for this reason that neither the body, mind, nor the soul can be classified as a person or as a human being since these capacities (with the exception of intellectual thinking) cannot be actualized in any one of them. For example, a human being has the capacity to see. This capacity to see requires eyes, optic nerves, and a visual cortex. These required organs do not exist merely because of the body for the body itself requires the soul for its existence and its potential capacities. So for a human being to see, the necessary and sufficient conditions for such an act require that both his soul and body interact. The body does not see, nor does the soul; it is the human that sees. Aquinas does not part ways with the dualists concerning post mortem existence. For Aristotelian/Thomism as well, the destruction of the body does not entail the destruction of the soul. Specifically what survives death is the soul existing independently of matter and functioning only through its rational faculty or the mind. Postmortem existence for the soul on this account is void of any sense experiences because these experiences require a body. As Jason Eberl points out:

> Such a deficient mode of existence does not entail that a human being ceases to be "human," that is, to exist as a rational animal, when he is composed of only his soul. A separated human soul has all the capacities proper to existence as a rational animal, namely intellective, sensitive, and vegetative capacities. Hence, though without his body a human being is unable to actualize many of his capacities, he remains a rational animal by virtue of his soul retaining all the capacities proper to such a nature.[82]

One serious problem with the Thomist view is that since the sperm and the egg exist prior to the body and soul, they seem to make the soul superfluous in so far as accounting for the body. This problem is easily noted by pointing out that the body is essentially the union of the sperm and egg. What more is added with talk of a soul? However, a Thomist may say the problem is not as serious as it appears. Like Aristotle, Aquinas affirmed the belief in three souls: the vegetative soul, the sentient/animal soul and a rational soul in tandem. The vegetative soul informs the matter in the womb resulting in a fertilized egg and eventually morphs into the animal soul from the same matter and, sometime later, God creates ex nihilo the rational soul. At this time, the rational soul informs the same matter that the animal soul is informing, and the animal soul ceases to be in the same

---

82. Eberl, "Aquinas on the Nature of Human Beings," 340–41.

manner that sperm and egg cease to be. Following Aristotle's lead, Aquinas holds that the rational soul informs the matter in the womb at 40 days for males and at 90 days for females. As a consequence, the rational soul takes on all the functions that were definitive of the previous vegetative and animal souls respectively. Contemporary creationists like Moreland and Rae who advocate Thomism dispense with the three soul hierarchy and hold that there is a certain organizing feature of the sperm and egg qua embryo that does not seem to be a feature of either the sperm or egg as separate entities. Rather for them, this organizing ability emerges not from the mere union of the sperm and egg, or from three souls, but from one rational soul that informs the matter of the sperm and egg. According to Moreland and Rae, "God directly instantiates the abstract property of being human and creates an individual human soul . . . [The sperm and egg] undergo substantial change and are incorporated into and subsumed under the new individuated essence to form one single substance."[83]

Moreland and Rae do not explain why this is just special pleading. Nevertheless, for Moreland and Rae, the rational human soul informs the sperm and egg and causes them to extend, as a composite whole, into a complex entity that has hands, feet and, among other things, the ability to think. As plausible as this reply is, it is at odds with cases such as conjoined twins. In these cases we are aware of two minds (seemingly implying two rational souls) and one body. This is not an easy conundrum for Thomists to solve.

Dispensing with theological metaphysics, Thomist John T. Noonan offers a purely biological conception of personhood at conception.[84] Noonan argues in a somewhat deductive manner that a human conceptus is a human person. He holds that the theological concept of ensoulment could easily be translated into biological language by substituting "human person" for "rational soul." Noonan explores five arguments that attempt to refute the moment of conception as the beginning of when human beings become ethically valuable beings. According to these five arguments a conceptus is not a person because it lacks any of the following five criteria: viability, lived experience with memories, being capable of eliciting emotions from other humans, sentience, and social visibility. After arguing that each falls short of being criteria for personhood, Noonan concludes with his view: "The positive argument for conception

---

83. Ibid., 220.
84. Noonan, "An Almost Absolute Value in History," 329–33.

as the decisive moment of humanization [personhood] is that at conception the new being receives the genetic code. It is this genetic information which determines his characteristics, which is the biological carrier of the possibility of human wisdom, which makes him a self-evolving being. A being with a human genetic code is a man."[85] Unfortunately Noonan has only explained the genetic causal condition of human value and when this "information" emerges. He did not establish that the effects of this information (our value) also exists at conception. Noonan's view as well faces the conjoined twin problem.

While both dualism and Thomism hold that personhood begins at conception or 40-90 days later respectfully, Scripture is silent on when God would causally connect the Cartesian "person" to the developing human body in the womb or inform prenatal tissue with a rational soul.

Nevertheless, some Christian scholars think otherwise. For example, Moreland and Rae cite Ps 51: 5: *Surely I was sinful at birth, sinful from the time my mother conceived me*. Moreland and Rae claim here that David is affirming his sinful nature as an embryotic person. Concerning the same verse pro-life philosopher Francis Beckwith argues:

> [T]he being at conception is the same person who will become the infant, the child, the adolescent, the adult, and maybe even a philosopher. In sum, it is clear that passages such as Psalm 51:5 are describing a person who is in the process of development, not a thing which is in the process of developing into a person.[86]

Moreland and Rae's and Beckwith's position that there is a continuity of personhood from conception to birth is dubious. Consider the Ps 51:5 passage; if dualism is the official view of the Bible where the soul is a separate substance, the text could not read that David was sinful from conception since it is his body that carries the sin, not the soul.[87] Contra Beckwith, it is unclear how a person can be in a state of development; it is completely clear how an embryo can be in a state of development. There are other questionable passages as well where Christians hold that personhood is an embryotic concept in the Bible.[88]

---

85. Ibid., 356.

86. Beckwith, *Politically Correct Death*, 140.

87. Dualism argues that God creates the soul; in this case, the soul could hardly be originally sinful.

88. Some have argued that the language of the Bible applies language of personhood to the conceptus. They cite such passages as Gen 4:1; Job 3:3; Luke 1:41, 44; Ps 139: 13-16; and Jer 1:5. Unfortunately these passages do no such thing. If Thomism

Non-reductive Materialism and Personhood

In contrast to the above views of personhood, a third recent view holds that personhood emerges sufficiently from the material substance in the womb of the mother. Proponents of this view claim that when the biological system (that starts as a composite of the sperm and egg) in the womb achieves a certain *structural complexity*, a person qua conscious individual emerges as a result. The person on this *materialist* view is not merely resultant of the system's configuration, such that it is nothing over and above properties possessed by the biological system's parts. Just as a magnetic field is not reducible to or constituted by the properties of the iron molecules that produce it, so too is the person not reducible to the brain. This is shown by the functional capacity of the person (its potential for intentionality, center of consciousness and qualia) that is over and above the properties of the biological system's parts, viz., properties and functions of brain cells. Emergentism was a popular view among some philosophers and scientists during the first half of the twentieth century.[89] Recent support for emergentism has been argued by Timothy O' Connor, Kevin Corcoran, Peter van Inwagen, William Hasker and E. J. Lowe.[90]

In contrast to the Thomist view, most proponents of emergentism describe the person as dependent on the body and sufficiently produced by the body, unlike the Thomist view which describes the body as dependent on the soul. What exists at conception for materialists is a human being. This human being continues its journey as a human being until it dies at

---

is correct about personhood, then the person does not begin until that time when God creates the rational soul, but this designated time is not at conception but sometime posterior to the existence of the sentient soul. If Cartesians are correct about the nature of a person, then a person is never the biological material in the womb. All that the passage in Jeremiah says is that God simply creates the person at some unspecified time prior to the creation of the embryo, which is not the person but its host. However, no passage in the Bible states exactly when this event happens prior to the womb. Commenting on Gen 4:1, which reads, "Now Adam knew Eve his wife, and she conceived and bore Cain, and said, 'I have acquired a man from the LORD,'" Beckwith, *Politically Correct Death*, cites Davis, who notes, "The individual conceived and the individual born are one and the same, namely Cain." See Davis, *Abortion and the Christian*, 35–62. (Despite Beckwith's citation, this reading is unwarranted. Is it Cain's body or a Thomistic soul that is the focus in this passage? The point is that it is not clear.)

89. See Broad, *Mind and Its Place in Nature*, chaps. 2, 3, 12, and 14.

90. O'Connor, "Agent Causation"; Lowe, "The Causal Autonomy of the Mental"; Corcoran, *Rethinking Human Nature*, 65–82; Hasker, "Emergentism."

some point later. Again, human beings become persons once they have a conscious capacity brain. If a Christian accepts this account of personhood, there are at least two problems with this view she must be aware of. The first problem is theological. While there is nothing incoherent in the notion of human personhood having an ontological material basis, there is the theological problem of disembodiment of the person after death. That is, if we are dependent on our physical constitution (i.e., being constituted by material bodies), then can we survive death? This is a serious problem, since the Bible clearly indicates our actual continued existence at the same time of the destruction of our material constitution, viz., the destruction of our body. Biblical evidence that human persons survive their body comes from Jesus' warning about death: "Do not fear those who kill the body but are unable to kill the soul; but rather fear Him who is able to destroy both soul and body in hell" (Matt 10:28, NASB). A dualist or a Thomist view of personhood intuitively fits better with passages like this.

Two responses have been offered by materialists. On the one hand, it is conceivable that God could, at the moment of death, continue our existence in another or new body we obtain that is causally connected to our corpse. Time does not permit a detail explanation of this post mortem existence of a material body, but it has been defended by Christian philosophers like Kevin Corcoran and Peter Van Inwagen.[91] This other body would presumably resemble in every detail the deceased body but at the same time is a continuation of the same human being.

The other problem is ethical. This problem concerns how a materialist can be pro-life at conception. Since the materialist denies that the human being is a person at conception and is a person only at some point later in the fetal stage of development, then it seems abortions are

---

91. For Corcoran, at death, God causes an immanent change in our body at the moment of death. In immanent causation, a state x of thing A brings about a consequent state y *in A itself*. In other forms of causation, such as efficient causation, the consequent state y would exist in another thing B. I can cause a window to break (efficient, external change) and I can cause myself to be healthier by exercise (immanent, internal change). This immanent change is the addition of new cells God creates that match in a one-to-one pairing with the cells in the dying body. Think of it this way. Each cell in your body usually gets replaced as they die at some point in time. Your skin cells today won't be the skin cells you will have next week. This "changing of the guard" never leaves you without some cells. For any change from old to new, there is a moment when you have double what you need. For Corcoran, this happens in an "all at once" transfer, resulting in two bodies. See Corcoran, "Physical Persons and Postmortem Survival without Temporal Gaps," 201–17. See a similar view by van Inwagen, "The Possibility of Resurrection."

permissible at conception. After all, since the ethical wrongness of an abortion seems minimally to depend on the existence of personhood, an abortion is not the termination of a person but merely the termination of a human being. This ethical problem may appear to be just for materialists, but it is essentially the same problem dualists have since they also deny that the embryo is a person.

Corcoran offers a response. He suggests that the metaphysics of materialism is in no more trouble concerning its compatibility with pro-life position than is dualism. They both, he argues, need to be supplemented with a theological thesis: (1) God intends every human person to be a soul-body composite or every human organism to constitute a person and (2) abortion is the wrenching apart of what God intends to be joined.[92] Now while the thesis of (1) and (2) can provide ethical justification for why it is wrong to abort an embryo and fetus in the womb, it is not clear that (1) and (2) are sufficient to justify the prohibition against destroying frozen embryos left over from previous IVF fertility treatments. The number of leftover embryos in the United States is estimated to be approximately 500,000.[93] If (1) and (2) are true, we are left with a very strange state of affairs given the existence of approximately 500,000 frozen embryos. The state of affairs of being frozen frustrates (1), and (2) entails that frozen embryos should remain frozen indefinitely unless implanted for fertility purposes. It is not at all clear what purpose this strange state of affairs serves for God, of course, given again that (1) and (2) are taken to be true.

Materialism qua Emergent Substance Dualism

A recent materialist extends talk of emergentism to include not just non-material properties but non-material substances. On this view, the person qua emergent conscious being need not be a physical body with emerging non-physical properties to be a person. This is William Hasker's position. Unlike other emergentists, Hasker does not consider the conscious mind a property of the body. Instead, the mind is able to maintain a separate existence as a substance after its emergence from the brain. Hasker holds that such a view must acknowledge the causal dependent relationship the

---

92. Corcoran et al., *In Serach of the Soul*, 174.
93. Smietana, "Leftover Embryos Lie in Frozen Limbo."

mind has on the brain and yet be able to explain post mortem existence. He writes,

> In the view I am proposing, the answer to these two requirements is found in an analogy between the mind (or soul) and the 'fields' (electrical, magnetic, gravitational, etc.) of physical science. If we take the magnetic field as our analogue, we may say that 'as the magnet generates its magnetic field, so the organism generates its conscious field '. The magnetic field is conceived, in keeping with the scientific realist assumptions of the proposed view, as a concrete physical entity, generated by the magnet but distinct from it. Certain states and/or processes in the magnet cause there to be a magnetic field; similarly certain states and/or processes in a living organism cause there to be another kind of field—call it the 'conscious field', or the 'psychic field', or (perhaps most provocatively) the 'soul-field'. Like the magnetic (or electrical, or gravitational, etc.,) field, the soul-field depends for its existence on the generating physical object; but like those other fields it is distinct from the object rather than identical with it. Like them, also, it is no mere epiphenomenon; it acts upon its generator as well as being affected by it.[94]

Hasker points out here that the notion of emergence and separate existence is not purely metaphysical or ghostly. Consider an electromagnet; it is a core with wire rapped around it. When an electric current is passed through the wire of the electromagnet something novel emerges that did not exist before, viz., a magnetic field. The magnetic field has properties that the electromagnet or electricity does not possess separately. It is not reducible to or constituted by the properties of the iron core and wire that produced it. The field extends out into space beyond the spatial dimensions of the magnet. Moreover, it can maintain an existence after the magnet is destroyed. In a similar but theoretical manner, so too can the mind have a separate existence from the brain. Like the electromagnet that generates a magnetic field that can exist posterior to the electromagnet, so too can the brain generate a conscious field that is able to exist posterior to what generated it. The only dependent relationship the mind has to the brain is in terms of an earthly function, not continued existence. Hasker describes his emergentism as combining the advantages of both Cartesian dualism and materialism. He refers to his position as *emergent dualism*. The ramifications of emergent dualism are as follows.

---

94. Hasker, "Emergentism," 475.

First, as a plus for this view, it does not face the theological gymnastics of standard materialism of Corcoran. Since the mind can maintain a separate existence from the body (particularly from the brain), post mortem existence is at least conceivable on Hasker's view.

Secondly, as a minus for this view, emergentism does not allow for personhood to exist until a certain complexity in the body has taken place, viz., when the brain becomes complex enough for consciousness to emerge. Obviously then, this substance emergentism as a metaphysical view cannot satisfy a pro-life position at conception. It has the same ethical problem materialism in general has concerning the prohibition of an abortion at conception. But if Corcoran's answers to this objection were sufficient for standard materialism, *ip so facto*, it would be sufficiently warranted for emergent dualism as well. However, Hasker faces the same problem if he adopts Corcoran's (1) and (2) thesis when applied to frozen embryos leftover from IVF. An alternative for Hasker, other materialists, and dualists who do not hold Corcoran's (1) and (2) thesis, is to hold that the frozen embryo is not a person or moral patient (since it is not sentient), but simply a human being with only potential value in virtue of its occurent ability to potentially be a moral patient or a person. This alternative attitude toward embryos would seem to allow for, for example, stem cell research, pending some yet to be determined ethical objection against stem cell research.

A Return to IVF

If the issue of frozen embryos is not problematic enough for views like dualism and materialism, IVF in general presents every view we have discussed with another conundrum. The success rate of an IVF transfer of an embryo to the uterus is proportionate to the number of embryos implanted. The more embryos implanted the more likely the mother will become pregnant. The embryos are transferred with the expectation that perhaps one out of, say, 5 implanted embryos will continue to live. This attitude towards IVF transfer implies that the medical staff is in compliance with the termination of several embryos for the sake of one successful pregnancy. To put the objection another way, doctors are sending embryos to their death since they know only one out of several will likely survive the transfer to the womb.

This is particularly an ethical problem for views that value the embryo as having equivalent value to that of an adult human person. We would not send several astronauts to the moon to ensure that at least one lands on the moon if we knew that only one is likely to return alive. It would appear that the double effect principle would be able to resolve this ethical dilemma since the IVF procedure meets the first three condition: a woman becomes pregnant, there is statistically no way transferring one embryo would be an alternative, and the death of the unsuccessful embryos is not intended. However, the fourth condition is not met and the deaths of the unsuccessful embryos are unwarranted in light of utility concerns. Perhaps then it is utility alone that should be the focus for a solution to the dilemma. A utilitarian would argue that there are several options for IVF transfer: transfer one, two, three, four, five, or whatever the maximum number would be to avoid a situation where all embryos are unsuccessful. The utilitarian would first point out that the actual outcome of an IVF transfer is uncertain, so the focus on probable success is imperative. As such, the option that results in the highest probable success rate of the embryos is the right option to choose. For the utilitarian, this is not a matter of placing a price tag on the life of the embryos nor for that matter is the IVF transfer like sending astronauts to the moon. As for the former issue, more disutility results when the embryos remain frozen or when the probability of any successful embryo is less than chance. In short, why transfer 5 embryos one at a time with a low success rate for each of them rather than transferring 5 collectively with a high success rate for at least one of them?

The Ethics of Abortion: Is Pro-choice an Ethical Position?

Now that we have looked at various conceptions of personhood, we can consider the ethics of having an abortion. Let us return to the two camps briefly described earlier, pro-choice and pro-life. Let us look at them in tandem. It will be argued here that the term "pro-choice position" is a poor choice of words as far as being an ethical position on abortion. Recall ethics essentially concerns what actions are right or wrong. Describing an action as right or wrong connotes that the action ought to be done if it is right and ought not to be done if it is wrong. By definition then, actions that ought to be done or ought not to be done necessarily entail a restriction of choices for the doer of the action. That is, if an action ought not to be done, this is equivalent to saying a choice to do the action is not available to some agent. Conversely, if an action ought to be done, this is equivalent to saying

affirmative action, the death penalty, and abortion   257

a choice not to do the action is not available to some agent. Simply put the commitment to a selected course of action is what it means to call an action an *ethical* action. Now to refer to an abortion as an *ethical issue* is to say either all/some abortions ought to be done or all/some abortions ought not to be done (or at least that they should or should not be permissible to do). It should be apparent here that talk of a "pro-choice" position on the ethics of abortion in the broad sense so defined, without normative restrictions, is incompatible with the normative language of oughts and ought nots. Recall that pro-choice is the view that an abortion should be a safe and legal option for all pregnant women. A pro-choice proponent cannot hold that an abortion is an ethical issue and at the same time hold that a pregnant woman can do whatever she wants with her pregnancy.

As a rejoinder, some proponents of the pro-choice position may say that they are not in favor of abortion on demand; rather, they hold, some abortions are wrong under some circumstances. She may say abortions after the 2nd trimester are wrong, partial birth abortions are wrong, or abortions done for convenience are wrong. Let us call these circumstances C. With this caveat, the pro-choice proponent has just nullified her pro-choice stance for two reasons. First, since this pro-choice proponent argues that some abortions are wrong, this judgment entails that these particular abortions ought not to be done and thus leaving it impossible for a pregnant mother under the circumstance C to have a choice in the matter. Secondly, the circumstances C, rather than the choice of the mother are what make the abortion wrong.

Now for proponents of pro-choice who insist on using the term "pro-choice" or who argue that the right to her body is what allows a pregnant mother "trump privileges" over any right to life the unborn may have, they should classify their position as a matter of subjective *prudence*, not ethics. If ethics is involved at all in this case, it is in defending the right the woman has to her body concerning any topic whether the topic is about her life or death (euthanasia) or the life or death of an embryo (abortion). Accordingly, abortions are neither right nor wrong; they are subjective prudential options if chosen. So having an abortion is a matter of what suits the pregnant woman's life the best as she sees it. In short, whether an abortion should occur turns on what the pregnant mother thinks is prudent for her to do with the unborn she is carrying. Talk of prudence fits better with the pro-choice advocate's defense of a high school pregnant young woman who concludes that it is prudent for her to abort her unborn in order to complete her final years in high school. Perhaps the young pregnant woman feels she would be encumbered if she had to take on a job if she were to also attend college in order to care for the eventual child. However, the choice to have an abortion, on this view, would not entail ascriptions of wrongness, rightness or even of ethical praise or blame. This approach to abortion of course ignores the metaphysics of what is being aborted, particularly when the choice to abort involves dismembered body parts (tiny hands, feet and crushed skulls in partial birth abortions). Pro-choice qua subjective prudence abstracts the abortion issue from the empirical world of the unborn (along with its dismemberment) to the conceptual world of ideals about rights to privacy, prudence, and autonomy.

In order for the pro-choice position to be salvaged as an ethical position on abortion, it must jettison the assumption that women have an *unconditional* choice to abort her unborn and, more importantly, that no abortions are wrong.[95] In other words, an abortion must not be looked at as an item on a menu. Here the pro-choice position must argue that an abortion is an ethical issue deserving of serious objective reflection for the sake of the mother and the unborn. Now pro-choice proponents could deny this claim, but then their position will not be an ethical position on abortion. As an ethical position the pro-choice position must decide when an abortion is ethically right, wrong, or permissible given the circumstances surrounding both the mother and her unborn rather than leaving its normative status completely in the hands of the mother's choice. On this view, the basis of the rightness, wrongness, or permissibility of an abortion must consider the value and interests of both the mother and the unborn. It may well be the case that some abortions do not involve the interests of the unborn (perhaps in cases involving an embryo) but surely this would not be the case for *all* abortions since some abortions involve fetuses that are moral patients (minimally a fetus has an interest not to feel pain). Again, what the pro-choice proponent must avoid is placing *all* abortions totally in the choice of the mother as if no abortion is wrong. With this said and despite their choice of words, we can now discuss pro-choice positions as ethical positions on abortion when we rename them *qualified pro-choice*: such views would consider the value and interests of both the mother and the unborn and be (a) pro-choice on abortions that are neither right nor wrong (where subjective prudence comes into play), (b) pro-abortion on abortions that would

95. Or at least it must argue that some abortions are right, e.g., to save the life of the mother due to a complicated pregnancy or a life-threatening disease.

affirmative action, the death penalty, and abortion 259

produce a greater good if performed, and (c) anti-abortion on abortions that would produce a greater evil than good if performed.

In an interesting qualified pro-choice argument developed by Judith Jarvis Thomson, Thomson comes close to fulfilling (a)-(c). Thomson's argument allows for abortion only in cases where a mother's pregnancy is forced upon her or is involuntary. In her 1985 essay, "A Defense of Abortion"[96] Judith Jarvis Thomson argues that even if the unborn is a person and has a right to life, "a right to life does not guarantee having either a right to be given the use of or a right to be allowed continued use of another person's body-even if one needs it for life itself." Thomson has in mind unborn persons who are conceived as a result of unconsensual sex, e.g., rape or incest. In defense of (a) Thomson holds that a woman is not ethically obligated to forgo an abortion in such cases; she has a choice to have one and to not have one.

In her argument Thomson draws an analogy between a woman who becomes pregnant against her will and a person who wakes up from a slumber and finds herself connected to a dying violinist. In the case of the dying violinist, Thomson asks you to consider waking up one morning and finding yourself connected via life supporting tubes to the dying violinist. While you were asleep, his fans (Society of Music Lovers), knowing he is on the verge of death, connect him to you in your sleep. When you awake and discover what has happened to you, Thomson asks whether you are obligated to remain connected to the dying violinist or not. To unplug yourself would result in killing an innocent life, viz., the violinist. For Thomson, since we did not have a choice in being plugged up to him, we are released of any responsibility if we decided to unplug him. At best we would be Good Samaritans if we allowed the violinist use of our body, but no moral obligation holds for us to do so. An ethical obligation for person A to save person B's life is nullified when person A is forced into a relationship with B in order to save B's life. So again, Thomson's thesis is that every person has a right to life, but this right does not extend to the forced use of another person's body. This is true even if the connection lasted for a day or nine months. She anticipates that most readers share her moral intuitions and concludes by analogy that a woman who is forced to conceive because of rape or incest, for example, also does

---

96. Thomson, "A Defense of Abortion."

not have an ethical obligation to remain connected to the unborn person inside of her womb.[97]

Thomson assures her readers that she is advocating the freedom to choose an abortion and not the right to an abortion. Contra some pro-choice advocates, Thomson argues that some abortions are wrong:

> First, while I do argue that abortion is not impermissible, I do not argue that it is always permissible. There may well be cases in which carrying the child to term requires only Minimally Decent Samaritanism of the mother, and this is a standard we must not fall below. I am inclined to think it a merit of my account precisely that it does not give a general yes or a general no. It allows for and supports our sense that, for example, a sick and desperately frightened fourteen-year-old schoolgirl, pregnant due to rape, may of course choose abortion, and that any law which rules this out is an insane law. And it also allows for and supports our sense that in other cases resort to abortion is even positively indecent. It would be indecent in the woman to request an abortion, and indecent in a doctor to perform it, if she is in her seventh month, and wants the abortion just to avoid the nuisance of postponing a trip abroad. The very fact that the arguments I have been drawing attention to treat all cases of abortion, or even all cases of abortion in which the mother's life is not at stake, as morally on a par ought to have made them suspect at the outset.[98]

Despite this distinction, pro-life advocate Francis Beckwith misrepresents Thomson's view by asserting that she does not see pregnancy as a *prima facie* good but rather as a *prima facie* violation of a woman's bodily integrity. He provides the illustration of a young woman involved in a car accident that is brought into a hospital because she is unconscious and has sustained injuries. When the doctors perform tests, they discover she is pregnant but supposedly she does not know she is pregnant, i.e., the doctors conclude she does not know because her diary does not indicate that she knows she is pregnant and her close female friend does not know she is pregnant. Beckwith asks, "what is the doctor's obligation to his unconscious patient? It would seem that, under these conditions, the

---

97. Similarly, if a woman voluntarily has vaginal sex, but takes prudent precautions against becoming pregnant (e.g., contraceptives), then if she becomes pregnant, the unborn does not have a right to her body. Hence, under these circumstances, it would not be unjust to abort the unborn.

98. Thomson, "Defense of Abortion," 65–66.

affirmative action, the death penalty, and abortion

doctor is morally required to perform an abortion to rid his patient of the 'massive intrusion' being imposed upon her by the unborn."[99] Certainly Thomson would disagree with this straw man illustration. Beckwith falsely assumes that the pregnant young woman would see her unborn as a "massive intrusion." It is presumptuous for Beckwith to make this claim. Even if we assume that the young woman was using a contraception and did not want to become pregnant, this assumption does not entail what Beckwith says it does, viz., that the doctor has an obligation to perform an abortion. Rather, what the doctor is likely to do and should do is wait till the young woman becomes conscious to discern what her choice is, which is what Thomson argues. Perhaps the young woman does not know she is pregnant but is not opposed to being pregnant. With this said, there are several noted problems with Thomson's argument.

First, it is not so obvious that no person has an ethical obligation to surrender freedoms to her body to ensure another person's right to life. *Rather what is certain is that no person has an ethical obligation to surrender freedoms to her body to ensure another person's right to life at the cost of her life*. Without question, no person should be required to surrender any of her own life essential organs to save another person. However, short of life threatening situations, restricting a person's bodily freedoms is in order when another person's life is the issue. Sometimes beneficence is obligatory, viz. when the agent's life is not on the line but some other person's life is. Imagine that you are walking along Lake Michigan and notice a person drowning. There is no one else there to assist but you. According to Thomson, the drowning person does not have rights to your body in this case, even if the person is drowning. But is this the case? While you freely decided to walk along the lake, you did not freely decide to place yourself in the position of rescuer. Nevertheless, as Kant would ask, do you have a duty to respond a certain way? It is safe to say that you would not be required to jump into the water to rescue the victim at the expense of your own life; however, you can throw the person a life jacket or place an emergency call to the fire department. Whatever the case, the victim has placed a demand on your body to respond to his grave situation. Thomson would allow us to ignore the drowning victim if we so chose. For Thomson, if we assisted, our assistance would not stem from justice, but from the goodness of our kind heart without duty. While you and the

---

99. Beckwith, *Defending Life*, 176.

person in Thomson's story are in different situations, you are both asked to use your bodies to save a life.

Secondly, it is not clear that Thomson's analogy holds; there are sharp differences between the plight of the violinist and an unborn. First, the unborn is naturally dependent on the mother for viability whereas the violinist is artificially dependent on the other person. Citing the natural dependency relationship the unborn has, that the violinist does not have, is telling when we consider the main issue, which is about Thomson's assumption that all persons have a right to life. Pace Thomson, if each human has a right to life, her argument for the permissibility of an abortion in cases of involuntary pregnancies makes the right unintelligible for unborns. Since we all have a right to life, obviously the right must be natural. The right comes about then by virtue of our coming into existence. No one can have a right to life if the conditions sufficient for the right to life are not attainable. Unless medical technology advances, there is no sufficient condition to exercise this right other than the mother's womb for persons classified as embryos and fetuses. Thomson seems to be unaware of this. Obviously, this right to life is *prima facie* and the embryo and fetus qua person forfeit the right when they jeopardize the mother's right to her life. Now as far as this right to life is assured from a post birth perspective for other persons, like adult human persons, a sufficient condition for it is merely a guarantee not to be killed as opposed to not to let die. Thomson specifies this condition when she says, "I have argued that you are not morally required to spend nine months in bed, sustaining the life of that violinist, but to say this is by no means to say that if, when you unplug yourself, there is a miracle and he survives, you then have a right to turn round and slit his throat."[100] In agreement with Thomson, the violinist thus cannot claim to have a *prima facie* right to life under the circumstances he finds himself, viz., being medically connected to another person. If the person unplugs him, she is simply letting him die, and while this is what is happening to an embryo or fetus, or even worse killed by physicians, again the difference is that the embryo and fetus have no other grounds to instantiate a right to life other than the womb. We have here a distinction with a difference.

Finally with the new name "qualified pro-choice," we can make sense of (b) when pro-choice advocates defend a pro-abortion stance on grounds of social utility. The argument typically goes the following way:

100. Ibid., 66

If abortions are restricted, the following disutility ensues: a poor woman who cannot afford contraceptives would be forced to give birth to a child she cannot afford to raise, be unable to attain further education for herself and thus be forced to accept the most marginal employment; without abortions rights for the poor, the population of the poor increases; and unless there is a fully reliable and safe contraception, women would be forced to be celibate unless they are also emotionally able to bear the burden of an unwanted pregnancy. Equally concerning is the psychological pain from rape. A rape victim should not be forced to give birth to a child she did not consent to. It will continually remind her of the culprit of the act and in turn lead her to resent the innocent child that resulted from the rape. Therefore, abortion under these circumstances would be in order or at least permissible.

To be sure, these negative consequences are warranted pending which view of personhood is correct that we have discussed. The views we looked at argued that the unborn (1) is a human being that is also a person at or near conception, (2) is a human being that becomes a person when the brain manifests mental states, (3) is a human being that is causally related to a person or (4) is a human being whereby a person emerges from it as an independent substance. It is unlikely that advocates of these utilitarian arguments would grant (1), and (2) and (4) after consciousness. However, some could and perhaps do, and hold that the well-being of the mother trumps the well-being of unborn qua person. At any rate, the point is that these negative consequences are warranted *iff* the unborn is not a person. Conversely these negative consequences are either unwarranted or problematic if the advocates of these utilitarian arguments acknowledge the unborn to be a person relative to personhood described in (1), (2), and (4). The main reason they are unwarranted or problematic is that they do not recognize the intrinsic or *prima facie* worth of an unborn person to any degree over against the worth of the mother's pains or pleasures. The problem here is not that an unborn person's life[101] should never be sacrificed for a greater good. Surely a fetus that is the result of an ectopic pregnancy should be sacrificed for the sake of its mother's life when its continued development would lead to the death of both of them. However, the qualified pro-choice utilitarian arguments (qua pro-abortion) just considered hold that the encumbered

---

101. I am using the term unborn person here to cover all the metaphysical views discussed. Even on substance dualism or emergent dualism, the person should be classified as unborn until the person's spatial location is not dependent on the womb.

pleasures and interests or inevitable pains of the mother count more than the encumbered pleasures and interests or inevitable pains of the unborn. This is a question begging assertion. Rather given that the unborn, if allowed to be born, is likely to outlive her mother, it stands to reason that it has more utility at stake than its mother. Moreover, there is a hidden assumption being made by these arguments that can only be empirically verified, viz., that there will not be any shift in attitude on the mother's end. For example, it is an empirical matter whether or not a mother will come to love her child even if it is a product of rape.

So to argue that a greater evil results if the child is born is rather premature. But even here, suppose much psychological pain results from carrying the unborn to full term and caring for it. Any advocate of an abortion for such a state of affairs is faced with an inconsistency problem. If it is ethically permissible for a mother to terminate the life of her unborn qua person prior to birth, why does she not have the same right to terminate the life of her child after birth? Why is the latter death classified as murder but the former death classified simply as ethically permissible death? We have here a *reductio ad absurdum*. If termination of a human being at 6 months is permissible then termination of a child at age 6 is equally permissible for the reasons given in the utilitarian arguments (again given that advocates of the utilitarian argument acknowledges the unborn to be a person). Consider, for example, a single parent mother is crippled from a near fatal car accident. As a result of the accident, she loses her job and now can only find marginal work due to her handicap. Under these circumstances, she is unable to provide a decent life for her child(ren). If we judge consistently here, the mother could kill her child(ren) because she has insufficient resources to care for child(ren).

Is Pro-life the Position of the Bible?

Let us turn our attention to the other side of the fence to the camp commonly known as pro-life. The pro-life position does not entail theism, for some of the views on personhood discussed do not presuppose God, viz., (2)-(4). With that said, many Christians, particularly evangelicals and Catholics, are opposed to abortions except in cases where the mother's life is threatened by the unborn.[102] As pointed out earlier by reference

---

102. I will not use the word baby in the discussion of abortion. Rather I have chosen the word unborn. The issue in the abortion debate is not whether the unborn is

to Clement and Tertullian, the early Christians held the view, in various ways, that the human soul is present at conception. Moreover, the early Church considered abortion homicide. We see evidence of this in *The Didache* and in *The letter of Barnabas* where the text condemns the abortion of a fetus and also infanticide of a new born. We see evidence of this also in the works of first-century writers Athenagoras and Municius Felix.[103] We find an exception to this prohibition against abortion in Rabbinical Judaism. Rabbinical Judaism prescribed embryotomy (the dissection of a fetus to aid in its delivery). This was done for the sake of the mother's health in complicated pregnancies. In the Talmud it reads: "When a woman giving birth to a child is in danger, the unborn child may be cut to pieces and removed, for her life takes precedence over the life of the unborn child" (*Mishna Oholot* 7:6).[104]

Again, the reason for this near absolute opposition to abortions is the belief in the sanctity or intrinsic value of human beings and the belief that human persons are present at conception. In essence, the Christian's belief in the sanctity of a human person follows from the biblical view that God created all human persons as the pinnacle of his creation; all human persons are made in God's image (Gen 1:26 –27). In broad terms, the normative Christian dictum asserts that the life of human persons should be preserved and thus human beings cannot be terminated for the sake of some other human person's goods, e.g., for the sake of particular psychological and physical pleasures of others. In essence this is to say Christians believe all human persons have a right to life. But this right to life is only *prima facie* for there are occasions as indicated earlier where preserving a human person's life requires the termination of another human person, e.g. terminating an ectopic pregnancy so that the mother does not also die. In the social and political milieu, what has just been described is called the standard "pro-life" position on abortion. Being "pro-life" is nearly a trademark of being a Christian or at least an ethically conservative Christian.

In recent times, however, there have been differences of opinion among Christians in regards to the circumstances for when abortions are permissible. Some Christians take exception to the so-called "standard

---

a baby or not but whether it is a person. Persons are those things (or at least human persons) that are identical to, emerge into, or exist in an embryo, fetus, infant, toddler, child, adolescent, and adult.

103. Gorman, *Abortion and the Early Church*, 47–62.

104. Anonymous, "Abortion in the Bible," 221.

view" of the pro-life position. They see it as too constricting. For them, the justification of abortions should be extended to cases of rape and incest. Some proponents of this view may classify it as a progressive pro-life position. While this broadening of the "pro-life" position has a sense of sensitivity for victims of rape and incest, it lacks any philosophical clarity. First, it is unclear how advocates of the progressive pro-life position can extend an exception for abortions in cases of rape when their platform against abortions is the sanctity of unborn life. To put the problem another way, if their objection to abortions is that unborn human beings are intrinsically valuable why does the intrinsic value of the unborn human beings diminish when they are a product of rape?

Secondly, it is unclear why progressive pro-life advocates consider rape grounds for a justified abortion but do not consider other utilitarian considerations, like an inconvenient pregnancy that threatens career and educational opportunities or an unplanned pregnancy where the mother is poor and won't be able to provide the basic needs for life for her unborn upon delivery. What progressive pro-life advocates fail to consider is that the issue of rape is an empirical matter. That is, it is an open question whether a baby born out of rape would lead to a life of permanent psychological pain for the mother. Like many traumatic experiences that humans face, the experience is initially unbearable. However, over time, the mother may come to terms with the experience. In this case, the trauma is acute and limited to a season. This is true particularly after experiencing a loss in the family or a divorce. If this is a plausible optimistic outcome after the traumatic experience of rape, it is hardly the case that the disutility from a season of psychological trauma outweighs the utility from the entire life of a person born as a result of rape.

Before going down the path of what the psychological future looks like for a mother bearing an unborn due to rape, pro-life advocates of every sort need not be concerned about being sensitive to the trauma of rape and the value of the unborn. An ethical dilemma ensues only if the unborn is actually a person rather than merely a human being. It is a matter of metaphysics. Only Thomism considers personhood to exist in the embryotic stage of a human being's existence. Even substance dualism does not classify a human in the embryotic stage as a person, or at any other stage of the human's earth existence. Dualists, to recall, consider the death of a human being unethical only because of a coexisting soul. Recall also, that when the soul becomes causally connected to the body, there is no way for a dualist to know.

affirmative action, the death penalty, and abortion 267

Is Pro-life Not the Position of the Bible?

A criticism could be made against the standard pro-life position being the biblical view of choice. The criticism comes in the form of two claims: (1) that there is no verse in the Bible that condemns abortions *per se* and (2) that the Bible does not ascribe value to the unborn.[105] Let's consider these claims. The first claim is usually not contested by pro-life proponents in so far as there being passages that directly point to a prohibition against abortion. There is reason, however, to think (2) true. The verse that is at the point of contention is Exod 21:22–24 which reads in the New American Standard Version and the Amplified Version respectfully:

> If men struggle with each other and strike a woman with child so that she gives birth prematurely, yet there is no injury, he shall surely be fined as the woman's husband may demand of him, and he shall pay as the judges decide. But if there is any *further* injury, then you shall appoint as a penalty life for life, eye for eye, tooth for tooth, hand for hand, foot for foot. (NASB)

And

> If men contend with each other, and a pregnant woman is hurt so that she has a miscarriage, yet no further damage follows, [the one who hurts her] shall surely be punished with a fine [paid] to the woman's husband, as much as the judges determine. But if any damage follows, then you shall give life for life, eye for eye, tooth for tooth, hand for hand, foot for foot. (Amplified Version)

Obviously the point of contention has been over whether the Hebrew phrase (yalad yatsa) should be translated as "birth prematurely" as in the NASB or as "a miscarriage" as in the Amplified Bible. The expected or natural word to use if the writer's intent concerned a miscarriage is the Hebrew word *shachol*. This is the selected word in Exod 23:26 and Hos 9: 14 where miscarriage is specifically understood. Moreover, the later use of the word "further" is not in the original text itself. The NASB, for example, italicizes it, as it should. With this exegetical information in hand, it is clear that any contrast being made is between an occasion when the mother and the premature child are not harmed (verse 22) and

---

105. In *Politically Correct Death*, Beckwith cites F. Michael Womack, who says, "[the word rendered miscarriage] is not the normal word for miscarriage. In fact, when used of children, the word refers to offspring and live birth" (*Politically Correct Death*, 144).

an occasion when the mother or unborn is harmed perhaps by death due to the struggle (verse 23–24). According to this reading (NASB), the unborn child's worth is actually valued on par with the mother.

Like religion, ethics is a polemic topic, particularly the specific ethical issues addressed in this book. As we conclude, if you happened to dismiss any position taken in this book, consider among other things whether your dismissal was foundationally a visceral reaction to a position, based on the narrative you were socialized into, or based on a certitude that the position you dismissed could not conceivably be true. If so beware the trappings of epistemic myopia.

Appendix

The purpose of the appendix is to provide background information to the chapters in this book so that you can make better sense of the logic and critical thinking content contained in them. The background information consists of two parts. The first part describes and explains the nature of critical thinking in a broad sense. Here we will take a formal look at arguments (in terms of their structure and ways in which to argue). The second part introduces and assesses informal fallacies. Let us begin section one and look at the definition of an argument.

What Is an Argument?

An argument is essentially a *relationship* between a proposition (or set of propositions) and some further proposition such that the former proposition(s) [viz., premises] is set forth as supporting, proving, or making probable the latter proposition [viz., conclusion]. In any given argument, the premises are understood to be true (or even hypothetically stipulated as true) or at least taken to be true by the person who composed the argument. The critical thinker should take note that an argument stands or falls on (*a*) the truth of its premises and on (*b*) whether or not the premises justify or prove the conclusion.[1] So while the conclusion of an argument may be true, if its premises are false or are unrelated to the conclusion in terms of justification, the premises of the argument have failed to *show* that the conclusion is true.

---

1. Notable exceptions to this description are arguments with necessarily true conclusions (e.g., nothing can begin its own existence or triangles have three sides). Necessarily true propositions follow from any claim whether the claims are true or not. Also, in valid arguments the premises need not be true to entail "their" conclusion. The premises need only show that *if* they were true, their truth necessarily entails the conclusion.

Recognizing Reasoning

Having a string of facts does not make an argument. Facts must be related to each other and show how they *lead* to the point you are trying to make. One way this is done is by providing propositions that are not merely true but, more importantly, they are sufficient justification for the conclusion being affirmed. Otherwise, your evidence may merely be an assertion of truth rather than justification for your conclusion. For example, stating claims that abortions are unethical because they are performed for convenience and cause certain health problems for pregnant mothers do not by themselves provide sufficient evidence that abortions are unethical. After all, driving to work as opposed to taking public transportation is done for convenience. Is driving to work therefore wrong? Also, radiation and chemotherapy cause certain health problems. Should cancer patients not undergo these treatments? Or recall the statistic that from 1930 to 1990, 4,002 people were executed in the United States and over 50 percent were black. This fact alone is not sufficient to draw the conclusion that the death penalty in America is racially biased. It could be that blacks commit more capital crimes than other ethnic groups.

Every argument has at least two propositions. The functional names for propositions in arguments are *premise* and *conclusion*. To reiterate, a proposition that functions to justify the truth of another proposition is called a *premise*. A proposition being justified by another proposition functions as a *conclusion*.

The Building Blocks of an Argument: Propositions

Now that we understand what an argument is, let us analyze the foundational element of every argument, a proposition. What are propositions? They are not sentences written on paper or statements spoken by someone. Sentences and the sounds that a person speaks are various ways of expressing propositions. For example, the propositions that are expressed by the English statements "I think, therefore I exist" can be expressed in other languages as well:

- In German as: *Ich denke, also bin ich.*
- In French as: *Je suis, j'existe*
- In Latin: *Cogito, ergo sum*

Whether a proposition is expressed by the above written languages (or others languages like Mandarin and Swahili) or expressed in other media (like chalk, lead on paper or a person's voice), the proposition remains the same. Essentially propositions are non-linguistic. They are the *meaning* behind the *spoken words* of a person and the meaning behind *written words* on paper or chalkboards. In the above example, there are five sentences but only one proposition behind them. The nature of every proposition is that it is either *true* or *false*. Thus propositions are not questions, emotional ejaculations or imperatives. Consider the following list of propositions on the left and non-propositions on the right:

- The Chicago Bulls is a bad team!
- The cat is on the mat.
- The snow is white.
- The man is tall.

- The pizza is great!
- Pink is a pretty color!
- Turn off the lights!
- Did you pass the test?

The Basis for Claiming That a Proposition Is True

As was just pointed out, propositions are either true or false. But how does a critical thinker know that a proposition is either true or false? There are four such ways:

Known to be true a priori

Known to be true a posteriori
- by common knowledge
- by expert authority
- by direct empirical evidence

Propositions that are known to be true *a priori* are known to be true *a part from experience* (i.e., independent of the five senses). To say that a proposition is *a priori* is to say that its truth is known *merely* by reason alone. Propositions of this sort are true by definition (e.g., *analytic* propositions) or known to be true once the relationship of the words contained in the proposition are understood. These propositions are self-justifying.

They need no proof beyond themselves. No amount of group consensus is required to verify them. Consider the following examples:

- A twin is a person who has or had a sibling
- The act of killing someone is wrong only if the act could have been avoided
- Rape violates the autonomy of its victim
- Every mountain has a valley
- Unmarried men are bachelors
- 2 + 2 = 4

Propositions that are known to be true *a posteriori* (or ones that are called *empirical*) are known to be true *because of evidence gathered by the five senses*. Propositions of this sort are known to be true *by common knowledge, by authority* or *by direct empirical evidence*. They cannot be known to be true by reason.

In an argument, the premises of your argument are considered evidence to support your conclusion. The conclusion does not justify itself. Premises are understood to be self-justifying or to require justification themselves before they can be used to justify the conclusion. When premises function in this later sense, they are called intermediate conclusions. As was recently stated, premises that are a priori need no justification and thus they can directly offer justification for their conclusions. However, while all a posteriori propositions require justification to affirm their truth, once justified their justification does not always need to be offered in an argument. There are two types of propositions that fit this description.

The first type consists of propositions known to be true by *common knowledge*. Common knowledge propositions are truths that have previously been verified and now their verification is known to society or the world at large. These kinds of propositions can be taken as givens (i.e., obviously true) because of the overwhelming number of eyewitnesses, consensus concerning their truth or evidence that verified their truth from different fronts. The phrase "preaching to the choir" expresses the meaning behind common knowledge. Let us take an example. The destruction of the World Trade Center on September 11, 2001, is common knowledge, thanks to copious eyewitness testimony and to the media's saturation of the event via video, magazines, and newspapers. To put the point another way, propositions that are common knowledge are propositions about the world such that a person cannot help knowing them to be true unless the person has been in a coma for a long time, in a foreign country that has no information network, or was just born yesterday. Consider the following examples:

- Barack Obama was the first person of color elected President of the United States.
- Germany executed over 5000 Jews during World War II.
- African Americans are decedents of African slaves.
- Pro-life proponents are opposed to abortions.
- Some infertile couples have children due to IVF technology.
- During the end of the twentieth century and the beginning of the twenty-first century AIDS became epidemic.

There is the potential to confuse a priori propositions with common sense propositions. A little elucidation may help. Some propositions known a priori are also known by common knowledge, e.g., all bachelors are unmarried men. The difference is that the former is not justified by experience although it is commonly known by most people. Moreover, not all propositions known a priori are known by common knowledge, e.g., conditionals that have necessarily false antecedents are true. Finally some propositions that are known by common knowledge are not known a priori, e.g., women and men have equal voting rights. In the above examples of propositions known by common knowledge, none of them can be known merely by reason alone; they are all known empirically. So to avoid confusion between propositions that fall into either category, let us refer to a priori propositions as propositions that can are known by reason alone although some of them as a matter of fact are known by common knowledge. Let us equally refer to common knowledge propositions as propositions that *cannot* be known a priori.

It should also be pointed out that the status of a proposition known by common knowledge is subject to change. In the above examples, some of the propositions may not be common knowledge in fifty years. In fifty years, for example, maybe only sports enthusiasts will know that Michael Jordan played basketball for the Chicago Bulls.

A second type of a posteriori proposition that can be presented without its justification is a proposition known to be true by *expert authority*. This type of proposition can be accepted as true if an expert has verified that it is true through research, experimentation or other means. A pharmacist who fills a prescription written by a physician does not question the written prescription. The pharmacist accepts the medical expertise of the physician such that he does not question whether the patient needs the medication or not. The pharmacist trusts that the physician has done an exhaustive examination of the patient and concluded that the patient requires the prescribed medication. In this case, the pharmacist takes the claim "drug X should be given to patient Y" as true by expert authority.

We can appeal to an authority to verify the truth of a proposition if the authority says the proposition is true. However, a critical thinker should take note that appealing to an expert requires that the expert is speaking on a subject on which he or she is an expert. Michael Jordan can speak as an expert on basketball, but not on golf or even Quantum Mechanics. As a scientist, Albert Einstein can speak as an expert on physics and mathematics, but not on reggae music or water polo. To reiterate, in all cases of authority, the authorities themselves directly verified what they claim to be true.

The third type of a posteriori proposition cannot be presented as true unless justification is provided. It is a proposition known to be true by *direct empirical verification* or what we may term, confirmation by facts in the world. Propositions that now have the status of common knowledge initially had to be verified by someone until they became known well enough by society at large where proof of their truth was no longer needed. Propositions that are known to be true because an expert authority confirmed they are true initially had to be justified by *direct empirical verification* by the expert. While all three types of a posteriori propositions are evidence based, this third type can never be used in an argument without the accompaniment of their evidence. In the above example of the pharmacist, the pharmacist accepts the correctness of the prescription for a given patient by authority. She knows that the physician has both examined the patient and knows what medication works for the patient's illness. However, the physician or some researcher had to directly verify that the medication works on people in general who manifest the same symptoms as the patient.

Hopefully you now understand the nature of an argument in terms of what one is and how to recognize one. In summary, an argument is reasoning or making an inference from one proposition to another proposition. Now some reasoning is better than other reasoning and some arguments are better than other arguments. Reasoning and arguments that fall into the latter categories are often tainted by what are called informal fallacies.

Informal Fallacies

If concepts are not clear, words do not fit. If words do not fit, the day's work cannot be accomplished, morals and art do not flourish. If morals and art do not flourish, punishments are not just. If punishments are not just, the people do not know where to put hand or foot.

—CONFUCIUS, *ANALECTS*, XIII:3

In this second part of the appendix we will take a close look at faulty reasoning, i.e., what is called a fallacy. There are many fallacies with various names that describe them. One of the earliest discussions of fallacies comes from the Greek philosopher Aristotle in his *Sophistical Refutations*, where he lists thirteen fallacies. A contemporary work that provides a helpful discussion of fallacies is T. Edward Dahmer's *Attacking Faulty Reasoning*.[2] Fallacies are either classified as formal or informal. A formal fallacy is committed when a person constructs an argument that has faulty form and structure.[3] An informal fallacy is committed when a person attacks or constructs an argument where the content of what is said is faulty. In so far as faulty reasoning is concerned, we will focus on informal fallacies.

---

2. Damer, *Attacking Faulty Reasoning*.

3. An example of a formal fallacy affirms the consequent of a conditional proposition in a three-proposition argument. Consider the following example:
    i) If I won a lot of money at a casino in Las Vegas, then I would wealthy.
    ii) I did not win a lot of money at a casino in Las Vegas.
    Therefore, I am not wealthy.
This argument is fallacious (invalid) because the premises could be true while the conclusion is false. How could the conclusion be false while the premises are true? Well, while you did not win a lot of money at a casino in Vegas, you can still be wealthy by other means. You could be wealthy because you were left copious money by inheritance, or you are a CEO of a computer company.

Fallacious Argument Construction

To remember, an argument consists of at least one premise and a conclusion. The conclusion of the argument is supposed to be inferred from the premise(s), such that the premise(s) is justification for the conclusion. When the construction of a person's argument is fallacious, such that the person commits a *fallacy*, the conclusion she draws does not follow from the evidence contained in the premise(s) of her argument. There are several ways that the premises of an argument can fail to justify the conclusion of an argument in this fallacious way.

Fallacies of Ambiguity

Equivocation: *Using an equivocal word in several inconsistent ways in an argument.*

This fallacy is committed when an equivocal word is used in an argument with the false impression that only one of its meanings is being used. An equivocal word is any word that can have several meanings. In each example, an equivocal word is being used in more than one way.

> What is in a mother is a *life*. It is a living human entity and not a part of the mother's body. All human *life* has a right to life. So, to abort the life in the mother's body is wrong.

> 1. Man is rational.
> 2. No woman is a man.
> Therefore, no woman is rational.

> The supporters of gun control legislation are the ones whose actions are coercive and smacks of intimidation. For if I own a gun and somebody takes it away from me by force, I am coerced.

In this first example, the word "life" is used in the first premise to describe a living being. Obviously this life is a human being since the second premise says so. However, the third premise's use of the word "life" means a human person since only persons have rights. In the second example, "man" is used in both of the premises. In the first premise, the word "man" is describing the whole of humanity. In the second premise, the word "man" is describing an adult male human. Neither is related to the other beyond containing the word "man." In the third example, the word "coercive" and "coerced" are equivocal. It is clear that the argument contains two senses of the word *coerce*. The sense of coercion in the premise, refers to coercion by physical force. The sense of coercion in the conclusion refers to coercion by law. Surely, if a person is forced to do something because the law requires them to do so, that person's action, by definition, ought to be forced, even if the action is against the person's will. But this sense of coercion is not being attacked in the premise. The focus of the premise is on a forced action that is illegal, i.e., robbery.

Fallacies of Irrelevance

All fallacious arguments in this category are non-sequiturs. In other words, their conclusion does not follow from their premises with any degree of relatedness.

Red Herring: *This fallacy is committed when attention is drawn away from the issue by some tangent issue.*

This fallacy is derived from the use of an actual herring. The story is told that escaping British prisoners would smear a stinking red herring across their trail and then venture off of it to decrease their chances of being caught by the hounds that were used to find them. At any rate, when a person purposefully or unintentionally "goes off the subject," that person has committed a red herring. Often what the person says has nothing to do with the issue being disputed. It is often committed in response to a question. Let us consider the following examples:

> Women should not be allowed to be medics in a war zone. Women are weaker than men and could not handle the enemy in a hand-to-hand conflict.

> When asked should the U.S. have gone over to Saudi Arabia to fight against Iraq in the Persian Gulf War, a person answers: "The U.S. was over there simply to protect their oil interest. This capitalist controlled government did not want anything to happen to the Kuwait oil supplies, so it sent our young men over there to protect it."

> When asked do gangster rappers have a moral obligation to refrain from explicit lyrics, a woman answers, "Rappers ought to be able to talk about shooting cops and about sexual promiscuity in their lyrics. And as far as them using the 'B' word, I don't have a problem with that. They are not talking to me because I know I am not a B———. I love what rap artists are saying; they are just keeping it real and telling it like it is in the hood ... you know ... word.

In our first example, the person acknowledges an obvious fact that women are, on average, physically weaker than men. However, this fact is unrelated to a woman's ability to treat the wounds of troops. Medical intelligence is the key here, not physical strength. In fact, as far as intelligence is concerned, commanding officers are often older than those they command, but this fact does not diminish their commanding ability. In the second example, the war objector may be right that the United States engaged Iraq militarily to secure the flow of oil to United States oil companies. If such were the case, the United States would be guilty of greed. However, the objector fails to see that individuals or even nations can act for the wrong reason but do what is right. Surely a nation that is aggressive against another sovereign nation should be stopped by diplomatic or military means. In the Persian Gulf War, this was the situation with Iraq against Kuwait. The United States and other nations that put an end to Iraq's aggression were right in what they *did*, viz., stopping Iraq. However, whether or not the United States was *motivated* to stop Iraq for ethical reasons or for reasons of economic greed is another matter. We can perhaps blame the United States for having the wrong motives but not for taking the wrong action. Finally, as for our last example, the supporter of explicit rap lyrics is way off the mark by noting the facticity of what the rap artists are saying. If "keeping it real" is ethical justification for what a person can state publicly, then any information that is factual can be stated publically without concern about its content, e.g., a person sharing publically the details of the sexual experience he had with his spouse. Moreover, this supporter of explicit rap music communicates that she is indifferent to woman being inappropriately addressed. Contrary to what this person says, rap artists do not discriminate among women; their lyrics refer to all women in derogatory terms.

Appeal to Hypocrisy: *This fallacy is also called Tu quoque or the "you too fallacy." It is committed when a person justifies their action by pointing out that their accuser is guilty of the same action.*

This fallacy is a version of the Red Herring fallacy. The person who commits it uses noted hypocrisy in the actions of the accusers to justify their position. As the old saying goes, two wrongs do not make a right. Consider the following example:

> A doctor says to a patient: "You shouldn't drink as much as you do. Drinking dulls the senses and reduces physical control." The patient responds: " I disagree, since you drink as much as I do."

The fact that the doctor is hypocritical is not evidence against his claim about drinking excessive alcohol.

Attacking a Conscientious Objection: *This fallacy is committed when a person dismisses an objection by making the relevance or importance of the objection relative to the person presenting it.*

When a person has very little to say in defense of their position, their last stand is often this fallacy. Without saying much in terms of substance, the person who commits it simply commands you to "look the other way and mind your own business." Do not confuse this fallacy with Paul's dictum concerning meat offered to idols in 1 Corinthians 8. Notice that the issue he is addressing has to do with how we behave in front of weaker brothers and sisters. Nowhere in the chapter is there a debate between believers concerning the morality of eating meat offered to idols. In fact, Paul says that eating meat offered to idols is permissible, but some believers do not know this. So, Paul says, do not eat meat in front of them because doing so causes them to struggle in light of their spiritual weakness. Paul presupposes that no argument or debate would take place. At any rate, consider a few more examples of this fallacy:

> "If you have a problem with gangster rap and hip hop music, then don't buy it. It is not for everyone."

> "You should not be concerned with what I do with my life. If you think what I do is wrong, then you shouldn't do it, but don't tell me I am wrong...To each its own. Mind your own business."

"If you have a problem with this medical procedure, then switch to another unit. It is not for everyone."

In each example, telling a person to keep their thoughts to themselves and to withdraw from doing the act they object to is not an objection to their position and does not make the problem go away.

Genetic Fallacy: *(1)Attacking a view because of its origin. (2)Presenting an argument with premises that appeal to an earlier context of a present issue.*

Genetic fallacies committed in the former manner dismiss an argument simply because the source of the argument is considered questionable. This is an inference commonly made. How often have you dismissed the claims made in tabloids you see in the checkout line at a grocery store? Tabloids are questionable sources of information and in general should not be trusted. But no matter how questionable a source is in terms of its factual content, its argument stands or falls on the basis of the justification offered for it. It is possible that even a tabloid can contain an argument that is justifiable. In other words, what could be challenged is not the coherency and warrant of the argument, but the truthfulness of the information in the argument. Claims are true because of the evidence that supports them, not because of their source. The German chemist, Friedrich Kekule, received inspiration for his discovery of the molecular structure of the benzene molecule from a dream he had. In the dream, Kekule dreamt of a snake chasing its tail. The snake resembled a loop and Kekule hypothesis that perhaps the benzene molecule was structured in a similar manner. As it turns out, the benzene molecule is shaped in a loop. Moreover, modern chemistry was derived from medieval alchemy, but these historical facts are not a basis for rejecting the truth claims of chemistry. At the end of the day, we all judge a book or argument without reviewing it. We do so in light of its source by inductive reasoning. If a Christian publisher, for example, has published books that defended either very liberal or very conservative theology, it is likely that the most recent books it publishes will also defend the same thesis. Nevertheless, it is equally true that at the end of the day, if we have not read a book, we can't say what is logically problematic or sound about the book even if we agree or disagree with the book's thesis.

Genetic fallacies committed in the latter manner confuse the contexts of two different situations such that the situations are considered the same situation. Suppose, for example, you are married and were at a party. A person finds your wedding ring objectionable because "in ancient times, men put ring bands on the fingers of their wives to symbolize the fact that the women were their property." More likely than not, you were not aware of this fact and did not wear the ring on your finger for that same reason. You do not see yourself as property of your husband. For you, the ring is symbolic of the commitment you and your husband mutually made to each other. As a result, the reason you wear the ring is not the same as that of the Ancients. While they can be charged with sexist ideologies, surely you should not be.

This second form of the Genetic fallacy can also be found in the debate over the celebration of Halloween. Consider the following argument:

> Children should not participate in such a demonic practice as Halloween. This holiday began as a tribute to Satan and dark, supernatural forces. Any parent who cares for his or her children would not let them go out on Halloween to receive treats.

This Genetic fallacy assumes that the child's involvement in Halloween is motivated for the same reasons as that of those who initially started the holiday a few centuries ago. For sure, children have totally different reasons for venturing out on October 31; they are motivated by candy, not by veneration to Satan and his cohorts.

Finally, consider this last example of a discussion between a martial arts instructor and a parent who wants to enroll her child in his class:

> Master Jae Kimm, I want to put my child into your martial arts class, but I am concerned about your eastern spiritual influence on my child. He really wants to learn martial arts . . . I don't know what to do.

In this example, the parent assumes that eastern Buddhist beliefs are still integral to the practice of martial arts. Historically, Buddhist priests in China prayed a lot on their knees and needed some form of exercise to strengthen their bodies. A martial art (Kung Fu) was invented for this purpose. Quite frankly, priests in Medieval European monasteries could also have invented a form of martial art for their religious practices. In either case, the physical dimension of a martial art is a completely separate matter from the place of its geographical, religious or philosophical origin.

Ad Hominem: *Attacking a person, not her argument, (1) because of her existing circumstances or (2) because of a character flaw she has.*

Because an ad hominem discredits an argument by attacking its source, it can be confused with the Genetic fallacy.[4] In general, this fallacy attacks an argument by discrediting the reliability of its author. The false assumption behind the first type of ad hominem is that a person's circumstances necessarily make their beliefs biased or ill-formed. This assumption questions (*a*) the objectivity of a person's motives or (*b*) the experience of a person's insight into some issue. In the former case, the phrase "of course you would say that…what else would you say" is often used by those who commit this form of the ad hominem fallacy. Consider the following example of (*a*):

> "I honestly cannot accept Dr. Jones' defense of affirmative action. Everything he said sounds impressive, but what else would he say . . . he's black."

In this example, the objection against affirmative action dismisses Dr. Jones' defense of affirmative action simply because of Jones' skin color. The objection assumes that all minorities of color automatically favor affirmative action. If Jones' argument for affirmative action is a bad argument, its problems will be discovered by an analysis of the argument, not Jones' skin color or ethnic identity.

Consider the following examples of (*b*):

> "I don't accept Dr. Janet Smith's analysis of male aggression in American society and how it is correlated with the high representation of males in prison. What does she know about male psychology . . . she is a woman."

> "Don't sign up for Dr. Feinberg's class on African American history in the U.S. He couldn't possibly tell me something I don't already know . . . he's white."

In both of these cases, the objections against the arguments are based merely on the circumstances of the persons who presented them. The objectors charge that the persons lack experience to address the subject matter, without evaluating what they say. Whether or not an argument is a good one has nothing to do with who presents it. Suppose Dr. Smith's presented her argument in a journal and falsely stated that her

---

4. To make clear the distinction between these two fallacies, a *Genetic fallacy* attacks the source of an argument when the source is not a person (e.g., a particular religious or political ideology, a text or even information systems like dreams and crystal balls). The *ad hominem* always attacks the source of an argument when the source is a person.

name was James not Janet, her objector could not use her gender against her. Suppose for the second example that Dr. Feinberg taught online and his ethnicity was unknown, then his objector could not use his ethnicity against him.

The false assumption behind the second type of ad hominem in our definition is that it fallaciously connects a person's scandalous lifestyle or character to the person's argument. Politicians often commit this fallacy. Instead of attacking their opponent's policy or argument, they call to mind, for example, their opponent's sexual affairs or their opponent's bigotry. A person's argument stands or falls regardless of their promiscuity or other vices of their character. For example, The Declaration of Independence should not be called into question simply because Thomas Jefferson owned slaves. Also, in like manner, Martin Luther King Jr.'s position on civil rights and social justice should not be called into question simply because of his extra-marital sexual affairs. Pointing to a person's lifestyle or character may explain why a person held the view he or she held; it does not show that the view is wrong. As Christians, if we did connect a person's personal failures and sins to truth claims that he/she asserts, we should have to reject parts of the Psalms since King David committed adultery with Beersheba. We should also reject other Old Testament books like the Song of Solomon and Ecclesiastes because of King Solomon's failures.

Appeal to Authority: *This fallacy is committed when a person appeals to an authority to verify the truth of a claim on a subject matter of which the authority has merely layman's knowledge.*

There is nothing fallacious about appealing to an authority to verify a claim. We know this from our discussion of authorities in the first part of the appendix. However, appealing to authorities on subject matters outside their field of expertise is fallacious. Although a family physician knows medicine, he is not an expert on heart surgery, neuropsychiatry or gastrointestinal diseases. The same holds true for a minister who, although he knows a great deal about religion, is not an expert on philosophy of religion to discuss such issues as the existence of God.

Fallacies of Assumption

Begging the Question: *(1) When the truth of something is assumed without any justification. (2) When a person assumes the very thing she/he is trying to prove.*

This first form of question begging is hard to detect. It is committed when a person begins with the truth of a claim as if it were a "given" or a brute fact. In other words, the person assumes that the claim is true by definition or is an established fact that goes uncontested. The person then reasons from it. Let us look at some examples:

> Miracles do not occur, so it is irresponsible for a nurse to say God healed a patient.

> Euthanasia is unethical because the Hippocratic Oath forbids doctors to administer deadly drugs.

In the first example, an objection is made against miracles. The objection claims that whenever medical anomalies occur, the events have natural explanations since *all events have natural explanations*. If this objection sounds suspect, it is. Nowhere does it offer any justification for the claim that all events have natural explanations; rather it assumes it. The objection would be cogent if it made the claim that natural explanations are more plausible to accept because they are consistent with our everyday experiences whereas miracles are not. The second objection assumes that because the Hippocratic Oath prescribes or prohibits an action X that X is right or wrong merely because it is prescribed or prohibited by the Hippocratic Oath. No argument is given for why the Hippocratic Oath demands this categorical allegiance.

The second form of question begging is called "arguing in a circle." The phrase "arguing in a circle" is often misused and misunderstood. Often when it is misused, the person using the phrase simply means that her opponent is not making sense. Actually the phrase means exactly what it says: A person attempts to argue for the conclusion of an argument by assuming the truth of the conclusion when it is disguised as a true premise in the same argument. Consider the following examples:

> Active euthanasia is morally acceptable. It is a decent, ethical thing to help another human being escape suffering through death.

Ethics is based on God because if God did not exist, then there would be no right or wrong.

I don't believe that a murderer ought to be allowed to live. Murderers have forfeited the right to live because anyone who murders another person has lost the right to live.

In all three examples the authors of the arguments simply restated their conclusion twice but in different words as an unproven premise.

From Ignorance: *Assuming something to be true since it has not been proven to be false or vice versa.*

This fallacy is committed either to defend or attack a belief in virtue of insufficient evidence on some particular point in dispute. The failure of an argument to defend itself should not be used as support for its rival argument. Politicians often commit this fallacy. For example, instead of explaining and defending their position on some social or economic issue, they attack the rival candidate's platform, concluding that since the rival's platform is bankrupt, therefore their own platform is the choice for the public. Consider the following example of sexism in an office:

The women in our office must be happy with their jobs, for none of them have ever complained about their jobs.

The fact that there is no sign of discontent among the women in the office does not entail they are happy with their jobs. One reason for their silence could be the fear of losing their job if they were to go public.

It is often tempting to destroy your opposition without offering any reasons why your own position is correct.

False Alternatives: *A person commits this fallacy in light of a claim he/she knows to be false such that the alternatives he considers to be true are too few. As a result the alternatives he has not considered may be true and the alternative he has considered may be false. A person also commits this fallacy when he/she assumes one of several senses of a word or phrase and thus rules out alternative definitions.*

Sometimes when there are only two possible answers to a question, an easy way to answer the question is to show that one of the possible answers is false, thereby proving the other possible answer to be correct. However, before you make this move, you should be sure that there are only two possible answers to a question. Failure to do so commits this fallacy. Often when a person commits this fallacy, the person fails to make a distinction between contradictory propositions (e.g., recognizing that either "All professors are nice" is true or "Some professors are not nice" is true but that not both of them are true and not both are false) and contrary propositions (e.g., recognizing that if something is not hot it does not have to be cold, it could be warm). Consider the following examples:

> If abortions are outlawed then poor, young women will
> be forced into back alleys abortions.

> Sarah said she was not pro-life. She must be a pro-abortionist.

What the author of the first argument does not acknowledge is that adoption is a third option. In the second example, the author of the argument assumes that a person is either opposed to abortions or in favor of them. What some pro-choice proponents argue is that while they are not in favor of abortion they think in some cases the choice to have one should be left to the mother's discretion.

Hasty Generalization: *Drawing a conclusion about a group or class without adequate information.*

Inductive reasoning involves a generalization about a set of something (a belief about all or most members of a set) based on what is known to be true about a subset of that set. Such an inductive inference is appropriate when the subset is large enough to make the generalization. However, when a person generalizes from a subset that is too small, the person commits a *hasty generalization*. Inferring a claim about a general population or class of things with an inadequate amount of information about a subset from the population or class allows for chance and anomalies to confound a person's generalization.

An obvious example of a hasty generalization is *stereotyping*. How often has someone said something to you about a particular class or group of things or persons and justified their belief on just their own personal experience. Consider the following examples:

> "Government welfare programs should be cut. Tax dollars are just going away to lazy people who don't want to work, like my neighbor living off of government housing."

"If I were you, I would not go into that neighborhood. I was robbed there last year."

The first example assumes that all people on welfare want to be on welfare and are lazy. In the second example, a person had an unfortunate robbery experience and assumes members of the neighborhood as a whole are likely to rob someone. The following example is a hasty generalization that does not involve stereotyping. It jumps to a conclusion about the effect of cigarettes on people based on an inadequate sample size:

"Smoking cigarettes does not harm people. Look, I am 90 years old and I have been smoking nearly all my life and I haven't developed cancer or any other health problems."

It turns out that cigarette smoking does cause cancer and other diseases; however, if this were an unknown fact, to discern that cigarettes do or do not cause cancer would have to be determined by observing more than one smoker. Obviously the smoker in the example is an anomaly. Perhaps his genetic makeup has made him immune to the ravages of nicotine. He is an exception, not the rule. Generalizations, to represent an entire group or class of things, must have adequate verification from particular samples of those groups and classes.

Straw Man: *Giving the appearance that you are attacking an argument when in fact you are attacking a weak version of it.*

In the 1970s a film won an Oscar for portraying a local boxer who had aspirations of winning the world heavyweight championship. The movie was *Rocky* and in the film the current heavyweight champion wanted to fight a local boxer because the odds were in his favor against the local boxer and the fight would make the champ look impressive with the easy win. First, he would have to build the hype about Rocky, the local fighter, and then defeat him. In the public's eyes he would look great once he defeated Rocky. In the movie Rocky (Sylvester Stallone) played the role of a straw man. A straw man is an opponent conceived to be a worthy opponent, but in reality is not. In Rocky, however, Rocky Balboa proved to be more than a straw man. Unfortunately, straw men can be found in arguments. They are recognized by their weak resemblance or misrepresentation of some actual argument or position held by someone who is being attacked. Because the straw man is weak, it can be easily defeated and makes its creator's position look strong. Consider the following straw men:

> "I'm a very controversial figure to the animal rights movement. They no doubt view me with some measure of hostility because I am constantly challenging their fundamental premise that animals are superior to human beings."- Rush Limbaugh
>
> "Many people complain that racism still exists in this country today. But this is not true, for seldom do you see lynching, cross burning, name calling and people actually hating each other."
>
> May 15—In October 1939, Nazi Leader Adolf Hitler issued an order, written in his own hand, ordering the extermination of those who were considered "unworthy of life." The order, entitled "The Destruction of Lives Unworthy of Life," stated that patients "considered incurable according to the best available human judgment of their state of health, be accorded a mercy death."
>
> Today, the Obama Administration is beginning to descend down that same road, promising to make the "tough choices" to cut entitlement programs such as Medicare and Social Security to save money—at precisely the time in which an increasing number of Americans are forced to depend on them as the economy slides deeper into Depression.

In the Limbaugh example it is ridiculous to hold that proponents of animal welfare actually think non-human animals are more intelligent that humans. If they claim anything, it is simply that non-human animals deserve equal consideration about their life interests. The second example misrepresents the view that racism exists in the world. Activists who are opposed to racism seldom mention racial prejudice of the KKK stripe. Rather they point to institutional discrimination in society, whether intentional or non-intentional or to racial prejudice that involves profiling at the victim's expense. In the last example, the author of this argument by analogy compares President Obama to the Nazi leader Adolf Hitler on who is worthy to live or die. It is a sad day when an American President is compared to Hitler, but the key problem with this argument is that medical coverage is never guaranteed in every case with currently existing insurance policies. So if the issue is about unlimited medical coverage, then currently existing insurance companies are also living out the spirit of Hitler.

Post hoc, ergo propter hoc: *This fallacy can be translated as "after this, therefore because of this." It is committed when someone falsely assumes a causal relationship between some event A and some event B without offering a justification for the relation.*

There may be a causal relationship between two events following each other temporally, but when no justification is given to support this relationship, the post hoc fallacy is committed. Consider the following examples:

> Ever since Sue has worked on the psych floor, meds have come up missing. She is a drug addict. I am going to report her to the charge nurse.

> Nuclear weapons have prevented any foreign threats against the U.S., for since we had them, no country has ever attempted to attack us.

Causal relations, in nearly every case, have explanations for how they exist. Without such explanations, events would be paired willy-nilly and be related to each other as "cause" and "effect" by chance. Thus in order for a person to say that two or more events are causally related, the person must be able to establish that the causal relationship exists. A person who commits this fallacy fails to realize that two events may simply be temporally correlated together. That is, coincidence may be the only reason why one event follows another. Perhaps the true cause of some event is not noticed. For example, in the above example concerning Sue, a disgruntle nurse may be stealing meds to shed unwarranted attention on Sue in order to secure her termination. In the other example, the reason why countries like Canada and Mexico have not attacked the United States may be because they have no desire to do so. As for other countries, the reason could be due to the size of the United States military. Conventional weapons can pose an equally potent deterrence.

Is-Ought Fallacy: *This fallacy is committed when a person assumes that something ought to be the case because it is in fact accepted by someone as being normative.*

Many people mistake factual truths for normative truths. To state a factual truth is simply to state how the world is at any given time. Thus to say everyone believes that rape is immoral is simply to state an empirical claim about a moral belief held worldwide. But it is a different matter whether rape is immoral. If this conflation of what is believed about rape and what ought to be believed about rape is correct, then if there was a universal acceptance of rape, it should to be permitted. This, of course, makes no sense. In short, any time someone attempts to approve of an action as ethically correct simply because it is accepted or done, the is-ought fallacy is committed. Consider the following three examples:

> "You can't say that there are moral absolutes! Take infanticide, for example. Some countries practice this. For them it is a norm. You can't go to those countries and tell them that they are practicing something immoral."

> "Abortions are legal according to the Supreme Court ruling of Roe vs. Wade. If there were something wrong with having a right to choose, it wouldn't be legal."

> "Don't complain about what my son said to your daughter . . . boys will be boys."

These examples return us to the humean objection discussed in chapter 3. However, the issue here is not that *ought* cannot be derived from *is*, but as these examples show, their authors assumed the derivation. Infanticide, abortion, and adolescent delinquency are either right, wrong, or neither but not because some individual or corporate group of individuals said so. If human fiat could ground normative affairs, then Supreme Court sanction edicts like "separate but equal" and Jim Crow laws ought to be enforced without objection during their establishment.

Slippery Slope Fallacy: *This fallacy begins an unjustified series of cause/effect relations. It is committed when a person has justification that some event A leads to some event B, but then assumes without justification that event A will eventually lead to some further events C, D, E, etc.*

A person commits this fallacy when he objects to a position or action because he believes, without justification, that the position or action will lead to some bad state of affairs. This fallacy is also known as the *Domino Effect*. Consider the following examples:

> Animal experimentation reduces our respect for life. If we don't respect life, we are likely to be more and more tolerant of violent acts like war and murder. Soon our society will become a battlefield in which everyone constantly fears for their lives. It will be

the end of civilization. To prevent this terrible consequence, we should make animal experimentation illegal right now.

Active Euthanasia proponents argue that active euthanasia should be allowed because of the poor quality of life of the terminally ill. But I argue that it should not be allowed. For if we allow it, then the next thing we would allow is the death of elderly people because their poor quality of life. Next we would put to death people who are autistic, schizophrenic or simply mentally retarded because of their poor quality of life.

Cloning human organs is immoral. For if we allow this type of cloning, the next thing those in the cloning camp will push is the cloning of entire humans. And for what purpose? To recreate some existing famous person.

Arguing that a state of affairs will cause or lead to a series of other state of affairs is not fallacious in and of itself. It is aptly appropriate to accuse someone of *The Domino Effect* or *Slippery Slope* if you can supply adequate justification for the unstoppable sliding effect. As you can see in these three examples, no justification was offered for the sliding. If anything, they give the appearance of paranoia concerning the issues they are objecting to.

Bibliography

Abbey, Ruth. "Rawlsian Resources for Animal Ethics." *Ethics & the Environment* 12, no. 1 (2007) 1–22.
Adams, Robert. "Divine Command Ethics as Necessary A posteriori." In *Divine Commands and Morality*, edited by Paul Helm, 109–19. Oxford: Oxford University Press, 1981.
———. "Divine Command Metaethics Modified Again." *Journal of Religious Ethics* 7, no. 1 (1979) 66–79.
Alston, William, P. *Epistemic Justification: Essays in the Theory of Knowledge*. Ithaca, NY: Cornell University Press, 1996.
———. "Some Suggestions for Divine Command Theorists." In *Christian Theism and the Problems of Philosophy*, edited by Michael Beaty, 303–26. Notre Dame, IN: University of Notre Dame Press, 1990.
———. "What Euthyphro Should Have Said." In *Philosophy of Religion: A Reader and Guide*, edited by William Lane Craig, 283–98. New Brunswick, NJ: Rutgers University Press, 2002.
Anonymous. "Abortion in the Bible." *Social Science* 55, no. 4 (1980) 221.
Anscombe, Gertrude E. M. "Modern Moral Philosophy." *Philosophy* 33, no. 124 (1958) 1–19.
Aquinas, Thomas. *Summa contra Gentiles*. Vol. 3/2, *Providence*. Translated by Joseph Rickaby. Westminster, MN: Carroll, 1950.
Arcidiacono, Aucejo, et al. "Affirmative Action and University Fit: Evidence from Proposition 209." National Bureau of Economic Research. http://www.nber.org/papers/w18523.
Aristotle. *Nichomachean Ethics* 1094a. In *Greek Philosophy: Thales to Aristotle*, edited by Reginald E. Allen, 384. 3rd ed. New York: Free, 1991.
Ayer, Alfred J. "Critique of Ethics and Theology." In *Language, Truth, and Logic*, 102–19. New York: Dover, 1952.
Augustine. *De doctrina Christiana*. Translated by R. P. H. Green. New York: Oxford University Press, 1999.
———. *The Spirit and the Letter*. In *Answer to the Pelagians*, translated by Roland J. Teske, edited by John E. Rotelle, 177–82. Hyde Park, NY: New City, 1997.
Bahnsen, Greg. *Theonomy in Christian Ethics*. Phillipsburg, NJ: Presbyterian and Reformed, 1977.
Barclay, Oliver. "The Nature of Christian Morality." In *Readings in Christian Ethics*, edited by David K. Clark and Robert V. Rakestraw, 1:41–49. Grand Rapids: Baker, 1994.
Beauchamp, Tom L., and James F. Childress. *Principles of Biomedical Ethics*. 2nd ed. New York: Oxford University Press, 1983.

Beckwith, Francis. *Defending Life: A Moral and Legal Case against Abortion Choice.* New York: Cambridge University Press, 2007.

———. *Politically Correct Death: Answering Arguments for Abortion Rights.* Grand Rapids: Baker, 1993.

Bedau, Hugo Adam. "Capital Punishment and Social Defense." In *Applying Ethics: A Text with Readings,* edited by Jeffrey Olen and Vincent Barry, 299–306. Belmont, CA: Wadsworth, 1999.

Benedict, Ruth. "A Defense of Ethical Relativism." In *Conduct and Character: Readings in Moral Theory,* 62–69. Belmont, CA: Wadsworth, 1995.

Bentham, Jeremy. *An Introduction to the Principles of Morals and Legislation.* Edited by J. H. Burns and H. L. A. Hart. New York: Oxford University Press, 1970.

Blackburn, Simon. *Essays in Quasi-Realism.* Oxford: Oxford University Press, 1993.

Bonilla-Silva, Eduardo. *Racism Without Racists: Color-Blind Racism and the Persistence of Racial Inequality in the United States.* Lanham, MD: Rowman and Littlefield, 2006.

BonJour, Laurence. *The Structure of Empirical Knowledge.* Cambridge, MA: Harvard University Press, 1985.

———. "Toward a Defense of Empirical Foundationalism." In *Resurrecting Old-Fashioned Foundationalism,* edited by Michael DePaul Lanham, 21–39. Lanham, MD: Rowman and Littlefield, 2000.

Boonin, David. *Should Race Matter? Unusual Answers to the Usual Questions.* New York: Cambridge University Press, 2011.

Bowen, William G., et al. *Crossing The Finish Line: Completing College at America's Public Universities.* Princeton: Princeton University Press, 2009.

Bowen, William G., and Derek C. Bok. *The Shape of the River: Long-Term Consequences of Considering Race in College and University Admissions.* Princeton: Princeton University Press, 1998.

Boxill, Bernard. "Equality, Discrimination and Preferential Treatment." In *A Companion to Ethics,* 333–42. Malden, MA: Blackwell, 1993.

———. *Blacks and Social Justice.* Totowa, NJ: Rowman and Allenheld, 1984.

Boyd, Richard. "How to Be a Moral Realist." In *Essays on Moral Realism,* edited by Geoffrey Sayre-McCord, 181–228. Ithaca, NY: Cornell University Press, 1988.

Brink, David. *Moral Realism and the Foundations of Ethics.* Cambridge: Cambridge University Press, 1989.

Broad, Charlie D. *The Mind and Its Place in Nature.* London: Routledge, 1962.

Brown, Michael K., et al. *Whitewashing Race: The Myth of a Color-Blind Society.* Berkeley: University of California Press, 2003.

Bruder, Carl E. G., et al. "Phenotypically Concordant and Discordant Monozygotic Twins Display Different DNA Copy-Number-Variation Profiles." *American Journal of Human Genetics* 82 (2008) 763–71.

Burstein, Paul. "Reverse Discrimination Cases in Federal Courts: Legal Mobilization by a Countermovement." *Sociological Quarterly* 32 (1991) 511–28.

Busenberg, Bonnie E., and Daryl G. Smith. "Affirmative Action and Beyond: The Woman's Perspective." In *Affirmative Action's Testament of Hope,* edited by Mildred Garcia, 149–80. Albany: State University of New York Press, 1997.

Carson, Donald A. *The Sermon on the Mount: An Evangelical Exposition of Matthew 5–7.* Grand Rapids: Baker, 1982.

Chisholm, Roderick. *Theory of Knowledge.* 3rd ed. Englewood Cliffs, NJ: Prentice-Hall, 1989.
Conklin, John E. *Criminology.* 4th ed. New York: Macmillan, 1992
Corcoran, Kevin. "Physical Persons and Postmortem Survival without Temporal Gaps." In *Soul, Body, and Survival,* edited by Kevin Corcoran, 201–17. Ithaca, NY: Cornell University Press, 2001.
———. *Rethinking Human Nature: A Christian Materialist Alternative to the Soul.* Grand Rapids: Baker, 2006.
Corcoran, Kevin, et al. *In Search of the Soul.* Downers Grove, IL: InterVarsity, 2005.
Corliss, Clark Edward. *Patten's Human Embryology: Elements of Clinical Development.* New York: McGraw-Hill, 1976.
Cosby, Bill. "Pound Cake Speech." Address at the NAACP's Commemoration of the 50th Anniversary of the U.S. Supreme Court's *Brown vs. Board of Education* at Constitutional Hall, May 17, 2004. http://www.rci.rutgers.edu/~schochet/101/Cosby_Speech.htm.
Craig, William Lane. *Does God Exist? The Craig-Flew Debate.* Burlington. VT: Ashgate, 2003.
———. *Reasonable Faith: Christian Truth and Apologetics,* Wheaton, IL: Crossway, 1994.
Craig, William Lane, et al. "The Debate: Is Goodness without God Good Enough?" In *Is Goodness without God Enough? A Debate on Faith, Secularism, and Ethics,* edited by Robert K. Garcia and Nathan L. King, 25–46. Plymouth, UK: Rowman and Littlefield, 2009.
Crimmins, James E., ed. *Utilitarians and Religion.* Bristol, UK: Thoemmes 1998.
Cummiskey, David. *Kantian Consequentialism.* New York: Oxford University Press, 1996.
Dayton, Donald W. *Discovering an Evangelical Heritage.* New York: Harper & Row, 1976.
Dionysius the Great. *Epistle XII—To the Alexandrians.* In *The Ante-Nicene Fathers: Translations of the Writings of the Fathers Down to A.D. 325,* edited by Alexander Roberts et al., 6:108–9. Grand Rapids: Eerdmans, 1969.
Donagan, Alan. *The Theory of Morality.* Chicago: University of Chicago Press, 1996.
Dow, David R. "Death Penalty, Still Racist and Arbitrary." *New York Times,* July 8, 2011, http://www.nytimes.com/2011/07/09/opinion/09dow.html?_r=0.
Eberl, Jason T. "Aquinas on the Nature of Human Beings." *The Review of Metaphysics* 58, no. 2 (2004) 340–41.
Ezorsky, Gertrude. "The Ethics of Punishment." In *Philosophical Perspectives on Punishment, edited by* Gertrude Ezorsky, xi–xxvii. Albany: State University of New York Press, 1972.
———. *Racism and Justice: The Case for Affirmative Action.* Ithaca, NY: Cornell University Press, 1991.
Farley, Reynolds, et al. "Stereotypes and Segregation: Neighborhoods in the Detroit Area." *American Journal of Sociology* 100, no. 3 (1994) 750–80.
Feagin, Joe R., and Clairece Booher Feagin. *Discrimination, American Style.* Englewood Cliffs, NJ: Prentice-Hall, 1978.
Feinberg, Joel and Jan Narveson. "The Nature and Value of Rights." *Journal of Value Inquiry* 4 (1970) 243–60.
Finnis, John. *Natural Law and Natural Rights.* Oxford: Clarendon, 1980.

Fiscus, Ronald J. *The Constitutional Logic of Affirmative Action: Making the Case for Quotas*. Durham, NC: Duke University Press, 1992.

Fletcher, Michael A. "At the Corner of Progress and Peril." *Washington Post*, June 2, 2006, A01.

Friedman, Howard Steven. *The Measure of a Nation: How to Regain America's Competitive Edge and Boost Our Global Standing*. Amherst, NY: Prometheus, 2012.

Fumerton, Richard. "Theories of Justification." In *The Oxford Handbook of Epistemology*, edited by Paul K. Moser, 204–33. New York: Oxford University Press, 2002.

Gauthier, David. *Morals by Agreement*. Oxford: Oxford University Press, 1986.

Gewirth, Alan. *Community of Rights*. Chicago: University of Chicago Press, 1996.

———. *Human Rights: Essays on Justification and Applications*. Chicago: University of Chicago Press, 1982.

———. *Reason and Morality*. Chicago: University of Chicago Press, 1978.

Glazer, Nathan. *Affirmative Discrimination: Ethnic Inequality and Public Policy*. New York: Basic, 1975.

Goldman, Alan H. *Justice and Reverse Discrimination*. Princeton: Princeton University Press, 1979.

Goldman, Alvin I. *Epistemology and Cognition*. Cambridge, MA: Harvard University Press, 1986.

———. "What Is Justified Belief?" In *Justification and Knowledge*, edited by George Pappas, 1–23. Dordrecht: Reidel, 1979.

Gorman, Michael J. *Abortion and the Early Church: Christian, Jewish and Pagan Attitudes in the Greco-Roman world*. Downers Grove, IL: InterVarsity, 1982.

Graham, Billy. *A Prophet with Honor: The Billy Graham Story*. Edited by William Martin. New York: Morrow, 1991.

Grudem, Wayne. *Systematic Theology*. Grand Rapids: Zondervan, 1994.

Grutter v. Bollinger, 539 US (2003), 3.

Grutter v. Bollinger and Gratz v. Bollinger. *Brief of Amicus Curiae, The Michigan Association of Scholars in Support of Petitioners*, January 16, 2002.

Gurin, Patricia, et al. "Diversity and Higher Education: Theory and Impact on Educational Outcomes." *Harvard Educational Review* 72 (2003) 330–66.

Harding, Sandra. "Rethinking Standpoint Epistemology: 'What Is Strong Objectivity?'" In *Feminist Epistemologies*, edited by L. Alcoff and E. Potter, 42–89. New York: Routledge, 1995.

Hare, Richard M. *Freedom and Reason*. Oxford: Oxford University Press, 1965.

Harris, Charles E. "The Ethics of Natural Law." In *Applying Moral Theories*, 95–122. Belmont, CA: Wadsworth 1986.

Harstock, Nancy. "The Feminist Standpoint: Developing the Ground for a Specifically Feminist Historical Materialism." In *Discovering Reality*, edited by Sandra Harding and Merrill Hintikka, 283–310. Norwell, MA: Kluwer Academic, 2003.

Hart, Herbert L. A. "Are There Any Natural Rights?" *Philosophical Review* 64 (1955) 175–91.

Hasker, William. "Emergentism." *Religious Studies* 18 (n.d.) 473–88.

———. *The Emergent Self*. Ithaca, NY: Cornell University Press, 1999.

Hills, Alison. "Defending Double Effect." *Philosophical Studies: An International Journal for Philosophy in the Analytic Tradition* 116, no. 2 (2003) 133–52.

Hobbes, Thomas. *Leviathan*. Edited by Michael Oakeshott. Oxford: Blackwell, 1960.

Hobbs, Eric E., and Walter C. Hobbs. *Contemporary Capital Punishment: Biblical Difficulties with the Biblically Permissible* in *Readings in Christian Ethics*. Vol. 2, *Issues and Applications*. Edited by David K. Clark and Robert V. Rakestraw. Grand Rapids: Baker, 1996.

Hochschild, Jennifer L. "Affirmative Action as Cultural War." In *The Cultural Territories of Race*, edited by Michele Lamont, 343-68. Chicago: University of Chicago Press, 1999.

———. *Facing Up to the American Dream*. Princeton: Princeton University Press, 1995.

Hohfeld, Wesley N. *Fundamental Legal Conceptions*. Edited by W. Cook. New Haven: Yale University Press, 1919.

Horgan, Terence, and Mark Timmons. "Troubles on Moral Twin Earth: Moral Queerness Revived." *Synthese* 92, no. 2 (1992) 221-60.

Hume, David. *Essays: Moral, Political and Literary*. Edited by Eugene F. Miller. Indianapolis: Liberty Fund, 1987.

———. *A Treatise of Human Nature*. Edited by L. A. Selby-Bigge. Oxford: Oxford University Press, 1978.

Jones, David Albert. *Soul of the Embryo: Christianity and the Human Embryo*. New York: Continuum, 2004.

Kaiser, Walter C., Jr. "Leviticus." In *The New Interpreter's Bible: A Commentary in 12 Volumes*, 1:985-1191. Nashville: Abingdon, 1994.

Kant, Immanuel. *The Doctrine of Virtue*. Translated by Mary J. Gregor. Philadelphia: University of Pennsylvania Press, 1971.

———. *Foundations of the Metaphysics of Morals*. Translated by Lewis White Beck. Edited by Robert Paul Wolff. Indianapolis: Bobbs-Merrill, 1976.

———. *Lectures on Ethics*. Translated by Louis Infield. New York: Harper & Row, 1963.

Kleingeld, Pauline. "Kant's Second Thoughts on Race." *The Philosophical Quarterly* 57, no. 229 (2007) 573-92.

Lawrence, Charles R., and Mari J. Matsuda. *We Won't Go Back: Making the Case for Affirmative Action*. Boston: Hougton Mifflin, 1997.

Lehrer, Keith. *Knowledge*. Oxford: Clarendon, 1974.

———. *Theory of Knowledge*. Boulder, CO: Westview, 1990.

Leonard, Jonathan S. "Antidiscrimination or Reverse Discrimination: The Impact of Changing Demographics, Title VII, and Affirmative Action on Productivity." *Journal of Human Resources* 2 (1984) 145-74.

———. "Employment and Occupational Advance under Affirmative Action." *Review of Economics and Statistics* 66 (1984) 381-84.

Levene, Malcolm I., and Frank A. Chervenak, eds. *Fetal and Neonatal Neurology and Neurosurgery*. New York: Churchill Livingstone, 2008.

Levinson, Ronald B. *A Plato Reader*. Boston: Houghton Mifflin, 1967.

Lewis, Clarence I. "The Given Element in Empirical Knowledge." *The Philosophical Review* 61 (1952) 168-75.

Locke, John. *The Second Treatise of Government*. Indianapolis: Bobbs-Merrill, 1952.

Lowe, E. Jonathan. "The Causal Autonomy of the Mental." *Mind*, NS, 102, no. 408 (1993) 629-43.

MacIntyre, Alasdair C. *After Virtue: A Study in Moral Theory*. Notre Dame, IN: University of Notre Dame Press, 1984.

Mack, Eric. "Affirmative Action: The New Racialism?" http://www.southerninstitute.info/civil_rights_education/plessy6.html.

Mavrodes, George. "Religion and the Queerness of Morality in *Rationality*." In *Philosophy of Religion: An Anthology*, edited by Louis P. Pojman, 561–69. 4th ed. Belmont, CA: Wadsworth, 2003.

Mikliszanski, Jacques K. "The Law of Retaliation and the Pentateuch." *Journal of Biblical Literature* 66, no. 3 (1947) 295–303.

Mill, John Stuart. "On Liberty." In *Utilitarianism and Other Writings*, edited by Mary Warnock, 126–250. New York: Penguin, 1974.

———. "Utilitarianism." In *Ethics: Selections from Classical and Contemporary Writers*, edited by Oliver A. Johnson, 260–81. 8th ed. New York: Harcourt, Brace, 1999.

Moore, George E. *Principia Ethica*. New York: Cambridge University Press, 1960.

Moore, Keith L. *The Developing Human: Clinically Oriented Embryology*. 7th ed. Philadelphia: Saunders, 2003.

Moreland, James P. *Universals*. Montreal: McGill-Queen's University Press, 2001.

Moreland, James P., and William Lane Craig. *Philosophical Foundations for a Christian Worldview*. Downers Grove, IL: InterVarsity, 2003.

Moreland, James P., and Kai Nielsen. *Does God Exist?* Nashville: Nelson, 1990.

Moreland, James P., and Scott B. Rae. *Body and Soul: Human Nature and the Crisis in Ethics*. Downers Grove, IL: InterVarsity, 2000.

Nagel, Thomas. "Equal Treatment and Compensatory Discrimination." *Philosophy & Public Affairs* 2, no. 4 (1973) 348–63.

Neffe, Jürgen. *Einstein: A Biography*. New York: Farrar, Straus and Giroux, 2007.

Nelson, G. Blair. "Men Before Adam: American Debates over the Unity and Antiquity of Humanity." In *When Science and Christianity Meet*, edited by David C. Lindberg and Ronald L. Numbers, 161–81. Chicago: University of Chicago Press, 2003.

Nielsen, Kai. "Ethics Without Religion." In *Introduction to Philosophy: Classical and Contemporary Readings*, edited by Louis Pojman, 555–61. Oxford: Oxford University Press, 2004.

Noonan, John T. Noonan. "An Almost Absolute Value in History." In *Bioethics: Principles, Issues, and Cases*, edited by Lewis Vaughn, 329–33. New York: Oxford University Press, 2013.

Nozick, Robert. *Anarchy, State, and Utopia*. New York: Basic, 1974.

O'Connor, Tim. "Agent Causation." In *Agents, Causes, and Events*, edited by Tim O'Connor, 173–200. New York: Oxford University Press, 1995.

O'Rahilly, Ronan, and Fabiola Miller. *Human Embryology and Teratology*. 3rd ed. New York: Wiley-Liss, 2001.

Origen. *Homilies on Joshua*. Translated by Barbara J. Bruce. Edited by Cynthia White. Washington, DC: Catholic University of America Press, 2002.

Peffley, Mark, and Jon Hurwitz. "Persuasion and Resistance: Race and the Death Penalty in America." *American Journal of Political Science* 51, no. 4 (2007) 996–1012.

Plantinga, Alvin. *Warrant and Proper Function*. Oxford: Oxford University Press. 1993.

———. *Warrant: The Current Debate*. New York: Oxford University Press, 1993.

Plato. *The Apology*. In *Greek Philosophy: Thales to Aristotle*, edited by Reginald E. Allen, 74–97. 3rd ed. New York: Free, 1991.

———. *Euthyphro*. In *Greek Philosophy: Thales to Aristotle*, edited by Reginald E. Allen, 57–73. 3rd ed. New York: Free, 1991.

———. *The Republic*. In *Greek Philosophy: Thales to Aristotle*, edited by Reginald E. Allen, 197–245. 3rd ed. New York: Free, 1991.

Plutarchus, Lucius Mestrius. *De Superstitione*. LCL 2. 1928.

Quinn, Philip L. *Divine Commands and Moral Requirements*. Oxford: Oxford University Press, 1978.
Rachels, James. "What People Deserve." In *Justice and Economic Distribution*, edited by John Arthur and William Shaw, 167–96. Englewood Cliffs, NJ: Prentice-Hall, 1978.
Rawls, John. *Political Liberalism*. New York: Columbia University Press, 1996.
———. *A Theory of Justice*. Cambridge, MA: Harvard University Press, 1971.
Regan, Tom. *The Case for Animal Rights*. Berkeley: University of California Press, 1983.
Regents of Univ. of Cal. v. Bakke, 438 US 311 (1978).
Reskin, Barbara. *The Realities of Affirmative Action in Employment*. Washington, DC: American Sociological Association, 1998.
Roe v. Wade, 438 US 311 (1978).
Ross, William D. *The Right and the Good*. In *Ethics: Selections from Classical and Contemporary Writers*, edited by Oliver A. Johnson, 362–79. 8th ed. New York: Harcourt, Brace, 1999.
Rothman, Stanley, et al. "Does Enrollment Diversity Improve University Education?" *International Journal of Public Opinion Research* 15, no. 1 (2003) 8–26.
Sartre, Jean-Paul. *Existentialism and Human Emotions*. New York: Philosophical Library, 1957.
Sayre-McCord, Geoffrey. "Deception and Reasons to Be Moral." *American Philosophical Quarterly* 26 (1989) 113–22.
Schmidt, Alvin J. *How Christianity Changed the World*. Grand Rapids: Zondervan, 2004.
Sellars, Wilfrid. *Science Perception and Reality*. London: Routledge, 1963.
Sher, George. "Reverse Discrimination, the Future, and the Past." *Ethics* 90 (1979) 81–87.
Shue, Henry. *Basic Rights: Subsistence, Affluence, and U.S. Foreign Policy*. Princeton: Princeton University Press, 1980.
Simon, Robert. "Preferential Hiring: A Reply to Judith Jarvis Thomson." *Philosophy & Public Affairs* 3 (1974) 315–19.
Singer, Peter. *Animal Liberation*. 2nd ed. New York: Avon, 1990.
———. *Practical Ethics*. New York: Cambridge University Press, 1993.
Smart, John J. C. *Utilitarianism: For and Against*. Cambridge: Cambridge University Press, 1973.
Smietana, Bob. "In Tennessee and Elsewhere, Leftover Embryos Lie in Frozen Limbo." *The Tennessean*, April 5, 2009, http://www.tennessean.com/article/20090404/NEWS06/90404026.
Sosa, Ernest. "Privileged Access." In *Consciousness: New Philosophical Essays*, edited by Q. Smith and A. Jokic, 238–51. Oxford: Oxford University Press, 2003.
Sterba, James P. *Affirmative Action for the Future*. Ithaca, NY: Cornell University Press, 2009.
Swinburne, Richard G. "Duty and the Will of God." *Canadian Journal of Philosophy* 4, no. 2 (1974) 213–27.
Tertullian. *A Treatise on the Soul*. In *The Ante-Nicene Fathers*, edited by Alexander Roberts and James Donaldson, 3:181–235. New York: Christian Literature, 1885.
Thernstrom, Stephan, and Abigail Thernstrom. *America in Black and White: One Nation, Indivisible*. New York: Simon and Schuster, 1997.

Thomson, Judith Jarvis. "A Defense of Abortion." *Philosophy & Public Affairs* 1 (1971) 47–66.

———. "Preferential Hiring." *Philosophy & Public Affairs* 2 (1973) 364–84.

Tooley, Michael. "*In Defense of Abortion and Infanticide.*" In *Bioethics: Principles, Issues, and Cases*, edited by Lewis Vaughn, 354–70. New York: Oxford University Press, 2013.

van Inwagen, Peter. "The Possibility of Resurrection." *International Journal of Philosophy of Religion* 9 (1978) 114–21.

Walker, Nigel. *Why Punish?* Oxford: Oxford University Press, 1991.

Warren, Mary Anne. "*On the Moral and Legal Status of Abortion.*" In *Bioethics: Principles, Issues, and Cases*, edited by Lewis Vaughn, 333–43. New York: Oxford University Press, 2013.

West, Cornel. *Race Matters.* Boston: Beacon, 1993.

Wise, Tim J. *Affirmative Action: Racial Preference in Black and White.* New York: Routledge, 2005.

Wolterstorff, Nicholas. *Justice: Rights and Wrongs.* Princeton: Princeton University Press, 2008.

Woo, Elaine. "Belief in Meritocracy an Equal-Opportunity Myth." *Los Angeles Times*, April 30, 1995, A1, A24–A25.

Yandell, Keith. *Christianity and Philosophy.* Grand Rapids: Eerdmans, 1984.

Scripture Index

Genesis
1–2   146n15

Exodus
1:15–21   93
21:12–14   228
21:22–24   267
21:23–25   221

Leviticus
20:10–21   228
20:22–26   229

Numbers
35:31   232

Deuteronomy
13:6–11   232
22:23   230
22:25, 28   230

1 Samuel
15:3   156

Psalms
51:5   250
137:9   156

Proverbs
17:27   33

Malachi
3:10   42

Matthew
5:3   176
5:27–30   231
5:43–48   172
6:19–20   165
7:1–4   4
10:28   245
14:14   175
16:25–26   164

Mark
2:23–28   179

Luke
10:27   160
14:11   176

John
8:1–11   230
8:32   23
12:46   50
14:17, 26   50

Acts

15:36–39	51
21:4	51
21:10	51

Romans

1:21–25	51
2:14–16	157
3:23	18
7:18	18
7:21–23	162
8:1–4	229
12:2	50
13:1–5	231

1 Corinthians

6:12–20	155
6:19	155
13	131
15:14–19	164
15:29–32	165–66

Galatians

2:11–13	51
3:28	170
4:19	42
5:22, 23	162

Colossians

3:11	170
3:12	176

Phillippians

2:3–8	176
4:8	131
4:19	42

James

4:6	176

1 Peter

2:9	131
5:6	176

2 Peter

1:3, 5	131

1 John

3:17	201

3 John

2	42

Subject index

50th Anniversary commemoration of the Brown vs. Topeka Board of Education Supreme Court Decision, 215
9th Commandment, 93

abortion, xiii, 6, 9–10, 18, 28, 31, 31n9, 50, 56–58, 66, 81, 106, 108, 133, 155, 180–81, 233–270, 286, 290
abstract liberalism, 190–91, 203
Adams, Robert, 140
adultery, 16, 167, 228, 230–33, 283
affirmative action, xiii, 10, 37, 50, 81
    NBA Draft Objection, 194–96
    Reverse discrimination, 156, 180, 182–89, 197–98, 216–17
    Role models, 209
african american males, 216
agape, 163, 171
Alston, William P., 29, 143–45
anal sex, 78
animal rights, 122–23, 288
Anscombe, Gertrude E. M., 132
Aquinas, Thomas, 75–79, 106, 119, 149, 245, 247–248
    View in three progressive souls, 245, 247–249
Arcidiacono, Aucejo, 209n39
Aristotle, 75, 115, 129–32, 175, 245, 248–49, 275
arranged marriages, 103
Athenagoras, 265
Augustine, Saint, 23, 158–59, 230, 244
autonomism, 5–8, 64
autonomy, 15–18, 83–86, 89–90, 102–04, 110, 117–24, 128, 132, 139, 151, 258, 202, 272
Ayer, Alfred J., 65–67

bad actions, 58–59, 61
Bahnsen, Greg, 142, 142n11, 143
Bakke, Allan, 184–86, 192, 204–6
Barclay, Oliver, 92n20
Beauchamp and Childress, 104
Beckwith, Francis, 250–51, 260–61, 267
beneficence, 56–57, 100–02, 104–106, 129, 143, 261
benevolence, 25, 129, 136, 141–43, 176, 200, 202
benevolent parent example, 140–41
Bentham, Jeremy, 90, 92n18, 94n21, 120–21
Biblical Absolutism Theory, 178
black church(es), 52, 214–15
blastocyst, 237
Bonheoffer, Dietrich, 19
Bonilla-Silva, Edwardo, 190
Boonin, David, 208
Bowen, William G., 210
Boxil, Bernard, 194
Bruder, Carl E. G., 236n71

Carson, D. A., 165n36
Categorical Imperative, 82–90, 99–100, 108
Cave Analogy, 44
Christian virtues
    faith, hope and love, 131
CIRP survey, 207
civil rights, 56, 109, 111, 114, 185, 187–88, 191, 214–15, 218, 283
Civil Rights Act of 1964, 185, 187
Civil Rights Movement, 114, 214–15
Clement of Alexandria on personhood, 243–45, 265
cognitivists, 66–67
coherentism, 28–30, 203

color blind racism, 190–91
compensatory rights, 116, 128
confidentiality, 103–04, 117, 117n41
confirmation bias, 33
conflict resolution, 25
contractual rights, 111, 116–18, 128
conventional judgments, 13–15
Corcoran, Kevin, 251, 252n91, 253, 255
Corliss, Clark Edward, 235
Cosby, Bill, 215, 218–19
Craig, William Lane, 138, 138n9, 140, 146, 147, 148–149, 151, 151n25, 152n27, 152
creationism, 244–245, 245n80, 38, 177
criminal justice, 198n22, 223–26
cultural relativism, xi, 10–17 see also ethical relativism
customs, 16

de facto defeaters, 27, 27n2, 34, 39
de facto myopia, 30, 43
death penalty, xiii, 9, 109, 128, 155, 180–81, 219–224, 225–33, 270; Atkins v. Virginia and the death penalty, 219; Louisiana v. Kennedy, 222
deificationism, 3–4
dejure defeater, 27n2
deontology, xii, 74, 81, 89, 92, 99–101, 119, 125, 128, 132, 152, 167
depravity, 5, 50–51, 135, 155, 161n34, 173n41, 229
Descartes, 29n6, 245
developments in the human being while it is in the womb, 237–38
The *Didache* and abortion, 265
dignity of humanity, 118, 128
Dionysius the Great, 176
dispositional and occurrent capacities, 242
divine metaethics (DM) thesis, 136–38, 177–78
DM dilemma, 137–44
Donagan, Alan, 81
doxastic assumption, 29
D'Souza, Dinesh, 191
dualist view of personhood, 246
Duderstadt, James, 205

Eberl, Jason, 248
Einstein, Albert, 53–54, 274
embryo, xiii, 28, 104, 181, 234–35, 235n67, 236–264, 255n102
emergent substance dualism, 253
emergentism, 251, 251n90, 253–4, 254n94, 255
emotivism, 65, 131n58
epistemic myopia, xii, 23, 27–41, 41n13, 42–55, 132, 155, 179, 268
epistemology, xi–xii, 10–15, 24, 28n3, 29n7, 38, 49, 51, 64, 75, 135, 153, 155, 177, 190, 203
Equal Employment Opportunities Commission, 184
equality, 52, 112, 114–16, 125, 156, 166, 171, 176, 182, 189, 191–92
ethical egoism, 80, 91, 91n15, 166–68
ethical relativism, 6, 15, 32, 83
ethical subjectivism, 8
eudaimonia, 130
Euthyphro, 136
external myopia, 30, 34–39
Ezorsky, Gertrude, 222, 223

fallacies, informal
 ad hominem(s), 48, 281–82, 282n4, 283
 appeal to authority, 283
 appeal to Hypocrisy, 279,
 attacking a Conscientious Objection, 279
 equivocation, 276,
 false alternatives, 285
 from ignorance, 285
 genetic fallacy, 280–82, 282n4
 hasty Generalization, 19, 286–87
 is-ought fallacy, 56–57, 57n2, 289
 post hoc ergo propter hoc, 289–90
 question-begging, 56, 56n1, 58, 154, 177–78, 222, 233
 red herring, 3, 3n1, 5, 277, 279
 slippery slope, 212, 290–91
 straw man, 33, 37, 91, 203–04, 261, 287–88
false promises, 89–90
Felix, Municius, 265
female castration, 16–17
fidelity, 79, 100, 103–104, 128

subject index 305

Finney, Charles, 52–53
Finnis, John, 76n2, 78, 78n5, 79, 79n5, 80, 80n7, 124
Fiscus, Ronald J., 185, 186, 197
Fletcher, Michael A., 216
foundationalism, 28, 28n3, 29, 29n6, 29n7, 29n8, 30
frozen embryos, 253, 255

genotype of a human being, 238
Gert, Bernard, 105
Gewirth, Alan., 81, 122
God
    difference between what God could do and what God would do, 139
God and ethics relationship
    The axiological question, 135–36, 145–47, 150–53
    The epistemic question, 135, 153–57
    The historical defacto question, 135–36, 166–77
    The metaphysical question, 135, 137–145, 153
    The motivational question, 136, 157–63
    The transcendental/utilitarian question, 136, 164
Golden Rule, 79, 91, 167, 171, 172n39
Goldman, Alvin I., 29n7, 196n20
good action, 59, 106, 149
Graham, Billy, 52–53, 53n20
Gratz v Bollinger, 183–86, 208
Greco=Roman world, 173–76
Grudem, Wayne, 146n15,
Grutter v. Bollinger, 204–06, 208, 210
Gurin study, 207

Harding, Sandra, 203
Hart, Herbert L. A., 122
Hasker, William, 251, 253–254
Herem, 156–157
historically black colleges, 208
Hick, John, 35
Hitler, 5, 12, 19, 36, 108, 163, 288
Hobbes, Thomas, 167–168, 168n37
Hohfeld, W.N., 110–111, 118
homosexual sex, 78
honesty, 103, 128–29, 131
honor killing, 12

human being, 181, 233–35, 235n67, 236–266
"human being" according to Aquinas, 247–49
Hume, David, 40, 41, 53, 65, 71–72, 73, 157–159
humility, 26, 53, 175, 175n45, 176
Hutcheson, Francis, 101, 157
hylomorphic union, 247–249

Imago Dei, 90, 145, 166
immanent causation, 252n91
Inappropriate action, 62–64
indiscernibility of identicals, 107, 148
infanticide, 173, 241, 241n77, 242, 265
instrumental value, 85
internal myopia, 28, 30–37, 39, 40, 48
intrinsic value, 84–86, 90, 99, 146, 166, 176–77, 265–266
IVF and abortion, 253–56

Jefferson, Thomas, 109–10, 114, 217–18
Jehovah Witness, 120
Jim Crow, and origin of, 13, 156, 187, 187n8, 188–90, 211, 214, 290
Johnson, Lyndon, 181
justice, 95–100, 110, 114, 116–17, 125–25, 144–45, 151–52, 157, 171–72, 180–82, 185, 196, 198, 199–201, 216–17, 219, 227, 231, 261, 283
Justice Harry Blackmun, 57
Justice O'Connor, 205–6
Justice Clarence Thomas, 210
Justice White, 57

Kant, 41, 41n13, 60, 80–86, 87–88, 89–93, 99–102, 105, 119, 122, 123, 152, 152n27, 261
Kant on acting according to duty, 82, 89–90
Kant on acting from duty, 82
Kennedy, John F., 39, 181
King Jr., Martin Luther
    I Have A Dream speech, 110
    Why We Can't Wait speech, 192
Kleingeld, Pauline, 41n13
Koper, 232–3

Lake Wobegon Effect, 34
Law of Hammurabi, 221
Leviathan (Hobbes), 167, 168n37, 169
Lewis, C. I., 29n6
lex talionis, 221, 221n52
libertarians, 113
liberty rights, 111, 112, 118
Locke, John, 73, 113, 113n37, 119
Lowe, E. Jonathan, 251
lying, 80, 86, 89, 92, 92n20, 93, 100
lynching, 35

MacIntyre, Alastair, 132
Mack, Eric, 203
Maric, Mileva, 53–54
Mavrodes, George, 160
maxim, 83, 87–89, 108n30, 123
McCorvey, Norma, 57
means, 83–86, 88, 106, 123, 130, 167, 169, 171–72, 180, 185, 188–89, 191, 200, 216–17, 220
metaethics, 1, 55–75, 136, 177
metaphysics, 10n4, 38, 170–77, 249, 253, 266
meter stick in Paris, 144–45
Michigan Mandate, 205–209
Mill, John Stuart, 90–92, 92n18, 94n21, 102, 104, 119–21, 152n27
minimization of racism, 191
Mishna Oholot, 265
Mismatch" hypothesis, 209–10
Moore, G. E., 67–68, 71, 149n23
Moore, Keith, 235–36
moral agents, 238–39
moral patients, 239, 241, 258
moral realists, 67–73, 138n8, 152n27
Moreland, James P., 149, 151n25, 249–250
Morton, Samuel G., 36
Mother Theresa, 165
MOTS, xi–xii, 2–21
murder, 7–9, 27, 83, 89, 107, 110, 112–13, 140–41, 154, 167–69, 174, 219–24, 228, 232–33, 264

Nagel, Thomas, 182
natural inclination, 60, 76
Natural law theory, 75–80, 106, 119, 124, 221
naturalistic fallacy, 67–68
naturalization, 191
Nichomachean Ethics, 115, 129
Nielsen, Kai, 138
nihilism, 148, 150, 214
non–cognitivists, 81, 84, 86
nonmaleficence, 102, 129
non-reductive Materialism and personhood, 251–253
Noonan, John T., 249
normative ethics, 1–2, 74–75
normative myopia, 31–53
Nozick, Robert, 124

O'Connor, Timothy, 251
O. J. Simpson trial, 36–37
objectification, 86, 102
Occupational Safety and Health Administration, 116
offensive action, 78
open question, 68–71
operational definition of cruel and unusual punishment, 222
O'Rahilly, Ronan and Fabiola Miller, 236
Origen, 157
original position, 125–127
other centered qua a means, 172
other centered qua an end, 172
ought, xii, 2, 6–7, 14–19, 55–64, 71–73, 107–09
ought implies can, 60

Peeping Tom acts, 97–98
perfect duties and imperfect duties, 89–90
personhood, 240–250, 250n88, 251, 252–264
phenotype of a human being, 238
Plantinga, Alvin, 27n2, 29n6

subject index

Plato, 43–44, 91n15, 136–137, 161, 174, 243, 245
Platonism, 144–145, 151–152
Plutarchus, Lucius Mestrius, 173
political rights, 112
Pontius Pilate, 24
Pope Dionysius of Alexandria on the early Church, 175–76
post mortem existence, 164, 245–47, 251, 253–54
President Roosevelt, 181
prima facie, 100–101
principle of double effect, 74, 106, 129
principle of equal consideration, 121, 169n38
principle of forfeiture, 129, 221–22, 228
principle of greater good, 128
principle of lesser of two evils, 128
privacy, 57, 96, 103–4, 112, 117, 117n41, 258
procedural rights, 115
pro-choice, 9, 37, 66, 181, 234, 234, 234n66, 256–63, 286
procreation, 77
progressive pro-life position, 266

qualified pro-choice, 258, 262–63

Rae, Michael, 248, 248n81, 249–50
Rahab, 93
Rawls, John, 81, 125–26
reductio ad absurdum, 91, 121, 187, 264
Regan, Tom, 122–23
Regents of the University of California v. Bakke, 184, 193, 204–5
The Republic, 44, 91n15
right and wrong action, 58–60, 60n4, 61–77
right claims in private relationships, 114
rights, 109–28
    justification of, 123–126
function of:
    interests theory" approach, 119–21
    will theory" approach, 119, 121–23
rights qua claims, 111
rights qua immunities, 118

rights qua liberties, 111, 117
rights qua power, 118
Ring of Gyges, 91n15
Roe v. Wade, 56–58
Roper v. Simmons, 219
Ross, W. D., 81, 100, 101
Rothman, Stanley, 206–7
rude action, 62

Sartre, Jean-Paul, 137, 149
Satan, 24, 281
Schmidt, Alvin, 174
Sellars, Wilfrid, 29n4
Shaftesbury, Earl of, 157
Shue, Henry, 113
Singer, Peter, 105, 121, 169n38
skepticism, xi, 4, 9, 9n2, 10, 25
Smart, J. J. C., 90, 97, 98
society, 9n2, 10, 10n3, 11–20
soul, 130, 239n73, 243–244, 244n80, 245–50, 250n87, 250n88, 251–64, 266
standard "pro-life" position, 264
standpoint theory, 49
Sterba, James, 182, 208
Stinney, George, 224
suicide, 41, 88–90
Sunday, Billy, 52
supervenience, 139
sympathy, 159–61, 175
syngamy, 235n67

Tappen, Lewis, 52
Thernstrom, Stephen and Abigail, 218
Thomism and personhood, 247–250, 250n88, 266, 250n88, 265
Thomson, Judith Jarvis, 182, 234n66, 259–62
traducianism, 244
tree of knowledge, 24
truth, 15, 20, 24–25
Tertullian, 243–44, 265

United States Department of Labor, 117
Universal Declaration of Human Rights, 112

Universalizability Principle, 45n16, 106–107, 107n29, 108–109, 128, 228
Utilitarianism, 90–99
    act vs rule utilitarianism, 93–99

vaginal sex, 77, 260n97
veil of ignorance, 125–26
viability, 57, 238, 242–43, 249, 262
virtues, 25–26, 41n13, 53, 69, 72–74, 101, 104n26, 127, 129–33, 175–76

Warren, Mary Ann, 240, 241, 241n77, 242–43
West, Cornel, 213–14
white flight, 199
Wise, Tim, 183
Wolterstorff, Nicholas, 110

zygote, 236–37

www.ingramcontent.com/pod-product-compliance
Lightning Source LLC
Chambersburg PA
CBHW050620300426
44112CB00012B/1591